British Generalship on the Western Front 1914–18

This book explores the British Army's response on the Western Front to a period of seminal change in warfare and, in particular, examines the impact of the pre-war emphasis on worldwide garrison, occupation and policing duties for the Empire's defence on the mindset of the Army's leadership and its lack of preparedness for a continental war involving a massive, unplanned increase in men and materiel. British generals, busy managing the army's expansion and inexperienced in continental war, were slow to reform. The reasons for the poor performance in the early years of the war are analysed. The high command rapidly learnt from the defeats of 1915–16 and performed much better in 1916–18, an especially formative period resulting in the promotion of a younger, more professional leadership and the development of the first truly modern system of tactics which has dominated wars ever since. During 1917–18 the Army's commanders and staff evolved and improved these new methods; developing a doctrine of combined arms and an operational style of attack employing limited-objective set-pieces to overcome the German defences. These developments of 1916–18 provided the tactical and operational efficiency to defeat the formidable German Army and turn defeat into victory.

Simon Robbins was awarded a PhD at King's College London for 'British Generalship on the Western Front, 1914–18'. He has worked in the Department of Documents at the Imperial War Museum since 1989. He is the author of 'Staff Officer, the Diaries of Walter Guinness (First Lord Moyne), 1914–18' with Professor Brian Bond and 'God's General: Cromwell the Soldier'.

Cass series: Military history and policy
Edited by John Gooch and Brian Holden Reid
ISSN: 1465–8488

This series will publish studies on historical and contemporary aspects of land power, spanning the period from the eighteenth century to the present day, and will include national, international and comparative studies. From time to time, the series will publish edited collections of essays and 'classics'.

Allenby and British Strategy in the Middle East, 1917–1919
Matthew Hughes

Alfred von Schlieffen's Military Writings
Robert Foley, ed. and trans.

The British Defence of Egypt, 1935–1940
Conflict and crisis in the Eastern Mediterranean
Steven Morewood

The Japanese and the British Commonwealth Armies at War, 1941–1945
Tim Moreman

Training, Tactics and Leadership in the Confederate Army of Tennessee
Seeds of failure
Andrew Haughton

Military Training in the British Army 1940–1944
From Dunkirk to D-day
Tim Harrison Place

The Boer War
Direction, experience and image
John Gooch, ed.

Caporetto 1917
Victory or defeat?
Mario Morselli

Postwar Counterinsurgency and the SAS 1945–1952
A special type of warfare
Tim Jones

(*Continued*)

British Generalship on the Western Front 1914–18

Defeat into victory

Simon Robbins

FRANK CASS
LONDON AND NEW YORK

First published 2005
by Frank Cass
2 Park Square, Milton Park, Abingdon, Oxon OX14 4RN

Simultaneously published in the USA and Canada
by Frank Cass
270 Madison Avenue, New York, NY 10016

Frank Cass is an imprint of the Taylor & Francis Group

Transferred to Digital Printing 2006

© 2005 Simon Robbins

Typeset in Times
by Integra Software Services Pvt. Ltd, Pondicherry, India

British Library Cataloguing in Publication Data
A catalogue record for this book is available from the British Library

Library of Congress Cataloging in Publication Data
Robbins, Simon.
   British generalship on the Western Front 1914–18 : defeat into victory /
Simon Robbins.
      p.   cm. — (Cass series—military history and policy,
   ISSN 1465–8488; 21)
   Includes bibliographical references and index.
   ISBN 0–415–35006–9
   1. Great Britain. Army—History—World War, 1914–1918.
   2. World War, 1914–1918—Great Britain.   3. World War,
   1914–1918—Campaigns—Western Front.   4. Command of troops.
   5. Great Britain. Army—Management—History—20th century.
   6. Great Britain. Army—Officers.   I. Title.   II. Series: Cass
   series—military history and policy; no. 21.
   D546.R55 2005
   940.4′1241—dc22

                                                     2004012401

ISBN10: 0–415–35006–9 (hbk)
ISBN10: 0–415–40778–8 (pbk)

ISBN13: 978–0–415–35006–8 (hbk)
ISBN13: 978–0–415–40778–6 (pbk)

To Sally, without whom this book would not have been possible, with all my love

Contents

Acknowledgements

The archivists and librarians of Churchill College, Cambridge; the Imperial War Museum; the Liddell Hart Centre for Military Archives at King's College, London; the National Army Museum; the National Library of Scotland; the Public Record Office (now part of the National Archives); the Royal Air Force Museum; the Royal Artillery Historical Trust; and the Scottish Record Office have all aided my researches and I am most grateful for their assistance. I have tried to allow the generals to speak for themselves without the distortion of hindsight and my extensive quotes have been fully acknowledged in the notes to each chapter and in the list of sources. Grateful thanks are due to the Trustees of the Imperial War Museum, the Liddell Hart Centre, the National Library of Scotland, and the Public Record Office and the Controller of HM Stationery Office. Every effort has been made to locate current holders of copyright in text, but I apologise for any omissions which may have occurred in this respect and would welcome information so that amendments can be made in future editions.

I wish to thank my father, Guy Robbins, and Betty and Roger Hedley-Jones for their support and encouragement; Andrew Humphrys, my editor at Frank Cass; and my fellow students, tutors and colleagues past and present in the Archives and the War Studies Department at King's College London and at the Imperial War Museum, notably in the Department of Documents, for their stimulation and assistance. I wish to thank Professor Brian Bond for supporting my efforts to finish my thesis and Professor David French and Dr John Bourne for encouraging me to publish it. Above all I wish to thank my wife, Sally, and my two sons, Jasper and Toby, who have inspired and made all my labours worthwhile. My indebtedness to my wife is inadequately acknowledged by the dedication of this book, for without her help and support this study could not have been completed.

Abbreviations

The following abbreviations are employed:

AA & QMG	Assistant-Adjutant and Quartermaster-General
ADC	Aide-de-Camp
AG	Adjutant-General
AIF	Australian Imperial Force
AMS	Assistant Military Secretary
BEF	British Expeditionary Force
BGGS	Brigadier-General General Staff
BGI	Brigadier-General Intelligence
BGO	Brigadier-General Operations
Bt	Baronet
CB	Companion of the Bath
CGS	Chief of the General Staff
CIE	Companion, Order of the Indian Empire
CIGS	Chief of the Imperial General Staff
C-in-C	Commander-in-Chief
CMG	Companion of St Michael and St George
CO	Commanding Officer
CRA	Commander Royal Artillery
CRE	Commander Royal Engineers
DAAG	Deputy Assistant Adjutant-General
DAA & QMG	Deputy Assistant Adjutant & Quartermaster-General
DCGS	Deputy Chief of the General Staff
DL	Deputy Lieutenant
DLI	Durham Light Infantry
DMI	Director of Military Intelligence
DMO	Director of Military Operations
DSO	Distinguished Service Order
FSR	Field Service Regulations
GCB	Knight Grand Cross of the Bath
GHQ	General Headquarters
GOC	General Officer Commanding

GQG	Grand Quartier General des Armees Francais
GS	General Staff
GSO1	General Staff Officer (1st Grade)
GSO2	General Staff Officer (2nd Grade)
GSO3	General Staff Officer (3rd Grade)
HE	High Explosive
Hon	Honourable
HQ	Headquarters
IGT	Inspector-General Training
JP	Justice of the Peace
KCB	Knight Commander of the Bath
KCMG	Knight Commander of St Michael and St George
KRRC	King's Royal Rifle Corps
MC	Military Cross
MG	Machine Gun
MGGS	Major-General General Staff
MGRA	Major-General Royal Artillery
MO	Medical Officer
NCO	Non Commissioned Officer
Oa	Operations Section A
Ob	Operations Section B
PBI	Poor Bloody Infantry
psc	Passed Staff College
PT	Physical Training
RFA	Royal Field Artillery
QMG	Quartermaster-General
RAF	Royal Air Force
RE	Royal Engineers
RFC	Royal Flying Corps
RN	Royal Navy
RNVR	Royal Naval Volunteer Reserve
SMO	Senior Medical Officer
SO	Staff Officer
UK	United Kingdom
VC	Victoria Cross

Sources

Records from numerous archive sources are referred to in the text, and they are given the acronyms below:

CAB	Cabinet
CCC	Churchill College, Cambridge
IWM	Imperial War Museum, Lambeth, London
LHCMA	Liddell Hart Centre for Military Archives, King's College, Strand, London
NAM	National Army Museum, Chelsea, London
NLS	National Library of Scotland, Edinburgh
PRO	Public Record Office of England and Wales, Kew, London (now part of the National Archives)1
RAF	Royal Air Force Museum, Hendon, London
RAI	Royal Artillery Institute, Woolwich, London (now the Royal Artillery Historical Trust)
SRO	Scottish Record Office, Edinburgh
WO	War Office

1   The army's ethos and culture

We are too near the events of the Great War to see them as our descendants will
see them, without prejudice and with fuller knowledge of the facts as a whole.
(Lieutenant-General Sir Noel Birch, 1920)[1]

History has given the British high command, during the First World War a bad
reputation and the public has a deep-seated belief that many of the British
offensives made between 1914 and 1918 led to needlessly heavy casualties for
negligible military gain. Since the guns stopped firing over eight decades ago,
the Great War has resulted in a large volume of literature of varied quality and
objectivity. The conventional image of that war is one of a senseless bloodbath –
a stark war of attrition conducted by unimaginative and incompetent generals
and lacking any tactical innovation. There is an almost indelible image of futility
produced by the heavy losses sustained on the Somme and at Passchendaele in
1916 and 1917, which puts the blame for the slaughter of British soldiers on the
Western Front directly at the feet of the British Expeditionary Force's (BEF)
commanders.

British generals are still caricatured as being incompetent, mistake-prone and
callous Victorians who did nothing to rectify their colossal errors. There remains
a tendency, when discussing the British Army's performance in 1914–18, to stress
internal factors, usually the incompetence of Haig, General Headquarters (GHQ),
and senior military commanders, devoting far more attention to the failures of
1915–17, notably the Somme and Passchendaele, than to the successes of 1917–18.
The fighting on the Western Front of the Last Hundred Days in 1918, culminating
with the German request for an armistice, the period on which Haig's claim to
greatness must rest, is still almost completely ignored.

In fact, technology and mechanisation, which led to improved tactics and strategy,
had unlocked the German defences and from August 1918 the British Armies had
triumphed in some of the greatest victories of British history. Analysis of the British
Army's internal failures does not explain the reasons for the successes of 1918.
The army's role as a colonial police force has often been regarded as a source of
institutional weakness, producing an army, which fought in 'penny packets',
lacked operational doctrine, was weak in staff work and under-gunned in heavy

artillery, and in particular unable to adapt at all, even slowly and inadequately, to the challenge of defeating the German Army on the Western Front.

The true story of the First World War and its tactics is not quite so mindless or simplistic as the critics would have us believe. The wars of empire in fact produced an officer corps with vast combat and active service experience. The intensity and range of professional opportunity offered by the pre-war British Army was enormous. It is difficult to reconcile the fit, adaptable, energetic, resourceful men who served as battalion, battery, brigade and divisional commanders in 1918 with the dogma-ridden and unprofessional commanders depicted by their critics. Indeed, in the second half of 1918, the BEF finally succeeded in integrating and combining infantry, artillery, armour, and aircraft to defeat the German Army.

It is now possible to provide a more balanced understanding of the war, replacing the cherished stereotype of a futile and blundering BEF with the perception that the British Army was tactically innovative during the second half of the Great War and able to learn from past mistakes as was clearly shown by its performance and the transformation of British fortunes in 1917 and 1918. How impressive developments in tactics, staff work, training, operational planning and all-arms co-operation were introduced, codified, and implemented and at what levels the British Army progressed along the 'learning curve' are some of the important questions which have to be considered and answered. By examining how strategic and technical innovation, effective co-ordination and planning were handled, it is possible to evaluate the performance of the British Armies in France.

For the most part, the commanders of the British Army have remained faceless, devoid of personality or character. The British military leadership is characterised as being led by unthinking automatons, part of a 'monolithic' war machine. This faceless and colourless portrayal of British commanders gives little recognition to individual military prowess, and, in the end, extends oversimplified caricatures of generals as Colonel Blimps. The results are a grossly stereotyped image of British commanders. A more balanced assessment of these men both as personalities and leaders is long overdue. Undoubtedly the war saw the emergence of a tougher and younger group of leaders during the war.

Haig had good reason to be proud of his triumph in November 1918 but British victories and defeats were fundamentally the accomplishments of a specific group of men. In many ways, Haig's subordinates are the forgotten men of the twentieth century. Haig's subordinates are far less well known than, say, Montgomery's lieutenants, because of Haig's dominating personality. While the battlefield commanders of the Second World War such as Montgomery and Slim became familiar names to the British people, Birdwood, Byng, Horne, Plumer, and Rawlinson remain relatively unknown. Increasingly, as the war progressed Haig's subordinates, resisting interference, played a major, and largely positive, role in winning the war on the Western Front but they have received little recognition or serious study.

To understand the British Army in 1914, one must comprehend something of the character and mentality of the officer corps, which was shaped by the ethos and culture of the Army's hierarchy. In this opening chapter, the British military leadership on the Western Front is examined as a group and 'social institution'. Every institution has a culture, the integrated pattern of behaviour that transmits knowledge and learning to succeeding generations, which can be observed in its distinctive behaviour. The Regular Army, largely cut off from British civilian society by the demands of foreign service and the distaste often displayed for army life by the middle and working classes alike, had its own unique style and identity. Who were the Army's leaders and what were their backgrounds, ethos and culture?

In an attempt to evaluate the breadth of background, education and experience of the men who formed the High Command of the British Army biographical data has been collected on a sample of 700 senior commanders and staff officers (SOs), who served on the Western Front at divisional level and above between 1914 and 1918. The overwhelming majority (89 per cent) were British Army officers, mostly serving officers (82 per cent) but also including a small number of retired officers (7 per cent), with the rest (11 per cent) being made up of a motley mixture of officers from the Indian Army, the Territorials, the Dominions, civilian life, and even the Royal Navy (RN)![2]

These war managers were born between 1854 and 1894, with 311 (44.5 per cent) being born in the 1870s; drawn from an Anglo-Saxon, Protestant, upper class or professional background. The British Army's elite shared an Establishment and Victorian upbringing, which provided a common social background and elaborate family ties. The leadership of the BEF were members of a privileged class enjoying social prestige based on family origin and service to the state, which supplied a strong group and cohesive morale. They were a cohesive group recruited from either an aristocratic and landed-gentry background (34.5 per cent) or respectable middle-class service families (35 per cent) and a significant minority (8.5 per cent),[3] such as Field-Marshals Lord Byng and Lord Cavan, Brigadier-General Hon A.M. Henley, and Major-General Hon W. Lambton, were members of the nobility. Others had aristocratic wives or family connections. A number of generals were close to the Royal Family, notably Lieutenant-General Sir William Pulteney (III Corps), who was a personal friend of the King,[4] and Field-Marshal Earl Haig, whose marriage to the Queen's lady-in-waiting took place in the private chapel of Buckingham Palace.[5]

The landed influence on the officer corps was still strong, with the gentry representing over a quarter (26 per cent) of the sample. The typical officer had the conventional upbringing of an upper-class Victorian gentleman. General Sir Walter Kirke, an SO throughout the war, had a typical background. The Kirkes had been the squires of Mirfield Hall, East Markham, Nottinghamshire, for several centuries but, unfortunately, the wealth associated with such an illustrious lineage had, as for many other gentry families, almost entirely evaporated by the time Walter Kirke was born.[6] The second son of a Colonel, Kirke went to Haileybury, leaving at sixteen to attend a crammer to pass into Woolwich where he won the riding prize. He took up polo and racing when in the Army.[7]

All the available biographical and autobiographical evidence underlines the continuing influence of old established families with a tradition of military service.

This elite was traditionally drawn from gentry with a military tradition and such families continued to serve King and Country as officers in the armed services. Major-General Sir Hereward Wake was one of the Wakes of Northamptonshire, who when they were not defending the Empire, resided at the family seat, Courteenhall. General Sir Walter Congreve came from an old Staffordshire family with a tradition of service in the army and a notable ancestor in the inventor of the rocket. The County families of Tyrone and Fermanagh in Ulster produced six Field-Marshals.[8]

It was a narrow world whose ethos and values remained those of the landed gentlemen, who moved in 'county' circles. Brigadier-General Sir James Edmonds noted that 'in 1914 the army was still very feudal in its status, and great personages, even great ladies, exercised the higher patronage'.[9] Personality and connections, rather than professional expertise, continued to exert a big influence in the Army. Many officers believed, as a result, that 'influential backing is more important than the possession of brains and professional ability'.[10] For example, Haig was accused of flaunting his royal connections,[11] and his rapid rise attributed partly by contemporaries to his links with the Royal family.[12] A number of generals, including Allenby, Hunter-Weston, Rawlinson, Robertson, and Smith-Dorrien, kept up a long correspondence from France with the King through his private secretaries. At lower levels, aristocratic officers such as Major-Generals Lord Loch and Hon W. Lambton also had contacts with the King and were reporting on operations.

The Army's values still espoused the traditional and leisurely lifestyle of the gentry and an officer was still expected to be a 'Gentleman', in an era when it was *de rigueur* for a 'Gentleman' to always carry a walking stick, which had replaced the sword as the symbol of belonging to the gentry.[13] Service served to confirm one's social status. Allenby, who looked like 'a typical young English fox-hunting squire',[14] joined the Army because 'other openings were limited, for commercial business was not in those days considered a suitable occupation for a gentleman'.[15] In Scottish society of the mid-nineteenth century, Douglas Haig's mother was regarded as having married beneath her class by marrying into trade (his father owned the Whiskey Distillers) and as a result he went to school in England and into an English cavalry regiment, the 7th Hussars, rather than into the Scots Greys,[16] and was referred to disparagingly as 'the opulent whiskey distiller'.[17]

General Sir John Burnett-Stuart, from the landed gentry in Scotland, was 'an awful snob' at Staff College, who allegedly socialised only with officers of the Rifle Brigade and Guardsmen.[18] If a person had the proper background as a gentleman, it could be assumed that he would have the proper abilities as an officer. Major-General Sir Robert Rice, 'a fine type of a loyal and determined English gentleman, ready to do his duty whatever required and regardless of his rank',[19] was the ideal officer. In 1914 Major-General Sir Frederic Glubb reminded his son 'that you are also a gentleman, a simple honest English gentleman – you cannot be anything better whatever you are'.[20]

Officers were 'expected to have more sense of chivalry and honour'[21] and conduct themselves in accordance with a code of behaviour based upon 'standards of morality, manners, and honesty, qualities we have been taught to regard as sacrosanct, and a peculiar heritage of our race'.[22] The Army's code was largely implicit and unwritten. A gentleman knew when he had broken the code. If caught transgressing the manners and morals which were stressed by the culture of the Army, resignation was expected. For example, Lieutenant-Colonel Charles Repington was forced to resign from the Army not for being either named as co-respondent in a divorce case in 1901 or incompetent but because he had 'broken a solemn written promise to a brother officer' and 'not behaved like a gentleman'.[23]

To be a gentleman was to fulfil the expectations of one's peers and often had little to do with professional competence. For example, when discussing the possibility of his removal from command of Second Army, Haig decided that 'Plumer is himself such an honest straightforward gentleman that I feel one ought to retain him if possible.'[24] Criticisms of senior officers reflected the prevailing ethos. Officers, such as Brigadier-General John Charteris, who 'behaved in anything but a gentlemanly manner',[25] were disapproved of and compared ill-favourably with those, such as Field-Marshal Viscount Byng, who was 'a perfect old courtier & gentleman in every way',[26] or General Sir Charles Fergusson, 'a perfect sahib'.[27]

Senior officers who had served in the ranks were rare but there were a few, notably General Sir Gerald Boyd, Major-General Lord Dugan, and General Sir William Peyton. Boyd was forced to obtain his commission through the ranks because he had failed to get into Sandhurst[28] while in Peyton's case he joined the ranks and was commissioned in the regiment of which his father was a Colonel.[29] The most famous ex-ranker, who made it to the very top of the Army despite his working-class origins, was of course 'Wully' (later Field-Marshal Sir William) Robertson and there was some disgust during the war at his lack of a gentleman's social graces.[30] Haig commented that it was 'much easier . . . to work with a gentleman'.[31]

The officer corps, educationally and socially exclusive, was dominated by the values of the gentry, whose family and social life was based very largely on horses and hunting. As Major-General J.F.C. Fuller noted, 'it was a delightful life, mostly duck-shooting and hunting in winter, and tennis and cricket in the summer'.[32] Sport was a central activity of officers, who had ample leisure time to indulge their passion for field sports and team games so characteristic of the public schools from which they came and were great enthusiasts for hunting, shooting, riding, and other outdoor sports. Most officers enjoyed playing sport of some kind, either individually or for regimental teams. Nineteen (2.7 per cent) of the sample particularly distinguished themselves at first-class sport. One SO noted that 'every senior officer with the forehead of an ape who can afford a horse thinks he is first a huntsman & then a soldier'.[33] Lieutenant-General Sir George Macdonogh was highly unusual in being no good at games, an indifferent horseman, and looking 'the embodiment of the Staff College "owl"'.[34]

General Sir Alexander Godley was typical in his all-round sporting interests: captaining the school Cricket XI; marrying a member of a famous Irish hunting family; being keen on all forms of sport; a noted rider, polo player and judge of horses; and Master, successively, of two garrison packs of hounds.[35] The obsession of Regular officers with sport also manifested itself in Divisional Race meetings and Horse Shows during the war. In 1917 the 33rd Divisional Race Meeting, consisting of 'seven events including two mule Races', was a miniature Epsom 'within 8 miles of 7th Div[ision] fighting hard at Bullecourt'[36] while the sports meeting of the 15th Division 'was very like an Agricultural Show, with jumping and musical riding and races on foot and mounted'.[37] The Cavalry Horse Show, besides being attended by 'a great gathering', produced 'an excellent lunch' with salmon and grouse.[38]

The Army's officer corps had been undergoing a social transformation since the mid-nineteenth century in which the 'landed class', in slow decline, was gradually being replaced by the middle class, which by 1930 held an absolute majority both in the officer corps as a whole and in its senior ranks. By 1912 the aristocracy and landed gentry constituted only 41 per cent of the entire officer corps and 64 per cent of the officers holding the rank of Major-General and above.[39] Men like Field-Marshal Sir John Dill, Major-General Sir Charles Gwynn, Field-Marshal Sir Douglas Haig, General Sir David Henderson, Colonel Richard Meinertzhagen, General Sir Charles Monro, and General Sir Cecil Romer, belonging respectively to distinguished families of ministers, academics, distillers, shipbuilders, merchant bankers, physicians, and judges, came from a professional or commercial rather than a gentry background.

Nearly a quarter (24 per cent) of the sample were from the professional classes. The broadening of the officer corps social background was gradual although to some extent accelerated by the Boer War and Great War. A significant proportion of officers were either sons of serving officers or had relatives in the services. This self-recruitment from among the sons of professional officers was extremely widespread among the British military elite. No less than 228 (32.5 per cent), nearly a third, of the sample were the sons of Army Officers,[40] notably Birdwood who was one of five sons to serve with the army in India.[41] Many senior officers also had brothers and relatives serving. Jacob was one of twenty-eight male members of his family who served in the East India Company's Army or the Indian Army between 1817 and 1926,[42] while Colonel B.C. Battye came from 'one of the well-known family who served India for generations'.[43] This resulted in a narrowing of the base of the British officer corps and the danger of officers becoming a self-perpetuating clique but had the advantage of an increase in the officer corps' professional identity.

In addition 79 (10 per cent) were sons of generals, implying an even tighter circle of recruitment. For example, General Sir Hubert Gough, coming from an Anglo-Irish family, which had abandoned the Church for the profession of arms in the eighteenth century and included a Field-Marshal, had a father and an uncle who were generals and had won the Victoria Cross (VC).[44] Thus, kinship provided a complex network of relationships within the Army's elite. The daughter of General Sir Francis Treherne married the son of Field-Marshal Sir Claud Jacob (respectively the Senior Medical Officer [SMO] and General Officer Commanding

[GOC], Meerut Division), the two families having known each other well in pre-war India, with the son of Field-Marshal Sir William Robertson as the best man.[45] Marriage to the daughter of a high-ranking officer was often a useful step in building a career, cementing professional ties with marriage. For instance, General Sir Eric de Burgh married the daughter of Lieutenant-General Sir Edward Fanshawe,[46] while Brigadier-General Sir John Gough, VC, wed the daughter of General Sir Charles Keyes, becoming the brother-in-law of Admiral of the Fleet Lord Keyes and Brigadier-General Sir Terence Keyes.[47] Similarly, Cavan and Byng and General Sir Noel Birch and Field-Marshal Lord Chetwode were brothers-in-law. Such relationships maintained the social exclusiveness of the Army's leadership.

Wealth was not necessarily synonymous with social status and, although some officers, such as Haig, were personally well off, many lacked financial *largesse*. Far from emulating the relaxed amateurism of the officers of the nineteenth-century gentry, these officers – often from a lower income group than their predecessors – were forced by their relative poverty to work hard and to take their careers as military professionals seriously. Burnett-Stuart, who won a scholarship to Repton, was aware that 'the state of the family finances made this rather important',[48] while Kirke had to leave Haileybury at the age of sixteen because of his failure to gain a scholarship.[49] Once in the Army, Kirke had to rely on his ability to buy and train horses for racing and polo, selling them at a profit, to finance his lifestyle.[50] Brigadier-General Sir Ormonde Winter resorted to the *shroff*, or local native money-lender, to finance his sport in India.[51] Field-Marshal Viscount Montgomery, as a bachelor with few expenses, helped his parents to pay the school fees of his younger brother.[52]

Lieutenant-General Sir Adrian Carton de Wiart was forced to seek active service abroad in Somaliland when his father crashed financially[53] and like Major-General Sir Frederick Maurice, 'a poor man'[54] with no allowance, had to live off his salary. Maurice and Brigadier-General E.G. Wace, both sons of Major-Generals, had to live off their own earnings and like Brigadier-General P. Howell, 'a poor man and keen',[55] were driven by economic necessity to take their profession seriously. Lieutenant-General Sir Launcelot Kiggell 'had practically no private resources and during his whole career was always undertaking extra work to support his family' with the result that as Chief of the General Staff (CGS) at GHQ he 'was an exhausted man'.[56] Whatever the sociological reasons behind the phenomenon, military professionalism developed gradually, slowly eclipsing the patrician-gentleman model.

Social change and the growing professionalisation of the officer corps, who increasingly saw the Army as a career rather than a pleasant hobby, had implications for the Army's performance during the war. It was easier for those with independent means to show the moral courage to risk professional ruin. In the First World War, Guardsmen and Cavalrymen with private means, such as Lord Cavan who was quite happy to retire to hunt with the Hertfordshire Hounds, were much more willing to criticise superiors and to resist orders whereas impecunious officers, such as Field-Marshal Sir Cyril Deverell, who could not afford to lose their jobs, were not.[57] General Sir Herbert Lawrence had 'one very strong asset', namely 'the independence of a civilian and the training of a soldier' having 'a very big job in civil life to go back to'.[58] As a successful banker outside the Army in peacetime, Lawrence could afford to be more independent than his predecessor, Kiggell, declaring that 'for myself, I care nothing and am quite ready to make room for a better man & take other employment'.[59]

Charteris noted that it was 'difficult for any regular professional soldier not to be influenced to some extent by considerations of his own future prospects'.[60] For example, when Major-General Sir Frederic Glubb, an officer with a wife, two children, and no private means, was placed on half-pay before the war it was 'no slight matter'[61] and Wace, who was 'very poor with a considerable family', was removed as General Staff Officer (1st Grade) (GSO1), 32nd Division during the war 'the loss of the comparatively high pay' was 'a bitter blow'.[62] Similarly, Major-General Sir Archibald Paris (Royal Naval Division) did not want to go back to being a Colonel and do routine duties.[63]

A strong desire by some officers to take advantage of a small window of opportunity in wartime to enhance their careers meant that careerism became a major problem during the war. Colonel C.J.L. Allanson remarked 'on the depressing extent to which soldiers, especially the ambitious Staff College type, cold-bloodedly regarded war as a professional opportunity' noting that when the war ended, General Sir William Bartholomew commented that 'it's ended a year too soon for me', thinking only of his lost chance of further promotion[64] while Burnett-Stuart, who was a Brigadier-General on the staff of VII Corps and GHQ, was always talking about people being 'in his way' for promotion.[65] Field-Marshal Sir Archibald Montgomery-Massingberd, as a rising SO during the war, was alleged to be eager to rise and determined to do so by agreeing with GHQ.[66] Such behaviour ate into the ethos of the officers corps.

Lieutenant-General Sir Desmond Anderson claimed that subordinates tended to cover up mistakes or inconvenient data and falsified reports in order to give a good impression and tell superiors what they wanted to hear, rather than the truth, in an attempt to appease the high command.[67] It is alleged that Field-Marshal Sir Henry Wilson ordered the destruction of operation orders issued by GHQ during the retreat from Mons in order to hide the panic, which had occurred during that campaign,[68] while Major-General Sir Hugh Bruce-Williams (37th Division) predated orders he had given and made untrue statements of events.[69] Similarly the Staff of the Fourth Army destroyed the War Diary of Fourth Army General Staff for 1 July 1916, and substituted a Narrative of Events in order to cover up the failure to exploit the success at Montauban by XIII Corps.[70]

One SO remarked that 'a feeling was created amongst those in the front line that to tell unpalatable truths' was 'unpopular with those above, and led to one being considered not to have the right amount of "The fighting spirit"' which 'undoubtedly led people to hesitate to tell the whole truth'.[71] Shoddy practices, such as falsification of reports and 'the whitewashing habit', prevented the high command from recognising 'the most valuable lessons' from the Somme in 1916 'which might have saved us from many of the futilities of Passchendaele in

1917'. Post-battle narratives by commanders, which 'did not always paint a true picture', failing 'to bring out some of the big lessons' were one reason for the failure 'to learn from our mistakes'.[72] On the Ancre in November 1916 one commander refused 'several times' to send on the reports by his Brigade-Major about the very poor conditions on the grounds that he would lose his job,[73] while another Brigade Major 'had to alter considerably a draft narrative, not because it was in any way inaccurate' but because his commander 'wanted certain incidents to appear in a more favourable light than they perhaps should have done'.[74]

Fear of dismissal when 'it was common talk that no divisional commander dared say his infantry were unfit to attack for fear of being sent home',[75] led to even more nefarious practices. One battalion commander admitted frankly after the war that he 'only renewed the attack' on Guedecourt in September 1916 'to save my reputation' and because he 'was more frightened of my superiors than even of the Germans'.[76] When unable to persuade the 14th Division of the impracticality of an attack on Delville Wood in August 1916, Brigadier-General P.C.B. Skinner (41st Brigade), hatched a plan with the commander of the 8/King's Royal Rifle Corps (KRRC) to launch a feint attack and then reported the position occupied.[77] When in April 1918 a battalion commander 'flatly refused to carry out' a 'futile' attack, his brigade merely reported that the counter-attack had failed.[78]

Nevertheless, many officers remained in less glamorous posts because they saw it as 'the right course for the general show' and regarded such 'days of grave crisis' as 'not time to think of one's own career'[79] although they fully realised that such action might be 'suicidal' and 'bad professionally' because it meant being left behind in promotion by friends and colleagues.[80] The GSO1, 30th Division was proud that his report on the operations of July 1916 was 'strictly accurate and not patched up as an *"apologia pro sua vita"*'.[81]

The careerism of a minority of officers was also counter-balanced by the social and cultural homogeneity of the officer corps which shared a close sense of community. Everyone knew each other either personally or by repute. Above all, 'the old Army was a small family affair'[82] in which an individual officer, Brigadier-General Philip Howell, could write to his wife that 'I seem to know everybody & everyone me', attend a conference with 'all the generals & staffs of the whole bally show' meeting 'hundreds of old friends', and be taken to have tea with Sir John French, the Commander-in-Chief, who explained 'the whole situation on the map'.[83]

From attending a particular school; Sandhurst or Woolwich; belonging to a particular regiment, or having participated in certain campaigns together; or Staff College, each officer had a small circle of acquaintances with whom he remained on intimate terms throughout his entire career. Friendships were particularly strong at regimental level. Field-Marshal Lord Alanbrooke, Lieutenant-General E.F. Norton, and Major-General E.O. Lewin, artillery SOs during the war became friends while serving together in 30th Battery, Royal Field Artillery (RFA).[84] Colonel A. Crookenden (GSO1, 11th Division) named his son after a friend in the same regiment who was killed in 1915.[85] These ties continued to be a strong influence on senior officers, such as Major-General Sir Reginald Pinney, who whenever visiting GHQ stayed or dined with Lieutenant-Colonel Sir John Dunnington-Jefferson, who had also joined the Royal Fusiliers.[86] This group cohesion was extended from regiments to divisions during the war. For example, the 51st Division was 'almost a family concern'.[87]

The Staff Colleges, the passport to high rank, provided a very important method of meeting fellow high-flyers and making life-long friendships.[88] Edmonds stated that the friends made at Camberley 'remained my closest friends for the rest of my life, eclipsing those of my school, Woolwich cadet and young officer at Chatham periods'.[89] The Staff College also widened an officer's contacts. Field-Marshal Sir Archibald Montgomery noted that 'two of the happiest years of my service were spent at the Staff College, where I made many friends in other branches of the Army'.[90] The closeness of the links between officers and their families can be seen in the friendship of Lieutenant-General Sir Basil Burnett-Hitchcock and Edmonds who served together for three years on the peace staff of the 4th Division, whose wives shared the same house when the war came, and whose children were at Oxford together and 'were almost one family'.[91]

An example of the friendships and networks made by officers can be seen by the careers of two officers. General Sir Sidney Clive, an SO at GHQ during the war, was 'curious how many people one knows' while lunching with five friends at XI Corps in September 1915; whom he had met during his service with the regiment (Grenadier Guards), at Staff College, the manoeuvres of 1913, during the war, and at GHQ.[92] Major-General Sir Hugh Tudor was at 'The Shop' in Woolwich with Major-General C.E.D. Budworth; a subaltern in India with Winston Churchill and General Sir Hubert Gough; in 'G' Battery with General Sir Percy Radcliffe, and with Field-Marshal Earl Haig on the Staff of Sir John French during the Boer War.[93] As the war progressed, the small numbers of the old Regular Army tended to be swamped by the more numerous territorials and New Army officers. For example, going on the leave boat to the UK, Edmonds discovered that 'as time passed I found that I knew fewer and fewer of the officers on board; from knowing every one in 1914, I was glad in 1918 if I saw the face of a single old hand'.[94]

With the close-knit Regular Army sustaining many deaths especially during 1914 and 1915, no senior officer was unaffected by the loss of colleagues and, indeed, 232 generals were killed or wounded during the war.[95] In early 1915 Sir John French haunted by the high casualties imagined that 'my room is becoming thick with the spirits of my friends'.[96] 'Wully' Robertson 'felt deeply' the death of Colonel Freddy Kerr, a close friend killed by a shell while he was a GSO1 (1st Division) on 31 October 1914.[97] Increasingly officers, such as Colonel Richard Meinertzhagen felt 'awful losing all of one's friends one after another' and saw each casualty list 'with a feeling of horror for the loss of another friend'[98] while Howell felt 'anger at losing my friends & anxiety to preserve the few who are left'.[99] Many officers also suffered the loss of close relatives: John Capper and Hubert Gough had brothers killed in 1915; Major-General Sir Robert Montgomery, Field-Marshal Lord Allenby, General Sir Walter Braithwaite, and Capper lost their only sons; while Herbert Lawrence lost both sons.

One outsider noted that the three pillars of General Lord Jeffreys' beliefs and loyalty were Eton, the Brigade of Guards and the Conservative Party.[100] These pillars contributed to the homogeneity of the British Army. The majority of the sample were in school during the last years of Queen Victoria's age.[101] The officer corps was not only dominated by public-school educated men, but they also came from a very narrow band of schools. For example, the bulk of the officers trained at Woolwich for the Royal Artillery and the Royal Engineers (RE) came from Wellington, Cheltenham, Clifton, Marlborough and Malvern while the Guards, Cavalry and Infantry officers at Sandhurst were supplied from Eton, Harrow and Winchester.[102] Nearly half the cadets at Woolwich in 1913 came from five schools (Wellington, Cheltenham, Clifton, Marlborough, and Winchester).[103]

This trend was also reflected in the Army's elite. Of the sample, over a seventh (93) had attended Eton while over a third (243) had been educated at one of five public schools (Eton, Wellington, Harrow, Marlborough, and Charterhouse) and over half (370) had attended one of ten public schools (Eton, Wellington, Harrow, Marlborough, Charterhouse, Winchester, Clifton, Cheltenham, Rugby, and Haileybury). Five public schools (Cheltenham, Clifton, Haileybury, Marlborough, and Wellington) founded to provide soldiers and civil servants for the Empire alone provided nearly a quarter (154) of the officers in the sample.[104] Sir Frank Fox even compared service at GHQ to 'such a life as studious boys might live at a Public School, if there can be imagined a Public School in which sport was reduced to the minimum essential to keep one fit for hard "swotting" '.[105]

At School, important links could be forged which would be useful in the Army both for senior commanders, such as Hubert Gough, who had been a contemporary at Eton of Field-Marshal Sir Philip Chetwode, Major-Generals Sir Neill Malcolm, and Sir Percy Hambro,[106] and junior officers, such as General Sir James Marshall-Cornwall, who was a contemporary, at Rugby, of Generals Sir Desmond Anderson, Sir Harold Franklyn, George Giffard, Arthur Percival and Sir Henry Pownall.[107] For others, acquaintance began even earlier. Colonel T.T. Grove was at Preparatory School with General Sir Charles Deedes, General Lord Jeffreys and Major-General O.H.L. Nicholson.[108] The 'Old School Tie' could also provide a point of contact between the regular and non-regular Officers. One temporary artillery officer following a visit from the Second Army commander (Plumer) was admonished for not being 'obsequious enough' and talking 'to the old man as if he had been a friend' by his Colonel who was unaware that they were both Old Etonians.[109]

Some officers, such as Major-General Sir Hugh Bruce-Williams, proclaiming Winchester the 'best school in the world', were aggressively proud of their school.[110] General Sir Sidney Clive, like his father an Old Harrovian, having heard in France that his wife had sent his son to Eton, returned to take him to Harrow.[111] Field-Marshal Lord Alanbrooke, who had gone to a private school in France rather than public school, was made to feel at Woolwich 'that I was quite out of the herd, I had missed something that they all had'.[112] Air Commodore L.E.O. Charlton 'was fully conscious that the Brighton College of his day was neither an Eton, a Harrow nor a Winchester; it was not even a Clifton, a Charterhouse or a Tonbridge' and 'it was many a long year before he could bring himself to admit without a certain embarrassment the precise locality of his *Alma Mata*'.[113] While some 73 (10 per cent) of the sample had been to University with Oxford and Cambridge by far the most popular Universities,[114] often, as in Haig's case, officers did not bother to take a degree, although Congreve (Pembroke, Oxford) was sent down for shooting the Junior Proctor in the head with an air gun.[115] Many officers resembled Haig who 'read few books and never a single novel'[116] and had 'few, if any, interests outside soldiering' other than polo and his family.[117]

The modern regimental system was at the heart of British military culture and its diversity of sub-cultures. Alanbrooke believed that his regimental service were 'some of the happiest and certainly the most carefree days of my life'.[118] Military dynasties were common as families became associated with regiments. For example, Major-General Sir Guy Dawnay served with the Coldstream Guards as did his father, his brother, and, eventually, his two sons while his brother-in-law, General Sir Sidney Clive, joined the Grenadier Guards as did his father, his brother, and his son. Officers were bound to their regiments by strong family ties, which owed little to grandiose ideas of nation or empire, but much to tradition, homogeneity and regimental pride. General Sir John Burnett-Stuart, a rifleman, stated in his memoirs that his proudest day came when he became Colonel Commandant of his Regiment's 1st Battalion.[119] SOs at GHQ, such as Generals Sir Sidney Clive and Sir Walter Kirke, tried to get back to their regiments without success.[120]

In an army which was permanently fragmented and thinly spread over a large Empire, a soldier's loyalty was to the concrete reality of the 'Regiment', not to the more abstract concept of the 'Army'. The regimental system, while promoting unit *esprit de corps* and cohesion, encouraged inter-arm rivalry and friction. When one Brigadier-General reported after the Battle of Cambrai that some drunken artillery officers had looted his headquarters, 'it raised an awful storm' and he and his Divisional Commander were put under pressure by the Corps and Army to withdraw the report, which he refused to do.[121] The fact that each regiment had its own traditions and habits formed a barrier to the development of new training or tactical methods and of the acceptance of centralisation by GHQ during the war.

With the advent of modern weapons the cavalry in particular felt itself to be under threat. The transfer of de Lisle from the infantry to a cavalry regiment, in an attempt by Lord Roberts to reform the cavalry after the Boer War, generated much opposition within the cavalry.[122] This defence of the cavalry arm prior to the war had been led by Haig and French. During the war, Beddington was accused by a senior officer, Lieutenant-General Sir Charles Kavanagh, of being '"a traitor"' to his arm, the cavalry, for advocating the abolition of the Cavalry Corps in 1916.[123] Allenby (Cavalry Corps) and his Brigadier-General General Staff (BGGS) (Howell) were reported to Haig by Major-General H.J.M. Macandrew (BGGS, Indian Cavalry Corps) as being 'despondent' regarding the possibilities of cavalry action in modern warfare.[124]

Such attitudes hindered any objective assessment of progress and fostered an extreme parochialism, which, according to Major-General J.F.C. Fuller, hampered the promotion of good officers, by replacing intelligence and professional knowledge with regimental favouritism.[125] It was the perception of many officers that belonging to an elite regiment could enhance an officer's prospects within the army. It was claimed that Major-General Sir John Davidson had 'the additional advantage' of being in the King's Royal Rifle Corps (KRRC),[126] while General Sir Francis Davies, as a Guardsman with 'a lot of influence', was thought capable of avoiding removal as a Divisional Commander after Neuve Chapelle.[127] The subsequent promotion of Davies to be Military Secretary at the War Office reinforced this perception. The rapid promotion of Bethell, the youngest divisional commander on the Western Front, was attributed to his belonging to Haig's old regiment, 7th Hussars,[128] although, in fact, Haig appears to have shown greater loyalty to his second regiment, the 17th Lancers, which formed the Guard of Honour at GHQ throughout his tenure as Commander-in-Chief.

The army was a small professional force designed primarily for a particular task: the defence of the Empire. Few of the officers in the sample were without imperial experience as only 123 (18 per cent) of 700 were not veterans and most had much more battle experience than their Continental counterparts. Of the sample 485 (69 per cent) had fought in South Africa (1899–1902), 73 (10 per cent) on the North-West Frontier (1897–98), and 64 (9 per cent) on the Nile (1897–99).[129] Most of the senior officers in the sample had obtained positions of influence as a result of their pre-war, colonial service. For example, of the four Inspectors-General of the King's African Rifles before the war, three, Major-Generals J.E. Gough, G.H. Thesiger, and A.R. Hoskins, served on the Western Front. Other officers, such as Generals Sir William Heneker and Sir Thomas Morland and Marshals of the Royal Air Force (RAF), Sir John Salmond and Viscount Trenchard, had also served with distinction in West Africa.

It is debatable whether colonial experience was of much use on the Western Front and General Sir Horace Smith-Dorrien bluntly complained that 'one could never become an up-to-date soldier in the prehistoric warfare to be met with against the Dervishes'.[130] At the turn of the century the British in Africa were still employing the square, notably against Fulani horsemen during the Kano-Sokoto expedition in Northern Nigeria in March 1903 and against the Dervishes of the Mad Mullah in Somaliland in April 1903. A large number of British Generals whose experience was bush-orientated had only a rudimentary knowledge of modern war. Typical were Major-General Sir Henry Lukin, who had fought in the Zulu War (1879), being severely wounded at Ulundi, in Basutoland (1881), in Bechuanaland (1896–97), and in the Boer War (1899–1902), and General Sir William Heneker, who had served in Benin and Nigeria (1899–1903), published a book on 'Bush Warfare' (1906) and was said to be 'more at home in a rough house than in civilised discussion or speculation'.[131] Although not 'educated' soldiers, men like Lukin, who was 'an experienced soldier' having 'commanded the Cape Mounted Rifles' during 'the last year of the South African War', possessed 'an abundance of sound common sense' and tactical flexibility.[132]

Physical robustness and initiative were required by officers on campaign against savage foes, especially those who found themselves in command of small forces in remote areas. Many officers became self-sufficient because of their experiences, notably Major-General S.S. Butler who 'had travelled from Baghdad through Arabia to Damascus disguised in native Arab costume'[133] and Meinertzhagen who, as a junior officer in Kenya, was one of 'three white men in the heart of Africa, with 20 nigger soldiers and 50 nigger police, 68 miles from doctors and reinforcements, administering and policing a district inhabited by half a million well-armed savages'.[134] Brigadier-General W.D. Wright won the VC at Rawia in March 1903 defeating the determined charges of the Emir of Kano's 1,000 horse and 2,000 foot with a small troop of Mounted Infantry, consisting of one officer and forty-four men. Major-General C.H. Foulkes thought nothing of journeying 175 miles with an escort of six Hausa soldiers, riding almost non-stop for three days and two nights, in order to capture the fleeing Emir of Kano despite a display of military might by at least 10,000 warriors.[135]

In defending the Empire the combined worldwide experience of the older officers and NCOs was formidable. While at Staff College 'there was hardly a corner of the British Empire but you could hear about it from someone who had been there, and hardly a small war of the past fifteen years but someone had taken part in it'.[136] General Sir James Marshall-Cornwall remembered that in his artillery brigade before the war in 1914 all the senior officers and even some of the subalterns had war experience and that, as a result, the field training was practical and taken very seriously.[137] Field-Marshal Lord Milne first came to the attention of Kitchener when serving at Omdurman while Lieutenant-General G.H. Fowke first came to prominence during the siege of Ladysmith.[138] The Regular Army was especially successful in producing at battalion and brigade level the drive, inspiring leadership and bravery of men such as Brigadier-General J.V. Campbell, who won the VC on the Somme in 1916; Major-General C. Coffin, who won the VC and the Distinguished Service Order (DSO) and Bar during 1918; Field-Marshal Lord Gort, who won the Military Cross (MC), three DSOs and the VC commanding battalions of the Grenadier Guards; Brigadier-General Frank Maxwell, VC, who was killed leading his troops from the front; and Brigadier-General (later Major-General) A.L. Ransome, who 'was quite willing and able to take a rifle and do a bit of the stabbing himself'.[139]

In many ways the army's own 'culture' reinforced the Colonel Blimp stereotype, which still prevails. Senior officers were often difficult and arbitrary in their behaviour towards subordinate officers, notably General Sir Richard Haking, who was 'a vindictive bully';[140] Lieutenant-General Sir Aylmer Hunter-Weston, who spoke to subordinate generals 'as if he was teaching a class of NCOs';[141] Major-General Sir Hugh Bruce-Williams, whose entrance caused 'a minor stampede' amongst his staff;[142] and General Sir Peter Strickland, a feared autocrat whose arrival caused his staff to exit in panic via the nearest window.[143] Senior officers, such as General Sir Bertram Sergison-Brooke and the Major-General Hon W. Lambton, were distinctly 'livery' in the morning and could not be approached until after luncheon[144] while others were notorious for their temper, notably Allenby, nicknamed 'the Bull';[145] General Sir Horace Smith-Dorrien;[146] Bruce-Williams, 'a blustering bounder';[147] Major-General Sir Oliver Nugent;[148] and Major-General H.L. Reed.[149]

One non-regular officer noted how 'the English professional officers of 1914' formed an 'isolated and self-contained body' which amazed him 'by their narrow professionalism and the extent to which they had preserved the outlook of the least intelligent and most snobbish type of late Victorian public-school boy'.[150] Senior commanders of the Great War 'retained an almost schoolboyish way of talking', using exaggerated terms about each other such as 'cads and bounders, rotters or stinkers' which did not represent a considered judgement but rather reflected 'the persistent adolescence characteristic of many regimental messes'.[151] For example, one officer called a fellow Brigade Commander 'a bounder and a cad, a bombastic fat buckstick'.[152]

Numerous stories illustrate the remoteness and Blimp-like qualities of the Generals at different levels of the hierarchy and the 'professional exclusiveness' of the old regular Army 'made it impossible for them to establish any contact with the civilians who formed the overwhelming majority of the officers in the line'.[153] Regular soldiers were often unable to unbend and found it difficult to establish relations of mutual trust with their own citizen soldiers, increasing the gulf between them and the New Armies. General Sir William Thwaites (46th Division), a Gunner with his eyeglass, ruddy complexion and fierce white moustache, could appear even to a regular SO as 'the very model of a modern Major-General' portrayed in The Pirates of Penzance.[154] Major-General Sir John Capper with 'a fanatical temperament' and 'holding the most archaic views on soldiering, government, and the conduct of life' epitomised the stereotype of Colonel Blimp being an 'extremely dogmatic' soldier who 'in arguing seemed rather to bark than talk', 'repressed rather than invited opinions, and would not tolerate argument'.[155]

The army disliked and distrusted showmanship of the type which generals such as Montgomery would indulge in during the Second World War. It was seen by officers, who exhibited an 'extreme reticence and horror of all forms of publicity', as 'bad form' to court the press by having one's photograph in the newspapers.[156] In marked contrast to the Second World War most of the senior officers, such as Haig, Allenby, and Plumer, were loath to address the troops.[157] Haig, in particular, was notorious for his inability to make a coherent speech.[158] Many generals, such as Major-General H.I.W. Hamilton (3rd Division) or Major-General W. Douglas Smith (20th Division), appeared taciturn, dour, and austere to their own SOs[159] let alone the troops they commanded.

Regular officers were slow to appreciate that the New Army made greater demands on their powers of leadership than the Old Army and tensions between the professionals and amateurs (like RN and Royal Naval Volunteer Reserve [RNVR] in the Royal Navy) continued well into the war. Senior officers proved unsympathetic in their professionalism to the New Armies and attempted to inculcate regular discipline, ill-suited to 'the type of war we were then fighting'.[160] Major-General Sir George Forestier-Walker (21st Division), 'very unpopular' and 'positively inhuman' to his troops, admitted that he had been impatient and had misjudged the differences in dealing with Regular and New Army troops.[161]

Many officers agreed with the sentiment that France was 'no place for amateur soldiers, of whom we have more than enough already'[162] and 'it became a joke that very simple language had to be used in instructing the officers and men of the New Army'.[163] One Divisional Commander complained about the 'sarcastic' and 'disparaging remarks' made in 1917 by Maxse (XVIII Corps) about the London Territorials of 58th Division, 'constantly comparing them with "teachers at a girls' school"'.[164] Field-Marshal Sir Henry Wilson believed that Kitchener's 'ridiculous and preposterous' New Armies were 'the laughing stock of every soldier in Europe',[165] and were 'a roughish lot with hardly a gentleman amongst the officers'.[166] Regular soldiers were particularly unfavourable towards the lax discipline of Colonial troops. For example, General Sir Archibald Murray noted that, although 'from a physical point of view a magnificent body of men', the Australians had 'no idea of ordinary decency or self control'.[167] Even Major-General J.F.C. Fuller, an innovative soldier, believed that the Canadians in 1914 were 'not an army but a mob, much worse than Kitchener's army'.[168]

Commanders at all levels were obsessed with saluting and regulations relating to uniforms and equipment. For example, Haig spoke to the Army and Corps Commander (Gough and Jacob) about 'the lack of smartness, and the slackness of one of its Batt[alion]ns in the matter of saluting when I was motoring through the village' where the 49th Division was billetted,[169] while Haig's staff complained to the commanders of the 16th and 33rd Divisions because troops failed to salute the Commander-in-Chief.[170] Lieutenant-General Sir Charles Fergusson took Cavan, his fellow Grenadier, to task for being improperly dressed, wearing the gold spurs of a guardsman when he was no longer a regimental officer.[171]

The Army firmly believed that 'discipline increases the self-respect of the individual and is shown by a smart and soldierly bearing, scrupulous cleanliness, good saluting, punctilious care of arms and the habit of unhesitating obedience to command'.[172] Obsessive behaviour gained intelligent Commanders reputations as martinets. Allenby (Third Army) was notorious for haranguing a dead body for not wearing a helmet;[173] Gough (Fifth Army) went round the trenches spotting dirty rifles;[174] and Hunter-Weston (VIII Corps) inspected the latrines whenever he visited a unit.[175] Haking (XI Corps) when inspecting a unit which had just come out of the trenches complained about the 'dirt on their clothes from hard work'[176] and inspected the 26th Brigade for 2½ hours in August 1916,[177] while General Sir Cameron Shute (V Corps) ordered troops to wear 'two head chains & burnished metal' for a parade.[178] In September 1917 the 37th Division insisted that 'a very high standard of smartness and cleanliness must be insisted upon throughout the training period'.[179]

In the eyes of one senior officer 'to concentrate on such trifles while neglecting serious matters showed a lack of a sense of proportion'.[180] This elaborate protocol and ceremony, which governed military life far more than that of civilians, formed a barrier between the army leadership and the New Army troops. A non-regular, regimental officer noted that 'the Old Army could not grasp that the New Army cared nothing for soldiering as a trade; thought of it only as a job to be done, and the more expeditiously the better'.[181]

Nevertheless, the social isolation of the army officer can be overdrawn. The more thoughtful officers were able to temper their professionalism with a more sympathetic approach. Haig, more flexible than many senior officers, preferred to stress the fighting spirit and keen determination of the Australians rather than their poor disciplinary record.[182] Generals such as Field-Marshal Lord Birdwood and Field-Marshal Lord Plumer with experience of Dominion troops were able to accept colonial ideas of discipline.[183] There are, moreover, many examples of the high regard held for senior officers at all levels of the high command. General Sir Horace Smith-Dorrien was an example of an officer who could speak with great eloquence to the troops and was greatly admired by regimental officers.[184] Plumer was someone who 'the men all love & admire', taking the trouble to get to know even his battalion commanders individually and gaining the confidence of the troops.[185]

Jacob (II Corps) 'made a great impression on the [8th] Division by finding time to see all the officers of each Brigade at Brigade Head Quarters (HQ) and to talk to each of them individually' in June 1917.[186] One Non Commissioned Officer (NCO) awaiting 'with no little trepidation' an interview with General Sir David Campbell (21st Division) for a commission was put at his ease 'with a kindly word' and emerged proud of his service with his battalion on the Somme.[187] Lieutenant-General Sir George Harper (51st Division), 'the most charming of men', won 'the genuine affection of all ranks' by being 'in constant touch with his troops, both in and out of the line' and was 'known personally to many of them'.[188] Lieutenant-General Sir Harold Walker (1st Australian Division), 'a waspish little bloke with a very quick turn of wit', maintained close contact with his troops and 'spent a lot of time chatting to them' wishing 'to know exactly what the men were thinking'.[189] Brigadier-General R. McDouall (141st Brigade) calling his troops 'a lot of lazy Buggers for not digging fast enough', removed his tunic and began digging beside them.[190]

Most of the senior officers of the BEF were part of a homogeneous and tightly knit group with its own sense of identity, ethics and standards. The interpretation that the social background of the officer corps was responsible for the failings of the Army in the First World War, while providing a possible answer for the shortcomings of some officers, remains dubious and conveys the impression of monolithic stupidity among the officer corps which is not convincing. Indeed, the fact that the army leadership of the First World War and the successful commanders of the Second World War came from the same social background makes untenable the interpretation that the social background of an officer corps dominated by the 'landed classes' explains the army's failures to meet the challenges of trench warfare or the suggestion that senior officers were incapable of adjusting to changing conditions. Enjoying the social activities of their class and era did not preclude soldiers from being professional once on the battlefield.

2 The decline and fall of an army

In truth the problem of semi-siege warfare . . . had never been studied by the General Staff in peace . . . , so we had to learn our lesson in the pitiless school of war.

(General Sir Noel Birch, 1930)[1]

The British Army, like the other armies involved from 1914, was unready for an unexpected trench war quite distinct from a 'traditional' war of movement. Unlike other European armies, the British Army was employed in worldwide garrison and policing duties for the Empire and, while excellent for colonial warfare, its small, professional organisation was ill-prepared for continental warfare, with its clashes between mass citizen armies. Birch noted that 'our army was to a great extent an amateur facing a professional army, and that those in command, in fact in all ranks from general to lance-corporal, had to train their men and fight at the same time'.[2]

In a repeat of the Crimean and Boer Wars the British Army, small by Continental standards, lacked the organisation for rapid expansion. The army leadership, trained in small isolated wars and with little experience of continental warfare, as a result of its pre-war role as an imperial police force, was severely handicapped when pitted against the well-trained and highly organised German Army. Kiggell remarked after the war that 'putting "new armies" up against highly trained ones, of such good stuff as Germans, is somewhat like putting up a village XI against the Australians'.[3]

Unlike the other major armies in 1914, which could concentrate their efforts on trying to absorb the lessons of modern warfare, the British had to cope with a rapid expansion of their professional army from a very small base. They faced the daunting task of raising and training a large and powerful army while deeply engaged in a major war, a task that other armies with their larger, conscript armies largely avoided. Yet in a comparatively short time, by 1917–18, all ranks, including the generals, had learnt to compete on equal terms. But a very heavy price was paid in casualties for such rapid progress.

In August 1914 Haig proposed that the BEF should not 'go over for 2 or 3 months' during which time 'the immense resources of the Empire' could be developed.[4] For political reasons, this good advice was ignored and, as a result, the first years of the war were a harsh and costly experience for the British Army. In 1915 and 1916 generals and staffs had to improvise formations from corps upwards and commanders at all levels lacked the operational experience to provide the necessary leadership. Looking back on the poor performance of the British commanders in 1914, General Sir Thomas Snow noted that 'we were one as bad, or I should say as ignorant, as the other' since 'none of us had the practice in handling such large bodies of troops, and the restrictions placed on the manoeuvre of troops in England had taught me many false lessons'.[5] Inexperienced in the operational art the British from 1915 launched a series of small-scale battles and costly, attritional attacks on unsuitable terrain 'with heavy losses and no decisive success'.[6]

The largest force put into the field during the lifetime of any serving officers had been the relatively small number, a peak of 45,000, raised for the Boer War.[7] The BEF was not organised as the 'sole strategic reserve for use as required in the Empire' until 1906; previously the Home Army 'had no real war organisation and was just a number of draft-finding units'.[8] In 1914, the British Regular Army at home consisted of only one cavalry and six infantry divisions and lacked even provisional planning for raising troops on anything approaching the Continental scale. Despite this the BEF expanded from 4 infantry divisions and 1 cavalry division in August 1914 to 11 infantry divisions and 5 cavalry divisions in January 1915; the cavalry remained static but the infantry divisions continued to expand in number to 22 in July 1915; 38 in January 1916; 55 in July 1916; 57 in January 1917; reaching a peak of 62 in July 1917.[9]

This ten-fold expansion in a time of war cannot be dismissed as an insignificant accomplishment. Nevertheless this was only achieved at great cost as the army was plunged into a spiral of decline from which it only recovered in 1917–18. As Macdonogh noted, 'the old British Army was destroyed at 1st Ypres'[10] and in these first months of the war the Regular Army lost a large percentage of its trained peacetime strength. The heavy casualties of 1914 and 1915 left the British with the Herculean task of revitalising the army at all levels, reconstructing the army at formation and unit level, and creating the weaponry necessary to win the war.

As General Noel Birch remarked, 'we had to learn our lesson in the pitiless school of war'.[11] Brigadier-General John Charteris noted 'we were learning our job by hard experience, and progress was on the whole rapid though costly', believing that battles such as Loos 'though unsuccessful, tactically or strategically' were justified by 'the lessons learnt and subsequently applied'.[12] As one battalion commander remarked on the Battle of Loos, 'everyone has to learn, staffs and troops alike, when faced with conditions so new as those of 1915'.[13] Marshal Foch thought that Haig's 'tremendous losses' on the Somme in 1916 were 'partly owing to having an untrained Army & Generals'.[14] The British Army had to undergo a steep 'learning curve' which 'during 1917 and 1918 led step by step to eliminating the omissions of 1916'.[15]

The weaknesses of an inexperienced army in controlling the battle at the operational level were exacerbated by the lack of cohesion and co-ordination at corps level. In marked contrast to the Canadian and Australian Corps, which with permanently allocated divisions and supporting arms possessed the inestimable advantage of homogeneity, enabling them to develop a cohesion in their training, the division remained the basic fighting formation in the British Army and the composition of corps was constantly altered as the operational situation demanded.[16] Moreover, it was 'not the policy of GHQ to keep divisions in [the same] Corps' in 1916 and Corps Commanders such as General Sir Walter Congreve who wished to retain divisions were not allowed to do so.[17] In mid-1916 XIII Corps concluded that the army 'has grown too big to think in Divisions' and that it was 'desirable that the Corps should be more generally recognised as the real "unit of attack"' and 'should exercise very close supervision and command over the plans and methods of divisional Commanders in order to ensure continuity and to avoid the repetition of methods which have been found to be erroneous'.[18] As early as October 1916 Kiggell had suggested the 'regrouping of Div[isio]ns in Corps and keeping [the] same Div[isio]ns in Corps'[19] but the idea was not developed.

As a result, in contrast to the Canadian and Australian experience, British formations were constantly broken up. Henry Wilson (IV Corps) listed 12 divisions which had been under him in 1916 on a relatively quiet front[20] while Maxse (XVIII Corps) 'hosted' 'no less than 30 British Divisions in 1917'.[21] General Byng (Third Army) complained to GHQ in August 1917 that 'the Divisions in a Corps are constantly changing'.[22] Rawlinson (Fourth Army) noted the difficulties of supervising training schools efficiently 'owing to Corps constantly changing their Divisions and areas'.[23] As late as October 1918 Major-General G.P. Dawnay (Head of Staff Duties at GHQ) was 'constantly being told by divisions moving from corps to corps and army to army that they are being taught differently – different doctrine and different methods – as they move from one command to another'[24] and Fergusson (XVII Corps) complained of the detrimental effect of 'this constant shuffling of divisions from one Corps to another'.[25] Experience showed that 'to work up poor divisions is impossible while they keep on shifting from Corps to Corps' whereas 'if Divisions were left in a Corps for a good long time one could work up Corps *esprit de corps*'.[26]

The system of rotating divisions through corps during 1915–17 gave Corps Commanders, who could further their own ambitions by proclaiming that the situation was more favourable than the more experienced divisional commanders judged it to be, little incentive to husband the divisions, which came and went with great rapidity. For example, Haking's disastrous attack (XI Corps) at Fromelles, which was 'a botch job'[27] and 'as good an illustration as there was of the *reckless extravagance in expenditure of life* which ruled the minds of some of the subordinate commanders, like Gen[eral] Haking, at this stage of the war', showed that 'the weakness of GHQ lay in not seeing that a Corps commander, left to himself, would also be tempted to win glory for his Corps by spectacular success, and would be prodigal in using the Divisions that passed through his hands for this purpose'.[28] Similarly the attack at Beaumont Hamel by the Fifth Army on 13 November 1916, was allowed against the protests of various Corps and divisional commanders and staff who pointed out the appalling conditions and the exhaustion and disorganisation of his troops,[29] because Gough was 'so keen and confident' that the Commander-in-Chief decided to permit the attack.[30]

With inexperienced commanders, staff, and troops the British Army during the period 1915–17 lacked the operational experience to conduct large-scale campaigns successfully and they found it very difficult to achieve the very ambitious plans pursued by the high command. As a result, poor or unrealistic planning and ineffective control of operations meant that too often the troops went into battle without the adequate preparation, fire support, logistic support and effective co-ordination which was necessary to perform successfully in modern battle against a well-trained and resolute enemy.

The best plans were doomed to failure unless the commanders at lower levels were thoroughly conversant with the ground, the men were fully briefed and were properly launched into battle. As early as December 1914 General Sir Archibald Murray, CGS at GHQ, warned that 'it is important' that 'orders be issued in sufficient time to enable subordinate commanders to become thoroughly acquainted with the situation and to make all necessary arrangements' and that 'should this not be possible it will usually be better to postpone the attack'.[31] With the expansion of the army and the largely 'amateur' status of the New Armies, this lesson had to be relearnt. One Brigadier-General noted that 'bad Staff work and want of co-ordination between Corps & Divisions' resulted 'in the many isolated efforts' failing because 'no attack could be successful if orders reach attacking troops too late for careful explanations to be given to subordinate commanders and plans to be carefully thought out'.[32]

Another lesson was the importance of preparation. One junior SO commented that the staff 'cannot say that their orders were always framed on sound tactics based on Field Service Regulations (FSR) Part I' and they 'could not expect the gallant and brave men to do what was impossible and to give them no sporting chance of a fight' wasting good officers and men in offensives which were ill-prepared and showed 'a total disregard of the opinion of Officers, NCO's and men who had to do it'.[33] After the war, Field-Marshal Viscount Montgomery noted that the more tired the soldier was 'the more it is necessary to ensure that he is given a good "kick off", and is launched on his task with a reasonable and sporting chance of success'.[34]

British operations in the Second Battle of Ypres were typical of the problems the 'amateur' British Army had to face while adapting to operations on a continental scale. The staff work of the Second Army in the Ypres Salient, exemplary in 1917, 'was very bad' in 1915 and divisions, notably the 50th, were thrown in without adequate orders or briefings.[35] Haig received reports from subordinates that 'the state of the British troops around Ypres is not satisfactory' with reinforcements being 'ordered into the fight without any preliminary reconnaissance or method' and counter-attacks being 'ordered over open ground, in daylight, which could not possibly succeed and only unnecessary losses resulted'.[36]

The poor management of operations continued at the Battle of Loos in September 1915 when no proper staff arrangements were made to clear the roads for the advance of XI Corps to exploit the initial success of the assaulting divisions.[37] Although Haig maintained that there was 'no avoidable delay' to the movement of the divisions of XI Corps through the administrative areas of I and IV Corps,[38] there is little doubt that poor staff work did indeed make the advance of the 21st and 24th Divisions on 25 September 1915 much more difficult than it should have been. The 21st and 24th Divisions were 'brought to the fight in an exhausted condition, due to bad Staff work' both behind the line where this fatigue was 'due in large measure to the lack of any efficient traffic control' and in the front lines by 'the utterly constant changes in orders'.[39]

The 64th Brigade (21st Division) was held up for over one and a half hours at Bruay railway crossing by a train accident and uncontrolled traffic.[40] The Guards Division had to wait at Marles les Mines for six hours because of the crowded condition of the road due to shocking staff work.[41] Forestier-Walker (21st Division), witnessing successive delays notably at the level crossing at Marles Les Mines, felt that even Regular Divisions 'would have had to do extraordinarily well' to cope with 'not only the enemy in front, but with the bad staff work of Higher Commands, the frequent counter-orders and the disgraceful lack of organised control in the district behind the Front line'.[42] According to Jeffreys, who witnessed 'the appalling confusion and congestion of the traffic' between La Bussiere and Noeux les Mines, 'the afterwards excellent system of traffic control of the army was evolved as a result of the lessons of that day'.[43]

Major-General Sir Frederick Maurice (Brigadier-General Operations [BGO], Head of Operations at GHQ) later admitted that 'for the night march of the 2 divisions which was through a congested area and crossed several lines of railway in which there was much traffic, GHQ should have made arrangements for assisting the march of newly formed divisions' and that 'this was a bad oversight on my part'[44] and as 'there was so much friction and discussion about the employment of the general reserve I ought either to have insisted on the First Army making arrangements for clearing the roads or seen to it myself'.[45] General Sir Robert Whigham (Sub Chief at GHQ) noted that there were also 'faults in the exercise of command and Staff work' by the inexperienced XI Corps HQ. Before the battle, First Army had been warned to help the New Army divisions by the CGS (Robertson) because 'in nearly every case the march discipline of the New Divisions when proceeding to the front to join armies has been noticed to be very indifferent' so there was no excuse for First Army to neglect traffic control.[46]

There were also complaints concerning the way in which the 28th Division was made to march to the Loos battlefield instead of being allowed to travel by bus and rail.[47] In a later attack on the Hohenzollern Redoubt on 13 October 1915, Major-General Hon E.J. Montague-Stuart-Wortley (46th Division) noted that the troops were hurried into the trenches to relieve the Guards Division and launched into the assault when 'the division had barely time to become acquainted with the actual position' and that 'the division suffered very heavy losses by an attack which was ordered to be made, contrary to appreciation of the situation' by the local commanders.[48]

During 1916–17 the problem of poor staff-work, the result of the inexperience of commanders and SOs, continued to dog the British, extending the time lag between the planning and execution, making them slow to react to events, and hindering the translation of their planning into reality. In March 1916 the recapture of the Bluff in the Ypres Salient emphasised that the 'preparation must be most careful and minute' with the troops selected to carry out the attack 'prepared and practised beforehand'.[49] The experiences on the Somme in 1916 and at Ypres in 1917 reinforced this lesson and commanders of divisions began to stress the necessity of giving subordinate units time to prepare their assaults noting that 'without it the bravest troops fail and their heroism is wasted' whereas 'with sufficient time to prepare an assault on a definite and limited objective' a well-trained division could 'capture almost any "impregnable" stronghold'.[50]

Many failures in attack on the Somme were caused by a combination of 'bad staff work – want of co-ordination – Infantry launched hurriedly into action – with insufficient knowledge of what was expected of them' and ignorance of the situation by the Higher Commands.[51] The failed attack by the 24th Brigade on Contalmaison on 7 July showed all the failings which so blighted the British performance in both 1916 and 1917, namely: 'insufficient preliminary reconnaissance'; 'lack of co-ordination between neighbouring units'; 'no proper liaison between units'; too many isolated bombing attacks along trenches instead of a 'well mounted, well gunned, simultaneous attack in strength and numbers across the open'; a 'lack of properly regulated and well timed Artillery support'; 'false reports of the situation'; poor tactics; and 'Brigade Headquarters too far back, out of touch with the immediate situation'.[52]

The tendency amongst higher commanders 'to allow too short a time between the issue of their orders for an operation and the time at which that operation is to take place' resulted 'in futile loss of life'.[53] Complaints of inadequate time to prepare and execute attacks during the Somme Campaign in 1916 to the BGGS of II Corps alone were numerous.[54] One Brigadier-General complained 'how most of the attacks made in those days were very hurried & without proper artillery preparation' and that attacks 'owing to the lack of time in getting orders given' were 'delivered piecemeal & for this reason failed'.[55] One regimental officer noted that the attack on Delville Wood on the 20th July 'was one of many instances of a hurriedly arranged, piecemeal attack going wrong' with orders being 'only received verbally at 10:30 p.m. on the 19th' forcing the battalion to deploy 'in the dark' and 'on totally unfamiliar ground without having a chance to see their objectives or lines of advance'.[56]

Brigadier-General H.C. Potter (9th Brigade) complained of many instances on the Somme 'of delay in transmission of orders failing to give subordinate commanders a fair chance of carrying out their orders', giving as an example the late arrival of orders on the afternoon of 22 July 1916 for an attack on Longueval, early the following morning which resulted in a failure[57] because the attacking troops 'were rushed into the attack at short notice with very little time to examine the ground'.[58] In another instance neither the 2/Durham Light Infantry (DLI) nor the 11/Essex had any time to carry out a reconnaissance and 'could only just get their troops into a suitable position to attack by zero hour' and although Brigadier-General R.J. Bridgford (18th Brigade) 'protested most strongly against this ill-advised scheme owing to the lack of time' he was ordered to continue.[59] At one extreme, the 41st Division sent out an impossible order for an attack in September 1916, which allowed no time for the assault to be prepared.[60] Pinney's 33rd Division was asked to attack Transloy at '48 hours notice' with the result that 'a soaked tired Div[ision]' was expected 'to do what wants 4 days preparation and fresh troops'.[61]

Inexperienced staff and troops ensured that the British Army was unable to react quickly to events and that any attempt to 'force the issue' by speeding things up resulted in disaster. The relatively untrained battalion and company commanders of the New Armies required '"nursing" into battle' and considerable time to reconnoitre the ground before attacking. Unlike the well-trained 'Old Army', they could 'not be hustled on and told to attack at an impossible hour'.[62] Tom Bridges (19th Division) warned that 'the new army wants lots of time & warning to do anything' and attributed the failure of his division at Bazentin-le-Petit to the lack of 'more time to prepare'.[63] Claims that it was 'the slowness of the New Armies which was the cause of the impasse in various parts of the battle field in the days following the main assaults' were refuted and the blame for failed attacks put squarely on 'the failure to give time to local commanders to organise their attacks' and the tendency to employ tired troops in attacks so that 'very heavy losses have been suffered and lives have been sacrificed to no purpose'.[64]

One major lesson from the Battle of the Somme was that 'the officers of the New Army take more time to digest orders and to pass them on' especially during the 'necessary preparations prior to an attack' and the better commanders, realising that there was no substitute for careful preparation and that 'when ample time was not given, attacks failed',[65] allowed time for reconnaissance by the divisional commander and his staff, liaison with other artillery and divisional commanders, to issue orders to sub-commanders, and to brief the battalions involved.[66] One Brigadier-General in July 1916 noted that 'the present staffs, from want of experience' did not know 'how long it takes for an infantry unit to carry out an order and get into position'[67] and 'the Corps apparently had no notion how long orders take to percolate through from the higher command to the Company Commanders'.[68] One battalion commander on the Somme noted that 'orders were often received by the batt[alio]ns after the time they were supposed to have been carried out' and that 'it never seemed to be realised by the higher authorities that after orders were received by the batt[alio]n Com[man]d[e]r, that Company Com[man]d[e]rs had to be collected, who again had to see their platoon Com[man]d[e]rs often widely scattered & difficult to get at'.[69]

To 'issue their orders in sufficient time to enable Battalion and Company Commanders to reconnoitre the ground to be attacked, make their preparations in detail and issue their orders', six hours was 'a minimum time for orders to pass from Corps to the Company Commanders and if less than that time is allowed adequate preparation cannot be made'.[70] But this minimum of six hours recommended by GHQ for orders to pass from Corps to Company HQ was considered by some divisions and corps to be 'greatly underestimated' given the conditions on the Somme.[71]

One division even suggested that 'operations orders should be issued 12 hours previously to all concerned',[72] while XIII Corps required that 'on average a period of at least 24 hours from the time Divisional Operation Orders are issued before the Platoon Commander in the front line is in a position to carry out his part in the attack'.[73] The Brigade Major of the 36th Brigade (12th Division) commented that 'it might take as much as six hours to go up from Brigade Headquarters, round two forward battalions and return' and that 'when the higher staffs issued these orders, often very lengthy and complicated, they did not ensure there was time for them to be digested below, and for orders to reach the troops who were actually to attack' giving the troops no chance of success.[74]

One SO noted on the Somme in November 1916 that 'it cannot be too well realised that you cannot change plans at the last moment, it takes hours for orders to reach front line, as wires [are] invariably cut by shell fire'.[75] Colonel W.H.F. Weber (GSO1 30th Division) complained that in the planning to capture Falfemant and Guillemont 'between 20 and 30 July the plan was changed or postponed no less than *ten* times' which involved 'one wild rush of visiting Corps & Divisions' while 'a request for a Barrage Map invariably accompanied each fresh change of plan'.[76]

The Somme was the nadir of the British Army. The Brigade Major of the 36th Brigade had 'the most bitter memories' of the Somme in 1916, commenting that it 'merely resulted in a useless loss of life and lowering of morale in the formations which took part in it' since 'the conditions, weather and in particular mud' made 'any real success out of the question'.[77] One sapper noted that 'the end of the SOMME battle, as seen by the regimental officer, appeared to be a pointless and depressing affair – a stale remnant of what had once been quite exciting'.[78] One company officer, later a battalion and brigade commander, complained of the 'failure of the Higher Command to cancel hopeless attacks which eventually made the troops feel that they were not being given a sporting chance'.[79]

Things began to improve in 1917 but nevertheless problems remained, partly because new, inexperienced commanders came out to the front repeating old mistakes and partly because 'the High Authorities never seem to learn lessons which are obvious to those who have to carry out their plans'.[80] At brigade level it was 'felt, perhaps quite wrongly, that the Staffs of the higher formations were not taking sufficient trouble to find out the true situation' and, although 'admittedly it was difficult for them in the limited time available, as even a Brigade Headquarters probably necessitated a long walk in the mud', they seemed 'time and again to ignore our reports and not to care that they were so ignorant, and to issue orders and instructions quite inapplicable to the real situation'.[81]

Too often the orders of the Higher Command were 'only a summary of the decisions taken at numerous conferences' which prescribed 'the choice of methods selected by (even) Battalion Commanders'. For SOs 'it was literally not possible both to effect the necessary personal touch with Formations to the flanks and to observe first-hand what one's troops were doing in front' since 'it was one constant stream of long motor rides over bad roads to conferences at which each new plan had to be examined and acted upon as it came along'.[82]

Colonel E.M. Birch noted that during the German withdrawal to the Hindenburg Line the Fifth Army advanced 'without real cooperation of formations or time given to them (as was the case in the early days on the Somme, when my experience as GSO 1 [25th] Div[isio]n was similar) to function properly'.[83] During operations of the 7th Division at Bullecourt the 22nd Brigade was not given enough time to prepare and 'was put into a night attack at very short notice' on 3 May and the 20th Brigade only received their orders late in the afternoon of 6 May when the troops 'had some miles to march, all arrangements for guiding onto the forming up tapes had to be made & the tapes themselves laid out' and 'the notice was too short to allow of any reconnaissance of the ground' for an assault on 7 May.[84] Birch also remembered, as GSO1 Fifth Army during the Battle of Arras in April 1917, 'how disgruntled I was at the sketchy & hurried way plans were made, giving recipients of orders no time to digest & act upon them', which 'was a repetition of the early days of the Somme fighting, resulting as then in much loss & little to show for it'.[85] One junior SO also noted that 'attacks were constantly being put in with insufficient time to organise them' when 'the wire about the Hindenburg Line was so strong that nothing short of a carefully prepared attack had any hope'.[86]

The failure of a very ambitious operation at Arras was the result of 'the lack of co-operation between units, and a lack of co-ordination from the higher command' which led to 'one futile attack after another, with appalling waste of human life'.[87] The attack by the 27th and South African Brigades of the 9th Division at Arras on 12 April 'was completely wiped out' because 'no doubt the Attack looked alright on the map, but viewed from the actual ground it was hopeless' with 'something like 1500 y[ar]ds of absolutely open ground to be advanced over in the face of an enemy well entrenched & well supplied with Machine Guns & Artillery'.[88] For 34th Division's assault at Arras on 29 April 'the orders for the attack were not issued from the Corps until early on the 27th April' and as a result 'the detailed orders did not reach battalions in time to enable adequate instruction to be given to the junior officers' most of whom 'were inexperienced'.[89]

One SO at Third Army during the Battle of Cambrai noted that 'all these attacks without proper preparation were pretty dreadful' especially as 'we did exactly the same at Loos'.[90] At Cambrai, the 2nd Guards Brigade was pushed into a hopeless and 'criminal' attack on Les Tone Wood and La Fontaine on 27 November despite the protests of its commander and Feilding (Guards Division), who 'got little backing from the Corps C[omman]d[e]r'.[91] But the lesson was gradually learnt. As a result of experiences at Ypres in 1917, the Second Army stressed that prior preparation, reconnaissance and close liaison by staffs were 'vital to the success of any operation'.[92] GHQ emphasised in early 1918 that each stage of the offensive had to be thought out, planned and rehearsed in every detail beforehand[93] while commanders such as Harper (IV Corps) reiterated in late 1918 that 'success in battle' was 'largely dependent on the care and forethought exercised by Commanders in laying their initial plans' and that most battles were 'won or lost before zero hour'.[94]

Other recurring faults emerged during the war. At some considerable additional cost in life and *materiel*, the British armies always fought for ground as much as to defeat the enemy. General Sir John Burnett-Stuart commented that 'ground came to have an exaggerated value, and that much fighting took place either merely to advance the line a fraction of an inch on the map without any tactical advantage, or to retain a bit of ground which was so commanded and exposed as to be worse than valueless, when often a much better position existed close behind it'. 'Clinging for months to bad and valueless positions became a fetish which it was worth no commander his place to disregard'[95] and those who surrendered ground voluntarily were likely to face severe disapproval. For example, when a withdrawal to a shorter line at Ypres rather than hold onto 'an impossible position' was ordered in May 1915 by the GSO1 on his own initiative, both General Allenby (V Corps) and General Plumer (Second Army) 'showed their disapproval by recommending, without any enquiry of the circumstances' the removal of Lieutenant-General Sir Henry Wilson (4th Division), causing much anxiety, 'heavy losses and ill success',[96] especially in 1915 and 1916.

These were invariably 'the general result of this policy of "hanging on at all costs" in unfavourable ground', resulting in an 'unduly large' casualty bill with the British 'losing heavily in life, fighting strengths, fighting efficiency, ammunition, equipment and, above all, moral' with the troops 'losing faith in the judgement and skill of those above them' and 'without sufficient corresponding gain'.[97] Typical examples of this policy was the failure of Sir John French to abandon the Ypres Salient, a policy advocated by Smith-Dorrien in 1915, which would have saved 100,000 casualties.[98] The British in early 1918 hung 'onto every yard of ground, whether it be to their advantage or not' and the failure to abandon the Flesquieres and Passchendaele Salients before the German Spring Offensive prevented subordinate commanders from being able 'to economize men and make the Germans attack us in conditions as favourable to ourselves as possible, that is to say on ground of our own choosing'.[99] The British in the end were forced by circumstances to abandon both salients. Edmonds believed that 'GHQ or Third Army hung on too long to the Flesquieres Salient so when the garrison did at last clear out it was forced N[orth] W[est] away from the Fifth Army and a gap between the Armies was created'.[100] Haig was considered to be much more flexible than many of his generals in refusing to hold onto useless ground or retaking lost ground if it was not worth the casualties.[101]

Another tendency was to commit troops in piecemeal assaults on narrow fronts. The more experienced British commanders were critical of the predeliction to carry out a 'nibbling' attack on a narrow front 'after a large attack in order to "straighten the line"' when the front could 'easily be straightened when the next big attack is carried out'.[102] The result was that the attacker lost 'far more men in the drawn-out original attack' than if he 'broke it off, and prepared for another'.[103] As early as December 1914, the British were taught the lesson that it was better to wait for a major offensive rather than trying to save casualties by gaining ground with 'small isolated attacks' which 'lost too many lives' to 'the subsequent most costly counter-attacks'.[104] But many generals remained wedded to 'minor and premature attacks' which 'when launched without adequate art[iller]y support or when sufficient time for preparation has not been possible, only result in useless waste of life and energy without inflicting on the enemy greater losses than we suffer ourselves'.[105]

One Brigadier-General noted that 'there can be little doubt that during the early days of trench fighting, and even later, we were too prone to make isolated attacks'.[106] General Sir Aylmer Haldane (3rd Division), a witness of the Russo-Japanese War, complained that he was forced to undertake three attacks in 1915, which failed because they had 'at best been gambles, and none of them had the odds in their favour which Napoleon insisted on as indispensable', and was highly critical of the '"holding" attacks' ordered by GHQ, 'silly shows' which asked 'men to sacrifice their lives uselessly' in attempting to pin down German reserves and frittered away men 'in absolute opposition to the principle of economy of force'.[107] Much anxiety and resentment stemmed from this mis-management of troops, which reinforced the perception of uncaring generals. Once established this reputation was very difficult to shake off.

After the Battle of Loos, one SO reported that 'events have proved the costliness or futility of attacks made by small formations such as brigades or even divisions, owing to the subsequent punishment by concentrated hostile artillery fire' and, noting that 'the troops hate these small efforts and go for them with small enthusiasm', recommended that any 'offensive should therefore be on a comparatively large scale – say with 6 to 9 divisions on a front of 5,000 to 10,000 yards'.[108]

Yet on the Somme, as before at Neuve Chapelle and Loos, 'the minor, but very costly piecemeal attacks' continued to be 'a feature of operations'.[109] The GSO1, 17th Division, felt that 'there was something very seriously wrong with our tactics, and methods, of attack' on the Somme in which the British 'squandered men' in the opening phase 'without inflicting commensurate loss on the enemy'.[110] The Germans were critical of British tactics on the Somme employing a series of 'almost continual attacks on a smaller scale to attain more limited objectives',[111] which, relying heavily on stereotyped attacks preceded by a heavy bombardment with little attempt at surprise, failed to exploit any initial success.[112] During the period of late July 1916 'piecemeal attacks were being made on small fronts' against 'the LONGUEVAL and DELVILLE WOOD salient'.[113] The isolated attack on Delville Wood by the 3rd Division in July 1916 'was a very great mistake' and was 'foredoomed to failure'.[114]

As a result, the infantry had no rest and 'it was impossible to consolidate or make the necessary preparation for any larger operation'. Experienced commanders were critical of 'the folly of such tactics' which were 'quite unsound and very costly',[115] noting that the attritional 'nibbling' tactics employed by the Fourth Army on the Somme in 1916 were very costly and 'hanging on and scratching forward from Bazentin was expensive work & we got well hammered'.[116] These numerous small, isolated attacks 'to straighten line prior to a big attack' were 'unnecessary' and 'very costly in valuable lives, munitions, and morale'.[117]

As one regimental officer noted, 'the most noticeable feature in the operations during this period was the almost invariable failure of small attacks' which led to the realisation that 'attacks on a large scale were as a rule much less costly in proportion and the ground gained was easier to hold owing to dispersion of enemy's artillery fire'.[118] Infantry Brigade Commanders 'very much resented the irritation of these minor attacks, after a series of big operations had come to an end' because 'in nine cases out of ten this "nibbling" was carried out by tired officers and men in (consequently) a very half-hearted fashion, and almost invariably meant heavy loss of life, and ended in disappointment & failure'.[119] One SO noted that, although 'constant isolated attacks' on Guillemont in August 1916, which ignored GHQ instructions, were 'extremely demoralizing to the Germans', better results 'might have been obtained by the Artillery leaving the front line to be held by a few outposts and thereby avoiding the terrible casualties these minor operations caused'.

Haldane maintained that instead of applying a policy of attrition employing 'piece-meal attacks', once the initial assault had taken place 'it would be much less costly to let things settle down' and instead 'of nibbling a small bit' to wait until 'the next general attack' as the attacker lost 'far more men in the drawn-out original attack' than if he 'broke it off, and prepared for another'.[120] One corps noted that the Somme operations 'have proved once again that small isolated attacks are usually doomed to failure' and noted that 'the French on our right attributed much of their success to the fact that the Commander of the VI French Army sternly set his face against any attempt at small isolated operations and hardly ever attacked on a narrower front than that of 2 Corps'.[121] Haig told Gough that it 'was better to wait than to start a series of small operations which could not have decisive results'.[122]

The problem, however, remained at Arras in 1917 where Fergusson (XVII Corps) threw away 'a lot of lives' on 'useless narrow front enterprises' at Roeux on the Scarpe,[123] as part of a series of 'numerous & isolated attacks on Roeux, the Chemical works and Greenland Hill' which made 'very sorry reading'.[124] Charles (BGGS, XVII Corps) maintained that 'the policy of tying the enemy down' to prevent him from moving his reserves elsewhere 'could equally well have been achieved by maintaining a strong and active force of artillery on our front' allowing 'the divisions who had taken part in the original victorious attack' to regroup and embark on a second stage of the Battle of Arras which 'would have achieved equally striking successes as they did on 9th April at a very much smaller cost in human life'.[125]

Major-General C.G. Fuller (GSO1, 29th Division) agreed on 'the futility of piecemeal attacks, beloved of the Higher Command, and abhorred by the Divisions and still more so by the B[riga]des & B[attalio]ns' whereas the adherence to general attacks would have ensured success at much lower cost in casualties.[126] The lesson was belatedly learnt in September 1917 when worried about 'the wisdom of making small attacks on farms and isolated strong points', Haig decided 'to stop Gough from going on with these little attacks' although Gough was resistant to this pressure.[127] In the victorious advance of 1918 very different tactics were employed. For example, Haldane (VI Corps) was warned by his Army Commander, in October 1918 to attack only on a broad front or with small raids and to avoid attacks on a narrow front.[128]

The penchant for launching piecemeal attacks was aggravated by a propensity to repeat assaults, which had failed, and to prolong battles rather than seeking to find alternative avenues of attack. One major reason for 'our painfully slow progress and heavy losses throughout the Somme battle' was 'the failure on the part of higher commanders to apply boldly the principles of "reinforce when successful"'.[129] Some commanders showed an unimaginative obsession for frontal attacks rather than by-passing strongpoints, which invariably resulted in heavy casualties. Haig felt that at Neuve Chapelle 'there is no doubt' that Willcocks and Joey Davies 'were impregnated with the old tactical idea that if during an attack any part of the line is held up, it is dangerous for the others (who are not held up) to press on' and 'hence no steps were taken to reinforce our tr[oo]ps [which] had met with success, and press forward and round the flanks of the points still holding out'.[130]

When the question whether the VIII Corps should in July 1916 'attack BEAUMONT HAMEL by direct assault or envelopment' was discussed by GHQ 'it was decided to attack it direct' because of the 'complication of [the] artillery programme' and the 'danger to our own troops from our own artillery or enemy' rifle fire.[131] Similarly, the plans in April 1917 of the 64th Brigade to bypass the Cojeul Valley – 'a death trap' – by capturing the neighbouring dominant features was ruined by the insistence of General Sir John Shea (30th Division) 'on "a continuous line of attack"' and as a result the 9/KOYLI were faced 'with an impossible task forced on them by Gen[eral] Shea's pigheadedness'.[132]

One Divisional Commander (Pinney) during the Battle of Arras in May 1917 found that his Corps Commander (Snow) was reluctant to abandon the concept of frontal assaults despite the opposition of the battalion, brigade and divisional commanders who favoured a flank attack.[133] Haig complained in August 1918 that the 32nd Division had lost 1,700 men in three days fighting 'due to having attacked the enemy in a prepared position without first reconnoitring to find out the best lines of approach, weak spots, in fact how best to attack it' so that 'our men came across uncut wire and were mown down by machine-gun fire'.[134] In September 1918 Haldane (VI Corps) was annoyed to find that the 62nd Division had taken a town 'by direct attack, and not by working round the rear as I wished, which would have been more effective and would have gained more ground'.[135] Here the probable explanation was that the Division's commander, Major-General (later General Sir Robert) Whigham, had only just taken command having spent most of the war as a SO at GHQ and the War Office. Lambert (32nd Division) as a veteran brigade commander on the Western Front should have known better, although he was a comparatively recent appointment as commander of a division.

There was no coherent, co-ordinated tactic other than battering on in the hope that the Germans would collapse and as a result each battle seemed to have developed a momentum of its own with Haig determined to continue with it whatever the circumstances. 'In the opinion of the intelligent man in the trench the prolongation of the [Somme] battle, and the final autumn attacks, were a mistake, and a waste' because of the poor ground conditions.[136] Unlike the Germans who in Spring 1918 'exploited any small breakthrough that they made and spread out behind such of our troops as had held their positions', the British 'generally had been accustomed to hammering away at the points which we had been unable to take at first'.[137]

Unfortunately, this attritional form of operations was persisted in throughout the campaigns of 1915–17. At Loos in 1915 attacks were continued into November when they should have been abandoned at the end of September;[138] on the Somme in 1916 Haig was 'bent on continuing the battle' until 'forced to stop by the weather' and indeed wanted 'to go on all through the winter'.[139] One SO later concluded that the Somme battle 'proved conclusively' that 'it is useless to attempt to maintain the momentum of the original attack if halts occur anywhere, unless ample time is given to the artillery to prepare for the next phase'.[140]

At Arras, repeated attacks were made along the Scarpe in May 1917 and this 'was another example of the same disastrous policy, of continuing the effort after all possible hope of success has gone'[141] and 'the many regrettable failures on the part of the British troops engaged' which were 'in strong contrast' to 'the fine successes achieved by the Canadians' at Vimy Ridge were mainly due to 'the use of tired troops'.[142] Lieutenant-General Sir Ronald Charles (then BGGS XVII Corps) noted that continuing the offensive proved futile as 'we had nothing but tired divisions who had lost pretty heavily in the initial attacks of the 9th, 10th & 11th of April, & it was quite evident, on the XVIIth Corps front, at any rate, that we were up against fresh German divisions who had no intention of retreating' and 'to hurl these depleted, & to some extent disorganised, formations against good troops who had had 3 or 4 days in which to place & dig in their machine guns was to ask for failure'.[143]

At Ypres in 1917, the offensive was allowed to continue into November, despite the protests in early October 1917 of Gough and Plumer who made it clear that they did not expect to see any further great strategic results from operations,[144] making 'rather doubtful victories' such as the capture of Passchendaele 'extremely costly'.[145] Similarly, after the initial success at Cambrai on 20 November 1917, the offensive was prolonged when success was no longer feasible.

There was a tendency within the high command of 'issuing orders without an accurate knowledge of the local situation and against the strong representations of commanders on the spot who had that knowledge'.[146] In a lecture on the lessons of the Battle of Loos, Montgomery (BGGS IV Corps) noted that once the planning process had been completed 'the less interference with subordinates the better' since 'mistrust and nagging at subordinates on matters of detail does an infinity of harm'.[147]

Unfortunately, this lesson was not learnt. One artillery commander complained that during the Battle of the Somme 'one was being harassed by Staffs from the rear a good deal', which 'added to the nightmare'.[148] The Staff themselves were also under pressure. When in September 1916 a postponement was reluctantly agreed to, allowing time for the XIV Corps to take Guillemont, there was talk of the BGGS (later General Hon Sir Francis Gathorne Hardy) 'being replaced by someone else as a consequence of this protest'.[149] Similarly, General Gough reported that the BGGS of Canadian Corps (later General Sir Percy Radcliffe) 'made unnecessary difficulties with bad results on the whole corps and also on neighbouring division'.[150] In such an atmosphere lessons were not learnt.

Aware of the need to maintain the tempo of operations, some sections of the high command were resistant to demands for more preparation. A number of generals at all levels of the hierarchy were quite prepared to browbeat and bully doubtful subordinates into carrying out their wishes and making sure that at lower levels of the command structure officers obeyed and implemented the approved policy. Examples of such commanders were Haking (XI Corps), Hunter-Weston (VIII Corps), and Lieutenant-General Sir Cameron Shute (V Corps). Haking constantly bullied and interfered with the planning of his subordinates, such as Air Vice-Marshal Sir Philip Game, the GSO1 of the 46th Division in late 1915[151] and reported Lieutenant-General R.G. Broadwood, 57th Division, for 'lack of fighting spirit',[152] when they tried to prevent the loss of lives in unprofitable attacks by their troops. Hunter-Weston unjustifiably removed Major-General P.S. Wilkinson (50th Division),[153] and Major-General P.R. Wood (33rd Division),[154] who was 'a victim to this bullying'.[155] Shute, 'a great thruster' with 'a rather ruthless nature',[156] continually harried in late 1918 his divisional commanders such as Major-General Sir Reginald Pinney (33rd Division)[157] and General Sir David Campbell (21st Division), who complained that 'the fortnight's bosh [sic] hunting to which he had looked forward all his Service had been absolutely miserable owing to Shute's fussing'.[158]

But during the Battles of the Somme and Third Ypres, Gough (Fifth Army) in particular was notorious for harassing subordinates into over-ambitious action, often breaking the chain of command by speaking directly to divisional commanders, and demanding that they implement unworkable orders. 'Very impetuous and difficult to get on with'[159] as well as being 'excitable & thoughtless & impatient', Gough was 'like a cat on hot bricks'[160] lacking respect for senior officers who did not come up to his standards and developing a tendency 'to fight with everyone above him as well as with the Boches'.[161] The death of his brother, Brigadier-General J.E. Gough, VC in early 1915, exacerbated Gough's almost irrational and unrealistic demands for speedy progress from his subordinates. One subordinate thought that Gough's 'temperament did not suite him for command' and when serving under him in France 'found him full of nerves & hunting his subordinates'.[162]

General Sir Edward Bulfin (28th Division) recalled serving under Gough at I Corps at the Battle of Loos as 'a sort of horrid nightmare' and did not 'want to serve under him again'.[163] On the Somme Major-General W.H. Rycroft (32nd Division) was said by his GSO1 (Wace) to be terrified of Gough and on receiving orders to return in October 1916 remarked 'wryly that it would be his undoing unless we went to Rawly's Army!' Lacking 'the kick in him to stand up to Gough, when all initiative was taken out of his hands', Rycroft was duly removed when his division failed in an attack on 18 November 1916.[164] During the planning for this operation on the Ancre, Wace (the GSO1) 'was furious at the time that the whole of these arrangements, even including the selection of Advanced B[riga]de HQ, were definitely laid down to us by Corps HQ *as the*

Army Commander's decision' or 'in other words Rycroft did not in effect command the 32nd Division' but 'was told what orders he was to issue, and he hadn't the spirit to say he would command his own Division'.[165] Other senior officers, such as Jacob (II Corps), Malcolm (his Major-General General Staff [MGGS]) and Percival (49th Division) were also alleged to be 'terrified' of him.[166]

By early 1917 Gough had gained the reputation of a commander who 'terrorises those under him to the extent that they are afraid to express their opinions for fear of being degomme [sacked]'.[167] Unlike good officers, such as Allenby and Plumer, Gough does not seem to have learned from the experiences of 1915–16. By early 1917 commanders such as Birdwood, who was 'very sick at going to the V Army',[168] Haldane[169] and Lambton were 'not at all keen' to go to Gough's Army.[170] By March 1917 junior officers felt that 'heavy losses & complete failure' were 'very typical [of] Gen[eral] Gough, who apparently does not care a button about the lives of his men'.[171] By mid-1917 there was 'little confidence' in Gough,[172] notorious for his 'encounters' with subordinates[173] and 'looked on as a bit of a freak'.[174] By late 1917 there was 'intense feeling against Goughy', who had made 'many enemies', with 'the formation of a sect of officers called the GMG which interpreted means "Gough must go"'.[175]

By late 1917 'no division wanted to go' to the Fifth Army[176] and most units hailed with relief a transfer to Plumer's Second Army.[177] In October 1917 Kiggell recommended to Haig that the Canadian Corps 'should be sent to General Plumer and not to Gough because the Canadians do not work kindly with the latter' who 'drove them too much in the Somme fighting last year' and again in November 1917 'of the strong wish of divisions not to be sent to Gough's Army'.[178] General Sir William Peyton (the Military Secretary) 'had told Haig three times that he was not only injuring himself but injuring also the cause by keeping Gough in command' but Haig was 'perfectly infatuated with him'.[179]

Like the Soviet Army between 1942 and 1945, the Army had to travel along a series of learning curves between 1915 and 1917 before victory was achieved in 1918. The nadir came on the Somme in 1916 but thereafter lessons were learnt and the Army gradually improved. That process was both painful and rather slow given the relative inexperience and small size of the British Army and its officer corps. The regeneration of an army, the development of a competent officer corps to command that army, and the articulation of an advanced military theory to govern all levels of war occurred in a short period of three years, but at a tremendous cost to the British nation. It is how the Army improved and developed which will now be looked at more systematically.

3 The brain of an army

Staff work (Divisional, Brigade, & Battalion)...was poor. The most competent officers were working on a scale and in conditions of which they had no experience, and they had to learn their job.

(Captain Pearson Choate, 1936)[1]

The tendency to concentrate on the mistakes made while the Army was adapting to *terra incognita* during the period 1915–17 has meant that the process by which the Army developed a war-winning staff in 1917–18 has been neglected. One of the biggest problems faced by the Army was to produce enough SOs capable of running the bureaucracy, producing the efficient command and staff methods at which the German Army excelled, and manning the staffs of the large formations required in continental warfare. Critics, such as Liddell Hart, have completely failed to understand that the skills demanded in the leadership of mass armies in an industrialised age were more managerial than the heroic generalship of the 'Great Captains'. By the end of 1915, on top of the divisional commanders and staffs required to man the forty divisional Headquarters, commanders and SOs had to be provided for three Army and nineteen Corps Headquarters, in France alone.

Clearly 'the difficulties and desire for change that have arisen during the war' were 'due chiefly to the rapid rise of both Commanders and SOs with absolutely no Staff experience' and while 'brains, ability and personal gallantry' were useful they could 'not compensate for lack of military knowledge, far less for lack of good staff training'.[2] While it was one thing to theorise about the achievement of good command and staff procedures, it was quite another to develop enough SOs with the talent for such large-scale operations. Major-General J.F.C. Fuller noted during the war that 'our weak point is our Staffs not the men'.[3] It was impossible to 'expect a General Staff only inaugurated 9 years ago, if so long, on a basis of 6 Divisions, and insufficient for that, to provide adequate SOs for 60 Divisions'[4] and 'to talk of 25 Corps is to talk like a madman or a fool' because it had 'taken our German friends 40 years to make 25 Corps'.[5]

Reforms at Camberley after the Boer War 'made the Staff College one of the most efficient places of military education in the world'[6] and one student, who qualified in 1913, concluded that 'as a result of what I had learnt at Camberley I was well equipped to deal with any situation that arose when I was a Staff Officer'.[7] A relatively small group of pre-war graduates of the Staff Colleges at Camberley and Quetta held most of the key positions in the BEF. However, early in the war it quickly became apparent that, owing to a shortage of well-trained and educated officers capable of undertaking the task of managing a hugely expanded army, the BEF lacked an adequate supply of well-trained SOs to equip the staffs of the new Divisions. Camberley and Quetta together could barely accommodate a minority of officers producing only 447 Staff College graduates in the 1914 Army List.[8] Of the sample, two hundred and eleven or just over a third (34 per cent) lacked any staff experience whatsoever prior to August 1914. Similarly only 92 (just under 15 per cent) had held the post of GSO1 or higher whereas 273 (nearly 74 per cent) had held lower staff posts such as General Staff Officer (2nd Grade) (GSO2) and General Staff Officer (3rd Grade) (GSO3). Edmonds noted that 'in 1914 there were very few trained SOs, that is men who had served on the staff of a command, a division, or a brigade with troops; and of these few more than half (including the best, such as George Morris, Adrian Grant-Duff and "Gussie" Geddes, who fell in action in 1914) were either killed or disabled in the early days'.[9] The few 'educated' officers who had attended Staff College prior to the war were thinly spread as the 'brains of the army' during the war.

Only 32 candidates were admitted to Camberley each year during the 1890s[10] compared to a 'year' consisting of 60 students in 1930[11] and 90 in 1952[12] respectively, nearly double and three times the number which passed through pre-1914. This meant that graduates were the elite of the army and certainly the year 1913 was a vintage one, including as it did two future Field-Marshals, Ironside and Dill,[13] who were to rise to the rank of Brigadier-General by the end of the war. In peacetime, this provided enough trained SOs to fill the relatively few posts available and assured a healthy competition for places. But this short-term policy relegated to regimental soldiering the unlucky majority who tended to resent ambitious colleagues who attended Staff College and in the long term meant that there was a severe shortage of qualified SOs during wartime when the army expanded enormously.

Another major flaw was the British Army's neglect of the operational aspects of modern war; namely the planning and staff work required for operations on a continental scale. SOs had little opportunity to hone their skills during peacetime. Neither army nor corps staff existed in peacetime, a condition imposed by the small colonial army, so that many duties had to be learned 'on the job'. The peacetime staff of a Division consisted of a General Staff Officer, a Deputy Assistant Adjutant-General (DAAG), a Commander Royal Artillery (CRA) and a Commander Royal Engineers (CRE) with other staff only joining on mobilization or for manoeuvres and training during every summer.[14] Since peacetime divisions were only allowed one GSO1,[15] they relied on the allocation of additional personnel before they were able to go to war. For example, 'the four additional SOs who were, on mobilization, appointed to the 4th Division were strangers to it' and having little experience or training were unable even to write operational orders.[16]

As a result, at first, the British Army was very inexperienced at the staff work required in warfare on a continental scale. One battalion commander noted that 'in the early stages of the war the Germans were better practised than were our staffs in the handling of large units'.[17] During the Somme in 1916 'staff work (Divisional, Brigade, & Battalion) in the earlier stages of the battle was poor' as even 'the most competent officers were working on a scale and in conditions of which they had no experience, and they had to learn their job', but in the later stages 'the Staff, having had an opportunity to learn, were just beginning to take hold of their job'.[18]

Staff officers were given a good technical training but little theoretical knowledge of how to operate formations above the divisional level. The task of the Staff College students 'was to learn the arts of lubrication' as they were 'to be greasers of the army machine, normal functionaries' and not 'as disciples of war and of wisdom'.[19] Field-Marshal Sir William Robertson, as Commandant, bluntly informed his students that they 'were at the Staff College to learn staff duties and to qualify for Staff Captain, not to talk irresponsible trash' on 'subjects of policy or strategy'.[20] One of the most able of the trained SOs, General Sir Charles Harington (MGGS Second Army), admitted that he had not been prepared to 'think in "Armies"', having 'never even in theory' contemplated the problems of commanding a force larger than the original BEF. Yet within less than two years of the outbreak of the war he found himself responsible for the staff work of an Army which 'two or three times in tenure exceeded thirty divisions'.[21] Harington blamed the British Army's many problems on the failure to develop 'a General Staff "doctrine"' in parallel to the big formations that had developed from nothing during the war and to standardise doctrine at army, corps and divisional level. The methods employed 'varied considerably' so that 'very divergent views are held and entirely different methods exist in the various Armies, Corps & Divisions'.[22]

This was the result of the fact that while Staff graduates held a majority of the highest posts their numbers were too few to establish an exclusive monopoly. Pre-war reform established the increasing dominance of Staff College graduates within the army, but a shortage of Staff graduates meant that entrance into the top military elite remained open to non-graduates, who were given posts of responsibility as a result of 'hands-on' experience and the army's rapid expansion during the war. Certainly as the BEF grew, the Staff College graduates (376 or 61 per cent of the sample) tended to dominate the Army's hierarchy. Nevertheless, there was a significant minority in the sample of commanders and SOs (239 or 39 per cent) who had not gone to Staff College. Staff College training was not a prerequisite for success. For example, successful brigade, division and corps commanders, such as Cavan, Jacob and Maxse, were not graduates and prevented the Staff College graduates from establishing a monopoly within the hierarchy and developing a standardised doctrine.

Of the eleven senior officers who held the posts of Commanders-in-Chief and Army Commander, eight (73 per cent) had attended Staff College whereas at corps and divisional level things were much more even. Progressing down the hierarchy the dominance of the Staff College diminished as the supply of graduates began to run out and only 27 (56 per cent) out of 48 corps commanders and 99 (51 per cent) out of 195 divisional commanders had graduated from the Staff Colleges. As the war progressed the proportion of divisional commanders who were Staff College graduates steadily dropped. During 1914, 84 per cent of divisional commanders had passed Staff College (psc). In 1916 the figure fell to 78 per cent and in the final year to 73 per cent.[23] By the latter stages of the war a number of officers who had not been to Staff College had received sufficient on-the-job training to make them efficient divisional commanders.

It was the older and younger officers who tended not to have been to Staff College. The senior officers, divisional and corps commanders such as Lieutenant-Generals Sir Charles Anderson, R.G. Broadwood, Sir John Keir, Sir Herbert Watts and Sir Charles Woollcombe; General Sir James Willcocks; and Field-Marshal Lord Cavan, had been able to make a career in the less professional era before the Boer War without attending Staff College while the junior ones, such as Field-Marshals Lord Montgomery and Lord Wilson; Lieutenant-Generals Sir Philip Neame, Sir Francis Nosworthy, and E.A. Osborne, who served as GSO1 of Divisions towards the end of the war, had not had a chance to attend before war broke out. Of the 293 (47 per cent) of the sample who were born in the 1870s only 83 (28 per cent) had not been to Staff College whereas of the 218 (35 per cent) born in the 1850s and 1860s and the 103 (16 per cent) born in the 1880s and 1890s 102 (46 per cent) and 56 (54 per cent) respectively had not attended Staff College.[24] An investigation by GHQ for the War Office in July 1918 showed that 'well over 50% of the divisional commanders had never been on the staff during this war' while 30 per cent had 'never been on the Staff at all'.[25]

More important for the functioning of the army's operations was a growing shortage of SOs as the war progressed[26] and Lieutenant-General Sir Richard Butler reported in 1918 that 'most of the higher staffs are double' the size of those of 1915[27] necessitating the employment of unqualified, non-regular officers on the staff as the Regular Army could not provide the numbers of trained SOs required. By 1918 the total number of Staff positions throughout the army had risen to some ten thousand.[28] The General Staff (GS) at GHQ in November 1917 concluded that 'the supply of trained SOs is falling short of the demand'.[29] In May 1918, GHQ stressed that 'it must also be realised by all Commanders of formations that the supply of trained SOs is getting very low and that Officers appointed to first grade appointments in future will not have had the same staff training, or experience on the Staff, as the Officers whom they replace'.[30]

These problems were exacerbated by the high casualties sustained by the small pool of qualified SOs during the first years of the war. Out of the 447 Staff College graduates in the army list of August 1914, 219 (49.2 per cent) were killed or died of wounds during the war including 180 Camberley Staff Graduates.[31] Among the many SOs lost early in the war were Captain J.B. Jenkinson (Brigade Major, 3rd Brigade) and Captain R.W.M. Stevens (Brigade Major, 9th Brigade) killed in August 1914; Colonel F.W. Kerr, Major G. Paley, and Captain R. Ommanney

(GSO1, GSO2, and GSO3 of the 1st Division respectively) and Lieutenant-Colonel A.J.-B. Percival (GSO1, 2nd Division) all killed by a shell landing on their Headquarters on 31 October 1914; and Captain G.M. James (Brigade Major, 22nd Brigade), killed in November 1914.

The problem of the shortage of qualified personnel was also worsened by the number of the SOs who proved incapable of standing the pace during the early period of the war. Both General Sir Archibald Murray in 1915,[32] who fainted in 1914 when he was told some bad news,[33] and General Sir Launcelot Kiggell, who 'was an exhausted man' by December 1917,[34] were relieved as CGS at GHQ on the grounds of ill-health. At a more junior level, Colonel F.R.F. Boileau (GSO1, 3rd Division), 'an exceptionally fine soldier and tactician', was announced to have died of wounds during the Retreat from Mons[35] when in fact he had gone 'quite off his head with strain & finally shot himself'.[36] Brigadier-General Sir James Edmonds (GSO1, 4th Division) broke down and 'threatened to shoot' the 4th Division transport drivers if they did not obey an order from GHQ to throw off all kit and baggage from the wagons to make room for tired men[37] and had to be replaced.

In addition, many officers who had attended Staff College prior to the reforms after the Boer War were not able to perform adequately as SOs during the war. Brigadier-General F.A. Buzzard became GSO1, 9th Division 'although he had been a failure as GSO2 with 2nd Division' and, proving to be 'indifferent', had to be replaced[38] after only two months in the post. Similarly, Lieutenant-Colonel L. Hume-Spry (GSO1, 50th Division in 1914–15) was described as 'the most completely brainless man'[39] and was soon sacked. Brigadier-General P.D. FitzGerald (GSO1, 2nd Cavalry Division) was 'completely idle and irresponsible' disappearing from his headquarters to go courting whenever the division was out of the line much to the consternation of his staff.[40] One Brigadier-General 'was amazed' by the 'monstrous appointment' of Brigadier-General A.G.A. Hore-Ruthven as BGGS, VII Corps regarding him 'as a thorough good sporting hard riding man with a minimum of intellect' who, although 'quite cool and collected', had 'not slightest idea as to what was going on or what he was going to do next'.[41] One regimental officer could not imagine how Major-General H.D. de Pree, who as BGGS, IV Corps was the '*bete-noir*' of 'Uncle' Harper (51st Division), 'got such a responsible job'.[42] One possible reason was that he was Haig's cousin!

The General Headquarters was forced in late 1914 to start 'making a list of all psc people not serving on the Staff'.[43] The shortages of staff meant that officers at GHQ spent much of the war trying to leave but were told that owing to the shortage of SOs their services were too valuable for them to be allowed to depart. When Clive requested a transfer from the staff to command of troops in June 1915, Sir John French refused remarking that 'he had let two go, & both had been killed within a week'.[44] Kirke's attempts to get out of the Intelligence Section in 1915 and 1916 were foiled because he could not be spared.[45] GHQ refused to sanction the offer of command of a battalion to General Sir Eric de Burgh because as psc his '"services could not be spared for regimental duty"'.[46]

Lieutenant-General Sir Launcelot Kiggell (CGS, GHQ) maintained that 'the needs of the Army and the Empire' made it 'impossible to let highly trained staff officers take up commands' as it was 'indispensable that staff work should be efficient and it will become still more so when we get the Germans into the open'.[47] When in 1917 Robertson, Chief of the Imperial General Staff (CIGS), wished to promote Marshal of the RAF Sir Edward Ellington to command of a Brigade, Kiggell insisted on his appointment as BGGS, VIII Corps because he was 'a trained SO and the number of these is running low' and GHQ had 'three BGGSs to find at present' whereas there were 'a large number of officers who have been through all the recent fighting who are well qualified to command Brigades and deserving of selection for such command'.[48]

By late 1916 Kiggell was worried that SOs 'holding the appointment of BGGS, GSO1, and equivalent appointments in the administrative branch of the staff, whom it has been necessary to keep on the staff for the good of the Service' should be given brevet promotion to compensate for the likelihood that 'the majority, if not all, of them would have been selected to command a Brigade' but for the fact that they 'possessed the necessary qualifications for staff employment'.[49] Moreover, it 'was much quicker and easier to reach the rank of B[rigadie]r-General by getting command of a Brigade, than by waiting to become the chief staff officer of an Army Corps, which is the lowest staff appointment carrying the [same] rank'.[50] It was also easier for a brigade commander than a BGGS to obtain command of a division as the SO had to command a brigade first in order to become familiar with modern conditions.[51]

Most SOs stayed in staff appointments throughout the war and few of the senior ones had any actual experience of front-line service during the war. There was certainly no policy of interspersing staff posts with tours of front-line duty as was the case in the Second World War. The few exceptions included General Hon Sir Herbert Lawrence who had the advantage of having commanded the 66th Division in 1917 before becoming CGS in December 1917; Lieutenant-General Sir Louis Bols, who had commanded a battalion and a brigade in 1914–15, before being appointed BGGS, XII Corps and then Major-General General Staff (MGGS) Third Army in 1915; Major-General Sir Reginald Hoskins who was 'a first rate' brigade commander before becoming BGGS, V Corps in 1915;[52] and Colonel E.R. Clayton who commanded a battalion for a year in 1916–17, before becoming GSO1, 2nd Division in 1918. A number of officers, such as Field-Marshal Lord Montgomery, Lieutenant-Generals Sir Philip Neame, and E.A. Osborne, who were relatively junior at the beginning of the war, rose to hold the post of GSO1 in 1918 having given gallant service in the front line in 1914 as regimental officers and thus gained first-hand experience of the conditions but once they were appointed to the staff they did not return to front-line service again.

Undoubtedly a shortage of competent SOs lowered standards. One disillusioned battalion commander believed that 'all the shell-shocked idiots of the British Empire were put to do staff work'.[53] There were a number of reasons for such perceptions. In contrast to the large SO Corps in the German Army, which allowed all division and most regimental staff positions to be held by highly trained members of this 'corps', the rapid expansion of the army meant that there was a severe shortage of trained staff. Many new SOs were seconded from front-line units, due to either wounds or meritorious service. Prior to the Battle of Loos, the 24th Division had 'no staff officer, who had acted in that capacity with troops in the field during the war' and although 'the GSOs I and II were serving regular officers, who entered on the war as regimental officers, both had been badly wounded in the first two months in France, and had spent months in hospital or convalescing' and neither 'had had any opportunity of appreciating to what extent everything connected with staff work before and during battle had developed in France, since the commencement of the war'.[54] Brigadier-General C.G. Stewart, the GSO1, 'was not well'[55] and both having 'been wounded in still open warfare on the Aisne and 1st Battle of Ypres' were in hindsight 'not well acquainted with what trench warfare attacks entailed'.[56]

In the early years of the war this decline in standards was made worse by a rapid turnover of staff. For example in 1916, Henry Wilson (IV Corps) 'lost my B[rigadie]r Gen[eral] GS, my 2nd Grade GS, my CRA, & my C[R]E & my Camp Comm[andan]t' in 1916.[57] As a result, some SOs achieved rapid promotion in the early years of the war. Brigadier-General John Charteris, who went from the rank of Captain in August 1914 to that of Brigadier-General in December 1915,[58] General Sir Richard Butler, who was promoted from being a Major on Smith-Dorrien's staff at Aldershot pre-war to be Chief of Staff of an army,[59] and Brigadier-General Philip Howell, who rose from Captain to Brigadier-General in two years,[60] all attained the rank of BGGS very rapidly. General Sir John Coleridge was able to rise from GSO3 to GSO1 very rapidly while serving with the 11th Division in just over a year owing to 'the death or wounding or illness of his superiors'.[61]

It would, however, be a mistake to think that an outdated minority of incompetents represented the Old Army's best officers. Many officers took their profession very seriously. The training at the Staff College had a great deal to do with producing a group of British generals and SOs capable of successfully leading armies against very proficient German forces. Those officers who attended Staff College in the late 1890s prior to the Boer War, such as Field-Marshals Lord Allenby, Lord Byng, Earl Haig, Sir William Robertson, and Sir Henry Wilson; Generals Sir Hubert Gough, Hon Sir Herbert Lawrence, Sir George Macdonogh, and Sir Henry Rawlinson; and Lieutenant-General Sir Launcelot Kiggell,[62] went on to hold senior posts at GHQ and Army level during the First World War.

Others such as Generals Sir George Barrow, Sir John Du Cane, Sir William Furse, Sir Richard Haking, and Sir Stanley Maude; and Major-Generals Sir Thompson Capper, H.N.C. Heath, O.S.W. Nugent, E.M. Perceval, H.G. Ruggles-Brise, and A.E. Sandbach held posts as divisional and corps commanders at home and abroad. The men, who left Staff College after the Boer War, were 'well-educated soldiers' and formed a new breed of professional SOs, who held most of the Staff posts at divisional, corps, and army level during the war. Their standard of ability was 'high' and their Staff College education gave them 'an enormously increased power of using our wits logically and with knowledge'.[63] These men were the backbone of the BEF in the war years and enabled the war to be fought. Their contribution to the winning of the war has been much neglected and ignored when British generalship during the war is roundly condemned as incompetent.

Staff College graduates such as Field-Marshal Sir Archibald Montgomery, Generals Sir Hastings Anderson, Sir Charles Bonham-Carter, Sir John Burnett-Stuart, Sir Lewis Halliday, VC, and Sir Charles Harrington, General Sir William Thwaites; Lieutenant-Generals Sir Louis Bols, Sir Basil Burnett-Hitchcock, Burnett-Stuart, Sir Sidney Clive and Sir Louis Vaughan; Major-Generals Hugo de Pree, Sir Charles Gwynn, and Hubert Isacke, held most of the Staff posts at divisional, corps, and army level. Later, batches at the Staff College produced men who held staff appointments at corps and divisional level, such as Field-Marshals Sir Thomas Blamey, Sir John Dill and Lord Ironside; Generals Sir John Brind, Sir Harry Knox, Sir Norman Macmullen, and Sir Percy Radcliffe; Brigadier-Generals Sir Archibald Home, R.H. Kearsley, and Sir Samuel Wilson.

Staff College graduates formed the spine of the BEF in the war years. For example, Brind (GSO1, 56th Division) 'was very much one of those who... made the Division what it was'[64] while McNamara (GSO1, 32nd Division) was one reason 'why the Division did so brilliantly'.[65] Lieutenant-Colonel H.E. ap Rhys Pryce (GSO1, 38th Division) 'was a thoroughly capable officer in every way', who 'in reality commanded the Division'.[66] Much of the operational effectiveness of the Australian and Canadian Corps sprang from the skill of their high-quality British SOs. All seven BGGS (Field-Marshal Sir Thomas Blamey; Generals Sir Charles Harington, Sir Percy Radcliffe, and Sir Brudenell White; Major-General Sir Charles Gwynn; Brigadier-General N.W. Webber; and Brigadier R.F.J. Hayter) of the Canadian Corps, the two ANZAC Corps and the Australian Corps between 1915 and 1918 were Regular officers who had been to Staff College. General Sir Brudenell White and Field-Marshal Sir Thomas Blamey, the two Australians who served as BGGS with the ANZAC or Australian Corps, were both regular soldiers and products of the Staff College. In the Canadian Corps, General Sir Arthur Currie insisted upon retaining British officers in the three senior staff appointments and singled out Brigadier-General N.W. Webber, his BGGS, for particular praise.

Lacking a large pool of their own SOs the Canadians employed the best British SOs, three of whom (Field-Marshals Lord Alanbrooke, Sir John Dill and Lord Ironside) later rose to become CIGS and Field-Marshals. The first Canadian GSO1 was not appointed until November 1917, and by the Armistice, one of the four Canadian divisions still had a British GSO1,[67] while two of the six Australian and New Zealand divisions still had a British GSO1. The Canadian and Australian Corps could scarcely have become operational without British assistance and the existence of its small caste of pre-war staff-trained officers such as Harington, Radcliffe, or Webber.

Inevitably staff work suffered, notably in 1915 and 1916 as junior staff posts were filled by inexperienced officers. For example, General Sir Ivor Maxse (18th Division) complained in 1915 that 'the Brigade Majors are inexperienced in staff work' and about one in particular 'who cannot write any sort of operation order and apparently cannot learn any routine work'.[68] An attack on Monchy by the 29th Division on 14 April 1917 'was another example of the dangers of inexperienced Staff Officers' in which 'the B[riga]de Major, who drew up the orders for the attack of the 88th B[riga]de was an excellent fellow, but very young' and 'in making out the orders, he omitted to detail troops to occupy the trenches vacated by the attacking troops a matter of routine' and 'as a result, when the Germans counter attacked, there was practically nobody in our front line at Monchy' and disaster nearly ensued.[69]

By 1916 there was a determined effort to train more SOs and slowly a corps of experienced and able SOs emerged. In December 1915 GHQ had 'started a small staff College' under Burnett-Stuart whose aim was 'to train junior staff officers'.[70] Bonham-Carter, commanded the Senior Staff School at Hesdin from October 1916 to April 1917, set up to help 'promising second grade SOs to fit themselves to fill first grade appointments in divisions by courses lasting six to seven weeks'. The officers trained by Bonham-Carter on the three courses held that winter, included an impressive array of talent who not only held the appointment of GSO1 of a Division or Army, providing a pool of useful SOs to back up the SOs educated at the Staff College at divisional level during the war,[71] but many of whom would have very successful careers after the war, notably Field-Marshals Viscount Montgomery, Lord Wilson; Lieutenant-Generals E.A. Osborne, Sir Philip Neame, VC, Sir Francis Nosworthy, Sir Arthur Smith; Major-Generals Sir Kenneth Buchanan, R.J. Collins, Sir Cyril Gepp, F.S.G. Piggott, and Hon P.G. Scarlett. Attending the Staff Course in 1917, Montgomery noted that the students 'all helped each other and acquired knowledge from each other'.[72]

By December 1916 the training of junior SOs was carried out either by attachment to formations within divisions or at the Senior and Junior Staff Colleges run by GHQ.[73] The Senior Staff School under Lieutenant-Colonel Bonham-Carter at Hesdin held a course for 20 officers training for senior staff appointments while the Junior Staff College under Lieutenant-Colonel R.A.M. Currie held two courses lasting six weeks for 50 officers training for junior staff appointments.[74] Having shut down during the operations of 1917, the two GHQ Staff Schools were re-opened on 1 October 1917 in Cambridge to train SOs during the autumn and winter of 1917.[75] Field-Marshal Lord Alanbrooke believed that the Cambridge Staff Course in March 1918 was 'the most excellent value'.[76]

From 1916 there was a growing meritocracy on the staff with a large number of talented, and often young, non-regular officers who served on the Staff, filling the posts of Brigade Major, GSO2 and GSO3. Some notable examples are Robin Barrington-Ward, Anthony Eden (later the Earl of Avon), Wilfred (later Lord) Greene, Edward Grigg (later Lord Altrincham), Walter Guinness (later Lord Moyne), Lord Howick, Oliver Lyttelton (later Lord Chandos), Basil (later Lord) Sanderson, the Earl of Stanhope, and Sir Charles Wright. With such talent it is difficult to sustain the argument that by the end of the war the Army had failed to employ the brains available to it outside the Regular Army. Although it is perhaps also noteworthy that most of these men, like the regulars, were public school educated holding similar interests and in the case of Lieutenant-Colonel J.C. Faunthorpe, the Military Director of Kinemategraph Operations at GHQ, a great athlete specialising in horse-racing, pig-sticking, polo, and big-game shooting. Some, such as Major-Generals K.D.B. Gattie, Sir Ralph Hone, F.E. Hotblack, and Lieutenant-General Lord Weeks, liked the Army so much that they obtained regular commissions. In March 1918, the Brigade Major of the 88th Brigade (29th Division), Captain J.K. McConnel, was only 23 while the Staff Captain, Gerald Pilleau, was 'a boy of 20'.[77] Anthony Eden was Adjutant of a battalion at 18 and Brigade Major of the 198th Brigade at 20.[78]

Although gradually the junior staff posts were filled by officers who had not attended Staff College, the higher staff posts remained the preserve of the Regular soldiers and there were certainly no civilian high flyers, the equivalent of men such as Toby Low (later Lord Allington), Sir Enoch Powell and Sir Edgar Williams who attained the rank of Brigadier GS during the Second World War. Early in the war Regular officers who had not been to Staff College saw 'little hope of advancement' on the GS, although administrative staff jobs with 'Q' were available.[79] Major-General Sir John Headlam echoed the resentment of many who were not part of the magic '"inner ring"'[80] formed by those who had psc when he wrote that 'to the Staff fanatic nothing counts in comparison with those magic letters' and that 'ten years of the most splendid service in war are as nothing when weighed in the balance against a week at Camberley'.[81]

A promotional ladder, from GSO3 to GSO1, was developed and climbed by officers such as Montgomery, Neame, and Grigg, who became GSO1 of Divisions in 1917–18 by dint of experience rather than by qualifications. Of the 275 men who held the position of GSO1 of a Division 57 (21 per cent) did not have psc after their name.[82] Until 1917, the post of GSO1 (Intelligence) at army level continued to be held by staff graduates. By 1918 there were exceptions like Lieutenant-Colonels S.S. Butler, F.S.G. Piggott (Fifth Army), and R.S. Ryan (First Army), which suggests the monopoly was breaking down but all these officers were still regular officers. C.H. Mitchell (Second Army), a Canadian Militia Officer, was the only non-regular to be GSO1 (I) with an army. Edward Grigg was the only civilian to become GSO1 of a division during the war. Lieutenant-Colonel A.N. Lee and Colonel H.W. Holland 'were the only two Territorial officers' to attain the rank of GSO1 at GHQ but as Territorials were given OBEs instead of the Companion of St Michael and St George (CMG) given to the Regular GSOs1.[83] The highest-ranking civilian was Sir Eric Geddes, formerly Manager of the NE Railways, appointed as Director-General of Transportation with the rank of Major-General in October 1916 to organise 'the working of the railways, the upkeep of the roads'.[84] Geddes was 'a most capable man' and 'a great success',[85] but did not challenge the military at their own competency.

The dominance of the Staff College elite was much more pronounced on the staff, as only graduates could be expected to perform to the required standards. All twenty-three (100 per cent) of the CGS at GHQ and the MGGS at GHQ and with the armies in the field were graduates. Of the BGGS at GHQ and with the Corps 95 and 93 per cent respectively were graduates while of the GSOs1 at GHQ and with the Divisions at the front 75 and 79 per cent respectively were also graduates.[86] Of the 76 men who held the posts of CGS, MGGS, BGGS, and GSO1 at GHQ only 13 (27 per cent) were not graduates and apart from one (a BGGS) all of these held the post of GSO1. Only 5 (7 per cent) of the 67 men who held the post of BGGS of a Corps had not been to Staff College while only 57 (21 per cent) who served as GSO1 of Divisions lacked the magic letters psc after their name.[87]

Early in the war the failure of the army's bureaucracy to achieve the required high standards meant that operations did not run as efficiently as the well-oiled machine of 1917–18. In particular, the principle of the Staff as servant of the troops had to be re-learnt and some SOs were too brusque or too domineering. Although able and hard-working, Bruce-Williams (MGGS Second Army) 'developed a rather objectionable manner to those under him in rank'[88] and was removed by Haig because he 'had caused much friction' and 'was not a good enough staff officer'.[89] There was much criticism of other senior SOs in 1915, notably Major-General Sir George Forestier-Walker (Second Army),[90] Lieutenant-General Sir Hugh Jeudwine (V Corps), and Major-General Sir Alistair Dallas (IV Corps).[91] Forestier-Walker was 'difficult both with superiors and inferiors and quite out of touch with his Corps' being 'always in the office',[92] while Jeudwine was 'often rude' and hated in his corps.[93] In dealing with peers and juniors, courtesy, consideration, and good manners were equally essential.

At a lower level arrogance exacerbated problems. Lieutenant-General Sir George Cory (GSO1, 51st Division), who seemed to suffer from a swollen head and 'hardly spoke' to his commander,[94] was duly replaced. Major-General Sir Reginald Pinney had to calm down one of his Brigadier-Generals who 'was crying with rage at imaginary slights' by GSO1, 33rd Division.[95] Lieutenant-Colonel F.H. Moore (GSO1, 29th Division) in November 1917 was 'an unpleasant person' and 'one of those persons who think that in order to be efficient one must be rude'.[96] In 1918 Pinney commented on his new GSO1, Lieutenant-Colonel M.O. Clarke, that 'his talents are A1, his manner is B4 & many resent it'.[97] It is significant that both Clarke and Moore lasted only a few months before being replaced as GSO1. Colonel Karslake (GSO1, 4th Division) was 'a capable officer, and impresses men with right ideas, but he has not got on as well as he should because of a sarcastic manner'.[98] It was known that the '"G" and "Q" branches [were] not on speaking terms in one Corps'[99] and Pinney had to warn his Staff that 'they were to help everyone & NOT get up rows between different branches'.[100]

The work-load sustained by the few experienced SOs was considerably increased. One Brigadier-General noted that 'the first principles of war were overwhelmed by a mass of detail which dispensed with individual initiative & any elasticity' giving as an example the orders issued by VIII Corps prior to 1 July 1916 a 'terrible document' of 76 pages issued with 365 Supplementary Instructions which 'had been endeavouring to legislate for everything' and noting that it took three days 'to reduce this enormous mass of instructions to some 8 pages & 5 maps of brigade orders'.[101] Of the October battles on the Somme the GSO1, 30th Division noted that 'there was never time during this period to manage anything'.[102] One solution for individual Corps, such as the II Corps in 1916, was to attempt to reduce the pressure of work on SOs and to 'draft instructions for reducing staff work in our staffs: fewer reports & returns; more liaison; less reduplication'.[103]

A persistent theme was the long hours required to keep that bureaucracy turning over. Life as a SO was not easy as critics and regimental officers imagined. General Sir Walter Kirke (GSO1, 4th Division) found the paper work to be intense and was up until 12:30 a.m.[104] while the GSO1, 17th Division complained that during the Somme 'the pace was terrific, averaging 16 to 18 hours work a day for the GI of a Division & I personally was tied terribly to my office'.[105] The senior staff of 20th Division during the attack on Guillemont on the Somme in 1916 remained in a 'dark office dug-out, lit by electric light' for 36 hours 'talking incessantly through the telephone sending messages and orders'.[106] During the advance in September 1918, Lieutenant-General Laurence Carr (GSO1, 51st Division) 'had only averaged 2 h[ou]rs sleep' during 'the previous five nights'.[107]

Field-Marshal Viscount Montgomery of Alamein (Brigade Major, 104th Brigade) with a routine of being woken at 5 am and working until 11 pm became 'very tired'[108] and by 1917 'was beginning to feel the strain a bit'.[109] Kiggell as CGS sent a circular round the sections of GHQ in early 1917 stressing 'the great importance' that SOs and clerks employed in all the offices 'should normally finish their work by 10 pm' in order to remain fit for offensive operations.[110] In January 1917, Haig 'urged the desirability of organising work in offices so as to allow Sunday to become as much as possible a rest day' as 'many excellent clerks and officers also are suffering from the continuous daily work'.[111] During the German Spring Offensive of March 1918, the BGGS of the III Corps became so exhausted that his duties had to be taken over for the night by the GSO1, 2nd Cavalry Division[112] while early in April 1918 Major G.M. Lee (Brigade Major, 41st Brigade) 'broke down under the strain' and was invalided home.[113] Colonel T.T. Grove (GSO1, 6th Division), having lost a lot of weight, was feeling the strain so much towards the end of the war that he asked for post at home but then withdrew his application as he could not bear to leave.[114]

The scarcity of trained SOs not only diminished significantly the efficiency of the staff in the BEF but also added to the pressure on commanders. As a result, there was a tendency for army commanders, such as Birdwood, 'to do the work which his subordinate Generals should perform',[115] while General Lord Rawlinson did 'a great deal himself' so that 'the proper staff are at somewhat of a discount'.[116] Edmonds noted that 'several divisional commanders' in 1918 'had to do their own staff work, and then go round the infantry brigadiers to tell them what to do'.[117] Haldane felt that he had 'to think of everything now that my staff is very different from what it was'.[118] Hunter-Weston (VIII Corps) 'devoted much of his time to the small details of administration that he should have left to Staff Officers and junior ones at that'.[119] Such methods made the staff inflexible. For example, while serving as GSO2, Indian Cavalry Corps Beddington discovered that the BGGS (Macandrew) had decreed that no orders were to be sent out without his prior approval and that as a consequence in his absence the other members of the staff were reluctant to send out draft orders warning of a pending move to subordinate units.[120]

More difficult to solve than the lack of SOs was the 'tremendous gulf between the staff' who 'lived in large chateaux miles behind the front' and 'the fighting army'[121] and the subsequent decline in good relations between the staff and the front-line troops. The staff 'were not welcomed because of the "approach" which was often in an "off hand red tab superior manner"'.[122] It would appear that the main cause of friction were the young, junior SOs holding the posts of Aide-de-Comp (ADC) and GSO3 who despite their lowly rank wore the Red Tabs of the GS. During the First World War all SOs were entitled to wear the red tabs and hat-bands of the GS but, during the Second World War, only full colonels and above were allowed to do so as a result of the hostility engendered amongst front-line troops by junior SOs.[123]

One junior SO, a non-regular, noted that when compared with the more experienced French and German Armies the Regular Army during 1915 and 1916 'tended to lead a secluded and relatively luxurious life far behind the firing-line where, immersed in office work, they had no time for personal contact with the front-line troops'.[124] As a result, considerable friction was generated between the staff and regiments in the front line during the war, which, by making it very difficult for the high command to be able to obtain accurate 'feed-back' from the front line, hindered the successful administration of reform and the introduction of new ideas. One junior artillery officer noted that 'the Staff had not the remotest idea of what conditions were like in the line'[125] and usually 'never went further than at the most Brigade HQ'.[126] During the whole time that the Cavalry Corps were in the Ypres Salient under the Second Army in mid-1915, 'not a single member of the Army Staff had come round to visit them and enquire into their needs'.[127] In May 1916, Haig noticed that 'in many divisions, the Staff does not circulate sufficiently amongst the brigades and battalions when operations are in progress'.[128]

The GSO1, 30th Division on the Somme noted that 'an effort to keep personal touch between Div[isiona]l H[ea]dq[uar]trs and the front-line troops would take a staff officer some 8 or 9 hours'.[129] The dangers of visiting the front for SOs were very real. For example, Lieutenant-Colonel J.A. Longridge (GSO1, 1st Division) was shot through the head and killed while visiting the front line in August 1916.[130] It is often forgotten that even staying back in the rear could be dangerous. For example, Lieutenant-Colonel F.E.L. Daniell (GSO1, 21st Division) was killed by a shell, which landed on his headquarters in February 1916.[131]

The lesson that senior officers must pay frequent visits to battle areas to be with the forward troops and commanders in order to make the on-the-spot assessments and decisions which would guarantee the success of operations was gradually absorbed. Good SOs found techniques to ensure that they kept in close contact with the front. On the First Army Staff it was the rule that 'every staff officer had to go out once every day (or night) and visit some unit' and that 'every position of the front held by the Army had to be visited at least once every week'.[132] General Sir Walter Kirke (GSO1, 4th Division) frequently went round the trenches with the CRE and the GOC, realising that 'its a good thing for the men to see the Staff pretty often' to prevent them thinking that the staff were 'leading a life of ease and luxury behind'.[133] Colonel W.H.F. Weber (GSO1, 30th Division) 'three times went right down to the front line to receive impressions' of operations to capture Trones Wood.[134] One Brigade Major did 'not get out enough round the line' because his Brigade Commander did 'not encourage it much' and it was only when his commander was replaced by a younger man that he was able to 'go out every morning', doing his office work in the afternoon.[135] Montgomery, while serving as a Brigade Major in 1916, had a routine of visiting the trenches in the morning and doing his office work in the afternoon[136] and while serving as GSO2, 33rd Division, in 1917 took it in turns with the GSO1 'to go out and visit the trenches' every other day.[137] Prior to the Battle of Loos, the GSO2 of the 21st Division 'had reconnoitred from the air 3 days before as far back as Pont a Vendin'.[138] By 1918 a number of SOs were employing aircraft in order to be able to travel about much more quickly.[139] GHQ noted in April 1918 that 'staff officers cannot satisfactorily retain touch with units belonging to their own formations or with other units on their flanks if they allow themselves to be bounded by their offices' and that 'they should make frequent personal reconnaissances in order to find out for themselves the situation both in front and on their flanks'.[140]

Another solution was the development of liaison officers, whose duty it was to keep their superiors informed about the conditions at the front, and, as 'undoubtedly when properly used' they 'proved of real value',[141] their employment gradually became universal. During the first years of the war 'the best use was not made' of liaison officers 'as they were not sent far enough forward' never going 'further forward than Brigade HQ'.[142] The GSO1, 32nd Division complained of 'the lack of liaison from back to front; we went back always to Corps HQ' having 'no recollection of Corps GS coming up to us to help & see how we were faring, & *never* further up ie to B[riga]des or to the men in front!'[143] At Third Army in 1916 there were three GSO3s who 'each had a Corps to look after and were supposed to know all about it and everything that went on in it, state of the trenches, etc'. But little notice was taken of their reports while the units regarded their visitors as spies trying to find fault rather than attempting 'to find out the real and actual conditions in the front line and to help as far as possible'.[144] Liaison Officers were often seen as 'the Army Commanders' private snoopers'[145] and when a 'learner' SO from Army HQ was found in his area by GOC 96th Brigade he 'was furious, & rightly so, that the Army should send up a sort of spy who never reported to Div[isional] HQ or to B[riga]de HQ either going up or coming back!'[146] One Regimental Officer noted how the Staff of the 91st Brigade were 'reduced to a state of perspiring nervousness' by a visit for tea by two officers from corps.[147]

As a result of experiences on the Somme in 1916, XIII Corps advocated that 'more use might, perhaps, be made of the French system of Liaison Officers' whose responsibility was 'keeping the superior authority informed of the situation and for verifying the position actually held by the infantry' and ensuring that 'the spirit of the orders of the superior authority is carried out by lower formations'.[148] The Fourth Army noted that it was 'essential' that divisional commanders should have liaison officers at brigade headquarters 'during important periods of operations' to keep them informed 'of all important events' and 'thus considerably relieving the work of the Brigade Staff'.[149] By 1917 the post of 'Intelligence Officer' at brigade headquarters had been evolved to keep them in touch with the front line,[150] and Plumer (Second Army) had officers living in sectors of the front line in order to keep him in touch with the troops.[151] By mid-1918 the troops of the 13th Brigade (5th Division) were visited regularly in the line by SOs from XI Corps.[152] In 1918 the 8th Division had an SO (GSO2), who 'was the principal liaison officer between the forward units and Divisional HQ', paying 'frequent visits to the forward troops'.[153]

Improving the quality of British staff work at all levels was essential. At his first conference with his army commanders in January 1916, Haig spoke on the importance of good staff work and the need for adhering to the principles of FSR.[154] During 1915–17, the staff work of the BEF gradually improved as the army absorbed the new, inexperienced SOs. By 1917 a number of formations had gained a very good reputation for their staff work and at army level in particular SOs formed close working partnerships with their commanders. For example, Rawlinson and A.A. Montgomery formed a close partnership at Fourth Army,[155] which was, apart from the partnership of Plumer and Harington at Second Army,[156] the best known commander and SO partnership at army level in the British Army during the war. In contrast to the Fifth Army, the Second Army in 1917 was renowned for 'wonderful organization and devotion to detail'[157] in its 'detailed preparation for the battle, down to battalion and battery level'.[158] Anderson Hastings, 'supreme as a Staff Officer', formed 'a strong combination' with Horne, 'a first-rate soldier', at XV Corps and then First Army[159] while Byng at the Third Army also formed effective partnerships with Bols and Vaughan.

Nevertheless, relationships were sometimes unhappy and problems could arise when commanders and SOs were unable to combine happily. In 1917 General Sir Hubert Gough and his MGGS, Major-General Sir Neill Malcolm, although old friends, proved to be a disastrous combination and the Fifth Army gained an unenviable reputation for poor organisation.[160] As things had 'not been running at all smoothly',[161] there was 'much discontent with Neill Malcolm', who 'accentuated and encouraged Gough's peculiarities, instead of softening them down',[162] and failed to control his restless army commander.[163] As a result as early as mid-1916, the combination of Gough and Malcolm had 'managed to put everybody's back up'.[164] In November 1916, Gough and his staff 'had simply no conception of the conditions in the forward area'.[165] By September 1917 even Haig was 'inclined to think that the Fifth Army staff work is not so satisfactory as last year'[166] and Malcolm left to command 66th Division. In 1918 Plumer held 'no high opinion' of Harington's replacement, Major-General Sir Jocelyn Percy, at 6 feet 3 inches 'a personality to be remembered',[167] who 'was not given the standing that was his due, and he had as a result on more than one occasion great difficulty in obtaining an essential service'.[168]

An 'outstanding' feature of XV Corps staff, which was a 'very happy family', was the 'intensive training for the issue of operation orders' by the BGGS (Hastings Anderson) who realized that 'it was all important in major operations that orders to units – smallest units – must reach them in plenty of time and that there must not be a second's delay to passing orders from Corps to Division & division to Brigade etc'.[169] As a result 'the staff work went like clock work' and the commander 'could get his orders carried out'.[170] Furthermore, as soon as 'a Division was ordered to join the Corps, one of the Corps Staff went at once to the Div[ision]'s HQ – even before it came into Corps area – to give maps, photographs, areas, traffic routes and in fact every scrap of useful information which could be circulated and digested during the move up'.[171]

The greatly increased mobility of their forces in 1917 and especially 1918 suggests that there had been a great improvement in the level of staff work. By early 1917 Corps Commanders, such as Du Cane, XV Corps, and Maxse, XVIII Corps, emphasised the necessity for a closer understanding between Regimental and SOs,[172] stressing that the Staff were 'the servants of the troops'. The staff were to 'avoid blaming subordinate Staffs unless their fault is grave' and above all to make sure that 'the troops have the earliest notice of matters affecting them'. It was also made clear that in order to help the troops the staff 'must be a happy family' and that there was to be 'no quarrelling between branches of the Staff'.[173]

By 1917–18 all British headquarters had gained greatly in the ability to exercise command; and had gained self-confidence too from their recent successes. Lord Cavan in October 1917 agreed with Haig that 'now the divisions understand the manner of making an attack, long delays for special preparations are no longer necessary'.[174] British staffs by late 1917 were able to assemble and deploy large numbers of men and equipment in a way which had not been possible in 1916. For the Battle of Cambrai seven assaulting divisions, five of whom 'had been concentrated in the back areas for training and were brought up to the front of attack by night moves', were supported by 1009 guns, of which 667 guns had to be moved in from other areas, and three Tank Brigades, which were moved to the front on 36 trains.[175] Staff procedures were appropriately flexible and unbureaucratic.

The General Headquarters warned in April 1918 that 'in warfare of movement it is neither possible nor desirable for Commands and Staffs, especially those of Divisions and Brigades, to carry out their functions with the facilities and the deliberation which have come to be looked on as normal in trench warfare'. Furthermore, 'it must be realized that it is necessary for headquarters to be prepared to dispense with heavy paraphernalia, to send away such officers and personnel as are not immediately necessary to the conduct of the battle, and to work as far as possible with a message book only'.[176] By the autumn of 1918, the staff work of the BEF had improved immensely and had become a smooth routine, based on much hard staff work, which was one of the factors in the victories of that year. Montgomery (GSO1, 47th Division) had 'to work out plans in detail for the operations' and to supervise 'all the branches of the Staff, and administrative arrangements' to ensure that:

> The day generally commences with an organised attack at dawn, after which we continue to work all day; then another organised attack is arranged for the next morning to carry us forward again, and so on. It means little sleep and continuous work, at night guns have to be moved forward, communications arranged, food and ammunition got up etc etc.[177]

With its colonial background, the British Army also had to develop a modern, professional and efficient staff system. This depended upon the stability of staff personnel, which was disrupted by a large turnover in the most senior staff positions during the period 1915–16. The practice of frequently replacing staff personnel prevented a long tenure in post, which provided continuity of thought and leadership on the staff. The commanders frequently did not trust their SOs, who lacked experience, and often usurped their functions reducing their status, lowering their morale, and altering the relationship between the commander and his staff. In contrast to the rapid turnover in the early years of the war when the staff were not in their posts long enough to provide needed direction to their formations, the lengthy tenures of the staff in the later years provided continuity of thought and leadership, in which officers became well versed in the functions of the staff.

British commanders and staffs had to learn how to run large-scale operations the hard way under combat conditions. Staff functions became more responsive and multi-faceted than ever before, demanding a high degree of teamwork, efficiency and knowledge. To achieve a 'staff culture' of greater flexibility and effectiveness, the British high command were required to improve its staff training, procedures and techniques. By 1918 the staff involved in the planning process at all levels were very experienced and well practised in working together having, in many cases, worked as a team in 1916–17. Their hard work, professionalism, flexibility, and abiding cheerfulness under great pressure throughout the final campaign were second to none.

4 Developing a professional leadership

In my opinion, the present circumstances in which the Army was placed justified the selection of the best and youngest men to fill the highest commands.

(Field-Marshal Earl Haig, 1915)[1]

The army was in transition during the period 1915–17 as both the commanders and their troops embarked on a learning curve, which would only be fulfilled with victory in 1918. During this transitional period there was a fundamental weakness at the top since the commanders at all levels were inexperienced or unfit for command. In the long term, the search for competent officers, regardless of arm, was of fundamental importance. The army hierarchy was dominated by officers (280) from the infantry who formed 43 per cent of the sample. Indeed 337 officers (55 per cent) had served with the infantry at some point in their career. The Artillery (112) were the next most dominant arm forming 17 per cent of the sample while officers who originated from the Cavalry (65), Engineers (64) and Guards (33) formed respectively only 10, 10 and 5 per cent of the sample. The Indian Army (46) and Dominion (32) officers provided respectively 7 and 5 per cent of the sample. When the war began a small group of 25 officers (4 per cent) were retired and served as 'dugouts'.[2]

In its exclusivity the army was compared to 'the Vatican Board of Cardinals'.[3] Regular officers dominated and only 22 (3 per cent) of the sample were not regular British or Indian Army officers, 15 of whom were Commonwealth officers (2 per cent) and 3 were RN officers! Non-regular officers (19) formed only some 3 per cent of the sample of whom 15 were Dominion officers (2 per cent) while the British non-regulars were very poorly represented with only 4 officers forming less than 1 per cent of the sample. Nevertheless the image that all senior Dominion officers were non-regulars is misleading as over half (17 or 55 per cent) were serving officers with their own Regular Forces.[4] Some, like Gellibrand and Russell, had served in the British Army while others, like Heneker and Hayter, were still serving in the British Army. Major-General G.P. Dawnay, himself a 'dug-out', concluded that 'such rot' was talked about non-regular soldiers not getting 'enough high appointments & that the Staff runs the war in its own interests, & doesn't want it to stop'.[5] Visited by the Minister of Education, who 'had recently expressed the opinion that officers of the New Army had not been promoted to high positions which they merit', Haig maintained that 'the truth is that we have more vacant appointments than qualified officers to fill them'.[6]

The cavalry held a prestige within the army's hierarchy which was proportionately much greater than the numbers of cavalry officers in senior posts. Although the cavalry in France played little active part in the war and represented only 10 per cent of the sample, a large number of commanders in the highest echelons were cavalrymen. Both (100 per cent) Commanders-in-Chief (Haig and French) and five (50 per cent) of the ten Army Commanders (Allenby, Birdwood, Byng, Gough, and Haig) were cavalrymen. Only 4 (40 per cent) of the Army Commanders (Monro, Plumer, Rawlinson, and Smith-Dorrien) were infantrymen.[7] The other Army Commander (Horne) was a gunner (10 per cent).

The dominance of cavalrymen at the top of the BEF's power structure is striking but at a lower level the picture was very different. At corps and divisional level, the infantry were dominant forming the largest group with 40 per cent (including Guardsmen, 62 per cent) of Corps commanders and 47 per cent (including Guardsmen, 55 per cent) of Divisional commanders appointed. The Cavalry forming the next largest group with 21 per cent of Corps commanders and 14 per cent of Divisional commanders appointed at the expense of the Gunners (15 per cent Corps commanders, 11 per cent Divisional commanders), Guards (12 per cent Corps commanders, 8 per cent Divisional commanders), and Sappers (4 per cent Corps commanders, 4.5 per cent Divisional commanders). The conclusions to be drawn from this evidence are clear: during the war years the British Army believed that service with the cavalry was second in importance only to service with the infantry when it came to training officers for command but the infantry predominated overall. The artillery came third.[8]

There was a drastic shortage of adequate officers for higher command at operational level compared with the French and German Armies during 1915–16, which meant that 'owing to the smallness of the old regular Army our divisions, army corps and armies were commanded by men of whom only a few had even handled a division'.[9] Of the sample of 700 officers who served on the Western Front during the war only 63 (9 per cent) had commanded a brigade, 28 (4 per cent) a division, and 9 (2 per cent) a corps prior to the war. General Sir Horace Dorrien-Smith, a veteran of the Boer War, was the only British general officer on the Western Front with personal experience of commanding a division in action before the war and only 34 (5 per cent) had commanded a formation of Divisional or larger size prior to August 1914.[10]

On returning to the UK to take command of the 18th Division, Maxse noted in November 1914 that none of his Brigade commanders had 'ever handled more than one battalion'.[11] Of the 23 divisional commanders on the Somme on 1 July 1916, only 3 had commanded even a brigade before the war, while of the 18 corps commanders, only 2 had commanded a division.[12] Their inexperience and that of their subordinates was inevitable and, as a result, mistakes were frequent and costly. In part because of their colonial background, corps and division commanders lacked experience when fighting at an operational level because 'their training had been in frontier wars and South Africa'.[13] One such commander was Major-General Sir Henry Lukin (9th Division), a South African, who had done well in bush-wacking expeditions in Africa, but whose knowledge of modern warfare was rudimentary.[14]

Other commanders, like Hamilton-Gordon, Pulteney and Woollcombe, were brought into Divisional and Corps commands from Britain because of their seniority. At a lower level, General Sir Tom Bridges' hair had 'gone grey with his quick rise from Sq[uadron] Leader in 4 D[ragoon] G[uards] on the Mons Retreat' to command of the 19th Division in December 1915.[15] Field-Marshal Sir Cyril Deverell rose from substantive Major to Major-General in about a year[16] while General Sir Peter Strickland obtained command of the 1st Division 'just 10 days over 2 years since I got Lieut[enant] Col[onel]!!!'[17] Haig promoted Jacob from Colonel to Lieutenant-General 'in about 18 months'.[18] The rapid expansion of the Army meant that majors were 'getting commands of Brigades as a matter of course'.[19] Such rapid expansion left formations at all levels of the army's hierarchy without experienced leaders.

For many, the war represented a new impetus for careers providing opportunities for advancement, which had previously seemed unattainable. Field-Marshal Earl of Cavan had actually retired in 1913 and had to be hastily recalled on the outbreak of war. Major-General P.R. Robertson, 'an able divisional commander', would not have attained the rank of Lieutenant-Colonel and command of a Battalion 'but for the opportune outbreak of the war'[20] while Jacob, commanding a battalion prior to the war, had been 'officially informed that there was no further employment for him and that he would be retired' in September 1914.[21]

Until the end of 1916 it cannot be said that there was a proper system of promotion based on professional expertise because there was no sustained reservoir of experience of continental warfare. During the period 1914–16 promotion to the high command and staff positions went mainly by seniority in the absence of any operational experience to influence decisions. Of the thirty Divisional commanders in the BEF in 1914 no less than nineteen (63 per cent) became Corps commanders, and six (20 per cent) were killed or invalided while only five (17 per cent) failed to become corps commanders, all of whom were rather elderly. Furthermore, five (17 per cent) became Army commanders. Of the twenty-five Brigade commanders in August 1914, only four (16 per cent), did not become divisional commanders while twenty-one (84 per cent) did so in the rapid expansion of 1914, 1915 and 1916. In August 1914 the three Brigadiers of the 4th Division, Haldane (10th Brigade), Hunter-Weston (11th Brigade), and F.M. Wilson (12th Brigade) 'were far and away better than the Brigadiers of other Divisions and all became Corps Commanders'.[22] Others were less lucky. General Sir Edward Bulfin (2nd Brigade) 'with his fine soldierly qualities' was one of Haig's 'stoutest hearted Brigadiers' and 'a tower of strength at all times'[23] but was wounded in 1914 and thus, having been removed from the promotion race at a vital time, did not get a corps until 1917.

Of the remaining 165 British and Dominion officers who obtained command of a Division on the Western Front between 1915 and 1918 only a very few, 20 (or 12 per cent), became Corps commanders; 145 (88 per cent) failed to progress to Corps level. In other words, those who commanded a division at the beginning of the war were particularly well placed for rapid promotion during the expansion of the army whereas those who attained this post later in the war were unlikely to progress further. Five (56 per cent) of the nine corps commanders in 1914 were promoted to command of armies, and one (Haig) became Commander-in-Chief at the end of 1915. This first group of corps commanders who went on to command armies must be seen as constituting a particularly privileged but rapidly upwardly mobile elite within the BEF. Of the 34 corps commanders who served between 1915 and 1918 only five (17 per cent) rose subsequently to army command.[24]

Even though few of this second generation of corps commanders managed to rise any higher than that level, they nevertheless perpetuated a relatively unchanging chain of command throughout the war. Those officers who were in the right place and rank in 1914 and 1915 and had good reputations, were able to move furthest up the ladder at a time when the Army needed commanders to step into the vacuum created by expansion. Once the initial expansion was beginning to slacken off in 1916 and ended in early 1917 promotion became slow and a matter of dead men's shoes once again. The rise by seniority meant that men often moved up in rank in spite of their personal qualities or competence because of the urgent need for 'educated' soldiers.

In 1915 Haig noted not only that the brigadiers, such as H.R. Davies, Lawford, Strickland, and Lieutenant-General Sir Herbert Watts, who were being promoted to command divisions were respectively 'a hard practical soldier', 'a hard fighting plucky soldier', 'a capable hard-featured officer', and 'a plucky hard little man' but also that Lawford and Watts were respectively 'endowed with no great ability' and 'no great brains'.[25] In particular Watts (later XIX Corps), although 'a fine leader and a delightful chief to serve'[26] and 'a hard fighter, a leader of men', was 'a distinctly stupid man and lacks imagination!'[27]

Both Cavan and Watts, as Divisional and Corps Commanders, had to rely heavily on their trained GS.[28] Lieutenant-General Sir William Pulteney, who 'was the most ignorant general' that his SO had served under during the war and could not be let out of his BGGS's sight as he could not be trusted to be left to his own resources,[29] nevertheless survived until early 1918. Like Wellington in the Peninsula, Haig had doubts about his senior officers' abilities, commenting in June 1917 that he had at last got five Army commanders 'who knew their business' whereas in 1916 only one did.[30] Progress in getting new blood into the high command proved difficult because of the relative shortage of experienced or capable men.

There were many more positions available for senior commanders and SOs in France than there were competent officers. Lacking a pool of experienced officers during the early days of the war, Haig could not show ruthlessness in replacing senior subordinates until there were officers to replace them. The overall average competence and inexperience of the officer corps did not allow him to make wholesale changes. Prior to the war in 1911, Haig was aware that 'there are a great many useless officers' who 'are just able to scrape along in peace time, but are quite unfit for the responsibilities which will come upon them in the event of war'.[31] Major-General J.F.C. Fuller noted that 'our regular army was an army of *dilettantes* & our new armies, armies of amateurs'.[32]

As early as 1914 Haldane removed three out of the four Battalion Commanders of the 10th Brigade, two of whom were arrested and cashiered for cowardice,[33] while Major-General E.C. Ingouville-Williams had sent home three of the four battalion commanders of the 16th Brigade, within three months of arrival in France, the fourth going on to command a Division.[34] Corkran (5th Brigade) reported in October 1915 that 'two of the COs in the brigade were tired and not very good'.[35] Henry Wilson complained in March 1916 that the 68th Brigade had '3 bad COs out of 4'.[36] Others had to be sent home to command Divisions of the New Army because they could not stand the pace, notably General Sir Ivor Maxse (4th (Guards) Brigade), who 'seemed to have lost his fighting spirit which used to be so noticeable at Aldershot in peacetime' and 'had not done well',[37] and Major-General R.H. Davies (6th Brigade), who 'seemed much changed, full of nerves', and 'very jumpy'.[38]

Many middle-ranking officers agreed in 1915 that 'all our commanders were too old'.[39] The presence of commanders at Brigade, Divisional and even Corps level who were 'old-fashioned and out of date in most things'[40] created friction and inertia within the army's machinery which prevented its smooth operation. Many of the older divisional commanders, such as Major-General Hon E.J. Montague-Stuart-Wortley (46th Division), who could not provide 'the necessary thinking' and took 'life very easily', failed to provide the leadership and energy required of front-line commanders.[41] At Loos in 1915 Stuart-Wortley was too far to the rear and should 'long ago' have been enjoying a pension 'instead of throwing away the lives of heroes',[42] while at Gommecourt in 1916 he was 'a worn out man who never visited his front line and was incapable of inspiring any kind of enthusiasm'.[43] The work ethic of some senior officers is characterised by the CRA of the 2nd Indian Cavalry Division, who 'looked upon his profession as a means of providing him with an easy going life connected with horses, hunting and good friends'.[44]

The shortage of officers necessitated the use of 'dugouts', such as Lieutenant-General R.G. Broadwood and Major-Generals C.G.M. Fasken, Sir John Ramsay, and C. Ross, as commanders at divisional level in 1915 and 1916. For example, Major-General Charles Ross (an instructor at the Staff College before retiring in 1912 to become a writer of military history) rejoined as a Brigade commander and, despite having 'very little experience of regimental soldiering or command', was promoted to command 6th Division in November 1915. He failed 'to exercise any command over his division, leaving his brigadiers a free hand to go their own way',[45] but managed to survive until August 1917 before being given a division at home. It was indicative of the rapid expansion of the army that officers of modest accomplishment, such as Ross and Ramsay, could be appointed to command of Divisions during 1915–16. It was not surprising that 'the new divisions under their old "dug out" generals' conducted attacks which 'just throw men's lives away' because the 'old gentlemen' were 'with no imagination, or no first-hand knowledge, & with minds far too "set" ever to learn new things'.[46]

At a lower level many younger, middle-ranking SOs, who were 'accustomed to taking soldiering very seriously even in peacetime',[47] had to 'carry' their seniors. Major-General Sir Cecil Bingham (4th Cavalry Brigade) 'was a charming rather elderly gentleman who was content to leave nearly everything' to Beddington, his Brigade-Major, who 'was in fact commanding the Brigade'.[48] Bingham later commanded a cavalry division and the Cavalry Corps. Field-Marshal Lord Montgomery (Brigade-Major, 104th Brigade) found that his Brigadier 'was an old retired officer' who was 'a very nice person but quite useless and it would be true to say that I really ran the Brigade, and they all knew it'.[49] In the 15th Division, where the commander, Major-General Reed, VC, was hot-tempered and his competency was in question, Lieutenant-Colonel W.N. Diggle, the GSO1, was 'exceptionally loyal' and kept 'things working very smoothly'.[50] The Army's swift expansion had removed too many experienced officers while bringing many others too rapid advancement.

Undoubtedly some senior officers were unfit both physically and mentally for the strenuous demands of war in August 1914. For example, one officer, who 'gloried in hock for breakfast & high living generally', had to refuse command of a Division in 1914,[51] while Lieutenant-General Sir James Grierson (II Corps), who left Southampton looking 'like a beef extract advertisement',[52] promptly died of a heart attack in August 1914 before he could see action.[53] Men of much sterner material were needed to perform under the 'tremendous strain' that senior commanders were enduring during the war.[54] Sir John French complained in 1915 that the strain and anxiety were 'most terribly wearing' and 'very trying' admitting that he 'had really begun to feel it horribly'.[55]

Many were unable to stand the pace. In July 1916 Brigadier-General H.F. Jenkins (75th Brigade) 'found the strain of command too much for his age & asked to be allowed to resign his command & to return to England'.[56] On the Somme in October 1916 Brigadier-General J.F. Edwards (71st Brigade) 'had to apply to be relieved of his command because he found it beyond his physical powers to go round his front line'[57] while Brigadier-General F.C. Carter (24th Brigade) resigned because 'his health is not too good and he feels too old for the hard work of a Brig[adie]r'.[58] Brigadier-General L.F. Philips (189th Brigade) 'had a complete nervous breakdown just before zero hour' at Beaumont Hamel in November 1916.[59] Lieutenant-Colonel George Powell commanding a battalion in the 18th Division on the Somme in July 1916 cracked up when in line for command of a brigade and had to be quietly sent home.[60]

To be effective, the British Army had to promote rapidly those officers with outstanding managerial skills and technical expertise. In June 1915 Haig felt that 'even if ample guns and ammunition, etc., be provided, progress will be disappointing unless young capable commanders are brought up to the front' and urged that 'some of the present captains should be chosen to command battalions, Majors Brigades, etc'.[61] In July 1915, Haig informed the Prime Minister (Asquith) of the 'necessity for promoting young officers to high command' and that 'to make room, some of the old ones must be removed' and, looking through the lists of Major-Generals in the army list for 'young, capable officers', recommended 'in order of seniority' Morland, Horne, Gough and Haking for command of corps believing that 'they should eventually be given command of armies'[62] and that 'the present circumstances in which the Army was placed justified the selection of the best and youngest men to fill the highest commands'.[63] Of the four generals mentioned all were commanding corps by the end of 1915 but only Gough and Horne were promoted to command Armies (in 1916).

Gradually as the war progressed the older commanders unfit for the strenuous life of trench warfare at Battalion, Brigade, and Divisional level were ruthlessly replaced by battle-hardened veterans. Brigadier-General F.J. Kempster (91st Brigade), an 'old boy [who] was useless and had received the boot in no uncertain manner', was replaced by Brigadier-General J.R.M. Minshull-Ford, 'a topping chap, a soldier both in appearance and being'.[64] During the Battle of Cambrai Brigadier-General H. Nelson (88th Brigade) 'fell senseless' to the ground during a German attack in early December 1917[65] and was replaced by the much younger Brigadier-General B.C. Freyberg, VC. A 'dug-out' having retired in 1909, Brigadier-General F.S. Derham (69th Brigade, 23rd Division) was replaced by the comparatively youthful Major-General T.S. Lambert who was over ten years younger and commanded the brigade for two years until May 1918 when he was given command of 32nd Division. Lambert 'was a first class soldier, who left nothing to chance and never hurried prematurely', and 'was close up to the scene of action, from whence he could watch the attack, and control by timely action its course'.[66]

Perhaps the most interesting example of the necessary clear out of the 'obsolete & incompetent officers who are always such a supreme asset to the enemy'[67] occurred on the Somme in April 1917 when a battalion commander, Colonel F. Rayner was '"degummed"' by his Brigadier-General E.W.S.K. Maconchy, who was promptly '"degummed"' by Major-General A.E. Sandbach (59th Division) who was himself '"booted"', and they 'all travelled on the same cross Channel boat' back to England! They were all considered too old for their jobs (Sandbach was 60, Maconchy 58, and Rayner 50) and were 'pushed out at the first chance',[68] as 'the 59th Division were out new from Home & somewhat inexperienced'.[69]

The personality of its commander was immensely important in the performance of a division. Haig considered that 'much also depends on the fighting spirit of the GOC Division' since 'the division is our real battle unit' and divisional commanders had to be 'able to inspire the unit with their own personal energy and fighting spirit'.[70] Hull was 'full of energy, dash and ambition'[71] and 'made the [56th] Division what it was' showing 'the extent to which the personality of the Divisional Commander permeates through a division'.[72] Haig noted that Lord Cavan (XIV Corps) 'spoke in high terms of Major-Gen[eral] Douglas Smith commanding 20th Division' which had become 'quite a different force' since his appointment and the improvement in the 33rd Division after the replacement of Landon with Pinney as its commander which proved how the performance of a division depended on the qualities and spirit of the commander.[73]

In contrast Haig noted that the 40th Division was 'a poor division' under Major-General Sir Harold Ruggles-Brise.[74] Sir Charles Fergusson (XVII Corps) claimed that under the 'mediocre' Reed the 15th Division had slipped 'from 1st to 3rd class' whereas, by contrast, Blacklock, 'a first rate commander', had made the 63rd Division 'one of the finest'.[75] According to Haig, Matheson, 'whose company was judged the best at company training before the war at Aldershot', had 'made the 4th Division into one of the best in the army'[76] while Sir Edward Fanshawe considered that the 3rd Division 'under Deverell was one of the best trained that ever came into the V Corps'.[77] Worn out and performing poorly on 1 July 1916, the 8th Division, which had been commanded 'damned badly' by his predecessor,[78] 'improved beyond all recognition' under Major-General (later General Sir William) Heneker,[79] who 'greatly improved' the division, which had been 'allowed to become sleepy'[80] and its esprit-de-corps 'at rather a low ebb owing to a series of unsuccessful attacks', and 'soon put our tails up'.[81]

From the Battle of the Somme onwards some effective commanders emerged within the BEF who had gained experience and were active in pursuing new ideas while the process of the weak and ineffective being weeded out by the high command continued. Young and experienced Brigadier-Generals were given command of divisions. Thus, 'most of the people who come out from home with the new Divisions are sent away fairly soon',[82] being replaced by younger officers who had already proved themselves while commanding Brigades. By 1916 it was becoming apparent that the performance of officers like Major-General W.G. Walker (2nd Division), who was 'a gallant soldier & a gentleman but without much tactical knowledge',[83] was not successful enough and that they needed to be replaced by more effective commanders, such as General Sir Peter Strickland (1st Division from 1916) who had 'a violent temper' and was 'unpleasantly rude',[84] but was 'an ambitious fighting-man with any amount of energy'.[85] By May 1918 the three brigadiers of the 1st Division, Brigadier-Generals G.C. Kelly, H.H.S. Morant, and W.B. Thornton, 'were young' but 'they had all proved their capacity in the field'.[86] Similarly, Major-General Sir William Fry, 'a cherry good-natured officer, [who] would probably execute orders better than he can make a plan',[87] brought the 30th Division out to France but was quickly replaced in command prior to the Battle of the Somme by a younger man. General Sir John Shea, who was 'a very smart fellow' with 'plenty of brains and energy'[88] was given the 30th Division but was nevertheless himself sacked in early 1917[89] and replaced by Major-General W. de L. Williams, who had commanded a brigade since 1915.

A pattern of renewal had been established. For example, Major-General Sir Ivor Philipps (38th Division), who 'had no training as a commander in the field',[90] was removed by General Lord Horne (XV Corps) on the Somme because he was 'ignorant' and lacked the required skills[91] and replaced by Major-General C.G. Blackader, commander of a Battalion between 1912 and 1915, and a Brigade in 1915. Blackader in turn made way for General Sir Thomas Cubitt, a younger man, who had commanded a Battalion and then a Brigade between 1916 and 1918.

Originally a regular soldier who had retired from the Indian Army before the war and was serving with the Pembrokeshire Yeomanry, Philipps had been promoted to command the 38th Division in early 1915 'over the heads of many more senior and meritorious officers' as a friend of Lloyd George and it was 'hardly surprising that he was ignorant, lacked experience and failed to inspire

confidence'. Under the command of Blackader and Cubitt the political atmosphere was eliminated and the division 'did extremely well'.[92] Haig ascribed the
improvement in the 38th Division 'which did so badly at Mametz Wood in July
[1916]' to the appointment of the 'excellent' Blackader as commander.[93] In
August 1918 General Shute (V Corps) reported that 'Cubitt commanding 38th
(Welsh) Division had done very well'[94] and in October 1918 Haig noted that he
had 'done particularly well as a divisional commander'.[95]

Similarly, the 50th Division demonstrates the process by which good men
were established in command of Divisions. Major-General Sir Walter Lindsay,
'a charming man but physically old and not an efficient commander of a division',
was sacked by Allenby (V Corps) in June 1915 and replaced by the exceptional
Cavan who before being promoted to command of the Guards Division in August
1915 reinvigorated the Division.[96] His successor, Major-General P.S. Wilkinson,
'a capable energetic commander'[97] and 'a sound, not brilliant' man, completed
the good work of turning it into 'a magnificent division'[98] before making way for
General Sir Henry Jackson, a younger commander who had already commanded
a Battalion and a Brigade, in March 1918.

As 'an immediate result' of the failure of the 32nd Division on the Ancre in
mid-November 1916, Major-General Rycroft who 'always gave one a feeling of
confidence and fair-play', the GSO1, and two Brigadiers including the 'very good'
Brigadier-General Compton, were removed[99] and replaced by more efficient and
younger men. Rycroft, a cavalryman, knew nothing 'at all about the PBI or how
to treat them'.[100] Rycroft was replaced first by Major-General Sir Reginald
Barnes (promoted from 116th Brigade), who fell ill, and then by Major-General
C.D. Shute who, although 'not popular' and 'very talkative and rather a gas bag',
had been recommended for promotion by Lord Cavan from 59th Brigade and
when later commanding the 19th Division 'did splendidly'.[101]

Shute worked for the 32nd Division 'hard but sensibly' and 'understood infantry
and their funny ways as none of the others did' and 'that is why the Division did
so brilliantly afterwards'.[102] On Shute's promotion to V Corps the division was
commanded briefly by Major-Generals J. Campbell and R.J. Bridgford, before
Major-General T.S. Lambert took over command until the end of the war. All had
been brigadiers since 1915. Major-General H.W. Higginson was given command
of the 12th Division in 1918 because 'he did very well as a brigadier in 18th
Division'.[103]

By 1917–18 a cadre of officers led divisions with a level of competence that
allowed them to compete with their German counterparts. Major-General
F.A. Dudgeon when appointed to command the 56th Division in August 1917 had
already commanded a battalion, April–August 1915, and the 42nd Brigade (14th
Division) for exactly two years from August 1915, serving at Neuve Chapelle,
the Second Battle of Ypres, Hill 60, Bellevaarde Ridge, the Somme, and Arras.[104]
This new blood provided a level of competence and professionalism, which made
sure that the British Army with a good balance of experience and relative youth-
fulness, was now, at last, well-run and able to attack with the high level of
performance which Continental warfare required.

By 1917 and 1918, one of the main attributes of a commander, whether at battalion, brigade, divisional, or corps level, was his ability to train his command and to pick subordinates who were also able to train their formations. Divisional commanders, such as Major-General Sir Reginald Pinney (33rd Division), spent much time interviewing or admonishing subordinate commanders and regimental officers, constantly looking for better officers to fill posts in his units, particularly as battalion commanders,[105] where necessary removing battalion commanders when they proved incompetent,[106] and recommending those suitable to command brigades.[107] New, younger commanders ruthlessly weeded out incompetent or unfit subordinates. For example, on taking command of the 8th Division, Heneker immediately sacked his CRA, two of his three Brigade Commanders, and the GSO2, who were not up to his standards.[108] He later also got rid of the third brigade commander and the Assistant Adjutant and Quartermaster-General (AA & QMG)!

Although there is no doubt that bad staff work and poor leadership contributed to the failures of divisions in the period 1915–17, the clear-out of senior officers was often unfair and drastic. Snow (VII Corps) felt that 'the whole proceeding was most unjust and to be regretted' and, although the sacked officers were replaced by more experienced men who had been through the fighting of 1914–15, this did 'not remove the injustice to those who suffered'.[109] Perhaps one of the most notorious removals was that of Smith-Dorrien, 'an exceptionally gifted soldier', from command of the Second Army in May 1915 because Sir John French, 'a much less able man', disliked him.[110] Major-General Sir George Forestier-Walker (21st Division) was also removed with 'quite unnecessary peremptoriness and harshness' by his Corps Commander (Fergusson) on the grounds of his unpopularity with the troops. This seriously damaged his career as he 'was relegated to the command of a Home Service division for about a year' and, although 'he managed to retrieve the situation to some extent' when commanding a division in Salonika, he retired immediately after the war in 1920 as a Major-General.[111]

In the cases of Lieutenant-General Sir Hew Fanshawe and Lieutenant-General Sir John Keir, who were removed from command of V and VI Corps respectively, Haldane felt that there were firm military grounds for removing them but that the arbitrary way in which their replacement was achieved caused friction and insecurity within the high command.[112] Lieutenant-General Sir Hew Fanshawe was 'quite ignorant of how to set about preparing to carry out an operation'[113] but, although agreeing that Fanshawe lacked 'enough experience to command a Corps', when sacked in June 1916, Haldane noted that 'there are other Corps commanders who are in like case' and survived in their posts.[114]

General Sir Aylmer Haldane noted that 'there are several Generals in our Army who, the moment anything goes wrong search for a scapegoat' which inevitably led to 'a general feeling of insecurity'.[115] Snow (27th Division) remembered that in 1915 'there was a great epidemic of stellanbosching' in which 'the higher commands were determined to whitewash themselves for the unsatisfactory state of affairs by making scapegoats of subordinates, and many brigadiers were relieved of their commands'.[116] For example, when Lieutenant-General Sir Edwin Alderson (Canadian Corps), who 'was at best a mediocre general',[117] was replaced by Byng, many Canadians, notably Currie (1st Canadian Division), were suspicious that Alderson had been removed as a result of his involvement in the controversy about the Ross rifle.[118]

Brigadier-General F.M. Carleton (98th Brigade) felt that he had been 'sacrificed to the ambitions of an unscrupulous general',[119] when removed from command on the Somme by Major-General H.J.S. Landon (33rd Division) who justified Carleton's replacement on the grounds that he lacked 'quick, practical methods of command, and a cheerful outlook which will communicate itself to the troops'.[120] Carleton's recent promotion to replace Strickland (promoted to 1st Division) was an example of how a 'change in command owing to promotion or casualties often had a marked effect on the value of a particular unit, and affected the battle'. Carleton 'although unmistakably a soldier, was a Cavalry man, and not exactly bursting with knowledge of infantry tactics, or experience of infantry in action' and as a result of 'friction between 98th Brigade and 33rd Division H[ea]dq[uar]t[er]s' was sent home 'but fought his case at the Horse Guards, and won his case, and later returned to the Front to command another brigade'.[121]

While some commanders needed to be removed, the 'hire and fire' syndrome, which affected the high command undoubtedly, had an adverse effect on both the troops and subordinate commanders. Whether the rapid turn-over of commanders was ultimately beneficial is debateable. As Lieutenant-General Sir Thomas Snow noted, 'throughout the war it was difficult to know how one's actions would be viewed by one's superiors' so that 'one was never sure whether for some particular action one would be promoted or stellanbosched'.[122] As late as October 1917, General Sir Charles Grant on getting command of a Brigade noted that 'indeed one rises and falls with great rapidity out here – uneasy in this respect is the humble slave who wears a Brigadier's uniform'.[123]

Early in the war corps and divisional commanders froze into inaction waiting orders from higher command displaying little initiative and allowing golden opportunities to slip by. One Company Commander complained in December 1915 that initiative was 'asked for, but woe to the man who displays it'.[124] Officers worried about the security of their own jobs were unlikely to be willing to experiment or innovate for fear of being removed if anything went wrong. Hence the care shown by some subordinates 'to avoid giving offence to superiors by hesitation to launch attacks when desired'.[125]

An example, of how savagely senior officers could object to 'the departure from an order in the presence of the enemy' was the reaction on the 1 July of Major-General Sir Oliver Nugent (36th Division), who 'was "Rigid" in so far as the obedience to *his* orders was concerned' and 'kicked up such a fuss about "disobedience"' threatening one of his officers, who had been forced to adapt his orders during the battle, with court martial for '"rank disobedience of orders"'.[126] Nugent was also reluctant to stop the hopeless attack of the 107th Brigade on his own responsibility.[127] Unsurprisingly, a lack of initiative at all levels was a persistent British weakness.

Gough complained that 'a great deal of time was lost, and many great opportunities lost also because we were so slow in preparing to meet a new situation' and

62 Developing a professional leadership

that 'throughout the army among the senior officers the spirit of energy, of resolution, & of initiative, was lamentably under-developed' and 'the value of time was not recognised'.[128] The oft remarked upon ponderousness of so many British operations may have owed something to the fact that boldness required commanders to gamble and the prospect of being sacked inhibited many from doing so.

Under intense pressure to conform many officers while showing great physical courage demonstrated little moral courage in the face of bullying by their seniors. Snow (VII Corps) was accused of being 'more frightened of GHQ than he was of the enemy'.[129] One impatient, SO concluded that too many generals were far more 'terrified of their own rules and regulations' than they were 'of the Germans; or of losing the war, or getting uselessly killed many thousand men'.[130] General Sir Havelock Hudson, whose 8th Division lost 'more than half his whole force' on 1 July 1916, was 'such a nice little man & very quick & sensible' but while he was 'quick enough to see what was going to go wrong' he had 'not quite enough personality to be insubordinate & refuse' pressure from above.[131] With quick decisions and prompt response essential in modern battle for success time was wasted in deciding the next move at every step and the resulting failure was inevitable.

Junior commanders were often placed in a cleft stick when given orders by seniors to make unsuitable assaults. Having 'no confidence in the plan' to attack the main Hindenburg Line in June 1917, Freyberg (173rd Brigade) went to see Lieutenant-General Sir Hew Fanshawe (58th Division) 'prepared to refuse to do it' aware that, although it was 'the duty of the commander to refuse to commit his men to a bad plan', if he did refuse, he would be sent home and another officer would be brought in at the last minute ignorant of the ground and the men. Freyberg remained at his post but the attack, as predicted, was 'a complete failure' with heavy losses.[132] By the period 1917–18 the learning process was less fraught and the problem of scapegoating diminished as the incompetent commanders at all levels were removed and replaced.

Fergusson (XVII Corps) noted that the 'constant shuffling of divisions from one corps to another' meant that 'a mediocre man very often goes on and on, because he is never long enough in one unit for the Corps Commander to feel justified in firing him out'.[133] For example, when the 2nd Division moved from the I Corps to the IV Corps in early 1916, Gough passed onto Henry Wilson his adverse but informal views on its commander, Major-General W.G. Walker,[134] who was later replaced. By 1917, however, continued assessment of the abilities of commanders had become more formalised replacing arbitrary sackings and allowing for the removal of mediocre commanders. The Fifth Army asked its Corps in September 1917 'to furnish a report on all divisional commanders who have been under your command from 31st July 1917' commenting on their 'fitness to command a division during active operations' and 'capacity for training a division'.[135]

Maxse (XVIII Corps) reported favourably on two commanders but adversely on two others. Major-General Sir Robert Fanshawe (48th Division) was 'a good average divisional commander and trainer' while Maxse had 'formed a high opinion' of General Sir George Harper commanding 51st Division, which was 'now one of the two or three best divisions in France' thanks to 'his intimate up-to-date knowledge of infantry tactics' and 'a masterly manner in active operations'. On the other hand, Lieutenant-General Sir Hew Fanshawe (58th Division) lacked the 'decision of character' to command during active operations, having 'little influence over his subordinate commanders' while Major-General G.J. Cuthbert (39th Division) had 'few ideas regarding the tactical employment of a division in battle' and, although 'a good disciplinarian of a narrow type', had 'little or no conception of training methods'. Both Cuthbert and Fanshawe refuted Maxse's adverse reports on them by complaining of Maxse's interference in the training of their divisions[136] but to no avail as both were removed from command of their divisions. According to Jacob (II Corps) Cuthbert had been 'inclined to be very obstinate & mulish' on the Somme in 1916.[137]

The process was a continuous one and by 1918 it was difficult to arbitrarily sack a divisional commander. When General Sir Walter Congreve (VII Corps) 'had reported unfavourably' on him, Brigadier-General F.W. Ramsay in temporary command of the 16th Division complained in February 1918 to the visiting Commander-in-Chief, who asked Congreve 'to go once more into the question, as Ramsay had done well as a brigadier'.[138] Ramsay was not confirmed in command of the 16th Division but given the 58th Division in June 1918.[139] In October 1918 Fergusson reported to Horne (First Army) that Major-General H.L. Reed, VC, was unfit to command 15th Division while praising the 63rd Division under Major-General C.A. Blacklock as the finest he had ever seen.[140] Reed was able to survive as his previous Corps Commander assessed him to be an 'above average Divisional Commander'.[141] By 1917–18 the older or less professional senior officers had been weeded out and replaced by those trained by experience at the front and with a greater commitment to professionalism. By September 1918, Haig felt that 'we have a surprisingly large number of very capable Generals' on whom 'are our successes to be chiefly attributed'.[142]

There was a steady flow of changes in the personnel holding senior commands at Divisional, Corps and Army level during the period 1915–18 as commanders were either incapacited, sacked or promoted so that between 20 and 33 per cent of commanders changed each year.[143] In the matter of generalship and professionalism, 1918 clearly demonstrated that the British had passed the nadir of incompetence and were at last coming into their own. Out of fifty-three British Divisions in France in late 1917 and 1918 no less than 36 (68 per cent) had had at least one change in command. In August 1917, for example, Major-Generals G.J. Cuthbert, C. Ross, and H.G. Ruggles-Brise (39th, 6th, and 40th Divisions respectively) were selected to command Divisions at home.[144] In another case Lukin (9th Division) 'compelled because of the grave illness of his wife to accept the offer of a tour of duty in England' was replaced by Tudor.[145] Others such as Major-General W.H. Greenly, 'who was very exhausted, broke down and had to hand over command' of the 2nd Cavalry Division.[146]

By 1917 GHQ was reluctant to give appointments to senior officers 'when they have not had recent experience' in France 'as the responsible Commanders are naturally anxious to get men who are absolutely up to date with the various peculiarities of this war'.[147] Haig was able to take his pick of 'a large number of brigadiers highly recommended for advancement, and who have commanded their Brigades in all the hottest fighting during the past eighteen months' and doubted whether it was possible 'for even the most gifted officer to suddenly take command of a Division before a modern battle and do justice either to himself or his troops'.[148] From 1915 younger and fitter commanders were gaining command of Brigades. For example, Brigadier-General Hon J.F.H.F.S. Trefusis had commanded the Irish Guards with 'great success' and as a result, although he was only a substantive Captain, Haig promoted him 'to command 20th Brigade'.[149] Brigadier-Generals Hon A.M. Arthur Asquith, the son of the Prime Minister, and B.C. Freyberg 'courageous and capable leaders' who were 'young men of exceptional ability and great promise'[150] both got Brigades in early 1917. In 1918 Brigadier-General G.H. Gater (62nd Brigade, 21st Division), a New Army officer and 'very highly recommended' by his superiors as 'a magnificent brigadier' who was 'quite exceptional', had 'been strongly recommended for a division'.[151]

Commenting on 'the strain of commanding a battalion in this kind of warfare', Haig believed that 'only young and strong men can stand it'.[152] Command of Brigades and Battalions was by the end of the war seen as a job for only the fit and energetic. One battalion commander in 1915 noted that it was 'a young man's war' and that 'no man over 50 should be further forward than the Division – a Brigadier should be under 50 – over that they are no use'.[153] Born in 1858 Derham was 'as too old' at sixty.[154] General Sir David Campbell, on being appointed to command of the 21st Division, 'on hearing the first time they met that Brigadier-General G.M. Gloster (64th Brigade) was 52 years of age, without further enquiry expressed the opinion that that was too old for a brigade command and had him sent home'.[155] One Brigade commander, who had been out in France as a Brigade commander since July 1915, wounded for the second time in March 1918, and evacuated home,[156] was not recommended to return to resume command of a brigade in the Field 'in view of his age' (56 years old) by the Military Secretary at GHQ[157] on the advice of his divisional, corps, and army commanders.[158] Lieutenant-General Sir John Keir (VI Corps) was sacked because he was 'over 60'.[159] Major-General Sir Edward Montague-Stuart-Wortley (46th Division) was too old at the age of 58.[160]

Brigadier-General A.B. Beauman was at the age of 29 the third youngest officer to be promoted to the command of a brigade behind two VCs, Bernard Freyberg and Brigadier-General R.B. Bradford.[161] Bradford was 25[162] and Freyberg was 28 when given command of a Brigade.[163] Asquith and Gater, both non-regulars, were in their thirties and old men in comparison! Brigadier-General G.S. Shephard, a model for Carruthers in Erskine Childers' *The Riddle of the Sands*, was only 31 when he was given command of 1st Brigade, Royal Flying Corps (RFC), in 1917 while Salmond obtained the rank of Major-General at the age of 36, becoming commander of the RFC in France in 1918 at the age of 37. Major-General H.K. Bethell was the youngest divisional commander on the Western Front at the age of 35.[164]

During the years of war the average age of general officers dropped as the emphasis was shifted to promotion by merit. The mean age of army commanders fell from 62 in August 1914 to 54 in July 1917, rising to 56 in November 1918; that of corps commander fell from 54.5 in August 1914 to 53 in November 1918; that of divisional commanders from 55 in August 1914 to 52 in July 1916, 50 in July 1917, and 49 in November 1918.[165] Not only, as one would expect, did the commanders became younger and more energetic further down the hierarchy but also the fall in the age of commanders became much more dramatic.

The British Army's particular weakness was at corps level. Haig complained that 'he had sent home more than a hundred brigadiers, but that he was forced to leave certain corps and divisional commanders in their appointments because he could not be sure of securing better ones'.[166] Haig had to allow men like Fergusson (II Corps), 'a smart-looking pleasant man' who got 'on well with his subordinates' but had no mental courage and caused 'too many difficulties',[167] and Pulteney (III Corps) who, while 'a plucky leader of a Brigade or even a Division', had 'quite reached the limits of his capacity as a commander' and had 'not, however, studied his profession sufficiently to be really a good corps commander',[168] to remain in their posts. Despite some unfavourable reports 'regarding his military efficiency' as commander of 15th Division,[169] Lieutenant-General Sir Frederick McCracken managed to be promoted to a corps. McCracken, who 'was quite pleasant and amiable, but weak and lazy, and left everything to his staff' with only 'imperturbability in the worst situations' as his strong point, 'was not found out and sent home' until March 1918.[170]

Some older corps commanders were indeed replaced but, given their seniority, which made it less likely that they were going to be sacked, and the difficulty of finding even half-competent corps commanders, many were able to linger. Field-Marshal Viscount Montgomery noted 'that the real people who were tired were the commanders behind; Corps Commanders were getting pretty old by 1917 and few of them knew what went on up in front', notably Snow (VII Corps) and Hamilton-Gordon (IX Corps).[171] Snow had failed at Gommecourt on 1 July 1916, having made little effort to reduce casualties for this subsidiary attack[172] and proved 'quite useless' at the Battle of Arras where 'he merely told his Divisions to get on with it' and provided 'no co-ordinated artillery plan'.[173] Hamilton Gordon (IX Corps) always appeared to be 'in his dotage'[174] and in a state of gloom and depression[175] but was not sent home until September 1918,[176] 'to make room for younger men'.[177]

By early 1918 the need for a clearout of Corps commanders was apparent and Henry Wilson as CIGS was very keen on adopting a scheme for 'turning out some of our senior Generals & starting a flow of promotion' and thus make it possible to promote younger men to command of corps and divisions.[178] Most of the Corps Commanders involved in the fiasco of the German counter-attack at Cambrai were 'retired shortly afterwards',[179] notably Generals Sir William Pulteney, Sir Thomas Snow and Sir Charles Woollcombe, who were unable to rise to the occasion showing little enthusiasm for the operations and were removed along with Generals Sir Frederick McCracken and Sir Walter Congreve in a purge of

Corps Commanders which took place in early 1918.[180] Congreve (VII Corps), who suffered from asthma, 'had not really recovered from having his arm blown off at the SOMME' or his son's death.[181] Woollcombe (IV Corps) was 'a first rate officer' but 'rather old in mind for an active corps in the field'.[182] By late 1918 unsuccessful corps commanders were quickly removed if unsuccessful, for example, when Rawlinson said 'that General Butler's arrangements had not met with his entire satisfaction' Haig 'directed Lawrence to arrange to relieve the III Corps complete, and to send General Morland and staff with three fresh divisions, now in GHQ Reserve to replace it'.[183]

To be effective the British Army had to promote rapidly those officers with outstanding managerial skills and technical expertise. Throughout the war but especially in 1917–18 the British Army was able to produce some highly competent corps commanders, who vied for accolades, notably the Earl of Cavan (Guards Division and XIV Corps), 'an exceptionally highly gifted commander'[184] and rated the best Corps Commander in France;[185] Jacob (II Corps), a 'first-rate'[186] and 'most efficient general';[187] de Lisle (XV Corps) 'one of the best Corps Comdrs';[188] Morland (X and XIII Corps) 'one of our best';[189] and Watts (XIX Corps) 'a born leader of infinite courage and coolness in action',[190] who 'had the name of knowing better than anyone exactly how much you could ask our infantry to do'.[191] One SO felt that 'except for Lord Cavan, Horne and Congreve were about the two best Corps Commanders in France' and that Jacob inspired 'great confidence in his capacity'.[192]

At Divisional level the Army also produced energetic and efficient officers such as Major-General C.A. Blacklock (63rd Division) who was 'thorough, and quite a first-rate commander';[193] Bethell (66th Division) 'a wonderful fighting soldier';[194] Major-General Hon W. Lambton (4th Division) 'a wonder',[195] who was 'full of brains and energy';[196] and Major-General Sir Cameron Nicholson (34th Division) whose behaviour during the Battle of Lys in April 1918 was 'magnificent'.[197] Haldane concluded that Deverell (3rd Division), Hickie (16th Division), and Shute (32nd Division) 'were the 3 best divisional commanders who served under me in the war',[198] while General Sir George Harper made the 51st Division into 'one of the two or three best divisions in France'.[199]

This cadre of competent leaders was slowly built up during the war and by 1917–18 the leadership required to win victory had been developed. As 'an experienced fighter' and 'a most likeable personality', who was 'full of sound common sense' and never 'rattled', but, above all, 'did not cling to steriotyped [*sic*] tactics if he saw something better',[200] Major-General Sir Henry Lukin (9th Division) was a typical divisional commander in 1917. By 1918 commanders had learnt to stand up for themselves and were certainly not just obedient *automata*. Colonel C.R.C. de Crespigny (1st Guards Brigade) expressed contempt for any senior officer and showed little respect for generals and the higher command.[201] 'Uncle' Harper (51st Division) was harshly intolerant of GHQ and of the orders that emanated from there.[202] Such officers were quite capable of standing up to bullying senior officers in 1917 and 1918 and to resisting undue pressure from above. A mature and experienced commander knew how to handle the tactical situation himself after ascertaining the facts on the ground and not to permit interference from any quarter.

In 1918 divisions were commanded by generals such as Major-General T.O. Marden (6th Division), 'a man of restless energy, and a first-class Regimental officer, with an exceptional knowledge of detail' who left no one 'in any doubt who commanded the division',[203] and Major-General Edward Feetham (39th Division), a commander with 'a reputation for great courage'[204] until killed in action in March 1918, was described by a fellow officer from the Berkshire Regiment as 'a very fine Regimental officer of the best type', who 'had seen much service in the Sudan and S[outh] Africa'.[205] They were far more typical of the very best type of British general than the old-fashioned stereotypes of lazy aristocrats and unthinking martinets.

5 The army's over-ambitious decision-making

> The result was a lack of realism and an excessive optimism, which the Brigadiers, naturally anxious about their own professional careers, were reluctant to challenge.
> (Sir David Kelly, 1952)[1]

For much of the war excessive optimism, not just a British phenomenon, was a psychological barrier to a realistic vision of the war, making it difficult for the British to assess accurately the German Army and to adjust to an unfamiliar continental warfare. The British high command's self-belief in refusing 'to conclude that by the rules of the game we were beaten'[2] and its ethos, expressed in the motto 'We'll do it. What is it?',[3] was its greatest strength, a powerful asset in motivating the army, when the other armies of 1914 all succumbed to mutinies. Believing in 'the relentless offensive spirit, which pursues its object with dogged determination till it is achieved',[4] most officers agreed with the sentiment that 'no matter what happens, this war has got to be won for once & for all even if it takes years to do it'.[5] But this was a two-edged sword as faith in victory too often degenerated in the early years of the war into a fatal lack of realism within the hierarchy, termed variously as 'the cult of optimism',[6] 'the "Cavalry Spirit"',[7] and the 'offensive spirit'.[8]

The official spirit, as in all army's, was one of optimism. GHQ stressed 'the great importance of a real spirit of determination being instilled constantly into regimental officers and men by all Corps, Divisional, and Brigade Commanders'.[9] In training officers and NCOs, senior officers especially valued 'a cheerful countenance' and emphasised the importance of being optimistic and enthusiastic at all times in order to foster the moral and *Esprit de Corps* of the Army.[10] Visiting GHQ in late 1916, one officer found that 'it is a relief to hear people speak optimistically again, after the way everyone at home is convinced that the war will last 5 years and that then we shall be beaten'.[11]

One division on the Somme in 1916 emphasised 'the importance of officers maintaining a cheerful attitude in dealing with their subordinates, even under distressing circumstances'[12] while one divisional commander spoke to subordinates 'about keeping cheerful instead of moaning about bad conditions which were made worse thereby'.[13] At a local, regimental level, raids were encouraged by the high command as a means 'of inculcating the offensive spirit into young troops and of giving them the moral superiority over the enemy that is so essential whether in offensive or defensive warfare'.[14] Corps commanders such as Birdwood tried 'to inculcate a real spirit of offensive' amongst his men.[15]

Pessimism was frowned upon since it was believed that 'a staff officer who allows a difficult task to depress him is useless'.[16] Commanders like Pinney tended also to disparage anyone they thought was 'a pessimist'.[17] Few were immune to this ethos and even realistic commanders, like Haldane, tended to be critical of officers such as Hamilton-Gordon, XI Corps ('the most melancholy-looking individual I know'), or Lieutenant-Colonel E.R. Clayton, GSO1, 2nd Division ('a doeful-looking customer'), who did not project the image of being 'a great thruster' such as Shute or 'full of energy and ideas' like de Lisle.[18] But during the early years of the war this ethos had an unhealthy effect, preventing officers at all levels from speaking unpalatable truths. In mid-1915 Philip Howell, 'an exceptionally brilliant officer' who 'had been largely responsible for the success achieved by the II Corps' on the Somme in 1916,[19] was called 'the most mischievous pessimist in France' by Major-General Sir Frederic Glubb (Chief Engineer, Second Army) and warned by Major-General Sir Robert Montgomery (CRA, Third Army) that 'by being so awfully pessimistic' he was doing himself 'a lot of harm at GHQ' and that to save his career he 'must cheer up'.[20]

Those officers who did not follow 'the party line' found their career jeopardised, reinforcing the tendency in other officers to tell their superiors what they wanted to hear. Haldane was warned by Major-General H.B. Williams (MGGS, Second Army) 'not to show my disapproval of what is proposed and not to do otherwise than advocate what is proposed!'[21] Allenby (V Corps) moved Lieutenant-Colonel Cuthbert Evans (GSO1, 3rd Division) back to regimental duties in 1915 because he was pessimistic and made difficulties.[22] In 1916 Brigadier-General John Charteris (Brigadier-General Intelligence [BGI], GHQ) informed Haig that Sir Henry Wilson (IV Corps) was pessimistic and should be removed when he questioned the prevailing optimism, stressing that subordinates 'in constant touch with the Germans' knew 'very well what fine soldiers they were'.[23] Divisional commanders such as General Sir Peter Strickland who had 'not written very cheerful letters' worried that they would be in 'trouble' if the censor read them.[24] Nearly sent home in March 1918 when the censor read a despondent letter to his wife, Brigadier-General C.H. Rankin was only saved by the intervention of Kavanagh (Cavalry Corps).[25]

As a result, commanders were pressurised into attacking despite unsuitable conditions and 'it was common talk that no Div[ision] CO [Commanding Officer] dared say his infantry were unfit to attack for [fear of] being sent home'.[26] When Furse and Tudor (GOC and CRA of 9th Division) suggested in July 1916 that 'it was sheer waste of life to advance further, until a general advance of the whole army was made' this advice 'was not well received'.[27] In the spring of 1917 Lieutenant-General R.G. Broadwood (57th Division) was reported for 'lack of fighting spirit' by his Corps commander (Haking) because he tried to prevent the loss of lives in unprofitable attacks by his troops.[28] In a climate where 'a lack of realism and an excessive optimism' prevailed Brigadiers, 'naturally anxious about their own professional careers, were reluctant to challenge' senior decisions[29] and for many officers, knowing that 'optimism pays in the way of promotion' to declare that 'we can break through the German line whenever we want to; that the Boches are absolutely *in extremis*' and that 'very soon we'll be in Berlin; that every thing we do is perfect'.[30]

More damaging still was the way in which a realistic review of planning was impeded by an unthinking assumption that the Germans 'must steadily & obviously go down hill: unless the Allies become very stupid or rash' which was accepted by many officers.[31] Prior to the Battle of Neuve Chapelle General Sir Horace Smith-Dorrien thought that the war would be over in March 1915,[32] while Major-General J.E.B. Seely believed in November 1915 that 'the German is the under-dog now'.[33] Although understandable in the first year of the war, such over-optimism was demonstrably unrealistic by 1917. Full of exhilaration, the British Army rushed headlong into over-ambitious offensives during the period of 1915–17.

Wishful interpretations of German intentions and capabilities percolated down from the highest levels of the hierarchy, reinforcing the tendency for British offensives to be over-ambitious. There was a tendency for the higher command to ignore unpleasant facts and to be 'sceptical of reports received from Battalions, Brigades and Divisions',[34] which contradicted their optimism and for Divisions to discount the value of much of the information coming from Battalions and Brigades because of the junior ranks of their Intelligence Officers.[35] Macdonogh complained that the Operations Section at GHQ 'cooked or suppressed' intelligence to suit their own 'preconceived notions' and 'systematically concealed' information from him in 1914.[36] Cavan (XIV Corps) concluded that the opinions of corps commanders on the Somme in 1916 'should have carried more weight' and that the advances of October and November should never have been attempted given the poor ground conditions.[37] Those who prophesied bad news, such as a German attack on Vimy Ridge in May 1916 or a German counter-attack at Cambrai in November 1917, were told by their seniors that they had got 'the "wind up"'.[38]

Both Commanders-in-Chief set the trend with their unrealistic optimism. 'Obstinate and unreasonable',[39] Sir John French 'believed what he wished to believe'[40] and 'never could believe that the Germans were not at the last gasp',[41] being always reluctant to pass on information which did not fit in with his plans during the campaign of 1914.[42] During the First Battle of Ypres, convinced that 'everything was going splendidly' and that 'the Germans were exhausted', Sir John 'got very angry, banged the table with his fist' when Macdonogh informed him that some fresh German corps were arriving, shouting 'How do you expect me to carry out my campaign if you keep bringing up these blasted divisions'.[43] Sir John remained 'ridiculously optimistic about German state of collapse' and in mid-1915 was 'convinced that the Boches are coming near the end of their reserves'.[44] Robertson (CGS, GHQ) struggled to get him 'in a better frame of mind & not so ridiculously optimistic about German state of collapse' yet informed a conference that he and Sir John French 'looked out above all things for optimists'.[45]

French's replacement as Commander-in-Chief brought no new realism because Haig was equally optimistic in his forecasts, convinced that German powers of resistance were diminishing and that a decisive victory was imminent. In the campaigns of 1916–17, being 'a strong man' and 'very determined', Haig did 'not always realise the limitations of his men' and his optimism 'obscured his judgement and led to heavy casualties in attempts to advance and decisively defeat the German Army, with insufficient means'.[46] For example, in June 1916 he informed the King that there were signs that 'the Germans might bargain for peace before the following winter',[47] believing that he could 'smash up the whole Bosh Army' on the Somme.[48] Despite the disaster of 1 July, Haig concluded that 'Germany is beaten'[49] and remained confident that the enemy was increasingly demoralised and 'not fighting so well'.[50] After the war Haig continued to claim that Germany was in a critical position in the summer of 1916 owing to the simultaneous Allied attacks on all fronts.[51]

The belief that 'the prospects of success' in 1917 were 'distinctly good'[52] was confirmed in Haig's eyes by successes at Arras and Messines. These battles 'undoubtedly produced a considerable moral effect on the German forces', which appeared 'much rattled'[53] and showing 'unmistakable signs of deterioration'.[54] Indeed, Haig informed his army and corps commanders in mid-1917 that 'the power of endurance of the German people is being strained to such a degree as to make it possible that the breaking point may be reached this year' and that 'one more great victory' would culminate in 'the collapse of Germany before next winter'.[55] Haig stressed that 'the present moment is very favourable for ending the war'.[56]

Haig believed that 'Germany was within six months of the total exhaustion of her available manpower'[57] and that 'further defeats in the field may have unexpectedly great results'.[58] In response to the 'grave misgivings' of Lloyd George (the Prime Minister) Haig stressed that his optimistic view of 'the very changed condition of the German Army since the commencement of the Somme battle last July' was 'justified by the present condition of our opponents' troops' and based on the German shortage of manpower, economic problems, and 'a marked and unmistakeable fall in morale of the German troops', which 'almost every week gives us fresh indications of the decisive effect of the Somme Battle on the German Army' and its 'very changed condition'.[59] By September 1917 he believed that 'the enemy is tottering and that a good vigorous blow might lead to decisive results'.[60] Such prophesies of doom were to come true only in 1918 and proved premature in both 1916 and 1917.

Haig tried to persuade Robertson (CIGS) that 'the German was now nearly at his last resources' and that 'the German Army was in reduced circumstances'.[61] Indeed, he complained that Robertson 'was most gloomy & pessimistic & talked d–nonsense', believing that the 'pessimistic estimates' issued by Macdonogh (a Catholic) at the War Office were 'tainted (ie Catholic) sources' and did 'much harm and cause many in Authority to take a pessimistic outlook, when a contrary view, based on equally good information, would go far to help the Nation on to Victory'.[62] In October 1917 Haig protested to

Robertson at the War Office's failure to point out evidence of poor German morale to the War Cabinet.[63]

The War Office was more adept at evaluating German intentions than GHQ and both Robertson (CIGS) and Macdonogh, Director of Military Intelligence (DMI) refuted the over-optimism of Haig and Charteris. Disagreeing with GHQ's calculations of the 'extent of depletion of enemy reserves' and observing that 'the diminution of German morale has been greatly overdone at General Headquarters', Robertson did not expect 'a great and definite victory involving the collapse of the German Army' in 1917.[64] Dismissing Charteris' claims that Germany was on the point of collapse, Macdonogh concluded that 'the morale of the German troops has not been affected by their reverses or by the adoption of a purely defensive role to such an extent as to make a decisive success for the Entente probable in the near future', emphasising that he could 'see no hope of exhausting the German reserves of personnel' and that 'the morale of the German people is as yet far from being broken'.[65]

Robertson implored Haig not to argue that 'you can finish the war this year, or that the German is already beaten'.[66] Macdonogh in particular warned that to publicise 'a low state of morale in the German Army' would lead the public to 'expect immediate great results, in which they will probably be disappointed' allowing the politicians 'to criticise our operations, run down the tactical handling of the troops' in 'a sudden revulsion of public feeling' away from 'undue optimism'. Macdonogh noted that 'the better the German morale, the finer the exploit of the British Army in defeating it'.[67]

As early as February 1917 the Earl of Derby (Secretary of State for War) urged that Charteris should be sacked[68] blaming him for rash and optimistic promises of a breakthrough made in the British and French Press.[69] Haig ignored this good advice, presenting an over-rosy view of the war which raised unfulfilled expectations and encouraged Lloyd George to sneer at Haig's 'optimistic views'.[70] Eventually, as Robertson and Macdonogh predicted, Haig's over-optimism rebounded as Lloyd George and the War Cabinet demanded an explanation for the successful German counter-attack which was launched at Cambrai on 30 November 1917 despite GHQ's reports that 'German morale was low and many German divisions of inferior fighting quality'[71] and Haig's assurances that 'the Germans are well on the down-grade in morale and numbers'.[72]

It is now clear that GHQ had miscalculated the effect of the collapse of the Eastern Front would have on the Western Front. In June 1917 Charteris argued that there was 'no reason to anticipate that Russia will make a separate peace' and concluded that 'Germany may well be forced to conclude peace on our terms before the end of the year'.[73] Charteris 'failed to appreciate the profound affect which the disappearance of the Eastern Front was bound to have on our position in the West, and he continued to encourage Haig by the prospects of an early victory, which had previously appeared to be within the bounds of possibility'.[74] GHQ underestimated the importance of keeping Italy and Russia in the war,[75] ignoring the warnings of the War Office.[76]

As late as October 1917, Haig was refusing to admit that Russia would collapse and contended that any German divisions transferred from the Eastern Front were likely to be of poor quality and unfit to take the offensive.[77] In short 'the highly optimistic estimates formed at GHQ in '16 and '17 of the waning strength of the Germans were proved to be all wrong' for, although intelligence showed that 'the Germans were undoubtedly very near the end of their tether up to the moment when the Russian Revolution upset all calculations', the biggest mistake made by GHQ 'was in not recognising the enormous effect caused by the Russian Revolution'.[78] Haig's forecasts 'had entirely miscalculated' the strength of German resistance.[79]

Blinded by optimism, Haig failed to grasp the fact that, although suffering much distress, the Germans were far from collapsing during 1916 and 1917 but rather were strategically on the defensive in the west while pursuing victory on the Eastern Front. In these calculations Haig 'placed the greatest reliance' on his BGI but Charteris 'regarded it as one of his duties to maintain Haig's morale by gilding the intelligence lily, a self imposed duty which eventually led to his downfall'.[80] Charteris was happy to distort facts,[81] notably removing all the more able-bodied Germans from a prisoner-of-war camp in order to impress his chief with the deterioration of the German troops.[82] Increasingly under the BGI's influence the opinions of Kiggell, Haig's CGS, also began to 'reek of Charteris'.[83] Reputed to be 'such a confirmed optimist that he was unable to weigh evidence objectively' and jumped to conclusions ahead of the information available,[84] Charteris was judged to be out of touch with events,[85] and to have an 'harmful' influence on Haig.[86] A turning point came when in December 1917 Kiggell reported that Charteris 'was much disliked in Corps and Armies' and Haig finally agreed to sack Charteris although insisting that 'no one had done or could do the Intelligence work better'[87] and that Lloyd George had plotted to remove Charteris because of his influence with the Press.[88]

As a consequence during the period 1915–17, the 'undue optimism of the higher command was one of the direct causes of failure'.[89] The planning process was 'too ambitious' with the result that 'in nearly every major operation in France the irrepressible optimism of the Higher Formations carried on the offensive beyond the point when from a balance sheet point of view, it had ceased to show a profit' because 'they never knew when to take their profit and stop'.[90] Only an 'unimaginative cult of the "offensive spirit"', which 'led to a disregard of the technique of stationary warfare', could explain 'this delusion about the "War of Attrition" and the bull-headed persistence in counting territorial gains of a thousand yards as worth any sacrifice of lives'.[91]

In particular, the overconfidence of the high command manifested itself in an underestimation of the supreme importance of secrecy and surprise for modern operations. Attempts to mislead the Germans in 1915–17 failed miserably given the all too obvious offensive preparations and poor security. The attack at Loos on 25 September 1915 was common knowledge not only in London but also to the enemy,[92] while during the St Eloi attack in March 1916 one divisional commander found that his operation was 'a general subject of talk'.[93] In April 1916 the DAA & QMG, 3rd Division was sacked for writing home that the British attack would be from Arras to the Somme.[94] Surprise prior to 1 July 1916 'was non existent' and the 'lack of secrecy or any effort to mislead' was one of 'the causes of this disaster'.[95] The British attack at Ypres in 1917 was an open secret[96] and one corps commander complained that a young SO at GHQ had actually informed his ADC about 'the big push up north to break the line'.[97]

Translations of German battle reports showed that the massive build up for the 1 July 1916, which gave numerous 'indications of an impending attack' to the enemy,[98] was spotted by German aeroplanes as early as February 1916.[99] At Beaumont Hamel the 'want of surprise' was 'the main cause of our failure' as 'the Hun must have known for weeks that an attack was pending' because 'our Artillery had been endeavouring to cut his wire'.[100] On the Somme lengthy preparations made concealment very difficult as there were 'masses of transport and men moving about in daylight, many in full view of the enemy' and the mass of guns made concealment 'out of the question'.[101] Similar lengthy bombardments prior to the Battles of Loos, Arras, Messines, and Ypres made sure that the element of surprise was 'completely lost'.[102] In January 1918, Lawrence bluntly concluded that 'hitherto, with the exception of the CAMBRAI operations, every intended offensive has become known to the enemy before it developed owing to changes in the organization, command, grouping and distribution of the forces to be employed'.[103]

Rawlinson was in no doubt that the 'very large number of casualties' in 1915 had been the result of 'faulty tactics and a misconception of the strength and resisting power of the enemy bred of a persistent optimism at GHQ' rather than any shortage of shells,[104] which was blamed by GHQ. For example, before the Battle of Loos in September 1915, 'everyone was too optimistic',[105] notably Haking (XI Corps) who assured his troops that once the German line had been broken there would be no resistance,[106] giving Regimental officers the 'altogether misleading' impression[107] that there would be 'very little opposition'[108] and that the enemy was badly defeated, which was 'a most regrettable travesty of the real facts'.[109]

Similarly before the Battle of the Somme, the high command was so 'misled by a faulty optimism'[110] that 'the whole plan of attack did not allow for any failure'.[111] Prior to 1 July 1916 VIII Corps (Hunter-Weston) 'were saturated with optimism over-emphasising the effect of the preliminary bombardment'.[112] Hunter-Weston 'was extremely optimistic telling everybody that the wire had been blown away' although they 'could see it standing strong & well' and that all they 'had to do was to walk into Serre',[113] announcing that the enemy's front-line trenches would 'be blown to pieces'.[114] The subsidiary assault on Gommecourt by VII Corps, 'inspired with unusual optimism',[115] was marred 'by the unwarranted optimism of the higher commands for an attack that never had any possible chance of being a success'.[116] General Gough 'became more and more optimistic as the day of the battle grew near'.[117] Haig believed that 'all the Corps Commanders' were 'full of confidence'.[118]

Even after the 1 July 1916 commanders remained unrealistic in their aims. Gough (Fifth Army), who was 'ultro optimistic',[119] promoted 'far reaching' plans,[120] while Haking (XI Corps), who 'was most optimistic',[121] had no doubts that the Germans on the Somme being 'very tired, confused & rather demoralized' were 'in a bad way'.[122] This 'undue optimism was one of the direct causes of failure' for XI Corps at Fromelles.[123] Similarly, one battalion attack on the Somme in August 1916 failed with heavy losses 'largely due to over optimistic reports about German moral' which lulled the troops, who had 'expected a sitter', into a false sense of confidence.[124]

Despite the bitter experiences of 1916 over-optimism continued in 1917 reinforced by communal loyalty of officers to the 'party line' and buoyed up by success early in the year. Before the Third Battle of Ypres, Field-Marshal Sir Claud Jacob (II Corps) addressing the officers of 25th Division 'talked the most arrant nonsense' concerning the plans of the Fifth Army 'to drive the Germans right out of Belgium'.[125] In late 1917 Field-Marshal Sir Cyril Deverell (3rd Division) was still 'very optimistic' thinking that 'the Germans are beaten and that the war may finish this year'.[126] Failure at Cambrai in November 1917 was caused by 'too great optimism in the higher command',[127] which meant that 'the fighting power and morale of the German Army were higher than expected'.[128]

The hierarchy's over-confidence and lack of realism created a situation in which too many senior officers were out of touch both physically and mentally with their subordinates. From 1916, GHQ were considered 'wholly inaccessible' and 'useless as guides, philosophers or friends' because of its 'complete isolation & therefore ignorance of what is going on'.[129] Although his staff stressed that 'he talked to numerous Regimental Officers, and saw and discussed affairs regularly with Battalion commanders and Brigade and Division commanders',[130] Haig was seen by his critics as being 'quite out of touch with the whole Army & even with his own Staff',[131] living 'an isolated life completely out of touch with his Corps generals and with the feeling of the Army'; seeing and entertaining nobody.[132] When attending periodical conferences with Army Commanders, Haig and his personal staff 'always brought their lunch with them and seldom if ever lunched at Army Headquarters',[133] limiting the chances for informal discussion. During the Battle of Ypres in 1917 Haig isolated himself on his private train with Kiggell and one SO and a few ADCs.[134]

None of Haig's senior staff, including Major-General Sir John Davidson (BGO) and Lieutenant-General Sir Launcelot Kiggell (CGS), ever went to the front.[135] Of Kiggell, one Brigadier-General remembered that 'we used to say on the Somme that he never ventured S[outh] of Amiens: no doubt a gross libel'.[136] Kiggell 'had not the slightest idea of the local conditions'[137] and when he did finally visit the front at Passchendaele after the battle he was shocked by the conditions and burst into tears.[138] Davidson's Operations Staff tended to remain in their offices instead of visiting Corps and Divisional HQ where they could have learnt much.[139]

Burnett-Stuart felt that 'several of the senior officers had been there so long that they developed an inferiority complex vis-à-vis the forward troops, and were shy of visiting them'.[140] Tandy (GSO1, Operations) admitted that his knowledge of the front line 'never consisted of more than that gleaned from official reports and telegrams from Armies, plus secondhand word pictures from Liaison Officers at the time'.[141] When General Sir Charles Bonham-Carter arrived as Director of Training, he 'was horrified by the lack of knowledge at GHQ of the conditions under which the fighting in the Ypres Salient was being carried out'.[142]

Henry Wilson, not an impartial observer, believed that Haig and his staff 'are completely out of touch with the Army' owing '*chiefly* to the fact Robertson & Haig abolished my system of Liaison',[143] which kept GHQ informed of conditions at the front, when armies were introduced in early 1915.[144] During the Battle of Neuve Chapelle in March 1915 a gap between the Meerut and 8th Divisions was unreported owing 'to faulty liaison work' between the Corps and the First Army because experienced officers such as Hugh Dawnay, Lord Loch, Frank Lyon, 'Mary' Price-Davies, and Jimmy Shea who had kept GHQ in touch with the front in 1914 had been 'replaced by quite inferior men, not psc', who were 'told nothing & know nothing & therefore are no use'.[145]

In 1916 'the importance of getting touch between GHQ and Corps by means of first class liaison officers' was ignored by Haig.[146] The Operations Staff under Davidson 'did not make proper use of the means at their disposal for keeping in close touch with the formations and units in front'.[147] Whereas close liaison could have allowed GHQ 'to get first hand information' of the situation at the front and to 'have heard the opinion of the troops',[148] liaison officers tended to visit formations rather than the front itself[149] and, as junior officers, could not override senior SOs.[150] Colonel E.M. Birch (GSO1, Fifth Army) remarked 'woe betide him who so much as hinted' to GHQ liaison officers in 1917 that mistakes were continuing in 'a repetition of the early days of the Somme fighting'.[151] At the time of Passchendaele and during the Battle of Cambrai, GHQ 'had not been sufficiently well informed of conditions at the front'.[152]

Effective liaison between GHQ and 'the sharp-end' was re-introduced by Dill at the end of 1917 when SOs with first-hand experience of the front and conditions at the front were appointed to the Operations Branch of GHQ[153] '"to maintain a closer liaison between GHQ and the troops in the line"'.[154] At last GHQ was able to link planning with first-hand information of the actual situation.[155] The liaison officers 'were carefully chosen and exceptionally able young officers' who visited 'the most forward troops' and returned 'to GHQ quickly with valuable information which would not have reached the Commander-in-Chief (C-in-C) through ordinary channels for some time', bringing GHQ 'in much closer touch with forward formations' during 1918.[156]

Haldane commented in March 1918 that VI Corps were 'visited much more frequently by S[taff] O[fficer]'s from GHQ than formerly'.[157] One liaison officer travelled by aeroplane to IX Corps on the Aisne and reported back to Haig.[158] Liaison officers 'short circuited' the long chain of command from brigade to GHQ by visiting the front 'to get the "atmosphere" of the fighting troops' and 'to "feel the pulse" of the whole great machine' taking 'the latest information' and 'a general view of the whole trend of the battle back to the C-in-C the same evening'.[159]

A common complaint after the war was that senior commanders did not visit the front. In 1916, Fifth Army staff 'had simply no conception of the conditions in the forward area' and were 'blissfully unconscious, living as they did, in a substantial chateau several miles behind the line'.[160] One regimental officer remarked that 'the Army or anyhow the Corps Commander at whatever risk ought occasionally to have come right up into the front line and seen the conditions for himself' and 'many of us felt that those responsible for the issuing of operation orders were out of touch with the real conditions under which the troops were to attack'.[161]

Another noted that 'I don't think the higher command quite realized the conditions under which the front line troops were existing'.[162] As a result the 'higher leadership was sadly lacking in ability to cope with the changing conditions of the campaign' and 'the instructions issued by higher authority hardly met the arduous conditions under which the troops were ordered to endure or to attack'.[163] Haldane (VI Corps) concluded that 'half the trouble during the war arose from senior commanders knowing nothing of the conditions at the front'.[164]

Haldane noted in 1915 that 'few divisional generals go to their front trenches'.[165] One divisional commander in the Ypres Salient in May 1915 'had never been outside his dugout for three weeks'.[166] Montague-Stuart-Wortley (46th Division) was notorious for rarely visiting his front line,[167] and 'there was always a feeling' against him 'for not going into the trenches'.[168] In July 1916, Furse (9th Division) had his HQ at Bruay some 7 miles from the front and seemed quite out of touch with the battle at Longueval.[169] While on the Somme the commander of the 123rd Brigade had no idea of the conditions at the front or the positions of his men.[170]

The custom of not leaving headquarters during operations was common at divisional and even brigade level.[171] One officer who commanded a company, battalion and brigade, complained that 'many CO's buried themselves in a Deep Dug-out & proceeded to write endless orders without keeping personal touch with their Batt[alions]' although there were brigade commanders, such as Bernard Freyberg, who 'was a brilliant exception',[172] and Frank Maxwell, who was often 'personally in no-man's-land seeing the alignment of troops for attack'.[173] One reason why senior officers did not visit the front from 1915 was a wish to preserve the lives of the limited numbers of trained commanders that were available.

In October 1915 after three divisional commanders, Major-Generals T. Capper, G.H. Thesiger and F.D.V. Wing, had been killed during the Battle of Loos, Robertson (CGS, GHQ) warned of 'the necessity of guarding against a tendency by senior officers such as Corps and Divisional Commanders to take up positions too far forward when fighting is in progress'.[174] This order was interpreted by many commanders to mean that 'owing to the scarcity of regular trained officers of the higher ranks, senior officers should be chary of exposing themselves unduly in the forward dangerous zone'.[175] To minimise casualties Nugent (36th Division) 'had laid down that no CO should go further than his battle HQ' on 1 July 1916.[176]

Even in 1917 the 'difficulty was to get commanders of divisions to go forward and take control of the operations' since 'they had been accustomed to sit behind trenches and command by the aid of the telegraph' and once the wires got broken 'they lost communication with their brigades who were advancing and fighting'.[177] Commanders at brigade and divisional level were expected to be accessible to the high command and it was 'anathema' for Brigadiers to 'move away from the telephone' ensuring that 'they become nothing better than ciphers perfectly unable to command their Brigades' as it was 'unpopular with higher authority' for Brigade commanders to visit the front because they were supposed 'to send them pretty messages of victory all the time'.[178]

One of 'the difficulties of commanders from div[ision]s upwards' was 'getting to know the actual situation *in time to take action*' and 'of even the front line formations (div[ision]s & b[riga]des) finding out the situation'.[179] By going forward, commanders often cut themselves off from their communications for a long time, as happened to one brigade commander at Loos when he was lost with his Brigade-Major for four hours.[180] Haldane (3rd Division) visiting Delville Wood in July 1916 after 'a very risky' journey found a 'state of confusion, which he could not rectify' and had to return having achieved nothing.[181] Effective commanders, such as Haldane, concluded that, despite the difficulties, they had to visit the front 'before ordering an attack, as the map does not show the difficulties of the ground and that makes all the difference'.[182] Haig noted that 'no one who has not visited the front trenches can really know the state of the exhaustion to which the men are now reduced'.[183]

As the war progressed the hierarchy's over-optimistic perceptions were increasingly challenged as front-line commanders became more realistic in their assessment of German durability. Birdwood (II ANZAC Corps) gave a typical opinion in early 1917 that 'things are certainly going well out here at present, but I still do not delude myself with any belief that the Germans are yet beaten, and that the war is over, for I am sure we have still very much before us both in time and fighting'.[184] Plumer thought German morale 'very much better than Haig & Kigg[ell] think' and that 'our men have no illusions on this point'.[185] In late 1917, the Second and Fifth Armies in Flanders expressed the predominant view when they informed Haig that a general demoralization of the enemy producing great strategic results could not be expected.[186]

Suspicion of 'exaggerated optimism in high quarters'[187] and the belief that 'the German defence is going to crack tomorrow, that his troops are demoralised' grew as bitter experience taught that 'we have not got the Germans beat yet and so it is useless talking of breaking their line and hunting them with Cavalry!!'[188] Senior officers came to 'always mistrust this kind of tonic from behind' believing that it was 'better to tell the men that they have a tough job'[189] and that prophesies of easy success were 'invariably wrong and do harm'[190] because 'over optimism rebounds'.[191] By 1917 pronouncements of impending victory had lost credibility with many commanders, who preferred from hard experience to believe that 'pigs may fly!'[192] According to Gough, army and corps staffs became more and more disillusioned with the tendency to indulge in wishful thinking and began to discount much that emanated from GHQ.[193] Germans offensives at Cambrai in November 1917 and in the Spring of 1918 had a further sobering effect on the British high command.

A greater realism went hand-in-hand with increased efforts to make contact with the troops. It should be remembered that good commanders and SOs at all levels kept in close touch with the troops in the front line. Smith-Dorrien (Second Army) regularly made personal reconnaissances of the ground in 1915,[194] while Major-General Sir George Forestier-Walker (21st Division) at the Battle of Loos came up to the front line 'to investigate personally' and walked 'along calmly with shells bursting literally all round him'.[195] In the last years of the war such visits to the front became the norm.

At army level Rawlinson (Fourth Army) visited the front 'one very early morning' in November 1916 and with Feilding (Guards Division) and Cavan (XIV Corps) 'walked about 40 or 50 yards in front of our own wire',[196] while Gough (Fifth Army) liked 'to see things for himself'.[197] Horne (First Army) visited Divisional HQs every day and cheered his subordinates up creating an atmosphere of confidence.[198] Allenby (Third Army) 'was constantly out in his car inspecting parts of the Army Area, visiting trenches, Divisional Headquarters, Hospitals, Ammunition dumps, etc.'.[199] Byng (Third Army) was always in close contact with the front[200] and Plumer (Second Army) travelled about his.[201]

At corps level, Jacob (II Corps) 'kept himself fully informed of all that was passing and in close touch with his subordinate commanders, so he always knew the situation of everyone and the condition of his troops',[202] while Birdwood made 'almost daily visits round the trenches'.[203] At Divisional level, Major-General Sir Amyatt Hull (56th Division) 'fully enjoyed' creeping round the new front line at Gommecourt[204] and Major-General W. Douglas Smith (20th Division) was quite happy to crawl round trenches to see things for himself.[205] At Arras de Lisle (29th Division) went upto the front 'most days' regardless of the shelling,[206] while General Sir Herbert Lawrence (66th Division) went round the trenches 'quite often'.[207]

In 1918 General Sir Walter Braithwaite (62nd Division) 'commanded his division from his horse, in the best open warfare style' in 'the closest personal touch with the situation', which enabled him to '"grip" his command'.[208] Major-General Lord Dugan (73rd Brigade) and Major-General Sir John Capper (24th Division) narrowly avoided capture by a German patrol while out visiting front-line posts unarmed.[209] At brigade level, Brigadier-General P.R. Wood (43rd Brigade) was right in the front line sheltering in a shallow trench from heavy, enfilade machine gun fire[210] while Brigadier-General W.H.L. Allgood (45th Brigade), 'used to go round his line *every* morning during operations either just before or just after dawn'.[211]

Commanders were also more willing to consult front-line subordinates. Tudor (9th Division) noted that 'later in the war a Divisional Commander's opinion was given due weight' as it was realised that they 'were in a better position than higher commanders to appreciate the situation on their own fronts'.[212] At army level, Allenby was prepared to listen to the advice of others,[213] while Rawlinson in November 1916 was persuaded by Feilding (Guards Division) and Cavan (XIV Corps) to abandon an attack.[214] Plumer took care to consult every corps and divisional commander's opinion in order to adjust his plans to local needs and opinions prior to the great success at Messines in 1917.[215] Byng was 'always ready to hear what one has to say about the difficulties which have to be surmounted' and did not 'force his own views' on subordinates or 'insist on an attack being carried out in accordance with his ideas'.[216]

The re-discovery of surprise, the chief feature of each offensive, became a major ingredient for success in 1918 as 'the experiences of the past two years' showed that 'the element of *surprise* forms a very leading factor in the preparation and execution of an attack'.[217] At Cambrai in November 1917, great care was 'exercised to guard against our intention becoming known prematurely, even to our troops'[218] and 'measures against leakage of information'[219] included keeping GHQ staff in the dark about the plan until late September 1917 and informing army commanders (except Byng) only on the eve of the attack.

As a result the British 'did in fact pull off a real surprise, not only on the Hun, but on the gossip-mongers round London dinner tables where to our shame and horror, we had learnt that all our previous Offensives had been discussed weeks before they had taken place'.[220] There was no preliminary bombardment or registration by the artillery and the infantry divisions, reinforcing artillery and tanks 'were moved as late as possible from distant billets by rail' and their arrival camouflaged and strictly regulated to prevent detection by the Germans.[221] Predicted artillery fire and the tank's ability to crush the formidable wire defences of the German Hindenburg Line made long wire-cutting programmes by the artillery, which negated surprise previously, no longer necessary.

The Battle of Cambrai became the model for the British attacks at Hamel and Amiens in 1918 when strategic deception became a major weapon in the British arsenal. The success of the Australian Corps at Hamel 'was largely due to the secrecy with which they were prepared' with 'every precaution' being taken 'not only to deceive the enemy and to do nothing to arouse his suspicion, but also to prevent our own troops from knowing that an attack was intended'.[222] Great care was also taken to preserve the secrecy during subsequent operations by Fourth Army at Amiens on 8 August 1918; by Third Army on 21 August 1918;[223] and by Second Army on the Clercken-Passchendaele Ridge in September 1918.[224]

Redeployment of the Canadian Corps was made 'with every conceivable precaution for secrecy' and deception measures such as installing dummy tanks, continuing normal radio traffic, and the movement of some Canadian units to the Second Army front in the Kemmel area,[225] which 'quite misled the Canadian troops', who 'spoke of the "coming offensive to retake Kemmel"!'[226] 'No outward preliminary preparations at all that could be spotted' were allowed and as a result the Germans 'were completely taken by surprise and demoralised',[227] enabling the troops to achieve 'their objectives quickly with very little loss'.[228]

From 8 August 1918 the British 'realized that the corner had been turned' and 'seized the initiative once more'.[229] Senior commanders such as Byng, Harper, Godley, and Rawlinson were 'confident that we shall get the Germans back to the

Hindenburg Line'.[230] By September 1918 the German was 'no longer the same man that he used to be' and, although he was 'still capable of putting up quite a good fight',[231] was 'on the hop' and 'thoroughly disorganised'.[232] GHQ concluded that with German resources badly over-stretched there was a unique opportunity to gain a decisive victory.[233]

By October 1918 there was 'little doubt that our breaking the whole of the Hindenburg systems of defence has had a great effect on the enemy' and he was 'ready to make peace on our terms',[234] being 'thoroughly demoralised' and at 'the end of his man power'.[235] By November 1918 'the Bosch infantry was not fighting well and handing itself in pretty freely' even though 'the artillery was pretty active'.[236] Unlike in 1916–17 there *was* a consensus that 'we have given the Germans a severe blow' obtaining 'the greatest victory which a British Army has ever gained'.[237] The optimism of the hierarchy was shared by front-line troops who with high morale just wanted to get after the Germans,[238] who 'fled like rabbits'.[239] But 'the training of four years' taught the British 'not to count our successes beforehand' even with 'the whole German line to the south tottering'.[240]

While Foch talked of still fighting in 1919, Haig believed that the Allies 'ought to hit the Boche *now* as hard as we could' in order to 'get peace this autumn',[241] calculating that the enemy's resistance could be 'completely broken' without 'another campaign next year'.[242] In September 1918 Haig travelled to London 'to impress on the Home Authorities the importance of hitting as hard as we could up to the mud time' but, while Wilson (CIGS) agreed that 'there was ample evidence of the deterioration of the Boch', Haig, handicapped by his previous over-optimism in 1916–17, had difficulty in persuading the Government.

In particular Milner (Secretary of State for War), who thought that Haig was 'ridiculously optimistic', was 'afraid he may embark on another Passchendaele', warning that 'if he knocked his present Army about there was no other to replace it'.[243] Fortunately Haig's optimistic views were now tinged with a new realism and more in tune with his subordinates. Indeed, Haig and his army commanders all agreed in October 1918 that 'the enemy is fighting a very good rear-guard action' and that '*the enemy has not yet been sufficiently beaten as to cause him to accept an ignominious peace*'.[244]

In the end the greatest strength of the British Army was its supreme self-confidence, which allowed it to keep going where all the other nations who entered the war in 1914 had suffered mutinies or collapsed. One of the British Army's most important achievements has gone largely unnoticed: namely, that the BEF's morale remained remarkably high till the end of the war. Optimism was necessary to carry through such a war. Before the British could defeat the German Army in 1918 they had to learn to temper their confidence with realism. A vital precursor to victory was that the army should have an objective and realistic analysis of the tactical possibilities and not, as one Brigadier-General complained, display 'rather a Micawber attitude of expecting something good to turn up'.[245] But the price of that lesson in 1916 and 1917, notably on the Somme and in Flanders, was a high one and Haig, in particular, must bear a heavy responsibility for the over-ambition, which prevented a satisfactory strategy being employed prior to mid-1917. On the other hand, Haig must be given credit for finally getting it right in 1918 and, showing great moral courage, in seizing the chance presented to him from August 1918 onwards against considerable opposition from the politicians and his fellow generals in London.

6 Training for victory

Officers and troops generally do not now possess that military knowledge arising from a long and high state of training which enables them to act promptly on sound lines in unexpected situations'.

(GHQ pamphlet, May 1916)[1]

Training the New Armies, which had been raised at the beginning of the war, so that they were capable of defeating the Germans presented a major challenge for the British Army. The formation, equipment, and training of the 30 divisions of the New Armies and the increase in strength of the BEF from 6 to 60 divisions in less than two years was a major achievement. Certainly, at first the British Army had neither the experience, training, nor ability to match the Germans in the tactical realm and 'in an army the greater part of which had had no experience of any war except this war of trenches, a certain lack of tactical sense was perhaps not to be wondered at'.[2] Against the skill of the Germans the British pitted inexperienced and undertrained troops. In September 1916 Foch noted simply that 'our Divisions were green soldiers & his were veterans' because the British Army had had to expand from '6 to 60 Divisions'.[3]

The daunting task of raising and training a large and powerful army while deeply engaged in a major war was considerably worsened by the rapid expansion of 1915–16. This process produced a 'lack of uniformity of training throughout the British armies in France' resulting in 'the unevenness of the worth of battalions' as late as April 1918.[4] The best solution would have been to expand the original eight Regular Divisions of the BEF 'by amalgamating less regular forces with it' to create 'quite a considerable Army'. But in reality it proved impossible to harness the 'undeveloped power' of the Empire when 'the bulk of our highly trained regular officers are at once carted off to France'[5] and killed 'in the first two months' of the war.[6]

The advice of Haig that the BEF should not 'go over for 2 or 3 months' during which time 'the immense resources of the Empire' could be developed[7] was ignored as it was widely believed that the war would soon be over. In November 1914 Haig reiterated that, since 'it will be many months before the new forces forming in England can take the field', British policy 'ought therefore to be to husband the strength of our present field army as much as possible'.[8] The failure to amalgamate the New Army Brigades and Battalions with Regular Divisions once in France to give them experience and raise their efficiency was a more culpable mistake.

The main value of the Regular British Army in 1914 was 'as a picked force of professional soldiers'[9] but, unfortunately, this expertise was not employed to provide 'a sufficiently strong nucleus of first rate trainers & leaders' to raise rapidly 'the standard of efficiency as a whole'.[10] 'All regular officers without exception' thought that 'the formation of new units is being overdone' and wanted existing Regular units to absorb the newly raised troops in the form of drafts,[11] mixing the 'very good army' of Regulars in France and the 'second rate army' of civilians to form one 'good army'. To do this, the alternatives were either 'to draft your reinforcements onto existing units' or to place plenty of regular officers and NCOs into the new units.[12]

Either method ensured an interchange of personnel in which New Army officers would learn from attachment to Regular units while allowing regulars, 'who have been through the mill' and were 'now rather stale', to take a well-earned rest while training the Yeomanry and New Armies.[13] Aware of the poor quality of the battalion and company commanders of the newly raised formations, Maxse urged in early 1915 the employment of junior captains and subalterns, who had gained priceless war experience with the BEF, to command battalions of the New Armies, which contained excellent raw material especially the junior officers who 'necessarily lack experience in leadership', and raise their skill levels.[14]

Aware of 'the danger of sending out the new army in corps or armies, whose staffs and officers have not got experience',[15] and of 'the necessity of using the troops by battns',[16] Sir John French, the Commander-in-Chief, supported by Haig (First Army) fought in January 1915 to replace Lord Kitchener's proposal to send out the New Armies as armies and corps with that of sending them 'out by Battalions or even Brigades, for incorporation in our existing Divisions and Corps'.[17] French won the agreement of the War Cabinet that 'the New Army will not come out in larger bodies than Divisions'[18] and that 'two seasoned brigades and one new brigade will form a division'.[19] Maxse also suggested that the twelve divisions of the First and Second New Armies should exchange two battalions in each brigade for two, experienced battalions as soon as they landed in France in order to create homogeneous Divisions.[20]

Unfortunately, this good advice was not acted upon. Kitchener refused to split up the New Armies and amalgamate them with the formations already in France maintaining that 'such a use of the New Army would ruin it'.[21] Instead 'whole brigades and even divisions' of the New Armies were 'coming out to take the field'.[22] This method of expanding the army contrasted sharply with the way in which the Dominions formed new divisions. Following the Gallipoli campaign, the Australians doubled the number of battalions by splitting the original existing units and using reinforcements to bring both halves upto full strength giving 'a veteran character and a feeling of brotherhood to the whole force'.[23]

The failure to mix the raw Kitchener Army troops with more experienced troops cost the army many lives.[24] The heavy casualties sustained by 'newly arrived units' in late 1914 demonstrated that there could be no 'real, rapid training unless the trainers are regular officers & men who have been through the mill' and that '10 per cent, 20 per cent even 30 per cent of the casualties' which had occurred in divisions newly arrived in the theatre 'during their first engagements, might have been avoided'.[25] The 'fatal policy of trying to form new units (big units, like divisions) instead of drafting onto old ones' resulted in 'a terribly big bill' in the form of heavy casualties and lost trenches even in formations like the 28th Division formed from 'real good regular battalions from India'.[26]

The older and more established divisions, for example, had a distinct advantage notably the 7th Division which was 'quite one, if not the best of the Divisions in our Army' whose arrangements for 1 July 1916 were 'particularly good' because they 'had a great deal of experience', having 'taken part in every attack from NEUVE CHAPELLE, FESTUBERT, LOOS'.[27] The failure to put reinforcements such as the 28th Division into the line gently as 'new boys' resulted in heavy casualties.[28] A huge 'waste of human material' within New Army formations such as the 34th Division, which had 'never done any good' and was seen as 'a "used-up division"' despite the 'd-ed good men' in its ranks, resulted from a shortage of leadership to provide the required training.[29]

Throughout the war the comparative low level of training achieved by the troops and their junior leadership was a serious problem. General Sir Reginald Stephens (5th Division) lamented that 'most of our troubles have come from our lack of training'.[30] The lack of training was reflected in the poor performance of the British Army. General Sir Ivor Maxse blamed 'the local success of the enemy' at Cambrai in late November 1917 on the 'lack of battle-training' in the infantry and the Machine Gun (MG) Corps.[31] While in September 1918 Harper (IV Corps) felt that 'it was evident during the earlier stages of the recent operations that British troops had not reached a sufficiently high standard of training to maneouvre successfully in the field throughout the varying stages of the battle'.[32]

The British 'fought the war after 1914 (or say 1915) with almost untrained men, and whenever we had to move, in 1917, and especially in 1918, the troops did not know how to do it, nor did the artillery know how to support them' and as a result there was 'unnecessary slaughter, and the non-attainment of objectives'.[33] One SO concluded that from the Battle of Arras in early 1917 until the end of the war, GHQ did not understand 'with what poor & untrained material we were fighting'.[34] Haldane (3rd Division) stated in early 1916 that 'the authorities quite forget that one's officers are young and those in command of companies have only about one year's service and cannot therefore show the knowledge and initiative of those we had earlier in the war'.[35] Owing to rapid promotion, 'most of the brigadiers and CO's now are not competent to teach'.[36]

The British Army had expanded too rapidly for the quality of its training and leadership to be unaffected and shortages of both within the New Armies were major obstacles to effective training on a large-scale. The Regular Army was 'dwindling at a most alarming rate' while the New Armies were 'increasing at an equally alarming rate'.[37] The Battles of 1914 at Mons, Le Cateau, the Marne, the Aisne, and Ypres 'practically wiped out the men of the original Expeditionary Force'[38] so that during the period 1915–17 the BEF was 'an army of amateurs – not professionals' – lacking the skills 'good enough to attack, break through, and carry on a pursuit'.[39]

Rapid expansion diluted the officer and NCO cadres to such an extent that the bulk of junior officers and the majority of other ranks who went into action had no pre-war service. General Sir Henry Rawlinson calculated in 1915 that owing to casualties the 'officers were at least 50 per cent less efficient than they were last Autumn and our troop leading is correspondingly less good' and this was having 'a marked effect on our fighting efficiency'.[40] A shortage of well-trained junior leaders was to be a major problem throughout the war. Commanders complained about the quality of the leadership at regimental level. Haldane (3rd Division) noted in early 1916 that 'the troops have been badly trained at home, there being few people with knowledge to do the work'[41] and GHQ noted that 'officers and troops generally do not now possess that military knowledge arising from a long and high state of training which enables them to act promptly on sound lines in unexpected situations'.[42]

In mid-1916 de Lisle (29th Division) complained that he was 'short of some good battalion commanders for training' the troops.[43] In late 1916 the poor quality of the regimental officers in the 57th Division rendered them unfit to command a platoon or to read a map,[44] while Rawlinson (Fourth Army) commented that on arrival in France the troops 'were very green and their officers want a good deal of training'.[45] Deverell (3rd Division) noted that 'a trained soldier can not be made in a few weeks and trained leaders require long training and practice' and that 'inexperienced officers and men must have experienced leaders immediately with them'.[46]

Heavy casualties exacerbated this problem in 1916–17. By late September 1914 the 4th Division had 'only one commanding officer left, all the other 11 having been either killed or wounded'.[47] Similarly by mid-1915 the 7th Division had lost the best of its officers and men and 'the ranks now contain many new hands who are inexperienced at the job'.[48] At the Battle of Loos, 5/Lincolns lost 22 officers and 460 men and 'with the exception of the MG officer, every officer in the battalion was killed or wounded' resulting 'in almost a complete lack of leadership for the battalion as a whole'.[49] Corkran (5th Brigade) reported in October 1915 that 'the *esprit de corps* of the old units were lacking in battalions' and that owing to hard fighting 'some of the battalions seemed to lack the fighting energy and morale which characterised the original units of the expeditionary force'.[50]

On 1 July 1916 the 11th Brigade (4th Division) lost its six COs and Brigadier-General as casualties (4 killed) and one battalion, 1/Somerset Light Infantry, lost 26 officers and 438 other ranks, including the CO and the Adjutant (both killed) and 'no single officer of those who formed up in the assembly trenches prior to the attack' was 'available for duty at the end of the day'.[51] The 23rd Division in August 1916 had 'great difficulties in getting Officers & NCOs of any standing at all', having 'lost about 5,000 all ranks' as casualties on the Somme.[52] At the end of 1917 after the Battles of the Somme, Arras, Ypres, and Cambrai 'the wastage in officers & NCOs, as well as men was appalling' and it was wonderful 'how battalions managed to carry on, subject as they were to a continuous loss of trained & experienced personnel'.[53]

By the autumn of 1915 'the majority of professional soldiers' in the line 'were either promoted NCOs or very recent products of Sandhurst'.[54] The dearth of experienced officers was a major disadvantage to the newly formed New Armies. The 'K3' Divisions, such as the 21st and 24th Divisions, were manned with untrained officers, especially subalterns, and lacked trained instructors as the best retired and 'temporary' officers had already been allocated to the 'K1' and 'K2' divisions and Cadet Battalions were not formed until early 1916 so that newly commissioned officers received no training before joining their battalions.[55] In the 24th Division there 'was a paucity' of the ex-regular officers while 'the younger ones were mostly the cast-offs of the Old Army owing to mental or physical disabilities'.[56] The 21st Division 'had one inherent weakness in the paucity of Regular Officers' so that when it 'landed in France, no Battalion had more than one Regular Officer besides the CO (who was in all cases a "Dug out")',[57] and 'the actual number of regular and ex-regular officers in the 13 Battalions was 14, exclusive of the Batt[alio]n Com[man]d[e]rs', practically all of whom were old Indian [Army] Dugouts.[58]

The problem of untrained regimental officers and NCOs is too often forgotten when discussing the performance of the generals. The efficiency of British units rested almost entirely on the small handful of regular officers, who after 1915 were forced to do the work of their junior officers and NCOs, having to train them as well as the men.[59] Owing to the shortage of experienced trainers during training in the UK, Forestier-Walker (21st Division) and his staff 'ran' not only the Divisional schemes but 'also conducted nearly all' the Infantry Brigade tactical exercises.[60] Much training was unsatisfactory because many of the young officers and NCOs had not learned how to teach their troops and regimental officers lacking 'a thorough grounding in military knowledge'.[61]

Williams (37th Divisions) reported that 'officers were often very tired when relieved' because 'with the present inexperienced troops the company officers are always on duty and so get little sleep when fighting is going on'.[62] Should these become casualties the efficiency of a unit tended to drop rapidly. For example, one officer on assuming command of the 9/KOYLI, found that, as a result of the heavy casualties sustained on the Somme including two COs and all the Battalion staff, 'no one left knows anything and all has to be organised'.[63] A major shortcoming affecting the quality of the British Army's training was a severe shortage of good NCOs. The loss of experienced NCOs in battle affected the performance of units; one platoon commander complained in August 1916 that when his platoon sergeant – 'one of the best NCO's in the Company' – got wounded the platoon 'wasn't anything like it was without him'.[64]

Haig commented in October 1915 that 'with the Territorial & new troops one misses the junior officers with some tactical knowledge & training' who could 'act on the spot at the right moment'.[65] One major reason for 'our painfully slow progress and heavy losses throughout the Somme battle' was 'the lack of initiative on the part of our Junior Regimental Officers and NCOs, due, of course, to lack of training'.[66] Stephens (5th Division) noted that 'the men were inclined to be trench-bound' and lacking in initiative so that having taken a trench they were 'quite satisfied to sit in it and hold it very much as if it were part of the old permanent line' rather then consolidating it against counter-attack and preparing for the next attack.[67] The Germans noted on the Somme in 1916 that the British junior leaders were not equal to their tasks demonstrating a tendency to panic, to surrender if cut off, and to suffer heavy casualties by employing large bodies of men in close order.[68]

In early 1917, GHQ noted that the advance to the Hindenburg Line was 'sticky' because the majority of officers and NCOs 'have had little or no experience in anything but trench warfare' and recommended that 'no opportunity should be lost, either by tactical schemes or otherwise, of teaching open warfare tactics and especially the use of ground to all officers and NCOs'.[69] Allenby (Third Army) believed that 'the companies having been so long in trenches were now like "blind puppies" and unable to see the features of the ground and take advantage of the cover afforded for turning out the enemy's machine guns'.[70]

'Three years of trench warfare had left its mark'[71] and it was 'a matter of comment at the time' that 'the stickiness of many operations' was 'not due to the mud but what was called trenchitis of the brain'.[72] Throughout 1917 'the German forces seemed to have more initiative than had the British' at junior leadership level with corporals and sergeants holding onto pillboxes or trenches 'determinately' whereas if 'our troops lost their officers too often they retired not because they had been beaten' but simply to 'receive orders from someone more senior'.[73] In early 1918, army commanders were still worried about the training of their troops; Plumer (Second Army) complained that his troops 'are untrained, with indifferent officers & although as brave as possible they simply don't know their business',[74] while Byng (Third Army) was anxious 'not so much from want of numbers as from want of training of men & of officers'.[75]

One Brigadier-General thought that 'the perfectly incredible ignorance of our jolly New Army' was 'absolutely inevitable' given that the expertise of the Regular Army had 'become instinct only by years of business, experience, & learning' whereas the New Army's training was 'surface deep at best'.[76] Whereas the Germans had personnel trained under national service and 'could therefore devote much more time and attention to thinking out new methods etc', the British 'had to do all that was possible against time with untrained civilians'.[77] British junior leaders, both young officers and NCO's, 'were just as gallant as the Germans, but were at great disadvantage' because of a 'lack of military sense and instinct'. 'Most of the Germans had gone through their 2-years' period of compulsory training & were real soldiers, with a well developed military instinct' whereas 'many of our young officers came straight from an office stool or some commercial employment' and 'could not be expected to be in the same class as leaders'.[78] The 'extraordinary lack of skill' shown by the British troops on the Somme reflected the fact that the percentage of the French troops who 'had had *no prewar* training' was 'at the very most 10 per cent and probably considerably less' whereas that of the New Army troops 'with *any prewar* training [was] at a maximum of 3 per cent or 4 per cent of the personnel'.[79]

Equally disastrous was the shortage of trained men, especially after the heavy losses suffered by battalions in the attritional fighting of 1916–17. General Lord Jeffreys (57th Brigade) complained in October 1916 that the drafts of reinforcements had not had much training[80] and indeed one Lance Corporal, arriving on the Somme with some reinforcements, '*did not know how to load his rifle*'.[81] By 1917, when 'large new drafts' of reinforcements formed 50 per cent of Brigades, commanders had to rely on 'short intensive training' to turn the new men 'into soldiers, as apart from brave men dressed in khaki'.[82] Reinforcements from home 'were but partially trained' because 'the period of training at home for infantry had been reduced, except for the Guards, to about three months'.[83]

As the war progressed the quality of the conscripts, who were either unreceptive, draft dodgers or very young troops, deteriorated in contrast to the volunteers of the New Armies in 1915 and 1916.[84] In December 1917 Haldane (VI Corps) received reports from two Commanders, Deverell (3rd Division) and Nicholson (34th Division), that the troops were fed up with the war.[85] The army 'was beginning to feel the strain of the heavy casualties and unpleasant conditions under which fighting was taking place on the Ypres front' and its morale 'was becoming gradually depressed'.[86] After the battles of March 1918 the British Army, badly depleted by heavy casualties, was receiving very young reinforcements, mainly of boys of 19[87] while many officers and NCOs were young and inexperienced.[88]

During the war the 'tight regimental system of reinforcements' broke down 'in the face of heavy and uneven Infantry casualties'.[89] A common complaint by battalion, brigade and divisional commanders was the disastrous effect on the morale and fighting qualities of the infantry of the 'hurried system of reinforcing units in the field', which resulted in battalions being sent reinforcements of 'men belonging to every kind of Corps other than their own'.[90] Regimental officers remonstrated at the 'pernicious habit of drafting officers and men of different regiments to fill up casualties often quite unnecessarily ie 50 Dublin Irishmen put into kilts in the Seaforths in the same brigade whilst in same draft 50 English recruits were sent to the Dublins'.[91]

Misgivings were also experienced by commanders that too much time was devoted to the construction of defences, fatigues and recreation to the detriment of training. As late as October 1918 a common complaint by Divisional and Corps Commanders was the lack of time and opportunity to train their men.[92] Training in France was made more difficult by additional factors, notably the 'great pressure' to avoid 'the destruction of crops' which was 'maintained by the French Authorities', whose reluctance to provide 'adequate areas' for training was 'extremely detrimental' to the training of the army. Finding the time and space 'to carry out training in back areas undisturbed' was equally difficult especially when Divisions in reserve 'almost without exception' were called upon 'to provide large working parties'.[93] The infantry were expected to supply men for fatigues and 'a host of other duties, which ought to be performed by men drawn from other sources than fighting formations about to go into action'.[94]

One Brigade commander complained that, although 'COs always live in hope of the Div[ision] being one day out of the line without any working parties to be found', a long rest of ten days for a battalion to train was a rarity except when 'training for a special operation'.[95] More typically 11th Division when resting 'only got two or three days training' before going back into the line again.[96] At Arras the 51st Division 'had a very serious lack of training' because it had been 'continuously in the line without rest since its arrival in France on 1st May 1915'.[97] In late 1917 the 34th Division was 'tired out and suffers from not having had a sufficiently long time out of the line for training'[98] while in the 20th Division 'one brigadier went so far as to say that he considered his men were not in a fit state to withstand a heavy attack'.[99]

From 1915 onwards the British were providing large-scale training in an ever-increasing number of schools of instruction for all ranks. The development of Army Schools was 'due to the individual effort' of General Sir Charles Monro (Third Army) 'who first originated the idea'.[100] Worried by the rapid deterioration in the standard of officers in France, Monro decided to set up an Army School,[101] establishing the Third Army School for the instruction of 50 officers and 50 NCOs in a month's course. By late 1915 and early 1916 the Third Army School of Instruction was attended by 100 officers and 100 NCOs for one month's course[102] and in April 1916, Henry Wilson (IV Corps) found it 'a most admirable place' and 'quite the best run school I have seen in this country', obtaining 'a lot of tips for our School'.[103]

This was destined to be the seed from which sprang not only the Third Army School but, later on, a school in each Army and dozens of Corps and Divisional Schools as well.[104] In early 1916 the types of schools and the lengths of courses run by corps and divisions varied tremendously[105] and many had been set up during the winter of 1915–16.[106] Haig noted in May 1916 that de Lisle (29th Division) had 'recently started a divisional school' when 'other divisions have had them going since November last'.[107] The Battle of the Somme re-emphasised the need for schools and by the winter of 1916–17, visiting various Divisional Schools, Haig was impressed by the good work that was being done to train young officers and NCOs as platoon commanders.[108] But as late as September 1917 there were only 17 Schools for 20 Corps.[109]

By 1917 a whole system of schools at army, corps, divisional and even brigade level had been established. The GHQ, Army and Corps Schools had been established in France 'to assist in the individual training of junior officers and NCOs'. The GHQ Schools dealt with special arms or services, for example the Machine Gun School, Anti-Aircraft Gunnery School, and the Physical and Bayonet Training School etc., while Army and Corps Schools had been established to train junior officers and NCOs to become 'efficient instructors'.[110] By December 1916, GHQ Schools included the School of Gunnery and the Senior Officers' School for Battery and Battalion Commanders respectively in the UK; the Machine Gun School at Camiers; the Junior and Senior Staff Schools at Hesdin;

the RFC School of Aerial Gunnery at Camiers and Carmont; the Cadet School at Blendecques for commissions from the ranks; the Wireless School at Campagne; 5 Base Training Camps at Etaples (2), Calais, Havre and Rouen; the Machine Gun Base Depot at Camiers; and the Physical and Bayonet Training School.[111] The Five Armies each had Schools for the Infantry, Artillery, Trench Mortars, Sniping, and Signalling, while Schools for Bombing, Musketry, Mounted Troops, and Lewis Gunners were at either Corps or Divisional level.[112]

Army Schools included the Infantry School to train company commanders and NCOs as well as commanding officers, the Trench Mortar School, the Artillery School, the Telescopic Sight School to train battalion sniping officers and NCOs, the Signalling School, and the Musketry Camp while the Corps Schools were the Combined Lewis Gun and Stokes Mortar School and the Signalling School. The Divisional Infantry School was to 'teach junior officers and NCOs to become platoon commanders and platoon sergeants'.[113] Every battalion was required from 1916 in accordance with GHQ's instructions to retain a permanent Instructional Staff, which did not go into battle.[114]

All these problems had a dramatic effect on the British tactical performance. Rather ironically given its poor reputation on the Somme and at Passchendaele, following reforms adopted after the Boer War, the BEF in 1914 was 'the most efficient body of troops that ever took the field'.[115] Impressed by its tactical expertise 'the Germans called the British professional Army "a perfect thing apart" '.[116] Indeed, General Sir Ivor Maxse claimed that before 1914 'our minor tactics were ahead of both French and German'.[117] Major-General G.P. Dawnay (MGGS, GHQ) agreed that the British 'were far ahead of the Continental Armies in tactics before the war' and that by 1918 the 'German and French tactics more and more closely follow the principles of our pre-war Field Service Regulations'.[118]

Unsurprisingly, British tactical methods at regimental level quickly deteriorated from the high standards of 1914 as the Regular Army ceased to exist and 'too much attention had been given in training the New Armies to "the bomb and the bayonet", and too little to the use of the rifle'.[119] One regimental officer noted 'the cult of the bomb was strong during 1916–17'[120] in which 'the men seem to have given up the rifle for those wretched bombs and can think of nothing but the latter when any enemy are about',[121] having the 'tendency to throw a bomb when a rifle could be used with equal, if not greater, effect'.[122] On the Somme 'owing to lack of training in the rifle & an over partiality for bombs', the troops 'could not hit the enemy' at 300 yards, when 'the Archers of Crecy would have made better shooting'.[123] It was very hard to get the men to use their rifles[124] as 'both sides at this period seemed to be suffering from the bombing mania'.[125] In late 1917 the fact that some troops 'had little skill in the use of their rifles and had inevitably lost confidence' was perceived as 'one of the factors that led to a definite lowering of morale, observed not only by anyone moving about the Army, but reported by censors'.[126] GHQ noted in early 1918 that in the past 'the importance of the bomb' had been 'unduly emphasized at the expense of the rifle and bayonet'.[127]

As the war progressed, the better commanders began to emphasize the crucial importance of musketry practice and slowly British tactical skill began to improve.

As early as July 1915 the Third Army stressed that 'all infantry battalions when at rest must be practised for at least ¼ hour daily in rapid loading and in rapid fire' and that 'the use of the rifle from behind all classes of cover with the least possible exposure must form part of the daily routine of training'.[128] In 1915 expecting his battalions to train at musketry for 'at least 2 hours per day' Heneker constructed 'a 50 yards range' for battalions to practice 'rapid fire and fire discipline by sections'.[129] One battalion commander issued an order that 'every man was to fire at least 50 rounds a day when in line' and eventually increased it to 100 rounds.[130] IX Corps noted that on the Somme 'some Brigades have realised that the rifle has been neglected during trench warfare and that more musketry training is required'[131] and 'undoubtedly this period was the turning point' marking 'a return of sane use of weapons and movement'.[132] Training in June 1917, 37th Division stressed that 'every effort must be made to raise the standard of musketry training throughout the Division'.[133] In the 9/DLI, rifle drill took place not only 'in reserve or out of the line but actually in the line'.[134] By early 1918 the 58th Division carried out musketry training in the trenches every day[135] while in the 42nd Division Sections were 'practised in firing five rounds rapid from their positions at least twice during their tour in the line'.[136] One Brigadier-General expected his men to be able to 'fire 15 aimed rounds a minute'.[137] In early 1918 GHQ emphasised that 'the rifle and bayonet are, and always will be, principal weapons of every infantryman' who were to 'use it freely and confidently to overcome opposition and repel counter-attacks'.[138]

This musketry training enabled the infantry to become self-reliant employing their own rifles to fight. Musketry practice 'by day and night' allowed one battalion to repel a heavy German counter-attack at Ypres inflicting 'enormous casualties'.[139] The 6/Northumberland Fusiliers in April 1918 employed the rapid musketry of the 'Old Contemptibles' in 1914 to drive off the enemy infantry, who came within 40 yards, 'with heavy losses'.[140] In a counter-attack in mid-September 1918 'whole platoons of the enemy infantry were simply mown down' by 'first rate troops', who were 'well trained in musketry', and the ground was 'covered with German corpses'.[141] This superb musketry can be compared favourably with the German reliance on the MG and the grenade and neglect of the rifle even late in the war.[142]

One complaint was that the troops instead of acquiring the tactical knowledge required in open warfare were 'over trained at Saluting, Close Order Drill in the ranks, Bayonet & PT and Bomb throwing'[143] because the infantry 'had so concentrated on bombing & sticking sacks with their bayonets'.[144] For example, General Sir William Heneker (8th Division) was 'rather too keen on spit and polish and outward appearance at the expense of efficiency with the weapons with which the men were armed'.[145] Platoon and section commanders also spent too much time teaching the mechanics of the Lewis Gun so that the 'tactical handling of the gun & dispositons of the teams in action are hardly ever practised'.[146] There was a tendency 'even at Lewis gun schools to concentrate too much on turning Lewis gunners into skilled armourers, far too much time being spent on teaching stripping and mechanism, and far too little on the tactical handling of the gun'[147] so that the troops became 'utterly "fed up" with the war'.[148]

General Sir Reginald Stephens (5th Division) worried that on the Somme 'our infantry has displayed the most magnificent courage but, I think it is admitted, a want of cunning'.[149] Major-General H.L. Reed (15th Division) complained that the troops 'suffered from want of knowledge on the part of junior leaders how to advance against MGs' and 'how to avoid bunching & crowding & so making the very best target for the boche Machine Gunners'.[150] In September 1918 Harper (IV Corps) noted that 'in the past the main efforts in training had been directed too much towards the training of the body and too little towards the training of the mind' with an over-emphasis on elementary training such as close order drill rather than on tactical work, training the men 'to act as individuals with an individual intelligence'.[151]

At the end of the Somme Battle, Fourth Army concluded that 'one of the principal lessons of the fighting of the last four months' was 'the need for more tactical training for Company and Platoon Commanders' to give them 'the necessary tactical knowledge and initiative to take advantage of initial success'.[152] As a result in April 1917 the Fourth Army issued a collection of tactical schemes setting realistic exercises for Company, Platoon and Section commanders to discuss, undertake and solve both indoors and outdoors,[153] which was quickly taken up by GHQ and re-issued to the whole Army,[154] and stressing the importance of Corps and Divisional Commanders ensuring that tactical exercises and instruction in billets were carried out during the winter 'to spread this essential knowledge of elementary tactics and the use of ground'.[155]

During operations at Ypres in 1917 Second Army emphasised that it was 'more and more evident that greater stress must be laid on training in open warfare to encourage initiative and power of leading in the ranks of Junior NCOs and Privates, which are so necessary when Officers become casualties'.[156] By the end of the war in November 1918 GHQ was clear that 'the success of an offensive campaign' depended not only on 'the will to go forward' but also 'the skill to go forward', in other words the 'offensive spirit' combined an 'eagerness to fight and the knowledge of how to fight'.[157]

In late 1918 Byng felt that 'by means of experience in this open air warfare – platoon and Co[mpany] commanders are improving in tactics to a very great extent'[158] and that 'our men are fighting better than they have ever done, and are killing more Germans'.[159] Hastings Anderson (MGGS, First Army) also noticed the 'marked improvement in minor tactics' and maintained that 'the proof lies in the reduced casualties with which we have been able to achieve successful results in dealing with the enemy's MGs and Rear Guards'.[160] Major-General Sir John Ponsonby (5th Division) commented that 'indeed one of the most gratifying features' of the operations after 21 August 1918 had 'been the way in which young officers of all services have been prepared to assume responsibility and act on their own'. There were also numerous examples of Privates and NCOs taking over command when the officers had been killed. This improvement in tactical handling of troops and initiative had been achieved despite the few opportunities for training since the Division had returned from Italy in April 1918.[161]

How was this improvement achieved? GHQ did not begin to respond to the challenge of training a mass army until late 1916. Henry Wilson, convinced of the importance of 'the education & training of Officers', 'straffed' Kiggell, the CGS at GHQ, in March 1916 'about giving us proper teachers for our schools' because 'the present casual arrange[men]ts are disgraceful'.[162] GHQ did not seem to be concerned with large-scale training ignoring the necessity of sponsoring training schools and the setting up of training schools and the evolution of ideas was left to the *ad hoc* efforts of senior commanders.[163] One Brigadier-General complained in early 1917 that 'most of what has been done in the training line in France is due more to individual efforts of Army, Corps, Divisions and Brigade commands than to any clear direction' from GHQ. Prior to 1917 there was little direction of training by Brigade and Divisional Commanders to ensure that 'a uniform system throughout' and, if a battalion was good, it was 'in spite of the Higher Commanders (e.g. Brigade and Divisional) in the Division'.[164] In December 1916, Haldane noted that 'at last GHQ had woken up' asking for proposals on the subject of organisation for attack whereas before it had always been the case that 'the initiative comes from below and not from above' because those in command had 'no experience of the fighting at first hand'.[165]

During 1916 'in some units not a single platoon was organised'[166] and many battalions were 'not organised in permanent sections and platoons' so that 'the men do not know to which platoon of section they belong' and subalterns were 'too frequently shifted from platoon to platoon and even from Company to Company'.[167] In January 1917, Montgomery (MGGS, Fourth Army) informed Butler (Deputy Chief of the General Staff [DCGS], GHQ) that, having 'talked to a great many of our Division and Brigade Commanders', he was 'quite certain that the general feeling in the Army is that GHQ must lay down a definite organization for a platoon, company and battalion, and that they must also lay down a standard form of attack for a platoon, company and battalion'. Cavan (XIV Corps) confirmed that 'any authoritative book of instructions for the training of the Platoon is not only necessary and urgent, but would be heartily welcomed by every Commander to whom I have spoken' and urged that 'no time should be lost in drawing up "Instructions for the Training of a Platoon for offensive action", as soon as possible'.[168]

Montgomery also noted that there was no universal doctrine in the British Army unlike the French Army, which was 'months ahead of us in practising these principles' and ensuring that 'exactly the same methods' were universally applied, and 'until you give us some guidance from above we shall be unable to catch them up'. Montgomery thought that there were 'plenty of experienced Divisional Commanders' notably Strickland (1st Division), Deverell (3rd Division), Maxse (18th Division), and Shea (30th Division) 'all of whom have commanded brigades, and two of them battalions, during the war' who could advise GHQ on training.[169]

A major innovation in early 1917 was the introduction of a training section at GHQ as the result of pressure from the Armies. In early 1917 Brigadier-General A. Solly-Flood, who had been appointed by GHQ to organise instructional classes for Lieutenant-Colonels and Majors in October 1916, was brought to

GHQ to inaugurate a Training Directorate for all arms and services in France in order to re-model the battle manuals of the British Army and revise tactical doctrine.[170] With plenty of front-line experience as commander of 35th Brigade and of training as Commandant of the Third Army Officers' School experimenting in late 1916 with new infantry formations,[171] Solly-Flood was ordered to 'inaugurate a Training Directorate for all arms and services in France' and provide 'for the co-ordination of all training whether carried out under GHQ, the Armies, the Corps or the Divisions'.[172]

As Head of the Training Branch (BGT), Solly-Flood attempted 'to ensure uniformity in teaching' by 'the issue of pamphlets laying down principles or in reporting lessons learnt during fighting' and by setting up 'in each Army a permanent demonstration platoon to show methods of applying principles of tactics in the best way under various conditions'.[173] The important reforms carried out by the new training Section at GHQ was the restoration of the platoon organisation as a focus for new tactical change, standardising recent innovation for the Army in manuals such as *SS143* and *SS144* issued in February 1917.

The experiences on the Somme laid the foundation for what would be the decisive tactical reappraisal in the BEF in the winter of 1916–17 and the tactics, which the British were to employ from the summer of 1917 onwards, had been formulated. *SS143* made official the new doctrine, which combined the weapons adopted by the infantry since 1914 into a self-contained unit capable of training and fighting on its own.[174] Hitherto the only manual available to Platoon commanders had been 'Infantry Training', which had been written pre-war and pre-trench warfare.[175] *SS143* was a vital milestone in tactics, making a changeover from the Victorian era of riflemen in lines to the twentieth-century era of flexible small groups built around a variety of weapons. The new edition of *SS143* issued in February 1918[176] was to be 'the manual upon which the victories of 1918 were won by the British and American Armies'.[177]

From 1916 onwards GHQ issued a large number of publications which, being regularly updated, were designed to aid the training of formations and units, notably on artillery in offensive operations (*SS98*); co-operation of aircraft with artillery (*SS131*); the training and employment of Divisions for offensive action employing the various combined arms (*SS135*); recreational training (*SS137*); the training and tactics employed by the infantry (*SS143*); communications (*SS148*); Instructions for training within Schools at GHQ, Army, and Corps level (*SS152*); Tactical Schemes to train junior officers and NCOs (*SS159*); the use of smoke (*SS175*); infantry and tank co-operation and training (*SS204*); and tank co-operation with other arms (*SS214*).[178] Another series of pamphlets entitled The Experiences of Recent Fighting, such as *SS111* (on gas), *SS119* (on the Somme), *SS158, 160–161* (on the battles which took place in the spring of 1917), *SS170–174* (on Messines), and *SS218* (on Hamel 1918) disseminating the lessons learnt in the battles of 1916–18. By the beginning of 1918 it cannot be said that GHQ failed to provide guidance because 'the principal *SS* publications to which Infantry Commanders should turn to for further information on the various branches of infantry tactics and organisations' included manuals on a multiplicity of technical and training matters.[179]

Yet it was felt by mid-1918 that 'the progress in obtaining uniformity of training was not rapid enough' and that the appointment of a general of high rank was required 'to compel Army and Corps Schools to adopt similar methods'.[180] Uniacke, Deputy Inspector General of Training from July 1918, observed that the Training Branch at GHQ had 'generally neglected the somewhat important matter of instruction' and 'still more the question as to whether instruction once given was ever properly applied'.[181] Montgomery (MGGS, Fourth Army) admitted in November 1918 that, although the 'system which has been evolved during the last three years' worked 'very well indeed in two out of the five Armies', in the other three armies the system had not worked so well because 'people have not done their job and have not taken sufficient interest in the show'.[182]

Dawnay (MGGS, Staff Duties at GHQ) argued that the German success in the Spring of 1918 'proved, above all things, the necessity for thorough training on the recognised tactical principles' and that, because 'there is no doubt that our own troops suffered from lack of sufficient training'.[183] It was 'a matter of the highest urgency to take steps to improve the efficiency of training throughout the Armies in France'.[184] Since the great administrative burden on the Training sub-section at GHQ made the installation of some further machinery 'very necessary', Haig, therefore, established an Inspectorate of Training to supervise training throughout the Armies in France and to ensure that the British Armies in France had 'adequate machinery to assist in bringing the training to a high pitch'.[185]

Maxse, an excellent trainer of troops, was appointed Inspector-General of Training (IGT) 'to assist the troops and their commanders' to train the Armies in France and 'if possible to help in co-ordinating the training in England and France' and was 'empowered to visit any formation, unit or training establishment' at 24 hours notice.[186] Organised to 'interpret GHQ doctrine as regards training and inculcate uniformity throughout the British Forces',[187] Maxse and his staff were to 'devote their energies to assisting Army and subordinate Commanders to improve the standard of training in all arms of the service'.[188] When an Assistant Inspector of Training (Major-General Lord Dugan) recommended the sacking of the Commandant and Chief Instructor of the X Corps School because they lacked drive and were too old, Maxse was able to appeal to the CGS (Lawrence) to ensure their removal despite the opposition of the Corps commander (Stephens).[189]

The appointment of Maxse as Inspector-General of Training in 'revolutionising the whole of the training arrangements', was intended by Dawnay to produce 'a renaissance in tactics' and a return to the 'old pre-war principles',[190] providing the bureaucratic machinery capable of producing uniform organisation and doctrine, which was such a feature of the German Army. This was seen by Hunter-Weston (VIII Corps) as 'one of the finest moves we made for the improvement of our Army'[191] and by Hastings Anderson (MGGS, First Army) as providing 'the benefit of uniform organisation in the battalion and training'.[192]

It has been claimed that Maxse, as IGT, 'radically recast the tactical doctrine on lines that followed but improved on the new German tactics'.[193] It is doubtful, however, that there was enough time to make a radical difference in the short time between Maxse's appointment in July 1918 and the beginning of the British counter-stroke on 8 August 1918. For progressive commanders little that Maxse taught was radically innovative. For example, having spent all day at a 'demonstration & lecture' by Maxse, Strickland (1st Division) saw 'nothing new in it'.[194] Maxse's main impact was as a conduit throughout the army for a more systematic dissemination of tactical doctrine, which had been developed in 1916–17. Solly-Flood, having 'introduced many drastic changes in Training & in methods of attack & defence' as BGT, later claimed that 'Maxse got all the kudos & all the rewards, but it was not he who did the work'.[195]

Solly-Flood had a point. The assumption that the Army lacked any structure for training the New Armies in France and suffered from an anarchy in training doctrine until mid-1918 ignores the fact that a large number of training schools were already established within the BEF and that a Directorate of Training had been in existence since early 1917, producing manuals and pamphlets and making a very significant contribution to victory. The increasingly skilled performance of the British on the battlefields of 1917 and 1918 rested on the training which began in some cases as early as 1915 but in all cases began in real earnest in late 1916 or early 1917, when the British Army began to concentrate much more on training after the jolt of the poor performance by many units on the Somme in mid-1916. Thereafter, there was much more emphasis on training as the war progressed and generals realised its overwhelming importance.

The phenomenon of a collapse in tactical expertise is often ignored in assessing the achievements of the British Army during the First World War. With a 'de-skilled' army it was very difficult for the British to defeat the well-trained German Army. It was not until late 1917, three years after the beginning of the war that the British were able to regain standards comparable with 1914 and to be on equal terms with the Germans. It is no small coincidence that a similar length of time was to pass until the Battle of Alamein in 1942 when the British were to find a winning formula in the Second World War. A new British Army rose swiftly out of the blood and mud of the Somme campaign. The events of 1917 provided the British commanders with further battle experience and, sound tactical theory aside, it was training within the schools system, which ensured the battlefield efficiency and tactical success of the British Army during 1917 and 1918.

7 Tactical innovation

The platoon was... an army in miniature, the Lewis guns supplying covering machine gun fire; the rifle grenadiers acting as artillery; and the riflemen making the infantry assault.

(Captain A.O. Pollard, VC, MC, DCM)[1]

To understand the processes by which the war was eventually won we need to unravel the processes by which the German Army was defeated and how one of the fundamental problems of the First World War for the high command, the need to integrate new technology and to shape doctrine in the light of technological capabilities, was solved by 1918. The First World War was shaped by dramatic developments in communications, transportation, and weapons technology and by the impact of that new technology upon tactics. The war on the Western Front, often portrayed as a mindless slugging match, was actually surprisingly dynamic at the tactical level. The failure to conduct significant manoeuvre at the tactical level was the root cause of the inability of armies to achieve strategic success during the First World War. Successful operational manoeuvre depended directly on success at the tactical level, specifically conduct of tactical manoeuvre. Much of the war was spent searching for the means to restore mobility to the battlefield and to smash the enemy's ever-more complex defences. To do this the British pursued several learning curves.

The British faced the problem of how to break down the German defensive system. This tactical problem was defined by one regimental officer, who had served on the Western Front, as 'how to surprise, overrun, and penetrate a well-sited defence system some four miles deep, the front edge of which was only a short distance from one's own, protected by massive wire entanglements and covered by the flanking fire of machine-guns and a wall of fire from artillery and mortars of all calibres sited in depth'.[2] Robertson (CGS, GHQ), outlining the British difficulties during the war, noted in 1915 that 'these Germans are dug in up to the neck, or concreted' in 'one vast fortress, without any of the disadvantages attaching to it' so that 'attack on a narrow front & we are enfiladed at once' while an 'attack on a wide front is impossible because of insufficient ammunition to bombard and break down the defences'.[3]

As early as September 1914 the 4th Division noted that 'the Germans handle their machine guns very skilfully'.[4] German MGs were 'most admirably handled' and 'most difficult to discover' causing 'more than half' of the British casualties at Neuve Chapelle.[5] Early in the war the British 'had not been able to find a satisfactory antedote' to MGs[6] but commanders, such as Rawlinson, were confident that, if they could 'only find a way of silencing these weapons', their task 'would be easy for their infantry are poor creatures, mostly *Landstrum*'.[7] The British had to slowly and painfully learn the best ways of overcoming what one SO called 'our arch enemies'.[8]

By the end of 1916, it was recognised that 'what have most impeded our advance during the recent fighting on the SOMME have been machine guns manned by alert and determined men, firing from shell holes and other positions which cannot be identified, behind, and well clear of, the enemy trenches'.[9] The Fourth Army concluded from the fighting of 1915–16 that 'the chief danger the infantry have to face is the machine gun' which to avoid the creeping barrage on the front and support trenches were now 'placed several hundreds of yards behind the enemy's front line' and 'difficult, if not impossible, to locate before the attack commences',[10] being 'hidden, not in substantial emplacements, but in grass, hedges, shell holes etc, where they are difficult to locate, and so destroy'.[11]

Once the infantry got beyond their carefully prepared artillery support, they were unable to exploit the initial success. This was first demonstrated by the failure to advance beyond the village of Neuve Chapelle to seize the Aubers Ridge in March 1915. As Haig's Artillery Adviser at First Army reported after the battle, the failure of the infantry to progress beyond Neuve Chapelle was not the result of a lack of determination but the result of the failure of the artillery to keep up with the infantry after the initial bombardment and to the strength of the German MG defences which were in depth behind their front line system.[12] The attempt to rush through the German defences, well entrenched and secured by MGs, failed because the strong-points or hinges, which had to be lifted before the defensive system could be toppled, remained intact.

In the most disastrous attempt to smash through the German defences on 1 July 1916, the infantry advanced 'to the attack in dense lines, almost shoulder to shoulder', casting aside all previous training based on fire and movement.[13] The lessons of the pre-war 'fire with movement' training, which emphasized that 'no movement towards the enemy can take place, in modern warfare, unless the advancing troops are covered by fire', were ignored and resulted in heavy casualties.[14] Major-General R. Wanless O'Gowan thought that 'GHQ did not quite trust the training of the Infantry' and was told by Sir Henry Rawlinson just before 1st July that 'the attack must be made in waves with men at fairly close intervals in order to give them confidence; this was wrong & entailed heavy casualties; the men would have done better in small groups & were quite well enough trained to adopt that formation' as the 31st Division had done 'quite a lot of musketry' and 'the results, although they did not come up to the Old Army, were not at all bad, especially in rapid firing'.[15] This lesson had to be relearnt during 1916–17.

The improvement in British tactical skill and the ability to penetrate the German defences in 1917 and 1918 was the result of the adoption of a platoon organisation, which gave the infantry its own weapons, and an emphasis on a return to fire and movement by innovative divisional commanders, such as Deverell (3rd Division), Stephens (5th Division), and Maxse (18th Division), during 1916. In September 1916, Stephens advocated a new platoon organisation of two rifle sections, including rifle grenadiers, a bomber section and a Lewis Gun section to replace the platoon of four rifle sections, which had been employed on the Somme.[16] Shea (30th Division) summed up the main lesson of the fighting on the Somme as being that 'the platoon will be the "fighting unit" and will be self-contained' and that 'the object of this organisation and training is to develop the use of all weapons in combination' with each platoon having Lewis Gunners, Bombers, Rifle-grenadiers ('its own "infantry artillery"'), and riflemen so as 'to exploit to the full and in combination all weapons, thus giving greater power of offence while if possible employing fewer men'.[17]

The new self-contained platoon was designed to exploit the increased firepower given to the infantry by the rifle grenade and the Lewis Gun, which was 'a very valuable addition to the firepower of a unit, especially in the attack',[18] to deal with enemy strongpoints and enable the infantry to fight its own way forward. In February 1917 GHQ laid down the organisation of the Battalion constructed around a platoon of one Lewis Gun Section, one Bombing Section and two Sections of Riflemen, as the 'unit for fighting and training' containing 'all the weapons with which the Infantry is now armed',[19] and provided guidance on formations for the infantry in assaults which had 'frequently been employed with success in recent fighting' and which were to 'be adopted throughout all Armies in France'.[20]

Within each platoon, the rifle-grenadiers and the Lewis-gunners formed the covering fire team while the assault team was made up of the hand-grenade section and the rifle section. By the summer of 1917 the platoon, considered 'the principal unit of the Army', was 'self-contained' and 'an army in miniature' with its own fire support with 'the Lewis guns supplying covering MG fire; the rifle grenadiers acting as artillery; and the riflemen making the infantry assault'.[21] One Divisional Commander noted that 'too much attention cannot, in my opinion, be devoted to training platoon and section commanders in the co-operation of Lewis Guns, grenades and rifle grenades for dealing with the hostile resistance'.[22] Abandoning the 'bomb', infantry tactics from 1917 depended on the rifleman and the Lewis gun working in combination and the German MGs ceased to intimidate.

SS143 recommended that the different weapons of the four sections should be used in conjunction with riflemen and bombers advancing on a flank while the Lewis gunners gave covering fire and rifle bombers opened up 'a hurricane bombardment on the point of resistance'.[23] An attack by the 1st Borders in January 1917 demonstrated such tactics. Establishing a barrage of rifle grenades from the front, Corporal Robins 'on his own initiative (but in accordance with previous training) moved round' the flank of the German strong point and brought 'his Lewis Gun into action enfilading the rear trench' in order to cut off and force the surrender of three German MGs.[24] The capture of Quarry Post by a company of the 5/Royal Berkshires (35th Brigade, 12th Division) during the Battle of Cambrai on 20 November 1917 'was an example of skilful use of all the infantry weapons of the period, a barrage of Stokes Mortars and rifle grenades smothering the fire of defenders'.[25]

By late 1918 the principles of fire and movement were recognised as the 'bedrock of infantry tactics' with the Lewis Gun section providing the 'fire' and the rifle section the 'movement', with each platoon divided into two rifle and two Lewis Gun sections.[26] The Training Leaflet No. 4 issued by Inspector-General Training (IGT) in October 1918 gave six drill formations for company and platoon commanders to train the two rifle and two Lewis gun sections of platoons in fire and movement.[27] GHQ also stressed that Lewis gunners as 'the framework of the infantry advance' were to 'be trained to push well forward with the leading riflemen' and that 'every effort must be made to teach them how to use ground and take advantage of cover'.[28]

The years 1917–18 saw a new flexibility in British attack formations as 'the infantry radically altered their tactics', in which 'two lines of skirmishers acted as an advanced-guard; loose groups followed, ready to manoeuvre against strong points'.[29] As early as July 1916, 30th Division noted that the 'best formation in which to advance' was within 'small handy columns'.[30] XIII Corps emphasised that 'small columns must be ready at once to manoeuvre round and attack in flank and rear any parties of the enemy or strong points which hold up the waves in front'.[31] In 1917, XVIII Corps advocated 'a more elastic infantry formation for the attack' employing platoons 'working in depth rather than battalions stereotyped in waves' so that behind the initial assault wave 'worms' of 'little columns of units in depth' were ready to 'stalk' the enemy 'on a narrow front close to the barrage'.[32] The Second Army noted that 'the waves of attacks' employed at Ypres in late 1917 did 'not give sufficient elasticity' to counter the new conditions being experienced[33] and abandoning linear formations advocated that the troops 'should move in small columns in file, the formation which the nature of the ground forces the men to adopt eventually'.[34]

Copying German infiltration tactics used at Arras, Ypres, and Cambrai in 1917 the 4th Seaforth Highlanders developed 'the "Dribbling" method of attack' in which, 'instead of advancing in waves parallel to the objective', the attacking troops were 'deployed in sectional columns in single file' and '"dribbled" forward in small numbers until close enough to their objective to launch the final assault'. The troops then advanced 'irregularly by short rushes' while others provided covering fire 'to pick off enemy machine gunners, and, by keeping up an accurate and deliberate fire' kept the enemy's heads down. Such methods were designed 'to reduce casualties' by limiting 'the targets presented to hostile machine guns'.[35] By early 1918 the platoon attacked with either one section thrown out as skirmishers and three sections advancing behind in single file or 'worms' or each section advancing in single file preceded by its two scouts.[36]

By late 1917 it was expected that 'one or two determined men' should be able to clear 'a fortified shell-hole' with the bayonet and four men could 'take a "Pill box" by fire and movement'.[37] By August 1918 Maxse's IGT staff believed that '3 men can be a fighting unit' capable 'of "stalking" a hostile light machine gun' by fire and movement.[38] Harper (IV Corps) advocated that platoons should first 'locate the machine guns by means of patrols' and then 'stalk them, under cover of Lewis gun and rifle fire, until within close enough range to hit the team or the gun with the bullet or rifle grenade'.[39]

Above all, frontal attacks were to be resisted. Acknowledging that the temptation for officers who saw an attack fail was to 'pour in more men is very great', Stephens encouraged platoon and section leaders in 1916 to think 'of a way to get round the flanks'.[40] The experiences of Divisions on the Somme showed that rather than reinforcing troops held up by 'carefully entrenched positions with well concealed MG emplacements', which was 'usually inadvisable', it was better to aid the progress of their neighbours 'by acting offensively and aggressively against the flank of the enemy who is holding them up'.[41] XIII Corps noted that 'all ranks' must have the idea of outflanking enemy resistance 'so thoroughly ingrained in them that they will be ready to press on to their own objective irrespective of what occurs on their right or left'.[42]

Stephens stressed in the training of the troops that 'any enemy resistance that is left must be overcome by their own weapons'.[43] The infantry were not to rely on the artillery or tanks but were to employ fire and movement at the platoon level to reach their objectives, making intelligent use of the firepower of the bomb, rifle grenade, rifle and Lewis gun to overcome opposition. One Divisional Commander in October 1917 commented that 'the French method of capturing strong points by working round them with Lewis Guns, which had been frequently practised in training, 'proved most successful'.[44] If held up by opposition, platoons were expected under the new doctrine to 'obtain superiority of fire and envelope one or both flanks' and also to help neighbouring units which were held up by employing fire and movement tactics.[45]

Experiences at Ypres confirmed that German strong points were 'inclined to surrender when the attacking parties begin to work round towards the rear of the buildings'[46] and that once attacking troops can outflank a fortified position 'the defence cracks up at once'.[47] Cator (58th Division) emphasised in September 1917 that the 'flank attack should be frequently employed in preference to the straight-forward frontal attack from one line to another' because 'it takes the enemy by surprise, strikes at his weakest point, his flank, and affects the morale of his troops, who do not put up such a strong resistance as when frontally attacked'. It was important that during training flanking manoeuvres 'should be thoroughly drilled into the men so that on meeting with a point of resistance it becomes a second nature to engage it from the front by fire with a portion of the party told off for its capture, while the remainder work round its flanks and behind it'.[48] XVIII Corps concluded that 'surprise is to be the first and chief consideration and all concerned should be reminded that the Germans put their hands up directly they are attacked from their rear', stressing that 'surprise is essential to success'.[49]

By late 1918 tactical doctrine emphasised pressing forward boldly without worrying about the flanks, and on bypassing the enemy's defences to maintain the momentum of the advance. As one division noted, failure to adhere to 'the principle of Infiltration' could mean that 'the whole advance of a Brigade' was stopped 'because one or two patrols have met with resistance'. Subordinate units were reminded that 'where one part of the line is held up, troops on the right and left should move on, and those points, where resistance is least or non-existent, should be used as means of filtering through supporting or strengthening forces'.[50]

IV Corps stressed 'the advantages of being able to manoeuvre reserve platoons into positions from which they can surprise the enemy from a flank' and the importance of mutual support, where neighbouring units held up by pockets of the enemy holding out would be assisted by a flank attack to clear such resistance.[51] Platoons were to capture their objectives, not stopping until organised resistance was met, regardless of their flanks and 'if one of the leading platoons is definitely held up, and the other is still making ground, the supporting platoons drive home the attack of the latter' in order to 'make a gap through which the supporting companies can penetrate'.[52]

By the end of the war GHQ emphasised that 'the idea must not be allowed to gain ground, however, that an offensive is impossible under any conditions without a barrage of great density or without the co-operation of tanks'. GHQ asserted that 'the infantry must never for a moment be permitted to consider that it merely exists to follow up an artillery barrage or to accompany a "tank battle"' but was adamant that 'the infantry must always be prepared to fight its way forward by means of its own weapons, making use of all cover available to facilitate its advance'. The successful conduct of a battle depended upon the rapidity with which local successes was gained and exploited. Attacks were to be 'pushed to the fullest extent possible' allowing an 'initial success' to be 'exploited at once by the bold and rapid intervention of all available troops' taking every advantage of the enemy's disorganisation by pressing the attack 'relentlessly at points where the enemy's resistance is weak' and employing reserves 'where progress is being made and not in places where the attack has been checked'.[53]

'Where an attack has completely failed' the assault 'should generally not be renewed until the defence has been shaken by further bombardment, by the infantry fire fight, by the bringing up of additional means of assistance to the infantry (e.g. tanks), or by an enveloping movement'.[54] By October and November 1918 the staff of the IGT were promulgating 'the system of exploiting the "soft spot"'[55] at battalion level in which it was emphasised that 'the enemy's defences will not be equally strong along the whole front' and that it was the task of platoons to 'find, penetrate and exploit' these 'soft spots'. Leading platoons were to push 'boldly forward regardless of open flanks' with the object of bypassing 'organized resistance' to exploit gaps in the enemy's defences and to outflank strong points and machine guns. This required initiative, determination, skilful leadership and, above all, co-operation among well-trained sections 'all steeped in the same doctrine and working to one plan'.[56] The 38th Division in the crossing of the River Selle in October 1918 employed these 'soft spot' tactics with great success.[57]

When open warfare returned in the final advance of 1918, it became even more important 'not to push frontally against his Machine Guns, but always to try to turn a flank'.[58] Any platoon, which was held up, was not reinforced but was to provide covering fire. At battalion level it was made clear that a supporting company 'does not reinforce a company which is definitely held up, it supports the company that is making progress' and that platoons were to be detached 'to attack in flank the enemy who are holding up neighbouring units'.[59] The weaknesses and holes in the enemy defences were to be exploited rather than reinforcing previous failures.[60] In November 1918, Braithwaite's IX Crops 'forced the passage of the [Sambre] Canal at two points' while putting down 'a barrage of smoke and gas on the rest of the front' and then by 'striking outwards, the defenders of the Canal were captured from the rear' by an attack which was 'a complete surprise'.[61]

The army could not just depend on superior infantry tactics to win the war but had to develop the means of either destroying or neutralising the enemy's defences – the obstacles to a successful advance by the infantry. The British spent 1915–17 searching for firepower to support the infantry's advance and the 'weapons system' to unlock the formidable defences on the Somme and at Passchendaele. In early April 1917 one corps commander noted that the key to success was a combined operation by the different arms because 'our present troops, excellent as they are for a regular attack on trenches, are not to be relied on when anything like open warfare supervenes' and 'they can only go forward safely covered by an artillery barrage and if possible with the assistance of tanks' since 'machine guns are the weapons that trouble most when open warfare comes' and 'with the present army, tanks, smoke and gas shell are needful to neutralize them'.[62]

By the end of 1917 the British had evolved tactics, which focused on employing combined arms to overcome the German defences. For example, the capture of the Westhoek Ridge by the 74th Infantry Brigade on 10 August 1917 took place under an artillery barrage supported by 36 MGs while the infantry surrounded and captured any strong points holding up the advance and then while the gains were being consolidated the inevitable German counter-attacks 'were annihilated by our artillery and machine gun fire'.[63] Employing a skilful combination of overwhelming firepower and new infantry tactics the British sought to undermine the German defence in depth and return some mobility to the battlefield.

The successful advance by the 51st Division of 1,000 yards towards Poelcappelle in September 1917, stressed 'the success of the methods employed to overcome the system of defence in depth by concrete "pill-boxes" and shell-hole posts' including incessant use of the rifle by the infantry, barrages by the artillery both to support the infantry and to neutralise the defences and counter-attacks, a barrage by thirty-two MGs, and the employment of twelve tanks.[64] Aircraft and tanks (new weapons developed during the war) formed with the artillery and infantry (the traditional arms) an all-arms team, which returned mobility to the battlefield.

Gradually different weapons coalesced into one weapons system in which co-operation between arms provided the solution to breaking through the German defences. Harper (51st Division) concluded in September 1917 that 'it is now proved that we can blow the Boches out of any line & then hold it against counter attacks'.[65] During 1917 generals like Plumer showed at Messines 'by use of siege methods' and at Broodseinde 'by attacking on a narrow front with a thousand yards' deep barrage, that a breach could be made',[66] employing the arms in combination.

By early 1918 this teamwork was well-established and the British sought 'to establish a mastery over the enemy's aircraft and artillery' and 'to protect the advance of our infantry against rifle and MG fire by a moving barrage of artillery and MG fire carefully organised in depth'.[67] Tanks were seen as one way 'to make up to a certain extent for the lack of training on the part of our troops, ie a poorly trained Division with Tanks will achieve what it would take a very highly trained Division to do without tanks'.[68] The operations of the 5th Division with the Third Army on 21–23 August 1918 provide an example in which the infantry, artillery and tanks worked in combination to overcome the German defences, notably the German wire and MGs, relying on the initiative of junior officers to overcome difficulties and exploit opportunities to advance or to aid the advance of others.[69]

Artillery, MGs, riflemen, and tanks had become the four elements of an offensive team, which were an essential part of any successful attack. The British high command believed that success could only result from the co-operation of all arms. By November 1918, GHQ outlined the now standard doctrine that the 'infantry must be practised in co-operation with the artillery, trench mortars, tanks, machine guns, and combat patrol aeroplanes, which accompany them in attack'.[70] When all these newly developed weapons began to work as a team as they did from 1917, the Germans were unable to find an answer to the sheer power of the British assault. During the advance after September 1918 'the thickest barbed wire entanglements were crossed, and the enemy seemed either disinclined or else incapable of stopping us when we attacked under a barrage'.[71]

The British began to develop use of MGs *en masse* to provide covering fire for their infantry as one solution to the enemy's own MGs. Machine guns were employed from the Somme in 1916 onwards 'for overhead fire to cover advancing infantry, for establishing barrages against counter-attacks and for holding in advance of captured trenches to cover consolidation' and to provide 'a machine gun barrage for a depth of 1,000 yards' freeing the infantry to deal with the enemy infantry.[72] Following the experiences of the Fourth Army in the German retreat to the Hindenburg Line, GHQ noted in April 1917 that 'the value of machine guns in covering the advance of troops with enfilade, oblique, or over-head fire was most marked' especially when employed 'well forward'.[73]

By August 1917 the British were 'well ahead of the enemy' in the use of 'barrages and covering fire, offensive and defensive, by massed machine guns' which had 'been brought to a high pitch of perfection' and could 'afford very great assistance to an attack' and 'render counter-attacks almost, if not quite, impossible'.[74] During the Third Battle of Ypres, MG barrages were employed in both the offensive, covering 'the advance of the infantry to each objective by searching the ground about 400 yards in front of the Artillery barrage', and the defensive, placing 'a protective barrage about 400 yards' in front of the objective while it was being consolidated.[75] By 1918 the main employment of MGs 'to provide covering fire for the attacking infantry' and 'to assist in the defence of the position won and to repel counter-attacks', as well as 'to inflicting losses on the enemy and to reducing his morale' with harassing fire by day and night, was well-established.[76]

Crucial to success was the development of artillery. By 1917 the British held 'the view that ground is gained by the artillery, that ground is defended by artillery, that battles are won by artillery and that battles are lost by lack of artillery'.[77] Against a strong enemy with interlocking defences there could be no hope of infiltration tactics without a devastating avalanche of shells to shatter the cement holding the corner stones of the defences together. Fourth Army noted the importance of artillery to the success of operations following its experiences on the Somme, contrasting the successes on 14 and 27 July, notably when the capture of Delville Wood 'was rendered a certainty by the enormous concentration of guns – 1 Gun to three yards – the Infantry assaulting under a barrage fired from over 200 Field Guns on a comparatively narrow front', with the failures to take Guillemont because of 'the difficulties of concentrating artillery fire'.[78] By 1918 'an effective 18-pdr. barrage' was considered to consist of one gun per 20 yards against defensive lines with dugouts and one gun to 15 yards against shell-hole positions.[79]

When criticising generals for employing long artillery bombardments to soften up the German defences, which put the enemy on full alert, it is often forgotten that the technology for predicted fire was first employed at Cambrai in November 1917 and was not available prior to that battle. From 1915 wire obstacles posed a difficult dilemma because 'to "strafe" it with artillery' simply led the Germans to expect an attack while if left uncut it was very difficult for the assaulting troops to enter the enemy's trenches.[80] These problems were not solved until the development of new artillery technology and tactics in 1917 which became an important ingredient in the formula of success in 1918.

By the end of 1915, British hopes lay in 'a greater development of artillery power rendered by an increased supply of guns and ammunition, and a greater experience in the handling of them' in order to produce 'a really crushing and stunning artillery bombardment' which 'once commenced, will continue in ever increasing volume, knowing no cessation or even pause until the time of assault arrives, and which will then advance like a wave in front of the infantry – overwhelming all in its path'.[81]

Although the Germans had noted an improvement in the way that the British artillery on the Somme had 'registered skilfully and inconspicuously',[82] the British still employed a long preparatory bombardment, which aimed at 'the demoralisation of the enemy and the methodical destruction' of his defences.[83] Haig 'undervalued the immense growth of the German defensive system' which could no longer 'be battered out of shape by a few hours' bombardment',[84] especially as, without the artillery resources of 1917–18, the Fourth Army 'were in fact short of artillery for the task' they 'were asked to achieve' and were 'trying to reach objectives which were out of the reach of our artillery'.[85]

Indeed, 'the inadequacy of the attack' and of 'the artillery massed' to support it 'was the major cause of the failure of the assault to penetrate more than a limited distance on the first day'.[86] It should be remembered that in 1916 the French forces on the Somme, enjoyed an enormous advantage in heavy artillery compared with Rawlinson[87] and that Foch, their commander, 'had heaps of heavy guns and went forward line by line on a time programme, and told his generals that if anyone went beyond 1,000 y[ar]ds he would turn him out', losing only 5,000 casualties compared to 70,000 lost by the British in July 1916.[88]

The Battle of the Somme produced one very important and successful development: the creeping barrage, which was employed on a large scale for the first time.[89] The attacking troops hugged the creeping barrage as closely as humanly possible in order to be 'on or under the edge of the artillery barrage and ready to rush the trench the moment the barrage lifts' as it was 'cheaper to lose men by our own artillery fire than to give the enemy time to bring his machine guns up from their dug-outs'.[90] The 19th Division concluded that to keep the enemy's MGs quiet 'an intense barrage must be put up just prior to the infantry assault' and 'so accurately timed that the infantry regardless of loss from an occasional "short" round, can advance under it and enter the hostile trench immediately the barrage lifts'.[91] This lesson was emphasised by other corps and divisions on the Somme and by the Fourth Army with the result that the employment of the creeping and stationary barrages, which moved forward according to a timetable, had been established by the end of 1916 as 'the best basis on which to operate'.[92]

To attain the optimum results very close co-operation was necessary between infantry and artillery, which took time to develop. At first close liaison between the artillery and the infantry was difficult to achieve. Poor co-ordination between units and liaison between infantry and artillery was exacerbated by the tendency to split up divisions and jumble up units piecemeal across the front. In his post-operations report Major-General Sir John Capper, concluded that the 24th Division 'was split up and in fact did not exist as a division during the fighting' at Loos, losing control of its artillery, and that its attack 'seems to have been unsupported by any special artillery fire, and to have been isolated'.[93] During the later stages of the Battle of Loos, General Sir Edward Bulfin (28th Division) was informed 'late on the night before the attack, which started at dawn' that 'the guns which had registered and been given their targets were to come out, and I had to put a new lot of artillery who knew nothing of the targets and had not registered' with the result that 'the whole show was hopeless'.[94]

One divisional commander on the Somme noted that 'with a few brilliant exceptions Heavy Artillery observers were too far back and too optimistic as to their probable performances' and advocated a closer liaison between the artillery and infantry.[95] Another noted the importance of the infantry being supported by its own divisional artillery because the tendency in which Divisions were 'of necessity put in very quickly one after the other' and 'very frequently' supported 'by guns of another division'[96] prevented close co-operation between the infantry and artillery. The Fourth Army after the Battle of the Somme came to the conclusion that 'it is distinctly advantageous that Divisions should be supported by their own Divisional Artilleries, under the command of their own CRAs'. The lesson that good artillery co-operation was vital seems to have been learnt quite well throughout the BEF by the later stages of the Somme but the Infantry were too often 'required to conform their movements strictly in accordance with the barrage programme'.[97]

This reinforced the tendency for tactics to be somewhat stereotyped and 'the Artillery programmes were sometimes inclined to be too "wooden", trust being implicit in the rather new Creeping Barrage'.[98] Edmonds noted that 'an artillery barrage was insufficient, it could not account for every enemy machine gun; even the creeping barrage, dropping ahead of the assault, when it came into practice in 1916, was insufficient, except when employed on an immense scale'.[99] Commanders were already becoming aware on the Somme in 1916 of the dangers of 'trying to do every attack by barrage and relying on stereotyped tactics' which meant that 'the Bosch always knows by our barrage where we are going to attack and when we are'.[100] Nevertheless, one Corps Commander complained in November 1918 that 'Div[isional] Gen[era]ls still, in some cases, will not move forward without an artillery barrage, and continue to order b[riga]des, to make certain laid-down bounds and "leap-frog" their troops during an advance', causing delay and taking away responsibility and initiative from brigadiers and their troops.[101]

As the war wore on, British doctrine laid great stress on the need for the troops to be able to operate independently because despite its great weight of fire the artillery was only able to neutralise rather than destroy the enemy defences. This coincided with a movement away from long bombardments and a return to the surprise bombardment, without registration from a mass of guns assembled secretly, which ushered in the employment of new tactics at Cambrai in November 1917.[102] This change took some time to become an established practice. The hurricane bombardment of 6–8 hours used so effectively by the Germans in March 1918 might have been employed by the British in 1917 but they were 'still obsessed with the idea that the total destruction of all enemy defences must be achieved before the attack' and were 'therefore still wedded to lengthy preliminary bombardments of several days which sacrificed all the advantages of surprise'. They only gradually learnt that 'the main advantages to be derived from Artillery fire was in its power of neutralising the hostile rifle, machine gun and artillery fire, as opposed to the destruction of trenches & obstacles'.[103] Unfortunately, the long preliminary bombardments employed in 1917 'inevitably indicated the general front of an intended attack and allowed the Germans to reinforce his artillery'.[104]

An attempt by Allenby (Third Army) prior to the Battle of Arras to achieve a surprise, by employing a short, sharp artillery bombardment of forty-eight hours rather than a week's bombardment which had preceded the Somme attack,[105] met much resistance, being opposed by GHQ as inadequate to deal with the German defences. Horne (First Army) wished to employ a long bombardment before the attack on Vimy Ridge and was supported by GHQ. General Sir Arthur Holland (CRA, Third Army), who had instigated this plan, was promoted to command the I Corps and replaced by a more conventional officer (Major-General R.St.C. Lecky) in order to lengthen the duration of the bombardment to forty-eight hours.[106]

The General Headquarters had some good reasons for opposing the idea of a short, intensive bombardment. Calibration in the field artillery was still rather elementary while flash-spotting and sound-ranging were not very far advanced. Without such aids the accuracy of unobserved fire attained at Cambrai and afterwards was scarcely possible. Moreover, the high rate of fire proposed for the short bombardment would have made observation of fire very difficult from the ground or from the air.[107] Also all the corps commanders and their chief SOs and most of the divisional commanders were hostile to the scheme,[108] and fellow Army commanders, such as Rawlinson, were also opposed to a forty-eight hour intensive bombardment.[109]

Yet in the final analysis Allenby was correct about the difficulties of wire-cutting because the wire on the Wancourt-Feuchy Line could not be cut in ten days, let alone two or four. The Army in 1917 remained divided about the best tactics to employ. While some, like General Sir Beauvoir de Lisle thought with hindsight that it was quite feasible for the troops to 'bullock through' with the aid of wire-cutters if the defence was adequately shell-shocked by High Explosive (HE) shells of large calibre guns and gassed (this was precisely what the Germans did in their great offensives in the Spring of 1918 when they did very little wire-cutting in the battle zone defences),[110] others, such as Haldane considered that there were not enough tanks available and that the wire, being 'exceedingly formidable', could not be cleared by a short bombardment alone.[111] General Sir Percy Radcliffe (BGGS, Canadian Corps) felt in hindsight that 'of course, we could never have got our infantry through the old established defences, such as Thiepval or Vimy, after only a few hours' bombardment'.[112]

Nevertheless, from 1916 onwards new tactics were developed which 'fixed the artillery doctrine which was to be followed for the rest of the war and which was to form the basis of post-war training'.[113] Following problems with the quality of the ammunition issued to the artillery on the Somme in 1916, when it was estimated that one shell in three did not explode,[114] the introduction of an instantaneous fuse was eagerly awaited to improve the performance of the guns employed on the Somme.[115] Moreover, use of the new 106 fuse ensured that the advance was not hindered by the destruction of the ground, which was so prevalent with the 'delay action' fuse used by the artillery upto 1917.[116]

Pointing out 'the paramount importance of the factor of accuracy' for the artillery when supporting the infantry, following the Battle of the Somme, the Fourth Army staff stressed the importance of calibrating guns and correcting for the temperature of charge and air; the barometer, the wind; and the wear of the guns as factors in providing accurate gun fire.[117] New equipment and methods of sound-ranging, flash-spotting, survey, calibration, and photography were gradually developed and employed in 1917.[118] By late 1917 the British artillery had become very efficient in employing such new techniques. By the end of the war the calibration of each field gun, a procedure available only to the Garrison Artillery before the war, gave the accuracy required.[119] All these improvements were the result of 'the slow evolution of an artillery doctrine, which had been going on for three years'.[120]

By mid-1918 the lessons of Cambrai had been learnt and Birch (as Major-General Royal Artillery [MGRA] at GHQ, Haig's Artillery Adviser) was stressing that a preliminary bombardment should not hinder the advance by turning the ground 'into a crater-field'.[121] By the end of 1918, in order to ensure the advantage of surprise, British doctrine stressed the importance of being able to *either* 'dispense entirely with a preliminary bombardment, and to rely upon other means, such as tanks, to crush passages through the enemy's wire and to prepare the way for the assaulting infantry' *or* to rely on a short bombardment 'of extreme violence' to ensure 'not so much the destruction of the enemy's defences as the demoralization of his troops, the neutralization of his artillery, trench mortars and machine guns, wire-cutting and the destruction of his observation stations, command posts and centres of communication'.[122]

Air power developed a new tactical function by providing observation for the British artillery, locating enemy defences and batteries, and reporting through 'contact patrols' on the positions of the advancing British troops. Ultimately, such developments and improvements in the handling of the RFC greatly assisted the better performance of the British artillery during 1917 and 1918. As early as September 1914 'much use had been made of observers in aeroplanes to locate the enemy's guns and trenches, as well as to direct the fire of our own artillery'.[123] By 1915 aircraft were already very important in providing 'the eyes' for the artillery, locating and reporting the positions of enemy targets.

As Haig noted, the 'excellent photos' taken by aeroplanes meant that attacks could 'all be planned out beforehand' in the minutest detail.[124] Before the Battle of Neuve Chapelle the Intelligence of the First Army employed air reconnaissance to obtain tactical information about the German defences.[125] Air reconnaissance was still in its infancy in early 1915 using hand-held cameras but it revolutionised military intelligence by enabling a close and complete picture of the enemy's defences to be provided with great precision.

From Neuve Chapelle in March 1915 onwards aerial photography provided photographic maps which gave a comprehensive picture of the whole German defensive system so that for the first time in history the British Army went into action with an intricate map of the enemy's defences.[126] During the Battle of Loos in September 1915 'constant air photographs were taken to try and locate machine-gun emplacements, strong points, etc, with considerable success' for the artillery.[127] During the Battle of the Somme the RFC issued 45,000 photographic prints while 19,000 negatives were taken.[128]

'The value of daily aeroplane photographs' which were 'taken and developed' each day was noted by the XIII Corps who also stressed the importance of close co-operation between the artillery and the RFC observers.[129] Fourth Army concluded that 'the great development in combined and artillery and aeroplane work' on the Somme required that 'increased importance' be given 'to thorough cooperation between these arms'.[130] Following the experiences of 1917, two manuals, SS131 and SS135, published in December 1917 and April 1918 respectively,[131] outlined the important contribution which aircraft provided for the all-arms team, notably locating targets for and directing the artillery's fire, reporting the dispositions of both the British and enemy infantry, and providing intelligence for the high command.

Ground support, another important facet of airpower, was also developed in 1916–17. The Germans noted that on the Somme 'the enemy's airmen were often able to fire successfully on our troops with machine guns, by descending to a height of a few hundred metres' and were keen to learn the 'lesson to be learnt from this surprisingly bold procedure on the part of the English airmen'.[132] By August 1917 low-flying aeroplanes were co-operating with the infantry by attacking the enemy's infantry, artillery, trenches,[133] and corps commanders, like General Sir Ivor Maxse, were advocating 'a more extensive use of low-flying aeroplanes' in order *not only* 'to attack strong points, nests of machine guns, infantry advancing or massing for counter-attack, and the personnel of enemy's batteries' *but also* 'to deal with the enemy's anti-tank guns and forward batteries' which otherwise would prevent 'the effective use of Tanks in large numbers'.[134] By late 1917 close air support was already commonplace.

During the German Spring Offensive low-flying aircraft played an important part, notably in March and April 1918 when the 'concentration of every available fighter on low-flying action' against the enemy breakthrough '"froze up" the German advance'.[135] The importance of air power and British dominance of the air was shown during the last months of the war when the RAF 'had the upper hand of the Bosch the whole time' and 'had some extraordinary good days on the back roads in the Bosch area shooting down guns and transport'.[136] At the end of the war GHQ noted that 'the essential preliminary to all other aerial work is to gain at least a local and temporary superiority in the air' but once that had been achieved 'offensive action against enemy troops and transport by means of machine gun fire and bombs by low flying machines' became 'feasible and must be vigorously undertaken'.[137]

The tank helped to give more mobility on the battlefield because as one Brigadier-General on the Somme commented 'they produced the effect of fire superiority for which we are otherwise entirely dependent on the artillery and produced it at the time and place required as the action progressed'.[138] Another Brigadier noted that the tanks provided the means once again 'to surprise, mystify, and hoodwink your enemy' for they 'could take the place of heavy guns, which would otherwise be wanted to cut the wire, and which would give the show away by their mere presence on the roads weeks before they opened fire'.[139] By early 1918 the tank ('a mechanically propelled armoured battery') was a major component in a successful assault, providing the mobility, security and offensive power with which 'to reduce resistance to the infantry advance' and 'to offer local protection to the infantry attack'.

Close co-operation between tanks, artillery, and infantry was essential to take 'full advantage' of 'the opportunities Tanks may create' and also to protect the tanks from enemy anti-tank guns.[140] GHQ maintained that 'tank units must be trained to co-operate with other arms in the attack'[141] and 'if tanks were to be used to the best advantage, there must be the closest co-operation between them and other arms'.[142] In breaking down 'organized resistance', the tank was allotted two separate roles in co-operation with the infantry, either to replace the barrage or to accompany the infantry to deal with particular strong points.[143] At the end of the war, doctrine decreed that 'in addition to assisting the advance of the infantry across the enemy's organized system of defences, the tank in open warfare was 'rapidly to exploit any success which had been obtained by disorganizing the enemy's reserves and breaking up his communications'.[144]

However, tanks were extremely vulnerable to enemy fire and mechanically unreliable in 1916–17 and an intense debate occurred within the British hierarchy over their employment. The correct operational employment of tanks was evolved in 1917 and gradually their strengths were acknowledged. GHQ concluded in December 1916 that 'in the present stage of development, tanks must be regarded as entirely accessory to the ordinary methods of attack, ie, to the advance of Infantry in close co-operation with the Artillery'.[145] At Arras in early 1917 'the tanks owing to shortage of numbers and poor tactical employment achieved very little'.[146] During the Third Battle of Ypres 'the Tank was being used outside its limitations'[147] and 'many were frittered away in the Ypres salient'.[148]

It was the tanks from 1917 and particularly in 1918, which in the close support role delivered the hammer punch allowing a breakthrough. In August 1917, Maxse was advocating that the employment of tanks 'to neutralize strong points, nests of machine guns and generally to facilitate the task of the infantry' and as a means 'of economizing man-power and minimising casualties'.[149] New artillery tactics combined with better tank techniques to provide the means to unlock the German defences but this was only made finally clear by the British success at Cambrai on 20 November 1917 and the great offensives of the Germans in the spring of 1918. At Cambrai, tanks were used in large numbers for the first time, making passages in the wire for the infantry and demoralising the German defenders.[150] They were, however, vulnerable to German machine gunners and artillery suffering heavy casualties.[151]

Many British commanders simply had not learned how to employ tanks properly. Although recognising that tanks were useful for mopping up and dealing with MGs, Lieutenant-General Sir Launcelot Kiggell in August 1917 felt that 'a check must be kept on the enthusiasts'.[152] As late as February 1918, when

Major-General Sir John Capper (Director-General of Tanks, War Office) came to breakfast to enlist his 'sympathy in Tanks', Rawlinson 'would have none of him'.[153] As late as July 1918 some of the Staff at GHQ were alleged to be not yet convinced of the tank's value and to be holding Haig back in developing them.[154] But attitudes did change. In June 1918 a converted Rawlinson was employing demonstrations to encourage 'the Australians to understand and appreciate the Tanks'.[155] Montgomery (MGGS, Fourth Army) was enthusiastic about the employment of Mark V tanks on 4 July 1918 at Le Hamel 'which helped enormously to save casualties'.[156]

By August 1918 Britain had 18 tank battalions in France to support 54 Divisions or a ratio of 1 to 3.[157] Haig himself notified Lawrence (CGS) in August 1918 that Byng's Third Army was to be provided with the latest Mark V tanks in order to 'carry out a surprise attack on as large a scale as possible with the object of breaking the enemy's front & disarranging his plans'.[158] Haig was generous in praising the Tank Corps for its contribution to the final victory, noting in his dispatch of the final months of the war that 'since the opening of our offensive on 8 August, tanks have been employed on every battlefield and the importance of the part played by them in breaking up the resistance of the German infantry can scarcely be exaggerated'.[159] Archie Montgomery noted in October 1918 that 'the tanks have been of very great assistance to us, and there is no doubt they are a great adjunct to an infantry attack, although they will not win the war by themselves, as some people seemed to think at one time'.[160]

The last two years of the war saw many innovative efforts to break the stalemate of trench warfare and restore manoeuvre to the battlefield. Those efforts did not bear fruit completely in 1917 and 1918, but the ideas behind them were taken up and improved forming the basis for tactics in the Second World War. These impressive developments in fighting efficiency during the war demonstrate that the British Army climbed a steep 'learning curve'. Lacking a trained army and modern equipment prior to this, the British had developed a modern doctrine of offensive warfare for the era of the MG and artillery fire by the end of 1917.

The emphasis was on flexibility and elasticity and much depended on the initiative of junior officers and battalion commanders. To do this took time and much training but the fact that the British Army was able to do so by 1918, forging a powerful weapon which was able to manufacture the victories of the Last Hundred Days, suggests that the British Army and its leadership was much more impressive and effective than a concentration on the poor performances of 1915–17 alone would suggest. The faults exposed by the failures during the period of 1915–17 serve as an important contrast to the successful application of all-arms co-operation in 1918. Prior to 1918 the British were seeking an unlimited breakthrough success, which was simply impossible to achieve at that time.

The tendency to see the British as 'enthusiastic but tactically incompetent schoolboys',[161] in contrast to German soldiers who are almost always perceived as incomparable tacticians ignores the British tactical expertise prior to the war and development during the war as part of a continuing learning curve. The tactical innovation achieved in 1916–17 has, unfortunately, been obscured by the lack of operational progress and heavy losses in the mud of Ypres in late 1917 and by the contrasting rapid German advance in the Spring offensive of March 1918. In reality in tactical affairs the Germans had been overtaken by the British tactics of late 1918 and were unable to provide an answer to their new firepower and tactics of infiltration.

8 A strategy for victory

It now runs like a well-oiled machine.
(A French General commenting on GHQ in 1918)[1]

In particular, this study looks at the development of British operational thought during the war, a subject that has been comparatively neglected. The concept of the operational level of war is employed here in the sense of the 'area between strategy and tactics which denoted the fighting of battles in a given theatre of operations in pursuit of the political objective of the war',[2] and as the 'grey zone once called Grand Tactics, the tactics of large formations', such as army groups, armies and corps.[3] One area of especially heated debate during the war was whether to employ breakthrough or siege operations to penetrate the formidable German defences.

The foremost strategic problem for the British high command during the early years of the war was that of conducting a successful strategic offensive and here was the biggest learning curve of all. The British high command lacked the experience at the operational level to control the large battles, which occurred during the Great War, and this was reflected in a poor operational performance during 1915–17. It was at this operational level that much of the damage to reputations would be inflicted and the British proved to be least well-equipped to adjust to the problems of trench warfare. This inexperience of the operational level was a recurrent problem dogging the British Army upto 1917, which explains the failure to gain tangible results until 1917–18. During this process the British Army was hobbled by a serious doctrinal controversy in which the Army's doctrine of seeking a quick, decisive victory had to adapt to conform to the harsh reality of tactical stalemate in the trenches. As a result of British weaknesses and inexperience at the operational level, stunning displays of all-arms co-ordination at Broodseinde and Cambrai were executed in something of a strategic vacuum, failing to provide the decisive victory craved so much by the high command.

Part of this learning curve required the development of GHQ from what was essentially an Army Headquarters into a large staff of the type, such as Supreme Headquarters, Allied Expeditionary Force (SHAEF) during the Second World War, capable of managing continental operations on an unprecedented scale. By

1918 the enormous staff of the Quartermaster General alone could be likened to a great modern industrial organisation such as Shell or ICI.[4] The growing pains of GHQ were reflected in the mediocre performance of 1915–17 while it is surely no coincidence that when GHQ was at last functioning properly in 1918 victory was finally achieved. The transformation of the BEF from a small, colonial army of some 220,000 soldiers in 1914 to a large, continental army of over two million men in 1918 capable of defeating the best army in the world, so often ignored by critics, was a unique British military achievement, which requires some explanation.

Handicapped and absorbed by the huge task of building a continental-scale army, the British lagged behind the Germans badly in developing the bureaucratic apparatus at GHQ to analyse problems, 'some branch whose chief duty it is to *think*', which was noticeably absent in the British Army in 1915–17,[5] and was not able to catch up with the dynamic leadership of men like Eric Ludendorff until 1918. As an institution GHQ was hastily and imperfectly improvised during mobilisation and did not function properly as the 'brain' of the army during 1914–15. Matters were made worse by personality clashes within the newly developed GS, which lacked the experience and organization to function properly until 1917–18.

Following Henry Wilson's outspoken behaviour during the 'Curragh Mutiny' in March 1914, Asquith's Liberal government had vetoed his appointment as CGS at GHQ by Sir John French and Lieutenant-General Sir Archibald Murray was brought in from 2nd Division to be CGS, although originally intended to be Quartermaster-General, and Major-General Sir William Robertson was given the post of Quartermaster-General. As a result, 'GHQ was almost entirely staffed from the MO Directorate', with Colonel G.M. Harper as GSO1, and having worked with Wilson (the Sub-Chief) for years they continued to regard him as their chief and looked to him for orders while Murray, the CGS 'a comparative stranger, knowing nothing of the plans drawn up with the French, was in a position of the greatest difficulty'.[6] Murray complained later that 'the senior members' of the GHQ staff 'ignored me as far as possible, continually thwarted me, even altered my instructions'.[7]

Matters were not helped by the fact that, although possessing a thorough knowledge of staff duties in general,[8] Murray was 'by nature petulant' and 'difficult to work with',[9] being cordially disliked by his subordinates[10] as 'incompetent, cantankerous, timid & quite useless'.[11] Murray and Harper were continually rowing[12] and on 24 August Harper 'let his personal feelings get the better of him' and 'stuck his toes in the ground refusing to do anything for Murray and consequently Lord Loch had to write messages even though it was not his job which caused a most unpleasant "atmosphere" as Harper resented it'.[13] Henry Wilson had to intervene to persuade Sir John and Murray from sacking Harper.[14] It was 'rather sad' and 'deplorable' that Murray was still making distinctions between members of the GS, and 'talking of "my men" and "his men" after working together for a month'.[15]

There were also complaints that French surrounded himself with a personal staff, including Colonel the Hon W. Lambton (Military Secretary), Colonel Brinsley Fitzgerald (Private Secretary), Lieutenant-Colonel Fitzgerald Watt and Captain

F.E. Guest (ADCs), who lived in his quarters in St Omer replacing his official staff. Few shared Sir John French's high regard for this personal staff who were seen by outsiders as being 'such awful courtiers',[16] 'very stupid' and 'making mischief like old women'.[17] One regimental officer felt that GHQ was 'full of the most extraordinary scallywags', who were 'no use to anyone & get in many people's way'.[18] Lord Esher warned Sir John French that this '"War Cabinet" requires strengthening' and that the King regarded his advisors as troublemakers.[19]

Sir John French required a strong personality as CGS to offset his limitations, notably his lack of staff experience. Murray was insufficiently robust for this role, fainting at one point 'when some bad news came in'[20] at St Quentin of Smith-Dorrien's decision to stand at Le Cateau on 26 August 1914. As a combination Sir John French and Murray were 'between them quite unable to size up a position or to act with constancy for 24 hours'[21] and often 'were out motoring & playing the ass all day'.[22] Murray became 'a cipher at GHQ'[23] with Sir John French ignoring his GS 'chiefly because Murray is incapable of managing them and getting any good work out of them'.[24] 'Rendered useless, because the CGS does not represent them',[25] GHQ was 'incapable of organising an attack on a large scale'.[26]

The performance of GHQ during the retreat from Mons when it panicked and fled from St Quentin to Noyon without notifying its change of address to the Corps,[27] was inglorious. Major-General Lord Loch, GHQ Liaison Officer with II Corps, felt that GHQ had 'lost their heads' and that 'an order giving authority for ammunition to be thrown away so as to carry men on wagons' had merely 'put the cap on the demoralisation'.[28] General Sir Aylmer Haldane (10th Brigade) witnessed the demoralising effect of 'such a mad order' on the 4th Division.[29] In early September 1914 the GS at GHQ were so 'in the depths of gloom', preparing to retreat to the Bay of Biscay,[30] that the French Liaison Officer with the British Army informed Grand Quartier General des Armees Francais (GQG) (the French HQ) that the BEF had lost all cohesion.[31]

When eventually sent home in January 1915 and replaced by Robertson,[32] it was felt that Murray had been 'intrigued out' by Henry Wilson, who 'got French influence to bear with Sir J. F[rench]'.[33] The French Government was indeed heavily involved in his replacement.[34] Robertson admitted after the war that, although tempted by the extra pay, he had not wanted the job because he knew that he was not the first choice and that the Commander-in-Chief had previously asked for Wilson to succeed Murray.[35] Like Murray, Robertson's influence was diminished by Sir John French's tendency to listen to Henry Wilson, who dined at French's personal table, while Robertson was relegated to a junior mess,[36] having no separate mess of his own, although his predecessor had lived with the Commander-in-Chief.[37]

As CGS, Robertson was hampered by an 'unofficial adviser', a rival 'of similar rank' but 'totally different temperament',[38] whose relationship with the Commander-in-Chief was especially close and cordial having been in his confidence in 1914 more than any other member of GHQ's Staff.[39] Wilson was believed to be an *agent provocateur* attempting to remove Robertson 'whom he dislikes'.[40]

Relations further deteriorated when the removal of Harper 'a close and trusted friend of Henry Wilson'[41] was 'carried out in a very untactful way',[42] fuelling a mutual antagonism[43] between Robertson, who was 'suspicious' and 'hostile',[44] and Wilson, who was 'rather upset by the changes made in his absence' touring the French front.[45]

Substantial changes in personnel were made by Robertson who, although accused of picking SOs like Perceval 'who will do nothing but just what they are told',[46] selected a team of talented SOs, such as Macdonogh (BGI), a man of 'many outstanding talents',[47] and Maurice (the BGO), who possessed 'quite exceptional talents'[48] and was seen by a French SO as one of the few flexible British SOs.[49] But problems remained, however, with the performance of GHQ as the central bureaucracy of the BEF during 1915. Despite their talent, these officers were inexperienced in the staff work required in continental warfare. Major-General Sir Frederick Maurice admitted after the war that difficulties were caused at the Battle of Loos by the inexperience of GHQ's Staff in operational matters.[50]

Maurice and his Operational Staff were very active in writing papers discussing the new tactical realities[51] but attempts by these officers to change tactics in 1915 floundered on the opposition of Sir John French, who continued to believe in the efficacy of the cavalry on the modern battlefield and 'still adhered obstinately to the idea of hordes of mounted men sweeping over Europe'.[52] He allowed his favourite, Haig, to continue to pursue the *chimera* of the breakthrough. French remarked that 'sometimes a Staff must be made to understand that a General intends to conduct a Campaign in his own way or not at all'[53] and Haig noted in March 1915 how Sir John made a point of seeing him alone in order to underline Robertson's lowly status as an administrator, who carried out rather than instigated policy.[54]

But, above all, Sir John French, '*un beau sabreur* of the old-fashioned sort'[55] and 'a brave fighting general' who was 'out of his professional depths',[56] failed to realise the necessity of employing GHQ as a well-oiled machine under his CGS ready to formulate and execute policy. Robertson complained that 'Sir John French chopped & changed everyday & was quite hopeless',[57] while Whigham (Sub-Chief) 'was very sick as he had to cancel & then re-write his orders'.[58] Indeed GHQ was split up for the Neuve Chapelle battle, the Battle of Aubers,[59] and again for the Battle of Loos when Sir John French established his advanced command post at an inaccessible chateau near Lillers, leaving his CGS (Robertson) and staff at St Omer, 25 miles away.[60] Sir John French was not a Staff College graduate and he tended to undervalue the crucial role in modern warfare of professional SOs.

French's successor as Commander-in-Chief, Haig, would not tolerate criticisms or suggestions from his staff very easily. When in October 1917, Colonel Rawlins frankly told him that if the Passchendaele offensive continued, no artillery would be available for a 1918 spring offensive, Haig reportedly went white with anger and said, 'Col[onel] Rawlins, leave the room'. When Edmonds agreed with Rawlins, Haig added: 'You go too'.[61] This was the only occasion when Edmonds heard anyone really stand up to Haig and tell him the truth, noting that he could make suggestions to Robertson or Macdonogh, but not to Haig.[62] Gough complained that in 1916–17 that 'Haig's conferences were too big & too formal & Army Commanders only attended to hear Haig's plans, never to discuss them' and 'there were not enough discussions, between the HQ Staff and the Army Commanders concerned, – when we could sit round a table with the maps before one, & really thrash out the problems'.[63] Most of the Army Commanders were reputed to be scared of Haig[64] and since it was not in his nature to seek counsel in 'marked contrast' to Allenby and Kitchener, who were open to advice, Haig was 'as a rule intolerant of any opinion that differed from his own'.[65] It was difficult for a subordinate to express criticism when Haig resented opposing views or gratuitous advice, telling Birdwood (Fifth Army) that 'I won't have anyone criticising my orders'.[66]

Haig's staff was 'an excellent machine, formed to carry out his ideas and intentions' but they initiated 'nothing'.[67] With his extensive staff experience Haig in many ways acted as 'his own Chief of Staff' and worked at his own house, away from the offices of the GHQ staff.[68] The actual incumbent, Kiggell, seldom contradicted his strong-willed leader and was more of a clerk than an executive instrument, having 'little to do except to see things go smoothly'. Although 'straight and charming', Kiggell was 'unknown to the Army' and 'neither organises nor assists the work of the Staff but, above all, would 'neither represent contrary views to Haig nor decide between contrary views when representing Haig'.[69]

'Tavish' Davidson (BGO, GHQ), although 'a charming fellow' and 'quite able', lacked the necessary drive and personality to influence the head-strong Haig and it was not until Brigadier J.G. Dill became BGGS, Planning in March 1918, that a permanent Plans sub-section was created to plan operations and a real grip was felt on the helm.[70] A small advance had been the formation of a small planning team, a special sub-division of the Operations Section at GHQ consisting of Lieutenant-Colonel C.N. Macmullen and Major Lord Gort as his assistant, created especially to study the problem of an offensive in Flanders in January 1917. But the advice of this section and that of Davidson (BGO) was often ignored, notably in the planning for Third Ypres.

It was not until 'a reorganisation of the General Staff at GHQ' occurred with the replacement of Kiggell (CGS), Butler (DCGS), Maxwell, Quartermaster-General (QMG), and Charteris (BGI) by Lieutenant-General Sir Herbert Lawrence, Major-General G.P. Dawnay, Lieutenant-General Sir Travers Clarke, and Brigadier-General Edgar Cox respectively, providing new blood and new ideas in January 1918, that strong direction and a well-balanced team emerged at GHQ.[71] Lawrence, the new CGS, was an 'able man' with a 'pleasant and tactful' manner remaining 'unflustered' at 'times of crisis' and whose judgment 'was always sound' and 'unerring in spotting the weak point of a case'. 'Cold and laconic', with 'outstanding ability', 'great strength of character and very clear judgement' and 'a really good business head', Lawrence was, unlike Kiggell, an impressive and significant figure.[72]

But above all he had 'had great experience in the front line' and as CGS Lawrence placed 'great stress on personal contact with formations in the field, and a great part of his time was spent in informal visits to Army, Corps and Div[isional] HQs'.[73] Lawrence was adamant that he would 'certainly refuse to act on the same lines as Kiggell, who had become rather like a superior ADC & was absolutely unknown in the army',[74] accompanying Haig on his visits to the divisions, corps and armies in the field and in his conferences with his French Allies and his Army Commanders[75] and insisting on having the right to attend all conferences between Haig and other SOs at GHQ.[76]

Having accepted Lawrence against his will, Haig soon began to appreciate him,[77] praising his 'cool judgement, equable temperament, and unfailing military insight'.[78] Very soon Haig had 'complete confidence' in Lawrence who was allowed greater responsibility, for example in July 1918 sending reserves to aid the French when Haig was absent in London.[79] Colleagues found that they no longer had to consult Haig on all matters as they could now get their 'work done with CGS' whereas beforehand they 'could get nothing done, as K[iggell] would not take responsibility'.[80] Undoubtedly 'with his virile personality Lawrence proved in the last year of the war a more stimulating support for the Commander-in-Chief',[81] running GHQ '"like a well-oiled machine"'[82] and providing 'complete coordination of planning & execution' for the first time.[83] Lawrence's integrity and wisdom certainly infused a new spirit into the General Staff at GHQ,[84] producing 'an atmosphere of smooth and effortless efficiency'.[85]

Haig was not only better informed but also better advised. According to Davidson, 'Haig & Lawrence never liked each other either before or after 1918, but for the war in 1918, they were a superb combination with the most supreme confidence in each other',[86] working very closely together in planning and execution of operations[87] notably 'the August offensive, which smashed the Hun and smashed him *so* badly that he never recovered, and from then on, it was success after another for us'.[88] In his final despatch Haig noted that Lawrence had shown 'an unfailing insight, calm resolution and level judgement which neither ill-fortune nor good were able to disturb'.[89]

At last GHQ had a team capable of fighting a modern war and much of the credit for its creation can be given to Lawrence, who reorganized the GS and promoted new and efficient SOs to key jobs at GHQ, such as Dawnay, an 'exceptionally able' and 'first rate man';[90] Dill, 'a splendid staff officer' with 'a brilliant brain' who was later CIGS;[91] and Cox, more realistic than Charteris, 'a very, very first class Chief of Intelligence', and 'probably one of the best military brains of his generation' whose impact 'at GHQ was striking'.[92] Lawrence himself was willing to delegate power to and open to ideas from such officers.[93]

The weakness of GHQ as an institution was reflected in the length of time needed to develop a strategy capable of winning the war. Regarding the annihilating battle as central to its war-fighting doctrine, the Army was ideologically opposed to siege warfare stressing that 'since the object of war can only be attained by the destruction of the enemy's field armies, all fortress warfare must be considered as subsidiary to that end', and advocated where possible 'an attack without recourse to siege operations'.[94] When faced with the strategic alternatives of either 'bite and hold' (siege) or breakthrough (conventional) operations, the Army leadership was predisposed towards the latter whereas the stalemate in the trenches increasingly necessitated commanders focusing on the former. For much of the war the high command was divided by this issue, which was only finally resolved in the second half of 1917.

In December 1914, one SO noted that 'opinion is gaining ground that the way to work is to capture a trench, organize its defence, and wait for a counter-attack, which is sure to come; so as to make the Germans lose heavier in the counter-attack than we lost in the attack'.[95] One battalion commander, Stephens, believed that 'the offensive actions of the past year have proved that it is impossible to break through either the German or the Allied lines, as they now exist, on the Western Front'.[96] The high command, notably Haig, insisted on pursuing the unrealistic aim of overrunning the German defences in one, huge blow in pursuit of 'the apparently impossible break-through'.[97] This was to be the *modus operandi* until late 1917.

In March 1915 Haig attacked at Neuve Chapelle 'with the definite objective of advancing rapidly (and without check) in the hope of starting a general advance'[98] in which the Germans were to be carried 'right off their legs'.[99] The operation at Neuve Chapelle was not planned as 'a very limited objective',[100] as the Corps Commander (Rawlinson) and his two Divisional commanders wished, 'a minor operation' whose conception was 'to capture a trench here, or a trench there', but as 'a serious offensive movement with the object of breaking the German line'[101] to capture Aubers Ridge.[102] Haig was convinced that a golden opportunity to push his reserves through to capture the Aubers Ridge had been squandered at Neuve Chapelle because of over-caution, believing that 'if Rawlinson had only carried out his orders and pushed on from the village at once, we would have had quite a big success'.[103]

A consistent advocate of siege tactics and limited objectives to wear down the Germans during the period 1915–17, Rawlinson opposed Haig's breakthrough strategy. By contrast, as a result of his experiences at Neuve Chapelle, Rawlinson, was 'content with capturing another piece out of the enemy's line of trenches and waiting for the counter attack',[104] believing that 'we can always take a line of trench 1000 yards long and hold it against counter attack' and that 'in doing so we ought to kill 4 Germans for every one of our own men' which 'raises our moral and lowers the enemy's' while inflicting 'heavy losses on the enemy'. Rawlinson was convinced that 'if we had not tried to do too much our losses would have been one quarter what they were and we should have gained as much ground', believing that 'it was not in the first assault that the casualties occurred but in the subsequent attacks on the various prepared keeps and redoubts which the enemy had constructed in the rear of their front line of defence'.[105]

Haig 'would have been better advised to content himself with the capture of the village instead of going on with the attack' in an attempt to break through and that 'had he been content with the village we should have gained just as much ground and reduced our casualties by three quarters'.[106] Such limited objectives did not, however, result 'in any decisive victory which could affect the final issue of the war' and 'only very slowly forces the enemy's line back towards their own frontier'.[107]

Noting that the British assault at Neuve Chapelle 'failed to penetrate the enemy's front', Du Cane (MGRA at GHQ) also advocated a series of limited attacks in which 'the first assault would be prepared and delivered as at NEUVE CHAPELLE' but 'should not be pressed so far as to carry the infantry beyond the range of artillery support' and 'the first step should then be consolidated, counter-attacks repelled and a fresh advance prepared for'. The next step would 'take place as soon as possible' with fresh troops and the process 'repeated till the enemy's resources are exhausted' and his resistance so weakened that 'a bid for decisive victory' could be launched.[108]

The GS at GHQ developed the concept of 'two distinct operations', namely 'the preparatory action' to use up the enemy's reserves and 'the decisive attack' to break through, 'carried out on the lines adopted at Neuve Chapelle'. The former, the 'bite and hold' operation, relied on the fact that 'once the ground won has been consolidated' the inevitable enemy counter-attack was 'likely to be far more costly to him than to us' and that 'a series of attacks in the same neighbourhood, if each is preceded by a careful registration of the objective by the artillery' would result in 'a slow but steady advance on our part from trench to trench, unaccompanied by very heavy casualties'.[109] Yet at the Battle of Aubers Ridge in April 1915 the same mistake was made of 'hammering at the enemy's defences' after the initial success losing 5,000 men for little gain whereas if the British had been 'content with the capture of the Village and stopped at the end of the first day' their losses 'would have been only 2300' having 'killed twice that number of Germans'.[110]

In mid-1915 Hugo Montgomery in the Operations Section A (Oa) at GHQ noted that each attack 'had been gradually brought to a standstill by the arrival of reserves on the defending side' and had merely pushed 'the line back for a short distance at the expense of very heavy casualties'. The enemy trenches resembled 'an elastic band which can be pushed back with sufficient force but which it is very difficult to break through'.[111] Faced with stalemate Montgomery also emphasised the distinction between 'a "wearing" attack' to 'gradually draw in all the enemy's reserves' and a decisive attack launched 'with a view to breaking through'.[112]

The debate about the efficacy of limited and unlimited objectives for an offensive was continued again during the planning before the Battle of Loos. Noting that the French had failed to take Loos village six months before and that the Germans had fortified the area with great diligence since, Rawlinson advocated a series of siege operations to wear down the Germans, being 'strongly of the opinion that the capture of Hill 70 cannot be undertaken successfully in one rush, but that it should be divided into at least two, if not three, distinct but consecutive operations' to take the German front line, Loos village, and then Hill 70 over a period of a week or ten days.[113]

Once again Haig refused to accept limited objectives and remained obstinately in favour of a dramatic breakthrough; announcing that 'the enemy is to be beaten on a certain length of front and driven out of it, and must not be allowed time to reform in rear of the captured trenches' by 'a *violent* and *continuous* action'.[114] Haig promulgated 'the principle that men must go forward as fast and as far as possible once the attack is launched'[115] and Gough (I Corps) stressed that 'this attack, by its suddenness and the size of the force employed, is aimed at capturing the enemy's second line, viz, HULLUCH-STAELIE-HAISNES, in practically one rush'.[116]

In post-battle assessments IV Corps felt that lacking 'the means wherewith to carry out the big thing, then the 1st Army should have given a limited objective',[117] outlining the risks and advantages involved between the alternative strategies. In 'the "all out" attack or the attempt to break through the enemy's whole system of defences at one rush', experience had shown that 'what we gain in the first rush is the easiest gain and very often much more than we are finally left in possession of' so that 'victory is almost as disorganising as defeat and no victory is more disorganising than one in which the attack is to go "all out" and units start with the intention of going forward until exhausted'.[118] By contrast a limited objective was 'by far an easier task' and offered a chance 'to inflict local loss on the Germans' or 'to draw in as many local reserves' but did not offer the same 'big results', which it appeared had so narrowly been missed at Loos.[119]

In December 1915 Stephens, now a brigade commander, was 'very thoroughly convinced that the surest way of obtaining decisive results is not by attempting to break through the enemy's front at one blow but by wearing down his power of resistance by a methodical advance from trench line to trench line on a very wide front'.[120] Thus, in 1915 the fundamental differences over operational methods, which were to dog British planning until late 1917, were outlined. The indecision over whether it was 'a problem of moving warfare, checked momentarily by field defences, as Haig thought' or a 'basic problem of siege warfare, the methodical approach and the blasting of a breach as Rawlinson believed',[121] had a fatal impact on the campaigns of 1916 and 1917, leaving a legacy of bitterness over British generalship during the war.

Yet ironically following the failure to break through at Loos Sir John French was replaced as Commander-in-Chief in December 1915 by Haig who remained the main proponent of the decisive battle. The GS at GHQ noted in January 1916 that 'the lesson of the war up to date is that a carefully prepared attack, if supported by an unlimited expenditure of munitions, causes more loss to the defence than to the attack in the first stages of the operation' but that 'owing to the depth and strength of the defences, the attack loses the advantages of the preparation and the artillery support which it started with'. The inescapable conclusion was that 'operations intended merely to cause loss to the enemy, *at a less cost to ourselves*, should not be pushed to the point where effective artillery support is lost and where disorganisation sets in'.[122]

Haldane (3rd Division) also advocated attacks 'with a limited objective' to make 'the enemy quit his front system of trenches and force him to move his heavy guns back' allowing the attackers to take advantage of the enemy's disorganisation to consolidate and prepare for another attack, envisaging a strategy of limited attacks 'on front after front of Corps or Armies, so that the enemy is constantly having to rebuild his line and shift or lose his guns' becoming disheartened and allowing the British to 'escape the heavy losses which invariably result from pushing on after the first day of attack'.[123] This was the operational method which was to prove to be very effective in 1918.

The War Office was also opposed to 'a big push' in 1916 as Kitchener preferred 'to continue small offensives with a view solely to killing Germans' on the premise that it was 'impossible' to finish the war in 1916 and that 'it would be unwise' to make 'an attack "au fond" incurring 50 or 60,000 casualties which could not be replaced'.[124] Robertson, now CIGS, concluded that 'we sh[oul]d not be helping the French by throwing away thousands of lives in knocking our heads against a brick wall'.[125] He tried to persuade GHQ that 'the road to success lies through deliberation' and 'nothing is to be gained but very much is to be lost by trying to push on too rapidly', believing that 'the thing is to advance along a wide front step by step to very limited and moderate objectives, and to forbid going beyond those objectives until all have been reached by the troops engaged'.[126]

Aware that all his Corps Commanders were opposed to an unlimited offensive on the Somme Campaign in 1916 and thinking it 'wiser to adopt the limited one and to look to winning this war in 1917',[127] Rawlinson pointed out that the depth and strength of the German defences in both the front and second defensive systems and in the 'strongly fortified villages' such as Mametz and Beaumont made a breakthrough unlikely to succeed. Convinced that a breakthrough involved 'very serious risks' and would leave the troops disorganised, without effective artillery, and vulnerable to the German counter-attack, Rawlinson once again advocated a series of limited advances, aiming 'to kill as many Germans as possible with the least loss to ourselves' by seizing points of tactical importance with good observation which would force the Germans to counter-attack 'under disadvantages likely to conduce to heavy losses' and take full advantage of the materiel superiority of the Entente over the Germans.[128]

Given the choice between a breakthrough battle to gain decisive results and a battle of attrition to inflict heavy casualties by limited but systematic advances, Haig maintained his stubborn obsession with the elusive decisive battle, planning 'to go for an unlimited offensive'[129] in order to overcome 'the whole of the enemy's defences in one rush as was attempted at Loos'.[130] Rawlinson predicted correctly that Haig was taking 'a gamble which involved considerable risks'.[131] Haig criticised the methodical advance being planned by the 18th Division because 'much valuable time' was being lost and insisted that instead the 'men should be training to go forward to the maximum of their power'.[132] He was also critical of Hunter-Weston (VIII Corps) who 'was only going to take the enemy first system to begin with, and proceed slowly stage by stage' believing that 'if he attempts to do it piece by piece, the enemy will bring on reserves (as the French have done at Verdun, though surprised at first) and the position will only be gained after great sacrifice of life'.[133]

Dismayed, when studying Rawlinson's proposals for attack, to learn that 'his intention is merely to take the enemy's first and second system of trenches and "kill Germans"', Haig determined that 'we can do better than this by aiming at getting as large a combined force of French and British as possible across the Somme and fighting the enemy in the open'.[134] Haig was still inclined 'to favour the unlimited with the chance of breaking the German Line' rather than an attack for limited objectives in the forlorn hope of 'breaking the line and gambling on rushing the third line on the top of a panic'.[135]

In comparison the French Army employed the limited tactics scorned by Haig and 'went forward line by line on a time programme', losing only 5,000 casualties compared to the 70,000 lost by the British early in July 1916.[136] Aware that the attack of the XIII and XV Corps at Montauban succeeded because 'their task was less ambitious', Major-General Hon William Lambton (4th Division) noted that in 'going for a big thing' in 'a very optimistic vein' everything 'had to go like clockwork'.[137] Haldane (3rd Division) concluded that, since 'the enemy can always recover from a frontal attack and hold another line', operations should concentrate on taking positions to 'cause the enemy continual loss' and to obtain good observation for the artillery, complaining that by 'seeking to win their objective quickly', GHQ had failed to assemble sufficient troops to take advantage of the lack of German reserves and were then forced to resort to the dubious tactic of attrition, 'pure "Bludgeon work"', which is so frightfully costly'.

Forecasting the strategy of 1918, Haldane advocated the launching of 'a great feint attack' on the Somme 'as the containing attack' to pin down German reserves before launching another surprise attack without a preparatory bombardment 'where the ground was suitable' and supported by massed tanks to destroy the wire in order to break through.[138] The tactical method of rigid adherence to time-tabled attacks was ill-suited to the breakthrough strategy adopted by GHQ but had distinct possibilities if allied to a strategy of limited objectives. The validity of limited objectives was to be shown later on the Somme by the successful attacks on 14 July and 15 September 1916, and at Vimy Ridge, Messines, and Hill 70 in 1917.

As the war progressed, there was considerable dissent and debate grew within the army, as an alternative theory of limited objectives emerged and gradually gained the ascendancy over the breakthrough as the preferred operational method, providing a template for generals, such as Montgomery, to follow in the Second World War. By early 1917 when the French under Nivelle 'talked about "breaking through"' British generals were sceptical having given up 'that catch word some time ago'.[139] The majority now believed that 'you cannot smash right through deep and strong defences in the course of a day' and a breakthrough 'in 24 to 48 hours' was 'most ridiculous' and 'entirely wasted the lessons of the last two years and a half'.[140]

Comparing 'the school of the Great Offensive, of large numbers on long fronts, for unlimited objectives' and 'the school of small and sudden offensives with comparatively small forces on limited fronts for limited objectives' and concluding that 'both schools were wrong, and have been proved wrong over and over again', Henry Wilson suggested that 'a middle course of big operations on long fronts for limited objectives' was 'by far the wisest plan', inflicting 'a maximum of damage to the enemy with a minimum loss to ourselves' and keeping him 'in a state of constant tension and anxiety'.[141] But the most important idea – a series of offensives along the whole front to exhaust and confuse the enemy, which was the winning Allied strategy in 1918 – had still to be fully formulated.

The doctrinal split within British operational planning came to a head during the planning for the Third Battle of Ypres in mid-1917. Lieutenant-Colonel

C.N. Macmullen, leading the small planning team created especially to study the problem of a Flanders offensive, advocated the employment of limited objectives carried out step by step within the range of powerful artillery support to capture the Passchendaele Ridge.[142] This coincided with proposals for a limited offensive in Flanders by the commanders on the ground, Plumer and Rawlinson,[143] who concluded that the lesson of the Somme was to refuse to allow the infantry 'to carry out an assault unless the hostile trenches had been absolutely pulverised' and to undertake 'only a very limited objective in depth'.[144] But Gough and Haig still had ambitious plans to smash through the German defence with one decisive blow.

In response to these ambitions Davidson (as BGO the Head of Operations at GHQ) outlined the limited operation, which was to prove so successful for the British in 1917–18 in unlocking the German defensive system, advocating 'a deliberate and sustained advance' divided up into 'a succession of operations' to a depth of 'not less than 1,500 yards and not more than 3,000 yards'. This 'deliberate and sustained advance' was designed not only to take advantage of the success of 'the first day's operations' when the enemy was in 'a state of disorganisation' but also to be 'in a position to deliver a second and well organised attack'. A limited objective for each successive step ensured that 'the infantry was not pushed too far and that the objectives are well within their reach' and that 'a good line of departure for the next operation' was secured since experience showed that 'with sufficient and efficient artillery preparation we can push our infantry through to the depth of a mile without undue losses or disorganisation'.

Davidson concluded that, if a series of such advances were repeated every two or three days and the momentum maintained, the cumulative pressure of the sustained succession of blows would destroy the German reserves without excessive demands being placed on the attacking infantry. Believing that 'an "all-out" attack' to break through was only viable when the enemy was beaten and in disarray, Davidson questioned the feasibility of a decisive offensive. Instead he promulgated a step-by-step advance with limited objectives under the artillery's powerful support to inflict maximum losses on the enemy strength and morale while reducing to a minimum the casualties and strain on the British troops.[145] Rawlinson also urged Haig 'to make Goughy undertake deliberate offensives' so that the troops did 'not go beyond the range of their guns or they will be driven back by counter attacks'.[146]

Davidson's plea for limited objectives faced much opposition from the proponents of the breakthrough. Gough contended that limited objectives did not 'reap all the advantages possible resulting from the first attack'.[147] Ambitious for 'an advance to THOUROUT and ROULERS' to inflict a 'decisive defeat upon the enemy',[148] Gough remained adamant that 'any thoroughly prepared attack can break through any defences which the enemy can devise' maintaining that 'the great initial success of the 1st July 1916, 13th November 1916, and 9th April 1917, are sufficient proof that this claim is not too great'.[149] Gough was confident of reaching the third objective (Green Line), an advance of 3,500 yards, and hoped to each the Red Line beyond the fourth (Black Line) with battle patrols.[150]

Haig over-ruled his own planners with 'the general intention of wearing out the enemy' and 'the strategical idea of securing the Belgian Coast and connecting our front with the Dutch frontier' by first capturing 'the bridgehead formed by the Passchendaele-Staden-Clercken ridge' and then pushing 'on towards Roulers-Thourout, so as to take the German coast defences in the rear'.[151] Whereas Macmullen, Plumer and Rawlinson 'had recognized that the problem before them was a siege operation and wished to proceed step by step', in a repeat of earlier 'rush tactics' Haig sought 'to silence the enemy's artillery and burst a way through in one assault'. Where 'the Operation Section urged a succession of limited attacks; the Fifth Army proposed to go as far as possible in the first rush, hoping to reach a depth of 5,000 yards, which would be beyond the range of all except the heaviest artillery, in 8 or 9 hours'.[152]

Once his breakthrough operations, because they had been 'ill-considered and the probabilities of success not sufficiently weighed', proved 'an expensive fiasco'[153] Gough was forced to repeat the small attritional attacks of the Somme while GHQ rethought its strategy. More receptive to Davidson's concept of limited objectives, Kiggell now considered that it was 'beyond dispute that we should so limit each advance as to ensure having fit and organised units at the end of it' and that the British should only 'go all out',[154] pushing the advance and the men 'to the utmost limits' when the enemy was beaten and 'so exhausted and disorganised that he cannot hit back effectively'. Kiggell now suggested that the offensive should consist of a series of consecutive blows in which 'our furthest objective must be not only within the power of our artillery, but within the power of our infantry' allowing the attacking troops to beat off the enemy counter-attacks and to 'exhaust the enemy as much as possible and ourselves as little as possible in the early stages of the fight'.[155]

In reply Rawlinson once again outlined the choice between 'a decisive battle with an unlimited objective' and 'a battle of attrition', which was 'by far the most suitable at the present juncture', noting that the British had failed 'to carry out a battle of attrition on absolutely definite lines, with successive objectives well within covering range of artillery and well within the physical capacity of the infantry'. Rawlinson contrasted attempts at breaking the enemy line at Loos in September 1915 and on the Somme in July and September 1916 (where 'although the crust of the enemy's defence was broken' the over-ambitious objectives had resulted in 'very heavy losses', 'disorganization from which it took many days to recover' and 'a disheartening effect on the morale of the troops, who felt that they had been called upon to carry out tasks beyond the limit of their powers') with limited operations at Longueval in July 1916, Vimy in April 1917 and Messines in June 1917 (where 'the objectives given were well within the physical capacity of the troops' and 'they reached their final objectives with their energies compara-tively unimpaired, and consequently, in a state to throw back any counter-attacks that were likely to be put against them').

Rawlinson advocated delivering 'a succession of carefully worked out hammer blows on the enemy at short intervals with the object of definitely beating him to his knees so that there is no question that his morale is finally broken'. By relying on his artillery, Rawlinson hoped to reduce the numbers of infantry assaulting, 'thus economising troops and saving valuable time' so that greater reserves were available for the next phase of the attack.[156] This strategy was implemented by Plumer's Second Army in September and October 1917 and the final offensive, which brought victory in 1918. Davidson's tactics prevailed as Plumer (Second Army) began a series of limited battles, which unlike previous battles planned as a single-action breakthrough formed a succession of 'bite and hold' operations to wear down the enemy over many days, leaving the breakout and exploitation until a later, final phase when the enemy was too weak to resist. Aware that German tactics relied on the defence in depth and counter-attacks,[157] objectives were selected to give 'the greatest advantages to defeat the enemy counter-attack', which were a 'real opportunity for inflicting loss on the enemy', and left the infantry 'in condition to consolidate and hold the points gained'.[158]

Plumer's tactics employed a methodical advance in steps with strictly limited objectives 'making four steps of approximately 1500 yards each with each division on a frontage of no more than 1000 yards' and 'to support them he wanted his allotment of artillery doubled, asking for 1,339 guns and howitzers for the offensive front alone'. The German defensive system 'failed with terrible losses against the systematic advances of Plumer'.[159] During the battles of the Menin Road (20 September), Polygon Wood (26 September), and Broodseinde (4 October), the scale of success was comparable with that of Arras or Messines in 1917 or Amiens in 1918.

The Battle of Broodseinde was 'by far the best thing the Second Army ever did',[160] notable as one of a growing number of 'black days of the German army', in which their entire front-line system was overrun with relatively light casualties to the attacker.[161] The success of Second Army's limited objectives, in which German policy of the counter-attack 'suffered heavy losses and was quite fruitless', forced a switch in German tactics to holding the front-line in force.[162] At last the British had got to grips with German defensive tactics by advancing in a series of steps. Each step set up the next by seizing jumping-off points for the next infantry assault and sites for the all-important artillery support while limiting the advance to a line which could be reached without tiring out the infantry and could easily be defended by infantry under the umbrella of the artillery's support.

The year 1917 'witnessed the turn of the tide' not only because 'those hammer blows were struck which led to the final victory in 1918'[163] but also because the correct operational methods had at last been adopted, using siege tactics, providing a glimpse of the succession of battles, which were to provide victory during the last Hundred Days of the war in late 1918. Unfortunately, this success has been overshadowed by Haig's stubborn refusal to cut his losses in October, once the weather had turned, continuing the battle into the now infamous Passchendaele stage, in which 'many thousand valuable lives'[164] were lost in 'rather doubtful victories'.[165]

British planning had finally abandoned the breakthrough as an operational method and a strategy of employing attacks on multiple axes was developed during 1918. In early 1918 Stephens (5th Division) proposed a strategy of 'many limited offensives carried out as quickly as possible one after the other – as fast as the guns can get there' but each offensive was 'to be sternly shut down after the first success' because 'we never lose many on the first day of a successful show, it's afterwards [that] the losses come' and the 'first days can be so prepared nowadays that they are bound to succeed'.[166]

Indeed, in marked contrast to Loos, the Somme and Passchendaele, the Battle of Amiens was closed down by Haig as soon as it was realised that the German resistance was hardening,[167] switching the main axis of attack to the Third Army area and attacking on the Scarpe on 21 August 1918.[168] Haig refused to carry out Foch's order to continue the Amiens offensive when informed by Lambert (32nd Division) of growing resistance and also postponed the attack on the Roye-Chaulnes front because Currie (Canadian Corps) and Rawlinson (Fourth Army) warned that it 'would be *a very costly matter*'.[169]

Haig's growth in stature is summed by Cruttwell who, although critical, concludes that 'Haig grew with disappointment and disaster, until he stood out in the last months of the war as a very great general' and notes the impact made at GHQ in 1918 by Lawrence, Haig's CGS, which is often ignored.[170] Haig had by mid-1918 begun to give effective army commanders, such as Byng, Horne and Rawlinson, and corps commanders, such as Currie, Haldane and Monash, greater participation in planning. For example, Rawlinson proposed the offensive at Amiens launched on 8 August to Haig and when Rawlinson suggested the discontinuation of the Amiens offensive Haig agreed 'without a murmur'.[171] Haig met his Army commanders prior to the Battle of Amiens alone with his CGS and 'had a general talk for 1½ hours' to discuss 'the policy and future plans of the Generalissimo (Foch)' and 'they appreciated the opportunity of being able to state their views to me personally instead of before a number of staff officers as on one of the periodical conferences with army commanders and staffs'.[172]

Haig met his five Army commanders and his CGS again on 30 August to tell them 'the general plan decided on by Foch' in order that 'they might realize that the enemy would be engaged by the Allied Armies on a very wide front from now on'.[173] Considerable power in the BEF had shifted to the army commanders, in particular to the experienced Byng and Rawlinson. Later, Haig sent Lawrence to see Horne and Currie, 'to tell them that I have no wish to attack the Queant-Drocourt line, if they have any doubts about taking it' since he 'was opposed to doing more attacking than was absolutely necessary'.[174] One of the most striking examples during the Hundred Days of a corps commander influencing the planning of an attack was the suggestion by Sir Walter Braithwaite (IX Corps) of an attack across the St Quentin Canal which led to 46th Division's brilliant success in storming the main Hindenburg Line on 29 September 1918. This flexible style of command, in which more authority was delegated to divisional commanders than previously in 1915–17, was crucial in the successful offensives of late 1918.

British doctrine stated that 'the development of active operations, whether undertaken by ourselves or the enemy, may normally be expected to take the form of a methodical and progressive battle, beginning with limited objectives and leading up by gradual stages to an attack on deep objectives in chosen portions of the front'. Each attack was one of 'successive steps in a continuous offensive' for carefully selected intermediate objectives which would 'best facilitate the reorganization of the infantry for the next stage of the attack' and final objectives providing 'a good defensive line well within the physical capacity of our infantry and the zone of effective artillery support' yet with the 'good observation over the enemy's defences' and suitable positions for the artillery, ready for 'the resumption of the attack at the earliest date possible'. It was emphasised that the offensive should 'be composed of several carefully prepared attacks' and carried out as 'a series of rapid blows, each delivered before the enemy has had time to reorganize after the previous one'.[175] This was possible because the tempo of operations during the Hundred days was much faster than in 1916–17. This was achieved by the greater availability of guns, ammunition and logistic support in 1918 than previously, which allowed large-scale operations to be conducted.

The doctrine followed by the British Army in the last, successful campaign of the war was summed up by GHQ as consisting of 'a series of attacks delivered on a wide front, but not necessarily on a continuous front' and employing 'a series of minor operations' to occupy the enemy's outpost zone in front of his main battle position 'in order to capture and to occupy suitable ground from which to initiate attacks on his main defensive system'.[176] Attacks were also made where a deep thrust would bypass any centres of resistance and was likely to unhinge the German defences.

For example, the 'capture of the high ground between Croisilles and Heninel' by XVII Corps (Fergusson) in August 1918, ensured that 'a door into the Hindenburg Line had been opened, so it was no longer necessary to make attacks along our whole front to take it' but that 'it ought now to be possible to pass troops through the gap already made, and take the Hindenburg defences in the rear'. Similarly, in August 1918 the 9th and 29th Divisions of XV Corps (de Lisle) took the Outersteene ridge 'which looks back into the back of the enemy's defended line'.[177] By September 1918 it is clear that the British understand the necessity of fighting separate operations to capture the outpost zone and the main battle position when the Germans were adopting a defence in depth giving the enemy two alternatives – either to 'continually give ground and to prepare new lines of resistance in rear – a policy he could not adopt indefinitely' – or 'to strengthen the force in occupation of his outpost zone and to accept battle in that area' with his troops 'exposed to the full power of the attacking artillery'.[178]

Attacks were be made as a series of interlinked thrusts on a wide front of 40–50 miles rather than on a narrow front as in 1917 in order to ensure that the Germans could not collect large forces of artillery on the flanks of the British offensive and to force the Germans to disperse their resources.[179] Archie Montgomery (MGGS, Fourth Army) described how after the Battle of Amiens on 8 August 1918, 'first of all the First Army, then the Third and then the Fifth' joined the attack,[180] stretching and confusing the enemy. In the final four months of the war the British Army captured more German prisoners than the American, Belgian and French armies combined.[181] By the end of October 1918 the British Army had 'engaged and defeated' 100 German divisions since 8 August 1918 while the Americans,

Belgians and French combined had beaten only 98.[182] The Fourth Army's campaign compared favourably in terms of captured prisoners and equipment and the smallness of their casualties 'with those of the Second World War in North Africa, Italy or Normandy'.[183]

The German Army had been defeated in the field as the result of a 'relentless and methodical hammering on a shaken enemy'[184] but also by the development and then execution of a sensible and effective operational strategy. At the operational level the British had discovered a very effective technique by mid-1917 to compensate for the deficiencies of training, which had so handicapped them in 1915–17. Rather than a single strategic thrust, a series of powerful successive multi-army strategic operations along several axes of attack were employed to destroy the German Army. This renaissance in British military thought in 1917–18 has been overshadowed by the horrific casualties of the Somme and Ypres. It provided not only the basis for the achievement of a British victory in 1918 but also for military development for the rest of the century.

Conclusion

The long succession of pyrrhic victories, which characterised the Allied campaigns on the Western Front, did irreparable damage to the credibility of an entire military generation who rose to high command in the British Army during the First World War. As a result, since the 1920s, British generals and senior officers have been stereotyped as Colonel Blimps who allowed their troops to be butchered through incompetent tactics and an abject slowness to adapt to change. Undoubtedly this Blimpishness, epitomised in the post-war Low cartoons and the more recent Blackadder television series, was one facet of the army which underpinned the great resolve and stubborn will to win required in modern wars and shown by the army's leadership in the long, hard campaign required to defeat Germany.

Unfortunately, this stereotype does little to aid comprehension of the inner workings of the army, or to understand how the traditions and bureaucracy, inseparable from all military hierarchies, affected the manner in which the war was conducted by the Army's leadership. British generalship was the product of a particular system, and not just the fruit of the peculiar idiosyncrasies and shortcomings of particular individuals at GHQ. Nor does it explain why it was that of all the armies, which went to war in 1914, the British was the only one that had not mutinied on a large scale or simply disintegrated by 1918. Unlike the continental armies of France, Germany, and Russia, the *raison d'être* of the British Army was to provide a garrison for an Empire, which was shielded from potential foes by a large and dominant Royal Navy. The rigours of defending the Empire had important consequences in shaping the identity of the elite of the British officer corps and in turn the conduct of the war.

The tempo of the learning curve quickened as the war progressed and can be divided into four specific phases: the opening period of mobile warfare (August–November 1914); trench stalemate while the army rapidly expanded (December 1914–June 1916); an interval of hot debate when the army realised the need for change and rapidly implemented new techniques (July 1916–August 1917); and a revolutionary phase which saw a qualitative shift or 'leap' causing a dramatic transformation in doctrine represented by the battles of Cambrai, Hamel and Amiens (September 1917–November 1918). The army had progressed along a number of learning curves in leadership, staff work, training, tactics, and operations and had radically overhauled its methods to evolve new techniques of warfare which would dominate the rest of the century. The emergence of a solution to the tactical and operational stalemate of 1914–17 can be traced through a series of learning curves, which when synthesised gave birth to a new, modern style of warfare.

The Somme marked the beginning of a steep learning curve in many areas, which was uneven but capable of carrying the army to victory, a major achievement that has not been properly appreciated. During the early years of the war, an inexperienced but over-confident hierarchy emphasised accomplishments rather than shortcomings. Realistic evaluations of German capabilities were too often replaced with bureaucratic optimism, the result of the unwillingness or inability of many leaders to examine previous mistakes closely even when there was enough critical information to show that over-optimism was unwarranted. The official 'party line' of optimism pervaded the hierarchy, which as a result lost touch with reality, tending to accept only that information that they wanted to hear and ignoring the warnings of subordinates. Under the prevailing climate of optimism professionalism was eroded; optimistic commanders were more likely to be promoted while the careers of subordinates who made realistic but pessimistic objections stagnated.

Attitudes in 1915–17 were epitomised by the way in which over-confident and over-ambitious generals were deluded by technology into an over-reliance on artillery and made little effort to achieve operational or tactical surprise, allowing the Germans to turn prospective breakthroughs into punishing and costly battles of attrition. Haig epitomised the faith that victory would be won and his flawed personality made him the most controversial general of the Great War. Haig's extreme optimism, excessive loyalty to friends such as Butler, Charteris, Gough, and Kiggell, and his inability to choose close subordinates with any judgement make him more likeable, but were fatal flaws for a 'great captain'. Growing realism from 1917 onwards made victory in 1918 possible. The turning points were the failure of the Flanders offensive in July 1917, the German counter-attack at Cambrai in November 1917, and the German *Kaiserschlacht* of March 1918, which convinced even Haig that the enemy should not be over-rated and encouraged him to introduce more realistic operational methods and re-emphasise the importance of surprise.

One factor in this change in emphasis was the replacement in 1916–18 of tired or mediocre commanders, paving the way for a new generation of professional soldiers. The evidence suggests that there was a learning process in the early years of the war as the army leadership struggled to come to terms with an unfamiliar situation and in 1915–17 younger, middle-ranking officers often had to 'carry' their superiors. Older and incompetent senior commanders and SOs were gradually replaced by more energetic men who had learnt many harsh lessons during the war. The leadership qualities of the British generals of the First World War as a group of men have been much disparaged. Painting the BEF's commanders as uniformly incompetent is both unfair and greatly exaggerates the case against the generals.

Although the British Army in the Great War did provide a number of examples of incompetence, the real weakness of the British leadership was inexperience of continental warfare and the severe dilution of that leadership by the rapid expansion of the army and the heavy casualties of trench warfare. Most senior officers had little practical experience of large-scale operations, having made their reputations policing the Empire in campaigns on the North-West Frontier or in Africa, and had little opportunity to learn before being thrust into battle. Their responses to fighting European armies were unsurprisingly conditioned by their colonial experiences. The heavy losses of 1914–15 made disastrous inroads upon the numbers of trained and experienced officers available. The shortage of experienced senior officers at all levels was a major factor in hindering the quick assimilation of complex lessons early in the war.

Many senior officers failed when confronted by the professionalism of the Germans in 1916–18 and were removed but as the generals gained experience through on-the-job training the turnover rate became relatively low. In the reconstruction of the British Army command, the criterion for promotion became ability on the battlefield and by 1918 a meritocracy based on promotion for able and experienced officers was established within the army leadership, which was open to debate and dissent and adapted decisions accordingly. The offensive of 1918 was entrusted to those officers who had shown their abilities in the short but terrifyingly intense battle-school of 1916–17. A growing professionalism within the army's elite enabled victory to be achieved by the British Army in 1918.

The offensive on the Western Front would not have succeeded without the solid performance of the British army, corps and divisional commanders, as well as their troops. The British Army was not an unchanging monolith composed of stupid Blimps that overwhelmed the Germans with sheer numbers, but rather a force that improved steadily during the war. By 1917–18 Britain had developed commanders who were thoroughly tempered by war, capable of coping with the complexities of modern operations and achieving effective parity in performance. This achievement plus the quantitative advantage more than compensated for any continuing tactical deficiencies.

The Battles of 1917 demonstrate that the BEF had learnt from the Battle of the Somme and that the British Army's art of attack evolved steadily during that period. The Battles of Arras, Messines, Ypres, and Cambrai clearly indicate that the lessons of the Somme had been learnt and represent a progression in tactical thought as further lessons were absorbed and then put into practice. Above all the use of combined arms was gradually developed and polished. These battles showed that the British Army possessed the techniques and weapons to break into any German defensive system but the problem of exploiting that initial success remained a major problem, as the heated arguments prior to the launch of the Third Battle of Ypres illustrated. The striking success at Cambrai with its return to surprise and an emphasis on concealing any preparation demonstrated the ability to learn from experience. Blending old and new techniques to produce revolutionary innovation Cambrai anticipated the successful battles of 1918 and of the Second World War.

The great strength of the British high command was that it was able to produce at all levels that minimum of high calibre commanders, such as Allenby, Byng, Horne, Plumer, Rawlinson, Currie, Maxse, Monash, de Lisle, Tudor, and Carton de Wiart, capable of attaining victory. The divisional commanders provided most of the operational leadership and were the key leaders. While recognising the weaknesses in the BEF's command system, the hackneyed stereotype of chateau generals requires revision. Over-concentration on Haig and his own clique at GHQ has over-shadowed the rapid progress made throughout the rest of the hierarchy. These very real advances have been obscured by the strategy imposed by the high command, which owing to over-optimism and an obsession with the breakthrough battle resulted in the attrition of the Somme and Passchendaele.

With its colonial background, the British Army also had to develop a modern, professional, and efficient staff system. This depended upon the stability of staff personnel, which was disrupted by a large-scale and rapid turnover in the most senior staff positions during the period 1915–16. The constant promotion and movement of personnel during the army's hasty expansion in 1915–16 resulted in a short tenure for most staff posts, which prevented any continuity of thought or leadership within the GS. The commanders frequently did not trust their SOs, who lacked experience, and often usurped their functions reducing their status, lowering their morale, and altering the relationship between the commander and his staff. In contrast to the rapid turnover in the early years of the war when the staff were not in their posts long enough to provide needed direction to their formations, the lengthy tenures of the staff in the later years provided continuity of thought and leadership, in which officers became well versed in the functions of the staff.

British commanders and staffs had to learn how to run large-scale operations the hard way under combat conditions. Staff functions became more responsive and multi-faceted than ever before, demanding a high degree of teamwork, efficiency, and knowledge. To achieve a 'staff culture' of greater flexibility and effectiveness, the British high command was required to improve its staff training, procedures, and techniques. By 1918 the staff involved in the planning process at all levels were very experienced and well practised in working together having, in many cases, worked as a team learning valuable lessons in 1916–17. Their hard work, professionalism, flexibility, and abiding cheerfulness under great pressure throughout the final campaign were second to none.

In the matter of the higher direction of war, the organisation of GHQ in 1914 had been essentially a hastily improvised Army Headquarters but developed slowly into a large staff organisation, similar to SHAEF during the Second World War, capable of managing a continental war on a scale never seen before. Under Robertson in 1915 and Kiggell in 1916–17 GHQ grew in size and complexity. One important step in early 1917 was the formation of a Training Section to give the staff a greater role in the development of tactical and operational doctrine. A further step in implementing the transformation of GHQ into a powerful 'military brain' at the disposal of the Commander-in-Chief was taken in early 1918 with the re-organisation of the staff under Lawrence, who oversaw a thorough overhaul of GHQ's organisation into an operational and planning monolith of more appropriate proportions. The staff at GHQ demonstrated a greater sense of professionalism and realism in 1918. GHQ's role throughout the war in disseminating new ideas and its willingness to embrace technological solutions should not be underestimated. GHQ was responsible for running the successful operations of 1918.

Poor training was probably the single most serious weakness of the British Army in 1915–17 and a continual handicap for all British units. Heavy casualties and the smallness of the pre-war army led to a collapse in the skill levels in 1915–16 as the well-trained regular officers and NCOs were replaced by amateurs. The New Armies had been hastily formed from volunteers who had no formal training and resulted in a lack of qualified leadership at all levels, both officer and NCO, leaving the army without a strong base of experienced leaders. While there were many outstanding exceptions, large numbers of the 'amateur' officer corps lacked professional knowledge, aggressiveness, leadership ability, and a professional commitment to soldiering. The rapid expansion of the army severely strained the British training system, which was largely based on a regimental system designed to train a small, professional army for colonial warfare rather than a large, conscript army for continental warfare.

This expansion had a pervasive, adverse impact on training, which was often disrupted by operational requirements. The low state of training was not only one of the major causes of the low level of battle effectiveness but also the greatest obstacle in improving that capability. Poor leadership seriously affected all efforts to create an effective fighting force, starting a cycle of poor training and poor fighting proficiency, which was a residual problem that lasted the whole war and a continuing source of concern for commanders at all levels of the hierarchy. Massive efforts were made to improve the quality of the troops by the establishment of a school system of training, which had to be developed from scratch.

One great problem was the lack of appreciation by senior officers, notably at GHQ, of the value of training schools, and a Training Section to produce training manuals and develop tactical doctrine was not set up at GHQ until early 1917. As late as 1916 the training provided in France was due more to individual efforts of army, corps, divisions and brigade commands than to any clear direction from higher command. Confident of victory, GHQ had neglected training and provided no central control of innovation in tactics, delaying the systematic introduction of new training methods and tactics until 1917. The period 1917–18 saw signs of greater flexibility at the tactical level and an increasingly successful standardisation of organisation and doctrine, which was such a feature of the German Army. The *ad hoc* development of doctrine and tactics by senior officers in the absence of any direction from GHQ during 1915–16 was in marked contrast to the efforts made by the high command in 1917–18 to improve training methods and to develop better tactics.

The entire process took years of work but was essential. Training schools had to be improvised quickly and during the period 1915–17 were expanded rapidly to train the great influx of recruits into the New Armies. The expansion of the British Army placed great demands on the new training schools, which expanded to offer training at GHQ, army, corps, and divisional level, teaching troops, notably officers and NCOs, how to operate new equipment and tactical techniques. Only through intensive training could divisions approach a common standard of battle effectiveness. Even a limited period of training made a tremendous difference in a division's efficiency.

The schools system was the most successful innovation of 1915–17, successfully developing the numbers of professionally competent officers and NCOs. Although at first providing little tactical knowledge or practice in combined arms warfare, the schools helped to create a standard of training for the whole army, raising the quality and competence of the junior leadership and turning out specialists in increasing numbers to satisfy the mounting demands for skilled instructors within the army. This laid a foundation upon which the British Army built during the last two years of the war steadily improving its efficiency and competence. The British Army of 1918 was well equipped and schooled by four years of hard campaigning.

Early in the war the British struggled to create a force with a coherent combined arms doctrine but by mid-1917 the BEF had found an operational style of attack employing the highly effective, limited-objective set-piece, under an umbrella of artillery deployed in enormous yet well-controlled quantities to support the infantry advance. Although cumbersome and imperfect, this type of set-piece, attritional battle was appropriate given the state of training and tactical effectiveness of the British armies and reflected the increasing *materiel* strength and tactical sophistication of the British Army from mid-1916 onwards.

By late-1917 the British had abandoned the idea of deep penetration and rapid exploitation. Attempting a strategic breakthrough against the German Army was extremely risky as the British found out to their cost on 1 July 1916 and 31 July 1917. Instead the British embraced the tactics of the limited objective attack which took a 'bite' out of the German defences, achieving break-ins that could be exploited to depths of up to two or three thousand yards and covered by the artillery. Once the assault had penetrated the outer crust of the German defences, the momentum of the attack had to be kept going in a series of 'digestible bites', with a pause between each 'bite' to build up gun ammunition, move guns forward and re-organise the troops. These were the 'stepping stones' that enabled the British to break-in into the German defences to some depth. The main lesson of 1916–17 was how to avoid too long a pause between 'bites' or phases, allowing operational sustainability and the tempo of the attack to be maintained. It took some time for the British to learn this valuable, operational lesson.

At Cambrai in November 1917 the problem of the tactical penetration of the front was resolved on the basis of well-organised co-operation between the combat arms, bringing the new infantry and artillery tactics together for the first time in large-scale operations. But the broader significance was that in applying these tactics and techniques it provided a blueprint, which the British would use to produce stunning results on the Western Front in the second half of 1918.

Massive British manpower, armour, air, and artillery superiority was employed in huge set-piece battles from late 1917 to 1918, which relied on careful preparation and the massive firepower provided by the combined arms of infantry, machine-guns, artillery, tanks, and aircraft to crush the German defences in depth.

Modern offensive forces, above all the large-scale employment of tanks and aircraft, opened up the possibility of overcoming the enemy's defensive systems. Employing the technique of the massive set-piece battle the British Army emerged victorious in November 1918. Overall the cautious firepower approach, which was adopted in 1917–18, was largely justified, since the 1916–18 experiences on the Western Front had demonstrated that simple numerical superiority was not enough to ensure Allied successes over the Germans. That the British Army had got from its 1916 nadir to a point in 1918 where it could take on the highly effective German Army, and consistently win, despite its limitations, was a tremendous achievement, of which British commanders were justly proud.

One factor inhibiting the performance of the British Army in 1915–17 was poor operational planning. By 1914 the British Army had evolved a tactical doctrine aimed at fighting a short war in Europe. This allowed it to develop doctrine within the existing colonial traditions, which shaped tactical responses to war during 1914–16. Training and doctrine on the cheap, a recurring theme in British military history, contributed to the poor quality of the available British generals and the operational failures of this period. Although the British Army possessed in the *Field Service Regulations* a doctrine, which provided the linkage between the strategic, operational, and tactical levels of warfare, doctrinal development was haphazard and largely the product of hasty improvisation rather than doctrinal debate and the exchange of ideas in peace.

British officers trained in colonial warfare had no experience of the operational level on a continental scale. The peacetime structure of the British Army did not encourage officers automatically to think in operational terms. Much of the controversy of the war years was much less concerned with the adoption of new weapons than with the choice between two radically different concepts of strategy, attrition and manoeuvre. In 1915–17 the emphasis was on ambitious attempts to break through the German defences and restore mobility whereas in 1917–18 faith was placed instead in set-piece battles to grind down the enemy.

Pursuing the *chimera* of the decisive breakthrough with great tenacity Haig's view of the offensive was frequently at odds with those of many military planners. Differences in opinion as to ultimate goal – a decisive or limited offensive – continued to haunt British planning until mid-1917. Haig placed strategic conditions on all his battles that hindered his commanders from making proper use of the new techniques that were available to them by 1917. Whereas Haig and Gough advocated a strategy of annihilation to crush the enemy and quickly achieve strategic ends, Plumer, Robertson, and Rawlinson pressed for restraint and adoption of a strategy of attrition to cope with the appalling destructiveness of modern war.

In advocating the concept of attrition during the Great War, generals increasingly assumed that in modern war victory could not be achieved by a single attack or a single, continuous offensive. Only when all the enemy's forces and means were exhausted in the struggle, and when they were unable to continue armed resistance, could final victory over the enemy be counted on. This conclusion regarding the inevitability of a protracted war was questioned by Haig who naturally gravitated towards a strategy of annihilation. Advocating a strategy of annihilation and over-estimating the power of modern artillery to devastate enemy defences and to produce a decisive breakthrough, Haig rejected the strategy of attrition.

Haig's conception of the offensive, which prevailed in 1915–17, resulting in over-ambitious offensives and attritional battles in which the British suffered needless casualties for little commensurate gain, is the one history remembers and one which dominates perceptions of the way the war was fought. Prior to Cambrai, Haig strung out his divisions and artillery along a broad front so that, in particular, the British offensives on the Somme and at Ypres lacked concentration and as a result failed to achieve decisive results. The war had become one of attrition, but the high command was dedicated to the idea, and therefore committed to the strategy, of a short war and a decisive victory. The unpopularity of a strategy of attrition until late 1917 is explained by the army's doctrine, which stressed that only the strategy of annihilation could provide victory, and appeared to be confirmed by its most recent experiences of large-scale war – the swift offensive operations leading to the fall of Pretoria during the Boer War.

But by mid-1917 the British had a masterplan for winning the war, which saw a shift from a strategy of annihilation to a strategy of attrition. The turning-point in the great strategic debate of the war between the contending strategic schools of attrition and annihilation was concluded in mid-1917 by the adoption of the concept of successive, limited operations. The pattern of Haig's methods of attack in 1917–18 in massing huge quantities of men and material to crush the enemy in a set-piece battle, closely resembled and were the model of military excellence for Montgomery's style of warfare in 1942–45. The impossibility in modern warfare of destroying an enemy army by a single blow compelled the British to achieve this by a series of successive operations.

The change in emphasis away from big battles in favour of successive, limited operations, begun during the Third Battle of Ypres as an *ad hoc* response to the switch in command from Gough to Plumer, became enshrined as official doctrine in mid-1918. Plumer's offensive represented a radical departure from the past British strategy and tactics. The attacks were characterised by massive co-ordinated assaults against German defensive positions with infantry, tanks and artillery. Plumer's success at Ypres rested on the lavish use of artillery and infantry to support tanks in a drive against a well-prepared German position, and was crucially important for the development of British tactics for the rest of the war.

By mid-1918, British operational methods had improved. Gone were the days of general advances on a broad front, instead, tanks, infantry, artillery, and aircraft were concentrated in key breakthrough sectors and breaches made in

German defences using massive artillery bombardments. Deception measures prevented the defenders from concentrating their resources, while constant air strikes disrupted enemy supply lines and delayed the movement of reserves. The large-scale and high intensity of simultaneous attacks over an extended area outpaced and overloaded the decision-making of their German opponent, resulting in the collapse of the German defensive strategy.

The abandonment of the breakthrough strategy in 1918 in favour of a series of inter-linked limited offensives, which gave the British more options in their axis of attack bypassing enemy strongpoints, returned considerable autonomy to its commanders in the field. The emphasis on securing limited objectives against counter-attacks meant that potential (but risky) opportunities to win battles were not exploited but the logic of attrition suggested that as long as the Allies avoided defeats, and thus sustained their own morale, sheer weight of numbers eventually would secure victory – a point ignored disastrously by Haig while planning his over-ambitious offensives during 1915–17.

By employing a new operational style based on a series of simultaneous and successive operations, which concentrated the available forces against several, narrow sectors of the front (rather than dissipating it evenly along a broad front) and limited the freedom of manoeuvre for the defender's reserves, the British managed to manoeuvre their wary opponent out of successive defensive positions in 1918 maintaining the tempo of the advance. Operations on a wide front, executed by the five armies co-operating with one another on a series of axes led to the creation of enormous breaches in the enemy fronts, which resulted in the enemy defence being chopped into pieces and destroyed piecemeal. The Germans became so disorganised that they suffered a series of successive strategic defeats.

At this operational level the object of the great British offensives on the Western Front in the second half of 1918 was nothing less than unhinging the enemy's entire defensive system. The victories from Amiens onwards, however ponderous, were genuine nonetheless, and the careful but unimaginative professionalism set the pattern for the British generalship until the Armistice, slowly grinding the enemy into submission by the inexorable logic of an attritional war of *materiel*. By 1918 the British operational art of war had come of age, as an evolution of *British* military thinking, which had been forged by the harsh realities of 1915–17. The war made the army more coherent and professional in its approach to development, doctrine, and training but, as the pragmatic approach had appeared to work during the war, there was no incentive to analyse the demands of modern command and no wide-ranging system of reform was advocated after 1918.

Although internal factors, such as the personalities and mistakes of Haig and his staff at GHQ, the over-optimism of the high command, and the culture of the pre-war Regular Army, were contributory factors to the mistakes made in 1915–17, neither the army's culture nor individuals can be blamed for the problems faced during the war. Inevitably Haig and GHQ must accept much of the blame for ignoring the importance of training until 1917 and implementing an over-ambitious strategy until late in 1917, by which time much damage to the army's reputation had been done. Haig merely personified much that was wrong with the army as a whole but it is clear that Haig's approach to operational planning and the atmosphere of fear engendered by GHQ abrogated constructive dialogue within the high command. But far more fundamental problems faced the army.

Rather than judging them, individually and collectively, as Colonel Blimps, it is important to remember that the generals expanded a small, professional army organised to garrison colonies into a large army of amateurs capable of facing and defeating the German Army, the best continental army in the world. When the British Army's colonial organisation, small officer corps, and large numbers of untrained and volunteer troops, are taken into account, it is clear that although some, notably Haig, Kiggell, Gough, Haking, and Charteris, did not perform well at different levels and periods of the war, the overall performance of the generals was very creditable overcoming many serious handicaps to win the war.

External factors, such as British inexperience of continental warfare, new technology, and tenacious German resistance provide a much more reliable means of understanding the problems faced by the British Army when apportioning blame for the heavy losses of the war. The poor British performance for much of the Great War cannot be blamed solely on the social background of the army elite and opposition to new ideas by reactionary senior officers, although resistance to change was a factor. The real explanation lies more in the unpreparedness of the small British Army in 1914 for a continental commitment.

This explains the inexperience in handling large formations and the practice of command and staff work which an European war entailed and in handling an organisation capable of managing such a war effectively. The role of the British Army as a garrison for the Empire, whose imperial role was dominated by worldwide policing duties, provides a better clue towards the problems the British generals had in adapting to the new conditions on the Western Front than any alleged rigidity and inflexibility amongst senior officers. Far-reaching consequences stemmed from this lack of experience of continental warfare, which was a factor of far greater importance than the social composition of the officer corps in explaining the failures of 1915–17.

Given the difficulties faced by the army it is not surprising that the path towards victory was not smooth and was at first painfully slow. Hindered throughout the war by the small size and inexperience of its military elite, the British had to improvise a Nation in Arms for the first time in their history. British generals were so busy learning to manage this tremendous growth of their army that they had little time to ponder tactical reforms. These institutional handicaps make the great victories of 1918 all the more remarkable. In the end a growing professionalism within its elite ensured victory for the British Army in 1918 and like the rest of the army, GHQ had achieved an organisation and expertise which allowed it to plan and implement a war-winning strategy.

Haig's mistakes, which in retrospect made the achievement of 1918 seem like a pyrrhic victory, should not obscure the achievements of his commanders and the British Army as a whole. What must not be forgotten is that Haig relied on his army, corps and divisional commanders and staffs to train the army and to implement his strategy and it was ultimately the learning process undertaken by these men during 1916–17, which allowed Haig to finally triumph in 1918. With hindsight this strategy could have been implemented some two years earlier in 1916 although it is doubtful if the results would have been quite so conclusive. German resistance was still very strong in 1916–17.

The Somme marked the beginning of a steep learning curve in many areas and the last two years of the war saw many innovative efforts to break the stalemate of trench warfare and restore manoeuvre to the battlefield. An important ingredient of British success was the adoption by the better British commanders of methods that had been proven by success in battle. Those efforts did not bear fruit completely in 1917 and 1918, but the ideas behind them were taken up and improved forming the basis for the tactics of the Second World War. Between 1917 and 1918, a revolution took place, which amounted to the birth of modern warfare. Some of the most innovative British generals had imbibed the lessons of their German and French counterparts but, better still, had transcended their mentors and taken theory and practice to a new level of excellence. All this was achieved while the army had to undergo a rapid expansion training and absorbing huge numbers of ill-trained soldiers, whose bravery was only matched by their inexperience.

Notes

1 The army's ethos and culture

1 Lieutenant-General Sir Noel Birch, *Artillery Development in the Great War*, The Army Quarterly, October 1920.
2 See Appendices 1 and 2.
3 See Appendices 7 and 8.
4 Field-Marshal Lord Kitchener to Field-Marshal Sir John French, 11 July [1915], French Papers 75/46/11, IWM.
5 The Countess Haig, *The Man I Knew*, pp. 36–37.
6 Brian St George Kirke, *General Sir Walter Kirke*, Part I: *Army Quarterly and Defence Journal*, Volume 115, No. 4, p. 442.
7 'General Sir Walter M.St.G. Kirke, GCB, CMG, DSO, DL, JP', undated, pp. 1–4, Kirke Papers, IWM.
8 See Professor Peter Gordon, *The Wakes of Northamptonshire*, pp. 174–197; Commander Sir Geoffrey Congreve, *The Congreve Family*, p. 1; Lieutenant-Colonel L.B. Thornton and Pamela Fraser, *The Congreves: Father and Son*, pp. 3–11; Field-Marshal Sir Archibald Montgomery-Massingberd, 'The Autobiography of a Gunner', *Journal of the Royal Artillery*, Volume LXXIII, No. 4, p. 292.
9 Brigadier-General Sir James Edmonds to Brigadier C.N. Barclay, 7 April 1950, Edmonds Papers I/2B/5a, LHCMA.
10 Edmonds, Remarks on the Staff College, undated, Edmonds Papers I/2B/6, LHCMA.
11 Lieutenant-Colonel William Vaughan to Sir Basil Liddell Hart, 21 February 1939, Liddell Hart Papers 11/1933/108, LHCMA; Edmonds, Memoirs, Chapter XIV, Edmonds Papers III/2/10, LHCMA.
12 Sir Basil Liddell Hart, Diary Note: Brigadier-General Sir James Edmonds, Liddell Hart, 1 February 1928, Liddell Hart Papers 11/1928/1b; Lord Geddes, *Unworthy Apolgia, National Review*, February 1953, p. 109, Liddell Hart Papers 15/2/23, LHCMA; Edmonds, Memoirs, Chapter XIV, Edmonds Papers III/2/10, LHCMA.
13 Major-General S.C.M. Archibald, Memoirs, p. 38, Archibald Papers, IWM.
14 Edmonds, Memoirs, Chapter XIV, Edmonds Papers III/2/13-14, LHCMA.
15 General Sir Archibald Wavell, *Allenby: A Study in Greatness*, p. 35.
16 See Duff Cooper, Haig, p. 166; Geddes, *Unworthy Apolgia, National Review*, February 1953, p. 109, Liddell Hart Papers 15/2/23, LHCMA; and Liddell Hart to Victor Bonham-Carter, 2 March 1964, Liddell Hart Papers 1/90/36, LHCMA.
17 Annotation by Major-General Sir Reginald Pinney, 2 September 1918, on a letter from Major E.J. Thompson, Haig's A.D.C. at GHQ, to Pinney, 1 September 1918, Pinney Papers, IWM.
18 Liddell Hart, Talk with General [Sir Henry] Karslake, 20 November 1936, Liddell Hart Papers 11/1936/107, LHCMA.

19 Field-Marshal Earl Haig, Diary, 8 November 1915, Haig Papers, WO256/6 PRO.
20 Lieutenant-General Sir John Glubb, *The Changing Scenes of Life: An Autobiography*, p. 26.
21 Field-Marshal Sir Archibald Montgomery-Massingberd to Major-General Sir Frederick Maurice, 15 May 1918, Maurice Papers 4/4/2/1, LHCMA.
22 General Sir Kenneth Wigram to Major-General G.P. Dawnay, 8 December 1946, Dawnay Papers 69/21/3, IWM.
23 A.J.A. Morris to *The Letters of Lieutenant-Colonel Charles a Court Repington CMG, Military Correspondent of The Times, 1903–1918*, pp. 6–10.
24 Haig to Field-Marshal Sir William Robertson, 18 February 1916, Robertson Papers 7/6/24, LHCMA.
25 General Sir Aylmer Haldane, War Diary, 8 March 1917, Haldane Papers Acc. 20249, NLS.
26 Brigadier-General P. Howell to his wife, 15 August 1915, Howell Papers IV/C/3/208, LHCMA.
27 General C.A. Milward, War Diary, 23 August 1914, Milward Papers 6510-143-1, NAM.
28 Colonel T.T. Grove, Memoir, p. 35, Grove Papers 6308-14, NAM.
29 Obituary of General Sir William Peyton, in Lieutenant-Colonel A.N. Lee's Memoirs, p. 134a, Lee Papers, IWM.
30 Howell to his wife, 10 April 1915, Howell Papers IV/C/3/135, LHCMA; Major-General Sir John Davidson to Major-General Sir Louis Spears, 19 March 1933, Spears Papers 2/3/8, LHCMA.
31 Haig, Diary, 13 February 1916, Haig Papers, WO256/8, PRO.
32 Major-General J.F.C. Fuller, *The Army in My Time*, p. 62.
33 C.M. Page to Edmonds, 25 August 1934, CAB45/136, PRO.
34 Obituary of Lieutenant-General Sir George Macdonogh by Edmonds, n.d., Edmonds Papers V/2/File 2, LHCMA.
35 Foreword by the Hon Eveline Godley, *Letters of Arthur, Lord Kilbracken, GCB, and General Sir Alexander Godley*, GCB, KCMG, 1898–1932, pp. 5–6.
36 Major-General Sir Reginald Pinney, Diary, 7 May 1917, Pinney Papers, IWM.
37 Lieutenant-Colonel A.N. Lee, Memoirs, p. 129, Lee Papers, IWM.
38 General Sir Sidney Muspratt, Diary, 1 September 1917, Muspratt Papers 86/22/1, IWM.
39 P.E. Razzell, *Social Origins of Officers in the Indian and British Home Army*, p. 353.
40 See Appendix 7.
41 Field-Marshal Lord Birdwood, *Khaki and Gown: An Autobiography*, pp. 25–26.
42 General Sir Charles Richardson, *From Churchill's Secret Circle: The Biography of Lieutenant General Sir Ian Jacob*, p. 1.
43 General Sir Charles Bonham-Carter, Autobiography, Chapter IX, p. 1, Bonham-Carter Papers 9/2, CCC.
44 Anthony Farrar-Hockley, *Goughie: The Life of General Sir Hubert Gough*, pp. 3, 383.
45 Richardson, *From Churchill's Secret Circle: The Biography of Lieutenant General Sir Ian Jacob*, p. 16.
46 General Sir Eric de Burgh, Memoir, p. 21, de Burgh Papers 7306-67, NAM.
47 Ian F.W. Beckett, *Johnnie Gough, VC: A Biography of Brigadier-General Sir John Edmond Gough, VC, KCB*, pp. xiii–xiv.
48 General Sir John Burnett-Stuart, Memoirs, Chapter I, p. 3, Burnett-Stuart Papers, LHCMA.
49 General Sir Walter Kirke, Memoirs, p. 1, Kirke Papers, IWM.
50 Brian St. George Kirke, *General Sir Walter Kirke*, Part I: *Army Quarterly and Defence Journal*, Volume 115, No. 4, p. 447.
51 Brigadier-General Sir Ormonde Winter, *Winter's Tales*, pp. 28–30.
52 Field Marshal Viscount Montgomery of Alamein, Notes on his letters and a letter to his mother, 10 April 1916, Montgomery Papers BLM1/57, IWM.

53 Lieutenant-General Sir Adrian Carton de Wiart, *Happy Odyssey*, pp. 45–46.
54 General Sir Charles Grant to Lord Rosebery, 20 May [1918], Grant Papers C41/24, LHCMA.
55 Brigadier-General Sir Archibald Home, Diary, 15 March 1915, Home Papers, IWM.
56 Liddell Hart, Talk with J.E. Edmonds, 7 June 1934, Liddell Hart Papers 11/1934/41, LHCMA.
57 Liddell Hart, Talk with [Major-]General [L.H.R.] Pope-Hennessey, 14 October 1933, and Talk with [General] Sir H. Karslake, 26 November 1936, Liddell Hart Papers 11/1936/111 and 11/1933/23, LHCMA.
58 Brigadier-General John Charteris, *At GHQ*, p. 286.
59 General Sir Herbert Lawrence to Maurice, 9 April 1918, Maurice Papers 4/5/12, LHCMA.
60 Charteris, *At GHQ*, p. 286.
61 Lieutenant-General Sir John Glubb, *The Changing Scenes of Life: An Autobiography*, p. 18.
62 Air Vice-Marshal Sir Philip Game to his wife, 6 December 1917, Game Papers PWG/16, IWM.
63 Major-General Sir Archibald Paris to Mrs Christine Pilkington, 30 March and 6 May 1916, Paris Papers, IWM.
64 Liddell Hart, Talk with Colonel C. [J.L.] Allanson, 19 August 1937, Liddell Hart Papers 11/1929/15, LHCMA.
65 Liddell Hart, Talk with General H. Karslake, 20 November 1936, Liddell Hart Papers 11/1936/107, LHCMA.
66 Liddell Hart, Talk with Edmonds, 23 September 1929, Liddell Hart Papers 11/1929/15, LHCMA.
67 Lieutenant-General Sir Desmond Anderson to Edmonds, 6 April 1936, CAB45/132, PRO.
68 Major-General Sir L. Pope-Hennessey to Liddell Hart, 28 May 1937, Liddell Hart Papers 1/579/3-4, LHCMA.
69 Liddell Hart, Talk with M. Cuthbertson, Liddell Hart Papers 11/1933/25, LHCMA.
70 Liddell Hart, Talk with Edmonds, Liddell Hart Papers 11/1931/3, LHCMA; Liddell Hart, 'Some Odd Notes for History', Liddell Hart Papers 11/1933/5, LHCMA.
71 Major-General G.M. Lindsay to Edmonds, 28 June 1937, CAB45/135, PRO.
72 Lieutenant-General Sir Desmond Anderson to Edmonds, 6 April 1936, CAB45/132, PRO.
73 Major L.W. Kentish to Edmonds, 19 November 1936, CAB 45/135, PRO.
74 Lieutenant-General Sir Desmond Anderson to Edmonds, 6 April 1936, CAB45/132, PRO.
75 [Major-General] F.A. Wilson to Edmonds, 26 November 1936, CAB45/138, PRO.
76 Brigadier-General H.H.S. Morant to Edmonds, 2 April [?1930], CAB45/136, PRO.
77 Captain L. Frewen to Edmonds, 13 April 1934, CAB45/133, PRO.
78 Lieutenant-Colonel M.C. Clayton to Edmonds, 3 March 1934, CAB45/122, PRO.
79 Lieutenant-Colonel F.H. Lister, Addenda to My Diary of 1st French Army Operations from 2 April to 12 August 1918, p. 2, Lister Papers, LHCMA.
80 Kirke, Diary, 21 December 1915 and 10 January 1916, Kirke Papers, IWM.
81 Colonel W.H. Frank Weber to Edmonds, 18 March 1930, CAB45/138, PRO.
82 Lord Moran, *The Anatomy of Courage*, p. 60.
83 Howell to his wife, 30 June 1916, 20 and 28 September 1914, Howell Papers IV/C/3/308 & 66-67, LHCMA.
84 Field-Marshal Lord Alanbrooke, Notes for My Memoirs, Alanbrooke Papers 2/1/55, LHCMA.
85 Mrs Mary Napier to Major A. Crookenden, 24 October 1915, Crookenden Papers, IWM.
86 Pinney, Diary, 31 May 1917, 20 January 1918, and 18 December 1918, Pinney Papers, IWM.
87 Brigadier-General Sir Standish Craufurd to Edmonds, 3 August 1944, CAB 45/118, PRO.

88 Karslake to Sir Basil Liddell Hart, 22 October 1936, Liddell Hart Papers 1/414, LHCMA.

89 Edmonds, Memoirs, Chapter XIV, Edmonds Papers III/2/26, LHCMA.

90 Field-Marshal Sir Archibald Montgomery-Massingberd, *The Autobiography of a Gunner*, p. 9, Montgomery-Massingberd Papers 159/1, LHCMA.

91 Edmonds to Liddell Hart, 25 November 1938, Liddell Hart Papers, 1/733/16, LHCMA.

92 General Sir Sidney Clive, Diary, 11 September 1915, Clive Papers II/2/47, LHCMA.

93 Major-General Sir Hugh Tudor, Diary of the War, 1915, pp. 19, 23, 31, 32; and 1916, p. 2, Tudor Papers, RAI.

94 Edmonds, Memoirs, Edmonds Papers III/11/14, LHCMA.

95 Frank Davies and Graham Maddocks, *Bloody Red Tabs: General Officer Casualties of the Great War, 1914–1918*, p. xii.

96 Sir John French to Mrs Bennett, 25 February 1915, French Papers 75/46/1, IWM.

97 Clive, Diary, 31 October 1914, Clive Papers II/1/50, LHCMA.

98 Colonel R. Meinertzhagen to Lieutenant-Colonel Sir John Dunnington-Jefferson, 28 May 1915, Dunnington-Jefferson Papers, IWM.

99 Howell to his wife, 28 September 1915, Howell Papers IV/C/3/229, LHCMA.

100 Oliver Lyttelton, Viscount Chandos, *The Memoirs of Lord Chandos*, p. 50.

101 See Appendices 4, 5, 16 and 17.

102 Lieutenant-General Sir Frederick Morgan, *Peace and War: A Soldier's Life*, p. 17.

103 Alan Shepperd, *Sandhurst*, p. 115.

104 See Appendix 4.

105 'GSO' [Sir Frank Fox], *GHQ*, p. 3 of the Foreword.

106 Obituary, *The Times*, 20 March 1963, Liddell Hart Papers 1/323/42, LHCMA.

107 General Sir James Marshall-Cornwall, *Wars and Rumours of Wars*, p. 4.

108 Colonel T.T. Grove, Memoir, p. 4, Grove Papers 6308-14, NAM.

109 Major R.P. Schweder MC to his wife, 19 December 1916, p. 110, Schweder Papers, IWM.

110 Guy Chapman, *A Passionate Prodigality*, p. 163.

111 Obituary of Brigadier Archer Clive, *The Times*, 17 April 1995, p. 17.

112 Field-Marshal Lord Alanbrooke, Notes for My Memoirs, Alanbrooke Papers 2/1/4, LHCMA.

113 Air Commodore L.E.O. Charlton, *Charlton*, p. 29.

114 See Appendix 6.

115 Commander Sir Geoffrey Congreve, *The Congreve Family*, p. 129.

116 Charteris, *Field-Marshal Earl Haig*, pp. 68–69.

117 General Sir Noel Birch to Field-Marshal Earl Wavell, 15 December, 1936, Allenby Papers 6/VI/24, LHCMA.

118 Field-Marshal Lord Alanbrooke, Notes for My Memoirs, Alanbrooke Papers 2/1/9, LHCMA.

119 General Sir John Burnett-Stuart, Memoirs, Chapter I, p. 6, Burnett-Stuart Papers, LHCMA.

120 Clive, Diary, 1 June 1915, Clive Papers II/1/140, LHCMA; Kirke to his wife, 2 February, 17 and 25 August, and 16 November 1915, Kirke Papers, IWM.

121 Brigadier-General Sir Standish Crauford to Edmonds, 3 and 25 August 1944, CAB45/118, PRO.

122 General Sir Beauvoir de Lisle, *Reminiscences of Sport and War*, pp. 121–124.

123 Brigadier Sir Edward Beddington, Memoirs, pp. 95–96, Beddington Papers, LHCMA.

124 Haig, Diary, 11 April 1915, Haig Papers, WO256/4, PRO.

125 Fuller, *The Army in My Time*, pp. 37–38.

126 Kirke to his wife, 6 February 1917, Kirke Papers, IWM.

127 Lieutenant-General Sir Henry Keary to his brother, Captain F.W. Keary, R.N., 23 April 1915, Keary Papers, IWM.

128 Pinney, Diary, 11 October 1918, Pinney Papers, IWM.
129 See Appendix 9.
130 General Sir Horace Smith-Dorrien, *Memories of Forty Eight Years Service*, p. 67.
131 Major-General H Essame to Liddell Hart, 27 January 1962, Liddell Hart Papers 1/269/107, LHCMA.
132 Haig, Diary, 29 April 1916, Haig Papers, WO256/9, PRO; Major-General Sir Hugh Tudor, Diary of the War, 1918, p. 3, Tudor Papers, RAI.
133 Haig, Diary, 9 June 1918, Haig Papers, WO256/32, PRO.
134 Meinertzhagen, *Kenya Diary, 1902–1906*, pp. 51–52.
135 Colonel A. Haywood, *The History of the Royal West African Frontier Force*, pp. 45–46.
136 Burnett-Stuart, Memoirs, Chapter IV, p. 45, Burnett-Stuart Papers, LHCMA.
137 General Sir James Marshall-Cornwall, *Wars and Rumours of Wars*, p. 6.
138 Obituaries of Field-Marshal Lord Milne, Lieutenant-General Sir Thomas Hutton Papers, LHCMA and Lieutenant-General Sir George Fowke, Lee Papers, IWM.
139 R. Cude, Memoirs, p. 156, Cude Papers, IWM.
140 Game to his wife, 8 and 20 December 1915 and 18 April 1916, Game Papers PWG/9 & 11, IWM.
141 Pinney, Diary, 24 December 1917, Pinney Papers, IWM.
142 Guy Chapman, *A Passionate Prodigality*, pp. 152–153.
143 C.P. Clayton, *The Hungary One*, pp. 168–169.
144 Oliver Lyttelton, Viscount Chandos, *The Memoirs of Lord Chandos*, p. 52; Lieutenant-General Sir Adrian Carton de Wiart, *Happy Odyssey*, p. 79.
145 General Sir George Barrow to Wavell, 3 June 1938, Allenby Papers 6/VI/16, LHCMA.
146 Field-Marshal Sir Archibald Montgomery-Massingberd, The Autobiography of a Gunner, p. 10, Montgomery-Massingberd Papers 159/1, LHCMA.
147 Major-General P.G. Whitefoord, Diary, 15 and 16 May 1918, Whitefoord Papers 77/2/1, IWM.
148 Captain Cyril Falls to Liddell Hart, 22 August 1964, Liddell Hart Papers 1/276/60, LHCMA.
149 Lieutenant-General Sir Arthur Holland to Field-Marshal Lord Horne, 12 October 1918, Horne Papers 73/60/2, IWM.
150 Sir David Kelly, *The Ruling Few*, pp. 98–99.
151 Geddes, Unworthy Apolgia, *National Review*, February 1953, pp. 109–110, Liddell Hart Papers 15/2/23, LHCMA.
152 General C.A. Milward, War Diary, 24 April 1916, Milward Papers 6510-143-5, NAM.
153 Kelly, *The Ruling Few*, p. 107.
154 Marshall-Cornwall, *Wars and Rumours Of Wars*, p. 40.
155 Extracts from *HQ Tanks, 1917–1918* by Captain the Hon Sir Evan Charteris, Liddell Hart Papers 15/2/6, LHCMA.
156 Notes by General Sir Ivor Maxse [January 1918], Maxse Papers 69/53/8A, IWM; Kirke to his wife, 11 February 1917, Kirke Papers, IWM.
157 General Sir Aylmer Haldane, Autobiography, Volume II, p. 366, Haldane Papers Acc. 20254, NLS.
158 Charteris, *Field-Marshal Earl Haig*, pp. 65–66.
159 General C.A. Milward, War Diary, 22 September and 16 October 1914, 28 June and 6 September 1916, Milward Papers 6510-143-1 and 6510-143-5, NAM.
160 Colonel R. Macleod, Memoirs, pp. 235–246, 380–381, Macleod Papers 1/1, LHCMA.
161 Lieutenant-Colonel K. Henderson, Memoirs, pp. 154, 178–179, Henderson Papers DS/MISC/2, IWM.
162 Kirke to his wife, 20 October 1914, Kirke Papers, IWM.
163 Edmonds, Memoirs, Chapter XXVI, Edmonds Papers III/10/8, LHCMA.
164 Major-General H.D. Fanshawe to Maxse, 58th Division A/35/6312, 29 September 1917, Maxse Papers 69/53/11, IWM.

165 Major-General Sir C.E. Callwell, *Field-Marshal Sir Henry Wilson*, Volume I, p. 178.
166 Game to his wife, 21 November 1915, Game Papers PWG/9, IWM.
167 General Sir Archibald Murray to Field-Marshal Sir William Robertson, 18 March 1916, Robertson Papers 8/1/14, LHCMA.
168 Fuller to his Father, 15 August 1914, Fuller Papers IV/3/141B, LHCMA.
169 Haig, Diary, 4 September 1916, Haig Papers, WO256/13, PRO.
170 Lieutenant-General Sir Launcelot Kiggell to Major-General W.B. Hickie, 5 March 1916, Kiggell Papers V/12, LHCMA; Major E.G. Thompson to Pinney, 1 September 1918, Pinney Papers, IWM.
171 Oliver Lyttleton, Viscount Chandos, *The Memoirs of Lord Chandos*, p. 46.
172 *SS143, The Training and Employment of Platoons*, 1918, GHQ OB/1919T, February 1918, Maxse Papers 69/53/11, IWM.
173 Major-General Cecil A. Heydeman to Wavell, 22 March 1939, Allenby Papers 6/V/32, LHCMA; Edmonds to Wavell, 23 June 1938, Allenby Papers 6/VI/33, LHCMA; Major-General Sir Lothian Nicholson, Diary, 5 March 1917, Nicholson Papers, IWM.
174 Liddell Hart, Talk with Broad, 12 February 1947, Liddell Hart Papers 11/1947/2, LHCMA.
175 [Major-General] Eric Harrison, *Gunners, Game & Gardeners: An Autobiography*, p. 51.
176 Pinney, Diary, 11 May 1916, Pinney Papers, IWM; see also Milward, War Diary, 9 May 1916, Milward Papers 6510-143-5, NAM.
177 Field-Marshal Sir Henry Wilson, Diary, 3 August 1916, Wilson Papers, IWM.
178 Pinney, Diary, 31 October 1918, Pinney Papers, IWM.
179 Lieutenant-Colonel J.G. Dill, *Notes on Training to be carried out in the Reserve Area*, 37 Division No G 3116, p. 2, 11 September 1917, Dill Papers I/3/2, LHCMA.
180 Lieutenant-General Sir Ronald Charles quoted by Liddell Hart, Diary, 2 February 1939, Liddell Hart Papers 11/1939/6, LHCMA.
181 Guy Chapman, *A Passionate Prodigality*, pp. 141–142.
182 The Memoirs of Major-General S.S. Butler, p. 5, Butler Papers PP/MCR/107, IWM; Field Marshal Lord Birdwood, *Khaki and Gown*, p. 309.
183 Colonel R. Macleod, Memoir, pp. 245, 256, Macleod Papers, LHCMA.
184 Lieutenant-Colonel T.S. Wollocombe, M.C., Diary of the Great War, pp. 38, 69, Wollocombe Papers, IWM; Lieutenant General Sir Arthur Floyer-Acland, Memoirs, p. 29, Floyer-Acland Papers, IWM.
185 Lieutenant-General Sir Thomas Morland to his daughter, 20 June 1917, Morland Papers, IWM; Rowland Feilding, *War Letters to a Wife, France and Flanders, 1915–19*, p. 163.
186 Brigadier Sir Edward Beddington, Memoir, p. 113, Beddington Papers, LHCMA.
187 I.L. Read, *Of Those We Loved*, p. 268.
188 N.G. Barron to Captain Cyril Falls, 8 January 1939, CAB45/116, PRO; Major F.W. Bewsher, *The History of the 51st (Highland) Division*, p. 273.
189 Major H.V. Howe to Captain E.W. Bush, 1 February 1972, Bush Papers 75/65/2, IWM.
190 Corporal H.W. Smith, Diary, 15 September 1916, Smith Papers, IWM.

2 The decline and fall of an army

1 General Sir Noel Birch to Brigadier-General Sir James Edmonds, 8 July 1930, CAB45/132, PRO.
2 Birch to Edmonds, 29 June 1938, CAB45/132, PRO.
3 Lieutenant-General Sir Launcelot Kiggell to Edmonds, 16 June 1938, CAB45/135, PRO.
4 Field-Marshal Sir Henry Wilson, Diary, 5 August 1914, Wilson Papers, IWM.

5 General Sir Thomas Snow, The Account of the Retreat of 1914, undated, p. 1, CAB45/129, PRO.

6 Field-Marshal Sir Archibald Montgomery-Massingberd, *The Autobiography of a Gunner*, p. 20, Montgomery-Massingberd Papers 159/1, LHCMA.

7 C. Barnett, *Britain and Her Army*, p. 347.

8 Major-General F.H.N. Davidson, Lecture to the Swiss Officers' Society, 1935, on the War Effort of the British Empire in the World War, 1914–1918, The War Office, February 1935, Davidson Papers, LHCMA.

9 Lieutenant-Colonel (later Major-General) R.M. Luckock, *Growth of British Troops in France, 1914–1918*, Staff College, Camberley, April 1920, Field-Marshal Sir John Dill Papers 3/2, LHCMA; see Appendix 16.

10 Lieutenant-General Sir George Macdonogh to Edmonds, 19 July 1938, CAB45/136, PRO.

11 Birch to Edmonds, 8 July 1930, CAB45/132, PRO.

12 Brigadier-General John Charteris to Edmonds, 24 February 1927, CAB45/120, PRO.

13 Lieutenant-Colonel R.E. Martin to Edmonds, 8 September 1926, CAB45/120, PRO.

14 Wilson, Diary, 12 November 1916, Wilson Papers, IWM.

15 Luckock to Edmonds, 8 August 1930, CAB45/135, PRO.

16 Colonel J.A. English, *The Canadian Army and the Normandy Campaign*, p. 16.

17 General Lord Rawlinson, Diary, 9 October 1916, Rawlinson Papers 1/7, CCC.

18 XIII Corps, Lessons Deduced [August 1916], p. 9, Montgomery-Massingberd Papers 47, LHCMA.

19 General Sir Aylmer Haldane, War Diary, 24 July 1916, Haldane Papers, NLS.

20 Wilson, Diary, Memoranda at beginning of January 1916, Wilson Papers, IWM.

21 Notes and Hints on Training, XVIII Corps No. GS 659, 10 February 1918, Maxse Papers, 69/53/8A, IWM.

22 Field-Marshal Viscount Byng to Advanced GHQ, 20 August 1917, WO95/365, PRO.

23 Rawlinson to GHQ (Training), Fourth Army GT 107, 28 October 1918, Montgomery-Massingberd Papers 91, LHCMA.

24 Major-General G.P. Dawnay to Major-General Sir A.A. Montgomery, GHQ, 31 October 1918, Montgomery-Massingberd Papers 91, LHCMA.

25 General Sir Charles Fergusson to General Lord Horne, 10 October 1918, Horne Papers 73/60/2, IWM.

26 Haldane, War Diary, 11 April 1918, Haldane Papers, NLS.

27 Wilson, Diary, 30 July 1916, Wilson Papers, IWM.

28 Captain Philip Landon to Edmonds, 2 April 1937, CAB45/135, PRO.

29 General Lord Jeffreys to Edmonds, 23 October 1936, CAB 45/135, PRO; Major-General G.M. Lindsay to Edmonds, 28 June 1937, CAB45/135, PRO.

30 Lieutenant-General Sir Launcelot Kiggell to Edmonds, 4 June 1938, CAB 45/135, PRO; see also Field-Marshal Earl Haig, Diary, 12 November 1916, WO256/13, PRO; General Sir Hubert Gough, *The Fifth Army*, p. 156.

31 General Sir Archibald Murray to First and Second Armies, 28 December 1914, Loch Papers 71/12/1, IWM.

32 Brigadier-General R. FitzMaurice to Edmonds, 7 November 1936, CAB45/133, PRO.

33 M.C. Ferrers-Guy to Edmonds, 29 June 1937, CAB45/116, PRO.

34 Field-Marshal Viscount Montgomery to Captain Cyril Falls, 8 October 1938, CAB45/116, PRO.

35 Major-General A.I. MacDougall, Diary, 4–13 May 1915, MacDougall Papers DS/MISC/92, IWM; see also Brigadier-General P. Howell to his wife, 27 May 1915, Howell Papers IV/C/3/167, LHCMA.

36 Haig, Diary, 2 June and 4 July 1915, Haig Papers, WO256/4, PRO.

37 Lieutenant-Colonel K. Henderson, Memoirs, pp. 162–164, Henderson Papers DS/MISC/2, IWM.

38 Haig to GHQ, First Army No. 194/15(a), 21 October 1915, Butler Papers 69/10/1, IWM.

39 Major-General Sir George Forestier-Walker to Edmonds, 24 January 1927, CAB45/120, PRO.
40 Major J. Buckley to Edmonds, 1 January 1927, CAB45/121, PRO.
41 Harold Macmillan, *Winds Of Change, 1914–1939*, p. 72.
42 Forestier-Walker to Edmonds, 24 January 1927, CAB45/120, PRO.
43 Jeffreys to Edmonds, 21 August 1926, CAB45/120, PRO.
44 Major-General Sir Frederick Maurice to Edmonds, 10 January 1926, CAB45/120, PRO.
45 Maurice to Edmonds, 12 January 1926, CAB45/120, PRO.
46 General Sir Robert Whigham to Edmonds, 9 July 1926, CAB 45/121, PRO; see also GHQ Instruction OAM 799 to First Army, 8 September 1915, WO95/158, PRO.
47 Howell, Diary, 11 October 1915, Howell Papers IV/D/12, LHCMA.
48 Major-General Hon E.J. Montague-Stuart-Wortley to Edmonds, 23 June 1926, CAB45/121, PRO.
49 Major-General Sir John Davidson to Maurice, 4 March 1916, Maurice Papers 3/5/25, LHCMA.
50 Major-General F.I. Maxse to II Corps, 18th Division in the Battle of Ancre, 1916, 18th Division No. G 274, 14 January 1917, paragraph 6, Maxse Papers, 69/53/8, IWM.
51 Brigadier-General R. FitzMaurice to Edmonds, 7 November 1936, CAB45/133, PRO.
52 Brigadier-General G.W. St Grogan, VC, to Edmonds, 10 April 1930, CAB45/134, PRO.
53 Major-General W.T. Furse to Major-General A.A. Montgomery, 9th Division, 26 July 1916, Montgomery-Massingberd Papers 47, LHCMA.
54 Howell, Diary, 17 July, 8 August, 31 August, and 2 October 1916, Howell Papers IV/D/13, LHCMA.
55 Brigadier-General F.G.M. Rowley to Edmonds, 22 October 1934, CAB45/137, PRO.
56 Captain V.C. Runcer to Edmonds, 11 December 1933, CAB45/137, PRO.
57 Brigadier-General H.C. Potter to Edmonds, 10 January 1934, CAB45/136, PRO.
58 Humphrey H. Prideaux to Edmonds, 5 December 1933, CAB45/136, PRO.
59 H.P. Pickering to Edmonds, 17 June 1935, CAB45/136, PRO.
60 Major-General A.I. MacDougall, Diary, 16 September 1916, MacDougall Papers DS/MISC/92, IWM.
61 Major-General Sir Reginald Pinney, Diary, 3 November 1916, Pinney Papers, IWM.
62 Major General F.I. Maxse to Major General A.A. Montgomery, 31 July 1916, Maxse Papers, 69/53/7, IWM.
63 Lieutenant-General Sir Tom Bridges to Field-Marshal Sir John French, 15 August 1916, French Papers 75/46/11, IWM.
64 Brigadier-General R.J. Kentish to 3rd Division, 76th Brigade No. B175, 3 August 1916, Montgomery-Massingberd Papers 47, LHCMA.
65 Major-General G.T.M. Bridges, Some Further Notes on the Recent Operations, by the Divisional Commander, 19th Division, 9 September 1916, Montgomery-Massingberd Papers 47, LHCMA.
66 Major-General J.S.M. Shea to Major-General A.A. Montgomery, 30th Division, 2 August 1916, Montgomery-Massingberd Papers 47, LHCMA.
67 Brigadier-General T.H. Shoubridge to Major-General F.I. Maxse, 30 July 1916, Maxse Papers, 69/53/7, IWM.
68 Brigadier-General F.G.M. Rowley to Edmonds, 22 October 1934, CAB45/137, PRO.
69 Lieutenant-Colonel C. Connell to Edmonds, 26 November 1929, CAB45/132, PRO.
70 IXth Corps, Notes on Information collected from various Sources including troops who have been engaged in the Recent Fighting, 31 July 1916, Montgomery-Massingberd Papers 47, LHCMA.
71 Lieutenant-Colonel C.P. Deedes, Notes on Experience gained during the Recent Operations, 2nd Division No. GS 1001/1/51, 16 August 1916, and Major-General W.G. Walker, 2nd Division No. GS 1001/1/52, 16 August 1916, Montgomery-Massingberd Papers 47, LHCMA; see also Brigadier-General A.R. Cameron, Questions relating to

an initial attack after lengthy preparation, X Corps, 16 August 1916, Montgomery-Massingberd Papers 47, LHCMA.

72 Major J. McD. Haskard, Notes on the Recent Operations, 19th Division No. G 48/27, 19 July 1916, Montgomery-Massingberd Papers 47, LHCMA; See also Lieutenant-Colonel R.M. Johnson, Notes on the Recent Operations – 2nd Phase: 20–30 July 1916, 19th Division, September 1916, Montgomery-Massingberd Papers 47, LHCMA.

73 XIII Corps, Lessons Deduced [August 1916], p. 10, Montgomery-Massingberd Papers 47, LHCMA.

74 Lieutenant-General Sir Desmond Anderson to Edmonds, 6 April 1936, CAB45/132, PRO.

75 H. Spender Clay, Diary, 17 November 1916, quoted by H. Spender Clay to Edmonds, 28 September 1936, CAB45/132, PRO.

76 Colonel W.H. Frank Weber to Edmonds, 19 October 1933, Extracts from Diary, CAB45/138, PRO.

77 Lieutenant-General Sir Desmond Anderson to Edmonds, 6 April 1936, CAB45/132, PRO.

78 Major-General C.G. Woolner to Edmonds, 2 April 1934, CAB45/138, PRO.

79 Brigadier-General S.V.P. Weston to Edmonds, 17 March 1937, CAB45/138, PRO.

80 Haldane, War Diary, 26 July 1916, Haldane Papers, NLS.

81 Anderson to Edmonds, 6 April 1936, CAB45/132, PRO.

82 Colonel W.H. Frank Weber to Edmonds, 19 October 1933, Extracts from Diary, CAB45/138, PRO.

83 Colonel E.M. Birch to Falls, 24 September 1938, CAB45/116, PRO.

84 Lieutenant-General A.N. Floyer-Acland to Edmonds, 10 January 1939, CAB45/116, PRO.

85 Colonel E.M. Birch to Falls, 24 September 1938, CAB45/116, PRO.

86 Major Hon D.G. Fortescue to Falls, 6 February 1938, CAB45/116, PRO.

87 Brigadier-General R.A.C. Wellesley to Edmonds, 14 August 1937, CAB45/116, PRO.

88 Colonel Sir George W. Abercromby, *April 12th 1917*, undated, CAB45/116, PRO.

89 Lieutenant-Colonel W.A. Vignolles to Falls, 10 February 1939, CAB45/116, PRO.

90 Major-General E.C. Gepp to Edmonds, 14 July 1944, CAB45/118, PRO.

91 Lieutenant-General Sir Bertram Sergison-Brooke to Edmonds, 6 December 1944, CAB45/118, PRO.

92 Notes on Recent Operations, Second Army No. GS 52/2 [November 1917], Montgomery-Massingberd Papers 93, LHCMA.

93 *SS135, The Training and Employment of Divisions, 1918*, GHQ OB 1635, January 1918, Montgomery-Massingberd Papers 92, LHCMA.

94 Lieutenant-General Sir George Harper, Guiding Principles Affecting the Attack, IV Corps, 23 October 1918, Maxse Papers 69/53/12, IWM.

95 General Sir John Burnett-Stuart, Memoirs, Chapter VIII, pp. 85–86, Burnett-Stuart Papers, LHCMA.

96 Field-Marshal Sir Archibald Montgomery-Massingberd, *The Autobiography of a Gunner*, pp. 16–18, Montgomery-Massingberd Papers 159/1, LHCMA.

97 Howell, Note on our position round Ypres, 28 May 1915, Howell Papers II/C/7, LHCMA.

98 Haldane, War Diary, 4 December 1917, Haldane Papers, NLS.

99 Ibid., 17 April 1918, Haldane Papers, NLS.

100 Edmonds to General Sir Hubert Gough, 21 November 1932, CAB45/192, PRO.

101 Haldane, Autobiography, Volume II, p. 430, Haldane Papers, NLS.

102 Haldane to Field-Marshal Lord Plumer, 16 April 1917, Spears Papers 2/2, LHCMA.

103 Haldane, War Diary, 19 July 1916, Haldane Papers, NLS.

104 General C.A. Milward, War Diary, 20 December 1914, Milward Papers 6510-143-1, NAM.

105 General Lord Rawlinson to Field-Marshal Lord Kitchener, 9 March 1916, Kitchener Papers WB/36, PRO 30/57.

106 Brigadier-General G.C. Kemp to Edmonds, 26 June 1926, CAB45/120, PRO.
107 Haldane, War Diary, 12 March, 25 April and 14 June 1915, Haldane Papers, NLS.
108 Major J.M. Elles, Notes on a further offensive, p. 2, 10 October 1915, WO158/17, PRO.
109 Brigadier-General R.J. Kentish to 3rd Division, 76th Brigade No. B175, 3 August 1916, p. 14, Montgomery-Massingberd Papers 47, LHCMA.
110 Major-General R.J. Collins to Edmonds, 7 February 1930, CAB45/132, PRO.
111 Montgomery-Massingberd, *The Autobiography of a Gunner*, p. 22, Montgomery-Massingberd Papers 159/1, LHCMA.
112 *SS478* (Translation of a German Document), *Experiences of the IV German Corps in the Battle of the Somme During July 1916*, GHQ Ia/20245, 30 September 1916, Montgomery-Massingberd Papers 49, LHCMA.
113 D.K. McLeod to Edmonds, 24 January 1935, CAB45/136, PRO.
114 Brigadier-General S.G. Craufurd to Edmonds, 19 November 1933, CAB45/132, PRO.
115 Haldane, War Diary, 26 July 1916, Haldane Papers, NLS.
116 Lieutenant-General Sir Tom Bridges to Field-Marshal Sir John French, 15 August 1916, French Papers 75/46/11, IWM.
117 Captain L. Frewen to Edmonds, 13 April 1934, CAB45/133, PRO.
118 Francis P. Heath to Edmonds, 29 March 1934, CAB45/134, PRO.
119 Brigadier-General Rudolf Jelf to Edmonds, 27 November 1934, CAB45/135, PRO.
120 Haldane, War Diary, 26 and 19 July 1916, Haldane Papers, NLS.
121 XIII Corps, Lessons Deduced, p. 13 [August 1916], Montgomery-Massingberd Papers 47, LHCMA.
122 Haig, Diary, 2 November 1916, Haig Papers, WO256/14, PRO.
123 Haldane, War Diary, 21 October 1918, Haldane Papers, NLS.
124 Lieutenant-General Sir Ronald Charles to Edmonds, 14 July 1937, CAB45/118, PRO.
125 Charles to Edmonds, 28 July 1937, CAB45/116, PRO.
126 Major-General C.G. Fuller to Falls, 8 July 1938, CAB45/116, PRO.
127 Haig, Diary, 7, 9, 10, 11 and 12 September 1917, Haig Papers, WO256/22, PRO.
128 Haldane, War Diary, 21 October 1918, Haldane Papers, NLS.
129 Lieutenant-General Sir Francis Nosworthy to Edmonds, 29 July 1935, CAB45/134, PRO.
130 Haig to Edmonds, 6 August 1925, Edmonds Papers II/4/39a, LHCMA.
131 General Staff, Precis of tasks allotted to Corps of Fourth Army, p. 7, undated [1916], WO158/19, PRO.
132 Brigadier-General H.R. Headlam to Falls, 9 June [1938], CAB45/116, PRO.
133 Pinney, Diary, 22–25 May 1917, Pinney Papers, IWM.
134 Haig, Diary, 16 August 1918, Haig Papers, WO256/35, PRO.
135 Haldane, War Diary, 1 September 1918, Haldane Papers, NLS.
136 Captain Pearson Choate to Edmonds, 26 March 1926, CAB45/132, PRO.
137 Brigadier-General A.P. Benson to Falls, undated, CAB45/116, PRO.
138 Haldane, War Diary, 14 November 1917, Haldane Papers, NLS.
139 Montgomery-Massingberd, The Autobiography of a Gunner, p. 23, Montgomery-Massingberd Papers 159/1, LHCMA; General Lord Rawlinson, Diary, 6 October 1916, Rawlinson Papers 1/7, CCC.
140 Lieutenant-General Sir Henry Karslake to Edmonds, 28 January 1936, CAB45/135, PRO.
141 Major-General G.M. Lindsay to Falls, 16 January 1939, CAB45/116, PRO.
142 Major-General W.L.O. Twiss to Edmonds, 18 September 1938, CAB45/116, PRO.
143 Charles to Edmonds, 14 July 1937, CAB45/118, PRO.
144 Major-General Sir Neill Malcolm, Fifth Army SG657/502, 1 October 1917, and Field-Marshal Lord Plumer, Second Army G 924, 30 September 1917, WO158/250, PRO.
145 Rawlinson, Diary, 19 September and 6 October 1917, Rawlinson Papers 1/7, CCC.
146 N.N. Menzies to Edmonds, 19 April 1934, CAB45/136, PRO.

147 [Brigadier-General A.A. Montgomery], Lecture given at Head-Quarters, 3rd Army, on 14th December, 1915 on action of IV Corps at Loos, 25 September 1915, WO95/711, PRO.
148 Colonel J.H. Bateson to Edmonds, 26 April 1936, CAB45/132, PRO.
149 General Hon Sir Francis Gathorne Hardy to Edmonds, 28 August 1934, CAB45/134, PRO.
150 Haig, Diary, 12 October 1916, Haig Papers, WO256/13, PRO.
151 Air Vice-Marshal Sir Philip Game to his wife, 10, 11 and 24 November 1915 and 8, 10 and 20 December 1915, Game Papers, PWG/9, IWM.
152 Sir Basil Liddell Hart, Talk with Colonel C.[J.C.] Allanson, 19 August 1937, Liddell Hart Papers, 11/1937/69, LHCMA.
153 Pinney, Diary, 23 February 1918, Pinney Papers, IWM; General Sir William Heneker, Diary, 24 February 1918, IWM.
154 Pinney, Diary, 27 November 1917, Pinney Papers, IWM.
155 Ibid., 28 November 1917.
156 Haldane, War Diary, 10 April 1918, and Autobiography, Volume II, pp. 436–437, Haldane Papers, NLS.
157 Pinney, Diary, 21 and 29–30 September, 2, 10–12, 22–26 and 29–31 October, 6 and 9 November 1918, Pinney Papers, IWM.
158 Ibid., 15 September 1918.
159 Haldane, War Diary, 30 June 1917, Haldane Papers, NLS.
160 Howell to his wife, 14 October 1914, Howell Papers IV/C/3/75, LHCMA.
161 Ibid., 19 March 1915; see also Brigadier Sir Edward Beddington, Memoir, p. 54, LHCMA.
162 Major-General Sir Richard Bannatine-Allason to Edmonds, 19 November 1931, Edmonds Papers II/2/257, LHCMA.
163 General Sir E.S. Bulfin to Edmonds, 11 December 1927, CAB 45/120, PRO.
164 Brigadier-General E.G. Wace to Edmonds, 30 November 1936, CAB 45/138, PRO.
165 Ibid., 30 October 1936.
166 Howell to his wife, 29 August 1916, Howell Papers IV/C/3/339, LHCMA.
167 Haldane, War Diary, 31 March 1917, Haldane Papers, NLS.
168 Rawlinson, Diary, 26 January 1917, Rawlinson Papers 1/7, CCC.
169 Haldane, War Diary, 30 June 1917, Haldane Papers, NLS.
170 Ibid., 10 September 1917.
171 Brigadier A.E. Hodgkin, Diary, Volume III, 14 March 1917, Hodgkin Papers P.399, IWM.
172 Brian Bond and Simon Robbins, *Staff Officer: The Diaries of Walter Guinness (First Lord Moyne), 1914–1918*, 23 July [1917], p. 162.
173 Major-General J.W. Sandilands to Edmonds, 14 August 1923, CAB45/192, PRO.
174 Brigadier-General C. Yatman to Edmonds, 23 May 1930, CAB45/132, PRO.
175 Rawlinson, Diary, 14 October and 1 November 1917, Rawlinson Papers 1/9, CCC.
176 Sir Basil Liddell Hart, Talk with [General Sir Charles] Broad, 12 February 1947, Liddell Hart Papers 11/1947/2, LHCMA.
177 General Sir Charles Harington to Liddell Hart, Diary Notes, 31 March 1927, Liddell Hart Papers 11/1927/1b; Liddell Hart, Talk with General Pope-Hennessy, 14 October 1933, Liddell Hart Papers 11/1933/33; Liddell Hart, Talk with Broad, 12 February 1947, Liddell Hart Papers 11/1947/2, LHCMA; C.R.M.F. Cruttwell, *A History of the Great War, 1914–1918*, p. 502.
178 Haig, Diary, 5 October and 8 November 1917, Haig Papers, WO256/24, PRO.
179 Edmonds, Memoir, Edmonds Papers III/12/17, LHCMA.

3 The brain of an army

1 Captain Pearson Choate to Brigadier-General Sir James Edmonds, 6 April 1936, CAB45/132, PRO.

2 [Lieutenant-General] Sir Richard Butler, Memorandum on 'Headquarters Units with a Division', 12 December 1918, Butler Papers 69/10/1, IWM.
3 Major-General J.F.C. Fuller to his mother, 27 March 1918, Fuller Papers IV/3/228, LHCMA.
4 Lord Esher to Field-Marshal Sir John French, 26 June 1915, French Papers 75/46/1, IWM.
5 Field-Marshal Sir Henry Wilson to General Lord Rawlinson, 16 September 1914, Maurice Papers 3/4/3, LHMCA.
6 General Sir Charles Bonham-Carter, Memoir, Chapter VI, pp. 4–6, Bonham-Carter Papers 9/1, CCC.
7 Brigadier Edward Beddington, Memoirs, p. 52, Beddington Papers, LHCMA.CHECK
8 Brian Bond, *The Victorian Army and the Staff College*, 1854–1914, p. 324.
9 Edmonds to Brigadier C.N. Barclay, 7 April 1950, Edmonds Papers I/2B/5a, LHCMA.
10 Edmonds, Memoirs, Chapter XIV, Edmonds Papers III/2/3, LHCMA; Regulations Respecting The Staff College, War Office, 1894, Edmonds Papers I/2A/1, LHCMA; Edmonds, *Four Generations of Staff College Students, Part I: 1896*, The Army Quarterly, Volume LXV, October 1952, p. 42.
11 Brigadier C.N. Barclay, *Four Generations of Staff College Students*, Part III: *1930, The Army Quarterly*, Volume LXV, October 1952, p. 49.
12 Major D.M.A. Wedderburn, *Four Generations of Staff College Students*, Part IV: *1952, The Army Quarterly*, Volume LXV, October 1952, p. 52.
13 Colonel T.T. Grove, Memoir, p. 29, Grove Papers 6308-14, NAM.
14 General Sir Thomas Snow, The Account of the Retreat of 1914, undated, pp. 2–3, CAB45/129, PRO.
15 Edmonds, Memoirs, Chapter XXII, Edmonds Papers III/7/4, LHCMA.
16 Ibid., Chapter XXIII, Edmonds Papers III/8/5, LHCMA.
17 Lieutenant-Colonel R.R. Gibson to Edmonds, 10 August 1926, CAB45/120, PRO.
18 Captain Pearson Choate to Edmonds, 6 April 1936 and 26 March 1926, CAB45/132, PRO.
19 Colonel Sir Thomas Montgomery-Cuninghame, *Dusty Measure*, p. 50.
20 Brigadier-General A.F.U. Green, *Evening Tattoo*, pp. 32–33.
21 General Sir Charles Harington, *'Tim' Harington Looks Back*, p. 53.
22 DCIGS [Major-General C.H. Harington] to CIGS [Field Marshal Sir Henry Wilson], 11 July 1918, Maxse Papers 69/57/11, IWM.
23 See Appendices 10 and 15.
24 See Appendix 8.
25 Major-General G.P. Dawnay to Major-General Sir Arthur Lynden-Bell, 27 July 1918, Dawnay Papers 69/21/3, IWM.
26 Lieutenant-Colonel K. Henderson, Memoirs, p. 151, Henderson Papers DS/MISC/2, IWM.
27 Lieutenant-General Sir Richard Butler, Answers to Questions Issued with Fifth Army No. GA 402/10, 29 January 1919, Butler Papers 69/10/1, IWM.
28 John Terraine, *Smoke and Fire*, p. 178.
29 GHQ, GS Note on Infantry Organisation, 28 November 1917, WO158/20, PRO.
30 General Sir Herbert Lawrence, OB/1329, 7 May 1918, WO95/370, PRO.
31 *Camberley Staff College Graduates Who Lost their Lives during the Great War*, Edmonds Papers I/2B/4a, LHCMA.
32 Field-Marshal Sir John French to Lord Kitchener, 25 January 1915, and to General Sir Archibald Murray, 25 January 1915, Murray Papers 79/48/3; Sir John French, Diary, 24 and 25 January 1915, French Papers 75/46/2; Major-General Lord Loch, Diary, 31 January 1915, Loch Papers 71/12/1, IWM; General Sir Walter Kirke to his wife, 9 February 1915, Kirke Papers, IWM.
33 General Lord Rawlinson, Diary, 30 October and 6 December 1914, Rawlinson Papers 1/1, CCC.
34 Bonham-Carter, Autobiography, p. 5, Bonham-Carter Papers 9/1, CCC; see also Rawlinson, Diary, 3 January 1918, Rawlinson Papers 1/9, CCC.

35 Lieutenant-Colonel T.S. Wollocombe, M.C., Diary of the Great War, p. 52, Wollocombe Papers, IWM.
36 Major-General Sir Frederick Maurice to his wife, 28 August 1914, Maurice Papers 3/1/4/10/ LHCMA; See also Loch, Diary, 28 August 1914, Loch Papers 71/12/1, IWM.
37 General Sir Aylmer Haldane, War Diary, 28 August 1914, Haldane Papers, NLS.
38 Field-Marshal Earl Haig, Diary, 29 August and 2 September 1915, Haig Papers, WO256/5, PRO.
39 Bonham-Carter, Autobiography, Chapter VII, p. 20, Bonham-Carter Papers 9/1, CCC.
40 General Sir Sydney Muspratt, Memoirs, pp. 59–60, Muspratt Papers, IWM 86/22/1.
41 Major-General J.W. Sandilands to Edmonds, 14 August 1923, CAB45/192, PRO.
42 Major-General D.N. Wimberley, Memoir, p. 107, Wimberley Papers, IWM.
43 Brigadier-General P. Howell to his wife, 14 December 1914, Howell Papers IV/C/3/ 95, LHCMA.
44 General Sir Sidney Clive, Diary, 1 June 1915, Clive Papers II/1/140, LHCMA.
45 'General Sir Walter M. St G. Kirke, GCB, CMG, DSO, DL, JP', undated, p. 4, Kirke Papers, IWM.
46 General Sir Eric de Burgh, Memoir, p. 10, de Burgh Papers 7306-67, NAM.
47 Lieutenant-General Sir Launcelot Kiggell to Lieutenant-General Sir Tom Bridges, 22 November 1916, Kiggell Papers V/61, LHMCA.
48 Kiggell to General Sir Robert Whigham, 4 January 1917, Kiggell Papers V/72, LHMCA.
49 Kiggell to the Army Commanders, 11 November 1916, Kiggell Papers V/59/1-2, LHMCA; see also Kiggell to General Sir Robert Whigham, 11 November 1916, Kiggell Papers V/58, LHMCA.
50 Maurice to his wife, 24 June 1915, Maurice Papers 3/1/4/196, LHCMA.
51 Major-General G.P. Dawnay to Major-General Sir Arthur Lynden-Bell, 27 July 1918, Dawnay Papers 69/21/3, IWM.
52 Haldane, War Diary, 27 September 1915, Haldane Papers, NLS.
53 Lieutenant-Colonel A.J. Richardson to Edmonds, 24 May 1930, CAB45/137, PRO.
54 Brigadier-General C.G. Stewart to Edmonds, 30 November 1927, CAB45/121, PRO.
55 Brigadier-General B.R. Mitford to Edmonds, 23 January 1926, CAB45/120, PRO.
56 Stewart to Major A.F. Becke, 3 August 1925, CAB45/121, PRO.
57 Wilson, Diary, 24 March 1916 Wilson Papers, IWM.
58 Henderson, Memoirs, p. 185, Henderson Papers DS/MISC/2, IWM.
59 Brigadier-General Sir Archibald Home, Diary, 15 March 1915, Home Papers 82/18/1, IWM.
60 Brigadier-General C.R. Woodroffe, Diary, 22 February 1915, Woodroffe Papers, IWM.
61 Henderson, Memoirs, p. 152, Henderson Papers DS/MISC/2, IWM.
62 E.K.G. Sixsmith, *Douglas Haig*, pp. 194–196.
63 Bonham-Carter, Autobiography, Chapter VI, pp. 9–11, Bonham-Carter Papers 9/1, CCC.
64 Lieutenant-Colonel R. Shoolbred to Edmonds, 11 June 1929, CAB45/137, PRO.
65 Brigadier A.C. Girdwood to Edmonds, 30 June 1930, CAB45/134, PRO.
66 Major G.P.L. Drake-Brockman to Edmonds, 7 February 1930, CAB45/132, PRO.
67 Colonel J.A. English, *The Canadian Army and the Normandy Campaign*, pp. 15–16.
68 General Sir Ivor Maxse to Brigadier-General H.C. Lowther, 18 November 1915, Maxse Papers 69/53/6, IWM.
69 Major-General C.G. Fuller to Captain Cyril Falls, 8 July 1938, CAB45/116 PRO.
70 Major-General Sir Frederick Maurice to his wife, 30 November 1915, Maurice Papers 3/1/4/264, LHCMA; Clive, Diary, 28 November 1915, Clive Papers II/2/97, LHCMA.
71 Bonham-Carter, Autobiography, Chapter VIII, pp. 24–28, Bonham-Carter Papers 9/2, CCC.
72 Field-Marshal Viscount Montgomery to his father, 13 April 1917, Montgomery Papers BLM1/58, IWM.
73 GHQ, Record of Army Commanders' Conference held at Rollencourt Chateau on Saturday, 9 December 1916, at 1 a.m., OAD 291/20, 12 December 1916, Haig Papers, WO256/13, PRO.

74 GHQ, Summary of Schools of Training for the British Expeditionary Force during Winter 1916–1917, undated [*c.* December 1916], Haig Papers, WO256/15, PRO.
75 Brigadier-General K. Wigram to Third Army, GHQ OB/1329, 28 July 1917, WO95/365, PRO; and Major-General R.H.K. Butler to Third Army, GHQ OB/1329/2, 7 September 1917, WO95/365, PRO.
76 Field-Marshal Lord Alanbrooke to his mother, 13 January 1918, Alanbrooke Papers 1/1/11/1, LHCMA.
77 Lieutenant-General Lord Freyberg, *A Linesman in Picardy*, Chapter VIII, pp. 4–5, CAB45/208, PRO.
78 Brian Bond and Simon Robbins, *Staff Officer*, pp. 11, 16.
79 Lieutenant-Colonel P.F. FitzGerald, Memoirs, p. 21, FitzGerald papers 79/35/1, IWM.
80 Lieutenant-General Sir Tom Bridges, *Alarms and Excursions*, p. 55.
81 Major-General Sir John Headlam to Major-General A.W. Bartholomew, 19 May 1919, Brigadier E.C. Anstey Papers 1159/2, RAI.
82 See Appendix 11.
83 Lieutenant-Colonel A.N. Lee, Memoirs, pp. 219, 224, 235, Lee Papers, IWM.
84 Haig, Diary, 24 August, 12 and 24 September, 7 and 27 October, 9 November 1916, WO256/12 and 13, PRO.
85 Ibid., 24 August 1916 and 7 May 1917, WO256/12 and 18, PRO.
86 See Appendices 11 and 12.
87 See Appendices 10–12.
88 Haldane, War Diary, 22 May 1916, Haldane Papers, NLS.
89 Haig, Diary, 27 May 1916, Haig Papers, WO256/10, PRO.
90 Clive, Diary, 8 February 1915, Clive Papers II/1/95, LHCMA.
91 Howell to his wife, 17 April 1915, Howell Papers IV/C/3/139, LHCMA.
92 Clive, Diary, 8 February 1915, Clive Papers II/1/95, LHCMA.
93 Howell to his wife, 7 August 1915, Howell Papers IV/C/3/203, LHCMA.
94 Haig, Diary, 5 June 1915, Haig Papers, WO256/4, PRO.
95 Major-General Sir Reginald Pinney, Diary, 13 April 1917, Pinney Papers, IWM.
96 Brigadier A.E. Hodgkin, Diary, Volume IV, 5 [November 1917], Hodgkin Papers P.399, IWM.
97 Pinney, Diary, 21 July 1918, Pinney Papers, IWM.
98 Haig, Diary, 20 May 1918 Haig Papers, WO256/31 PRO.
99 Lieutenant-General Sir Ivor Maxse, XVIII Corps Staff Conference Agenda, 1 February 1917, Maxse Papers 69/53/8A, IWM.
100 Pinney, Diary, 24 December 1917, Pinney Papers, IWM.
101 Brigadier-General H.C. Rees to Edmonds, 14 November 1929, CAB45/137, PRO.
102 Colonel W.H. Frank Weber to Edmonds, 20 April 1936, CAB45/138, PRO.
103 Howell, Diary, 4 October 1916, Howell Papers IV/D/13, LHCMA.
104 General Sir Walter Kirke to his wife, 3 April 1917, Kirke Papers, IWM.
105 Major-General R.J. Collins to Edmonds, 7 February 1930, CAB45/132, PRO.
106 General C.A. Milward, War Diary, 3 September 1916, Milward Papers 6510-143-5, NAM.
107 Lieutenant-General Laurence Carr to his wife, 5 September 1918, Carr Papers, LHCMA.
108 Field-Marshal Viscount Montgomery to his father, 11 March 1916, Montgomery Papers BLM1/39, IWM.
109 Ibid., July 1917, Montgomery Papers BLM1/61, IWM.
110 Kiggell to the Branches of GHQ, 19 January 1917, Kiggell Papers V/983/2, LHMCA.
111 Haig, Diary, 3 January 1917, Haig Papers, WO256/15, PRO.
112 General Sir Eric de Burgh, Memoir, pp. 14, 16, de Burgh Papers 7306-67, NAM.
113 Major-General Sir Cyriac Skinner to Edmonds, 20 December 1926, CAB45/193, PRO.
114 Colonel T.T. Grove, Memoir, pp. 40–41, Grove Papers 6308-14, NAM.
115 Haig, Diary, 2 September 1916, Haig Papers, WO256/13, PRO.

116 Air Vice-Marshal Sir Philip Game to his wife, 3 December 1914, Game Papers PWG/4, IWM.
117 Edmonds to Brigadier C.N. Barclay, 7 April 1950, Edmonds Papers I/2B/5a, LHCMA.
118 Haldane, War Diary, 13 September 1915, Haldane Papers, NLS.
119 Bonham-Carter, Autobiography, Chapter IX, pp. 26–27, Bonham-Carter Papers, CCC.
120 Brigadier Sir Edward Beddington, Memoir, pp. 87–88, Beddington Papers, LHCMA.
121 Montgomery to Colonel Sir Henry Abel Smith, 7 August 1969, Haig Papers 347/64, NLS Acc. 3155.
122 Paul Maze to 2nd Earl Haig, undated, Haig Papers 347/12, NLS.
123 Major-General S.C.M. Archibald, Memoir, p. 135, Archibald Papers, IWM.
124 Sir David Kelly, *The Ruling Few*, p. 107.
125 G.P. MacClellan to Edmonds, 15 October 1936, CAB45/136, PRO.
126 Paul Maze to 2nd Earl Haig, undated, Haig Papers 347/12, NLS.
127 Haig, Diary, 2 June 1915, Haig Papers, WO256/4, PRO.
128 Ibid., 14 August 1916, Haig Papers, WO256/12, PRO.
129 Colonel W.H. Frank Weber to Edmonds, 20 April 1936, CAB45/138, PRO.
130 General Sir Peter Strickland, Diary, 18 August 1916, Strickland Papers P.362, IWM.
131 Lieutenant-Colonel K. Henderson, Memoirs, p. 182, Henderson Papers DS/MISC/2, IWM.
132 Lieutenant-General Sir Richard Butler to Edmonds, 1 May [?1926], Haig Papers, WO256/7, PRO.
133 General Sir Walter Kirke to his wife, 4 July 1917, Kirke Papers, IWM.
134 Colonel W.H. Frank Weber to Edmonds, 18 March 1930, CAB45/138, PRO.
135 General C.A. Milward, War Diary, 4 and 23 April 1916, Milward Papers 6510-143-5, NAM.
136 Montgomery to his mother, 7 May 1916, Montgomery Papers BLM1/43, IWM.
137 Montgomery to his father, July 1917, Montgomery Papers BLM1/61, IWM.
138 Comments by Brigadier D. Forster, 12 April [1926], CAB45/120 PRO.
139 See for example, Field-Marshal Lord Alanbrooke to his mother, 27 July 1918, Alanbrooke Papers 1/1/11/26, LHCMA; General Sir John Burnett-Stuart, Memoir, p. 81, Burnett-Stuart Papers, LHCMA.
140 GHQ, T/9, *Notes on Recent Fighting No 4, Staff Duties*, 13 April 1918, WO58/70, PRO.
141 Bonham-Carter, Memoir, Chapter VII, pp. 15–17, Bonham-Carter Papers 9/1, CCC.
142 Ibid., pp. 15–17.
143 Brigadier-General E.G. Wace to Edmonds, 30 October 1936, CAB45/138, PRO.
144 Brigadier G.R.P. Roupell, V.C., Memoir, September 1916, p. 15, Roupell Papers GR3, IWM.
145 Bonham-Carter, Memoir, Chapter VII, pp. 15–17, Bonham-Carter Papers 9/1, CCC.
146 Wace to Edmonds, 30 October 1936, CAB45/138, PRO.
147 Major C.C. May, Diary, 30 April 1916, May Papers, IWM.
148 XIII Corps, Lessons Deduced [August 1916], p. 9, Montgomery-Massingberd Papers 47, LHCMA.
149 Appendix 6, Liaison, to unsigned and undated memorandum, possibly draft for Fourth Army GS 400 [December 1916], Montgomery-Massingberd Papers 93, LHCMA.
150 Sir David Kelly, *The Ruling Few*, pp. 94–96.
151 Sir Basil Liddell Hart, Diary Notes, 31 March 1927, Liddell Hart Papers 11/1927/1b, LHCMA; General Sir Charles Harington, *Plumer of Messines*, pp. 316–317.
152 Major W. Wilberforce to Edmonds, 10 July 1933, CAB45/119, PRO.
153 Brigadier G.R.P. Roupell, VC, Memoir, p. 2, Roupell Papers GR5, IWM.
154 Haig, Diary, 8 August 1916, Haig Papers, WO256/7, PRO.
155 Field-Marshal Sir Archibald Montgomery-Massingberd, *The Autobiography of a Gunner*, p. 18, Montgomery-Massingberd Papers 159/1, LHCMA.
156 Bonham-Carter, Autobiography, Chapter IX, p. 29, Bonham-Carter Papers, CCC.

157 Brian Bond and Simon Robbins, *Staff Officer*, p. 162.
158 Anthony Eden, *Another World*, p. 135.
159 Bonham-Carter, Autobiography, Chapter IX, pp. 27–28, Bonham-Carter Papers, CCC.
160 Ibid., pp. 3–4.
161 Rawlinson, Diary, 11 and 13 October 1917, Rawlinson Papers 1/9, CCC.
162 Edmonds, Memoirs, Chapter XXVIII, Edmonds Papers III/12/16, LHCMA.
163 Howell to his wife, 17 April 1916, Howell Papers IV/C/3/139, LHCMA.
164 Ibid., 24 July 1916, Howell Papers IV/C/3/325, LHCMA.
165 General Lord Jeffreys to Edmonds, 23 October 1936, CAB 45/135, PRO.
166 Haig, Diary, 18 September 1917, Haig Papers, WO256/22 PRO.
167 Edmonds, Obituary of Major-General Sir Jocelyn Percy, *The Times*, 25 August 1952, Edmonds Papers V/2, LHCMA.
168 Bonham-Carter, Autobiography, Chapter IX, pp. 29–30, Bonham-Carter Papers, CCC.
169 Major P.J.R. Currie to Edmonds, 23 April 1930, CAB45/132, PRO.
170 C.M. Page to Edmonds, 25 August 1934, CAB45/136, PRO.
171 Currie to Edmonds, 23 April 1930, CAB45/132, PRO.
172 Pinney, Diary, 10 March 1917, Pinney Papers, IWM.
173 Lieutenant-General Sir Ivor Maxse, XVIII Corps Staff Conference, Agenda, 1 February 1917, Maxse Papers 69/53/8A, IWM.
174 Haig, Diary, 1 October 1917, Haig Papers, WO256/23 PRO.
175 Major C.A.L. Brownlow, Notes on the Battle of Cambrai, Nov[ovembe]r 1917, undated, pp. 4, 6, 7, and 9, CAB45/118, PRO.
176 GHQ, T/9, *Notes on Recent Fighting No 4, Staff Duties*, 13 April 1918, WO58/70, PRO.
177 Montgomery to his mother, 3 September 1918, Montgomery Papers BLM1/65, IWM.

4 Developing a professional leadership

1 Field-Marshal Earl Haig, Diary, 26 July 1915, Haig Papers, WO256/5 PRO.
2 See Appendices 3 and 2.
3 Major-General J.F.C. Fuller to Sir Basil Liddell Hart, 22 September 1926, Liddell Hart Papers 1/302/100, LHCMA; see also Oliver Lyttleton, Viscount Chandos, *The Memoirs of Lord Chandos*, p. 45.
4 See Appendix 2.
5 Major-General G.P. Dawnay to his wife, 26 July 1918, Dawnay Papers 69/21/3, IWM.
6 Haig, Diary, 11 February 1918, Haig Papers, WO256/27, PRO.
7 See Appendix 10.
8 Ibid.
9 Sir David Kelly, *The Ruling Few*, p. 107.
10 See Appendix 9.
11 General Sir Ivor Maxse to Brigadier-General H.C. Lowther, 18 November 1915, Maxse Papers 69/53/6, IWM.
12 John Terraine, *Smoke and Fire*, pp. 114–115.
13 'General Sir Walter M. St G. Kirke, GCB, CMG, DSO, DL, JP', undated, p. 5, Kirke Papers, IWM.
14 Kelly, *The Ruling Few*, p. 107.
15 Brigadier-General F.A. Maxwell, Diary, 20 May 1916, Maxwell Papers 7402-25-17, NAM.
16 General Sir Charles Bonham-Carter, Autobiography, Chapter VIII, p. 4, Bonham-Carter Papers 9/2, CCC; Lieutenant-Colonel K. Henderson, Memoirs, p. 198, Henderson Papers DS/MISC/2, IWM.
17 General Sir Peter Strickland, Diary, 1 June 1916, Strickland Papers P.362, IWM.
18 Brigadier-General P. Howell to Sir Montague Turner, 7 July 1916, Howell Papers IV/C/2/233, LHCMA.

19 General Sir Walter Kirke to his wife, 25 September 1915, Kirke Papers, IWM.
20 Colonel T.T. Grove, Memoir, p. 42, Grove Papers 6308-14, NAM.
21 Brigadier Sir Edward Beddington, Memoir, pp. 92–93, LHCMA.
22 General Sir Thomas Snow, The Account of the Retreat of 1914, undated, p. 4, CAB45/129, PRO.
23 Haig, Diary, 20 and 27 September 1914, and 1 November 1914, Haig Papers, WO256/1, PRO.
24 See Appendix 19.
25 Haig, Diary, 26 February, 22 April, and 5 May 1915, Haig Papers, WO256/3-4, PRO.
26 Bonham-Carter, Memoir, Chapter VIII, p. 3, Bonham-Carter Papers 9/1, CCC.
27 Haig, Diary, 9 May 1916, WO256/10, PRO.
28 Bonham-Carter, Autobiography, Chapter VII, p. 24, and Chapter VIII, p. 2, Bonham-Carter Papers 9/1 and 9/2, CCC.
29 Ibid., Chapter IX, p. 1.
30 General Lord Rawlinson, Diary, 14 June 1917, Rawlinson Papers 1/7, CCC.
31 Haig to Lieutenant-General Sir Launcelot Kiggell, 31 August 1911, Haig Papers 328e, NLS.
32 Major-General J.F.C. Fuller to his mother, 27 March 1918, Fuller Papers IV/3/228, LHCMA.
33 General Sir Aylmer Haldane, War Diary, 4, 5 and 15 September 1914, Haldane Papers, NLS.
34 Grove, Memoir, p. 33, Grove Papers 6308-14, NAM.
35 Haig, Diary, 23 October 1915, Haig Papers, WO256/6, PRO.
36 Field-Marshal Sir Henry Wilson, Diary, 2 March 1916, Wilson Papers, IWM.
37 Haig, Diary, 6, 14 and 17 September 1914, Haig Papers, WO256/1, PRO.
38 Haig, Diary, 27 August, 18, 22 and 24 September 1914, Haig Papers, WO256/1, PRO.
39 Brigadier-General Sir James Edmonds to Spencer Wilkinson, 15 March 1916, Edmonds Papers II/2/133, LHCMA.
40 Field-Marshal Viscount Montgomery to his Mother, 10 April 1916, Montgomery Papers BLM 1/41, IWM.
41 Air Vice-Marshal Sir Philip Game to his wife, 19 and 20 November 1915, Game Papers PWG/9, IWM.
42 Colonel J.C. Wedgwood to [H.H. Asquith], 28 November 1915, Lord Barlaston Papers JCW/3, PP/MCR/104, IWM.
43 Brigadier-General Frank Lyon to Edmonds, 10 June 1929, CAB45/135, PRO.
44 Field-Marshal Lord Alanbrooke, Notes for My Memoirs, Alanbrooke Papers 2/1/70, LHCMA.
45 Grove, Memoir, p. 47, Grove Papers 6308-14, NAM.
46 Howell to his wife, 21 June 1915, Howell Papers IV/C/3/183, LHCMA.
47 Henderson, Memoirs, p. 152, Henderson Papers DS/MISC/2, IWM.
48 Beddington, Memoirs, pp. 83–84, Beddington Papers, LHCMA.
49 Field-Marshal Viscount Montgomery of Alamein, Notes on his letters, Montgomery Papers BLM1/1, IWM; see also Montgomery to his Mother, 10 April 1916, Montgomery Papers BLM1/41, IWM.
50 General Sir Arthur Holland to General Lord Horne, 12 October 1918, Horne Papers 73/60/2, IWM.
51 Major-General Sir Reginald Pinney, Diary, 13 July 1917, Pinney Papers, IWM.
52 Major-General J.F.C. Fuller to Sir Basil Liddell Hart, 6 May 1937, Liddell Hart Papers 1/302/246, LHCMA.
53 Major-General Lord Loch, Diary, 19 August 1914, Loch Papers 71/12/1, IWM; General C.A. Milward, War Diary, 17 August 1914, Milward Papers 6510-143-1, NAM.
54 Lieutenant-General Sir Arthur Lynden-Bell to Sir Basil Liddell Hart, 7 September 1937, Liddell Hart Papers 1/466/1, LHCMA.

55 Field-Marshal Sir John French to Mrs Bennett, 18 February 1915, French Papers 75/46/1, IWM.
56 Lieutenant-Colonel E.N. Snepp to Edmonds, 30 July 1930, CAB45/137, PRO.
57 Grove, Memoir, p. 44, Grove Papers 6308-14, NAM.
58 Rawlinson, Diary, 13 March 1915, Rawlinson Papers 1/1, CCC.
59 Brigadier Harold M. Sandlilands to Edmonds, 20 November 1936, CAB45/137, PRO.
60 Wilson, Diary, 29 and 31 July 1916, Wilson Papers, IWM.
61 Haig, Diary, 25 June 1915, Haig Papers, WO256/4, PRO.
62 Ibid., 8 July 1915, Haig Papers, WO256/4, PRO.
63 Ibid., 26 July 1915, Haig Papers, WO256/5 PRO.
64 Major C.C. May, Diary, 24 February and 11 March 1916, May Papers, IWM; see also Bonham-Carter, Autobiography, Chapter VIII, p. 5, Bonham-Carter Papers 9/2, CCC.
65 Brigadier-General H. Biddulph to Edmonds, 22 September 1944, CAB45/118, PRO.
66 Brigadier-General G.W. St G. Grogan, VC, to Edmonds, 10 April 1930, CAB45/134, PRO.
67 Major-General J.F.C. Fuller to his father, 21 January 1916, Fuller Papers IV/3/177, LHCMA.
68 Lieutenant-Colonel A.N. Lee, Memoirs, p. 125, Lee Papers, IWM.
69 Lieutenant-Colonel L.W. Lewer to Captain Cyril Falls, 10 January 1939, CAB45/116, PRO.
70 Haig, Diary, 27 October and 7 November 1915, Haig Papers, WO256/6, PRO.
71 Brigadier-General Frank Lyon to Edmonds, 10 June 1929, CAB45/135, PRO.
72 Lieutenant-Colonel R. Shoolbred to Edmonds, 11 June 1929, CAB45/137, PRO.
73 Haig, Diary, 23 June and 27 October 1916, Haig Papers, WO256/13, PRO.
74 Ibid., 24 April 1917, Haig Papers, WO256/17, PRO.
75 General Sir Charles Fergusson to General Lord Horne, 10 October 1918, Horne Papers 73/60/2, IWM.
76 Haig, Diary, 20 May 1918, Haig Papers, WO256/31, PRO.
77 Lieutenant-General Sir Edward Fanshawe to Edmonds, 10 November 1936, CAB45/133, PRO.
78 General Sir William Heneker, Diary, 20 August 1917, Heneker Papers, IWM.
79 Lieutenant-Colonel A.A. Hanbury-Sparrow to Edmonds, undated, CAB45/134, PRO.
80 Haig, Diary, 4 March 1917, Haig Papers, WO256/16, PRO.
81 G.F. Richards to Edmonds, 20 April 1936, CAB45/137, PRO.
82 General Sir Walter Kirke to his wife, 25 September 1915, Kirke Papers, IWM.
83 Wilson, Diary, 24 February 1916, Wilson Papers, IWM.
84 Major-General S.C.M. Archibald, Memoir, pp. 127–128, Archibald Papers, IWM.
85 Captain Pearson Choate to Edmonds, 6 April 1936, CAB45/132, PRO.
86 Haig, Diary, 15 May 1918, Haig Papers, WO256/31, PRO.
87 Ibid., 8 April 1916, Haig Papers, WO256/9 PRO.
88 Kirke to his wife, 25 September 1915, Kirke Papers, IWM.
89 Haig, Diary, 23 and 25 April 1917, Haig Papers, WO256/17, PRO.
90 Ibid., 17 January 1916, Haig Papers, WO256/7, PRO.
91 Bonham-Carter, Autobiography, Chapter VIII, pp. 13–14, Bonham-Carter Papers 9/2, CCC.
92 Major G.P.L. Drake-Brockman to Edmonds, 7 February 1930, CAB45/132, PRO.
93 Haig, Diary, 19 December 1916, Haig Papers, WO256/14, PRO.
94 Ibid., 25 August 1918, Haig Papers, WO256/35, PRO.
95 Ibid., 17 October 1918, Haig Papers, WO256/37, PRO.
96 Bonham-Carter, Autobiography, Chapter VII, pp. 20–22, Bonham-Carter Papers 9/1, CCC.
97 Haig, Diary, 23 March 1916, Haig Papers, WO256/9, PRO.
98 Bonham-Carter, Autobiography, Chapter VII, pp. 20–22, Bonham-Carter Papers 9/1, CCC.

99 Lieutenant-Colonel H.J.N. Davies to Edmonds, 10 November [1936], CAB45/133, PRO.
100 Brigadier A.C. Girdwood to Edmonds, 30 June 1930, CAB45/134, PRO.
101 Haig, Diary, 12 August 1915, 28 April 1916, and June 1917, Haig Papers, WO256/5, 9, and 19, PRO.
102 Brigadier A.C. Girdwood to Edmonds, 30 June 1930, CAB45/134, PRO.
103 Haig, Diary, 8 May 1918, Haig Papers, WO256/31, PRO.
104 Major-General F.A. Dudgeon, Mss Notes on his Career, n.d., Dudgeon Papers 86/51/1, IWM.
105 Pinney, Diary, 22 April, 8 May, 1 September, 20 October 1916; 12 and 16 July, 1 September, 17 December 1917; 1, 4–5 April, 23 May, 11, 14–15, 21 July, 22 September, 14 October 1918, Pinney Papers, IWM.
106 Ibid., 8 August 1917, 3 October and 8 November 1918.
107 Ibid., 28 November 1916.
108 General Sir William Heneker, Diary, 27 and 31 December 1916, Heneker Papers, IWM; see also Beddington, Memoir, pp. 106–107, Beddington Papers, LHMCA.
109 Lieutenant-General Sir Thomas Snow, Memoir: 27th Division, Nov[ember] 1914 to June 1915, p. 25, Snow Papers 76/79/1, IWM.
110 Bonham-Carter, Autobiography, Chapter VII, p. 19, Bonham-Carter Papers 9/1, CCC, see also General Sir Aylmer Haldane, War Diary, 7 May 1915, Haldane Papers, NLS.
111 Henderson, Memoirs, pp. 178–179, Henderson Papers DS/MISC/2, IWM.
112 Haldane, War Diary, 30 June and 7 August 1916, Haldane Papers, NLS.
113 Haig, Diary, 22 and 23 June 1916, Haig Papers, WO256/10 PRO.
114 Haldane, War Diary, 6 April and 25 June 1916, Haldane Papers, NLS.
115 Ibid., 24 February and 30 June 1916, Haldane Papers, NLS.
116 Snow, Memoir: 27th Division Nov[ember] 1914 to June 1915, p. 25, Snow Papers 76/79/1, IWM. 'Stellenbosched' was the term used in the South Africa War for those removed from command in disgrace.
117 Daniel G. Dancocks, *Sir Arthur Currie: A Biography*, p. 68.
118 A.M.J. Hyatt, *General Sir Arthur Currie: A Military Biography*, pp. 55–57.
119 Brigadier-General F.M. Carleton to his wife, 28 August 1916, Carleton Papers, IWM.
120 Major-General H.J.S. Landon to XV Corps, 33rd Division R1, 28 August 1916, Carleton Papers, IWM.
121 Captain Pearson Choate to Edmonds, 6 April 1936, CAB45/132, PRO.
122 Snow, Memoir: 27th Division Nov[ember] 1914 to June 1915, p. 25, Snow Papers 76/79/1, IWM.
123 General Sir Charles Grant to the Earl of Rosebery, 31 October 1917, Grant Papers C41/2, LHCMA.
124 Major C.C. May, Diary, 13 December 1915, May Papers, IWM.
125 Sir Basil Liddell Hart, Talk with Colonel C. Allanson, 19 August 1937, Liddell Hart Papers 11/1937/69, LHCMA.
126 Brigadier-General F.P. Crozier to Edmonds, 23 March 1930, CAB45/132, PRO.
127 Captain Cyril Falls to Liddell Hart, 22 August 1964, Liddell Hart Papers 1/276/60, LHCMA.
128 General Sir Hubert Gough to Edmonds, 18 March 1944, CAB45/140, PRO.
129 Liddell Hart, Talk with General Edmonds – United Services Club – 22 April 1937, 23 April 1937, Liddell Hart Papers 11/1937/30, LHCMA.
130 Brigadier-General P. Howell to his wife, 18 August 1915, Howell Papers IV/C/3/188, LHCMA.
131 Howell to his wife, 3 July [1916], Howell Papers IV/C/3/188, LHCMA.
132 Lieutenant-General Lord Freyberg, *A Linesman in Picardy*, Chapter V, pp. 16–18, CAB45/208, PRO.
133 Lieutenant-General Sir Charles Fergusson to General Lord Horne, 10 October 1918, Horne Papers 73/60/2, IWM.

134 Wilson, Diary, 24 February 1916, Wilson Papers, IWM.
135 Major-General Neill Malcolm, MGGS, to Lieutenant-General Sir Ivor Maxse, Fifth Army GA 720/39, 22 September 1917, Maxse Papers 69/53/11, IWM.
136 Lieutenant-General Sir Ivor Maxse to Fifth Army, XVIII Corps No. GS 82, 27 September 1917, Maxse Papers 69/53/11, IWM.
137 Field-Marshal Sir Claud Jacob to Edmonds, 20 December 1936, CAB45/135, PRO.
138 Haig, Diary, 15 February 1918, Haig Papers, WO256/27, PRO.
139 Ibid., 17 August 1918, Haig Papers, WO256/35, PRO.
140 Lieutenant-General Sir Charles Fergusson to General Lord Horne, 10 October 1918, Horne Papers 73/60/2, IWM.
141 Lieutenant-General Sir Arthur Holland to Horne, 12 October 1918, Horne Papers 73/60/2, IWM.
142 Haig, Diary, 20 September 1918, Haig Papers, WO256/36, PRO.
143 See Appendix 18.
144 Pinney, Diary, 24 August 1917, Pinney Papers, IWM.
145 John Buchan, *The South African Forces in France*, p. 156.
146 General Sir Eric de Burgh, Memoir, pp. 14, 16, de Burgh Papers 7306-67, NAM.
147 General Sir Launcelot Kiggell to Brigadier-General H.S. Sloman, 6 March 1917, Kiggell Papers, LHCMA.
148 Haig to Field-Marshal Sir John French, 20 August 1917, French Papers 75/46/11, French Papers, IWM.
149 Haig, Diary, 2 September 1915, Haig Papers, WO256/5, PRO.
150 General Sir Hubert Gough, 'My Story', *News Chronicle*, 18 November 1936, Liddell Hart Papers 1/323/26, LHCMA.
151 Brigadier-General S.E. ('Tom') Hollond to Lieutenant-General Sir Ivor Maxse, 7 October 1918, Maxse Papers 69/53/11, IWM.
152 Haig, Diary, 13 May 1918, Haig Papers, WO256/31, PRO.
153 Brigadier-General E.M. Morris to Lieutenant-Colonel A.N. Lee, 21 July [1915], Lee Papers, IWM.
154 Wilson, Diary, 3 March 1916, Wilson Papers, IWM.
155 Henderson, Memoirs, p. 185, Henderson Papers DS/MISC/2, IWM.
156 Brigadier-General Hon R. White, late commanding 184th Brigade (61st Division) to Lieutenant-General Sir Ivor Maxse, 30 September 1918, Maxse Papers 69/53/11, IWM.
157 Major-General Sir Harold Ruggles-Brise to The Secretary, War Office, 23 May 1918, Maxse Papers 69/53/11, IWM.
158 Major-General Sir Colin MacKenzie to XI Corps, 61st Division No. Q88, 11 May 1918; Lieutenant-General Sir Richard Haking to Assistant Military Secretary (AMS) First Army, XI Corps No. A/923/13, n.d.; General Sir Henry Horne, First Army, to the Military Secretary, GHQ, 18 May 1918, Maxse Papers 69/53/11, IWM.
159 Haig, Diary, 8 August 1916, Haig Papers, WO256/12, PRO.
160 Air Vice-Marshal Sir Philip Game to his wife, 1 August 1915, Game Papers PWG/12, IWM.
161 Brigadier-General A.B. Beauman, *Then a Soldier*, p. 57.
162 Colonel W.D.B. Thompson, Biography of Brigadier-General R.B. Bradford VC MC, p. 3, IWM.
163 Paul Freyberg, *Bernard Freyberg, VC*, pp. 102–103.
164 Brian Bond and Simon Robbins, *Staff Officer: The Diaries of Lord Moyne, 1914–1918*, p. 16.
165 See Appendices 13, 14 and 15.
166 Edmonds to Brigadier C.N. Barclay, 7 April 1950, Edmonds Papers I/2B/5a, LHCMA.
167 Haig, Diary, 19 December 1915 and 20 February 1916, Haig Papers, WO256/8, PRO.
168 Ibid., 11 May 1916, Haig Papers, WO256/10 PRO.
169 Ibid., 4 August 1916, Haig Papers, WO256/12, PRO.

170 Henderson, Memoirs, p. 188, Henderson Papers DS/MISC/2, IWM.
171 Montgomery to Captain Cyril Falls, 8 October 1938, CAB45/116, PRO.
172 F.H. Walers to Edmonds, 9 September 1929, CAB45/132, PRO.
173 Montgomery to Captain Cyril Falls, 8 October 1938, CAB45/116, PRO.
174 General Sir William Heneker, Diary, 23 May and 3 June 1917, Heneker Papers, IWM.
175 General Lord Jeffreys to Edmonds, 31 July 1931, CAB45/123, PRO.
176 Wilson, Diary, 8 September 1918, Wilson Papers, IWM.
177 Haig to his wife, 5 September 1918, Haig Papers 152, NLS Acc. 3155.
178 Wilson, Diary, 20 February and 7 March 1918, Wilson Papers, IWM.
179 Major-General C.G. Fuller to Edmonds, 7 January 1945, CAB45/118, PRO.
180 Haldane, War Diary, 8, 10 and 15 November 1917, 27 February, 12 March, and 22 May 1918, Haldane Papers, NLS.
181 Major-General J.W. Sandilands to Edmonds, 14 August 1923, CAB45/192, PRO.
182 Haig, Diary, 13 and 27 February 1918, Haig Papers, WO256/27, PRO.
183 Ibid., 22 September 1918, Haig Papers, WO256/36, PRO.
184 Bonham-Carter, Autobiography, Chapter VII, p. 21, Bonham-Carter Papers, CCC.
185 General C.A. Milward, War Diary, 10 July and 12 August 1916, Milward Papers 6510-143-5, NAM.
186 Haig, Diary, 9 September 1915, Haig Papers, WO256/5, PRO and Howell to Sir Montague Turner, 7 July 1916, Howell Papers IV/C/2/233, LHCMA.
187 Bonham-Carter, Autobiography, Chapter IX, p. 31, Bonham-Carter Papers, CCC.
188 Major-General Sir Hugh Tudor, Diary of the War, 1918, p. 36, RAI.
189 Howell to his wife, 20 June 1916, Howell Papers IV/C/3/303, LHCMA.
190 Bonham-Carter, Memoir, Chapter VIII, pp. 1–2, Bonham-Carter Papers 9/1, CCC.
191 Lieutenant-General Sir Edward Fanshawe to Edmonds, 29 June 1935, CAB45/123, PRO.
192 Beddington, Memoir, p. 92, Beddington Papers, LHCMA.
193 Lieutenant-General Sir Charles Fergusson to General Lord Horne, 10 October 1918, Horne Papers 73/60/2, IWM.
194 Lieutenant-General Sir Gordon Macready, *In the Wake of the Great*, p. 25.
195 Kirke to his wife, 4 July 1917, Kirke Papers, IWM.
196 Ibid.
197 Major-General Sir Walter Constable-Maxwell-Scott to Edmonds, 14 February 1933, CAB45/124, PRO.
198 Haldane, War Diary, 10 April 1918, Haldane Papers, NLS.
199 Lieutenant-General Sir Ivor Maxse to Fifth Army, XVIII Corps No. GS 82, 27 September 1917, Maxse Papers 69/53/11, IWM.
200 Major-General Sir Hugh Tudor, Diary of the War, 1918, pp. 3, 31, Tudor Papers RAI.
201 Harold Macmillan, *Winds of Change, 1914–1939*, p. 79; Oliver Lyttleton, Viscount Chandos, *The Memoirs of Lord Chandos*, p. 41.
202 Philip Gibbs, *The Pageant of the Years*, pp. 190–191.
203 Colonel T.T. Grove, Memoir, p. 48, Grove Papers 6308-14, NAM.
204 Colonel J.C. Wedgwood to [H.H. Asquith], 28 November 1915, Lord Barlaston Papers JCW/3, PP/MCR/104, IWM.
205 Lieutenant-General Sir Frederick McCracken to Edmonds, 13 June 1935, CAB45/124, PRO.

5 The army's over-ambitious decision-making

1 Sir David Kelly, *The Ruling Few*, p. 107.
2 Field Marshal the Earl of Cavan to Captain Sir Basil Liddell Hart, 4 April 1928, Liddell Hart Papers 1/155/1, LHCMA.
3 Lieutenant General Sir Tom Bridges, *Alarms and Excursions: Reminiscences of a Soldier*, p. 73.

4 Brigadier-General J.P. Du Cane, BGGS III Corps, to 4th Division, III Corps G 340, 13 January 1915, Montgomery-Massingberd Papers 38, LHCMA.
5 Brigadier-General C.R. Woodroffe, Diary, 20 October 1914, Woodroffe Papers, IWM.
6 Comments on Loos Draft by Brigadier-General C.G. Stewart, 19 January 1926, CAB45/121, PRO.
7 General Sir Aylmer Haldane, War Diary, 3 March 1915, 24 February 1916, and 13 June 1916, Haldane Papers, NLS; General C.A. Milward, War Diary, 26 August 1914, Milward Papers 6510-143-1, NAM.
8 Kelly, *The Ruling Few*, p. 107.
9 Lieutenant-General Sir Launcelot Kiggell to Field-Marshal Lord Plumer, 8 May 1917, Kiggell Papers II/11/2, LHCMA.
10 Brigadier-General R.J. Kentish, *The Maxims of the late Field-Marshal Viscount. Wolseley and the Addresses on Leadership, Esprit de Corps & Moral*, Gale & Polden, 1917, pp. 31–32.
11 Air Vice-Marshal Sir Philip Game to his wife, 4 December 1916, Game Papers PWG/14, IWM.
12 Lieutenant-Colonel R.M. Johnson, Notes on the Recent Operations – 2nd Phase: 20–30 July 1916, 19th Division, September 1916, Montgomery-Massingberd Papers 47, LHCMA.
13 Major-General Sir Reginald Pinney, Diary, 8 November 1916, Pinney Papers, IWM.
14 Policy on the Army Front for 1918, Fourth Army No. 161 (G), Section III, 30 January 1918, Montgomery-Massingberd Papers 61, LHCMA.
15 Field-Marshal Lord Birdwood to Colonel D. Rintoul, 23 July 1916, Birdwood Papers WRB/1, IWM.
16 General Sir Charles Bonham-Carter, Memoir, Chapter VI, pp. 6–7, Bonham-Carter Papers 9/1, CCC.
17 Pinney, Diary, 21 September 1918, Pinney Papers, IWM.
18 Haldane, War Diary, 21 June 1916, 24 August 1918, 10 April 1918, 2 June 1917, Haldane Papers, NLS.
19 Lieutenant-General Sir Francis Nosworthy to Brigadier-General Sir James Edmonds, 29 July 1935, CAB45/134, PRO.
20 Brigadier-General P. Howell to his wife, 18 and 19 July 1915, Howell Papers IV/C/2/195-196, LHCMA.
21 Haldane, War Diary, 22 August 1915, Haldane Papers, NLS.
22 Brigadier-General Cuthbert Evans to Haldane, 13 August 1915; Haldane, War Diary, 16 and 31 June 1915; 1–3, 8 and 12 August 1915, Haldane Papers, NLS.
23 Lieutenant-Colonel J.D. Belgrave to Edmonds, 20 February 1929; Major-General H.D. de Pree to Edmonds, 20 January 1929; and General Sir Charles Deedes to Edmonds, 21 January 1929, CAB45/139, PRO.
24 General Sir Peter Strickland, Diary, 5–11 March 1916, Strickland Papers, IWM.
25 Field-Marshal Earl Haig to General Sir George Greaves, 12 March 1918, Haig Papers Acc. 3155, No. 147, NLS.
26 F. Wilson to Edmonds, 26 October 1936, CAB45/138, PRO.
27 Major-General Sir Hugh Tudor to Edmonds, 2 December 1933, CAB45/138, PRO.
28 Sir Basil Liddell Hart, Talk with Colonel C. Allanson, 19 August 1937, Liddell Hart Papers, 11/1937/69, LHCMA.
29 Kelly, *The Ruling Few*, p. 107.
30 Howell to his wife, 19 July 1915, Howell Papers IV/C/2/196, LHCMA.
31 Howell to his uncle, Sir Montague Turner, 7 July 1916, Howell Papers IV/C/2/233, and to his wife on 4 July 1916, Howell Papers IV/C/3/311, LHCMA.
32 Haldane, Diary, 15 March 1915, Haldane Papers, NLS.
33 Major-General J.E.B. Seely to Colonel J.C. Wedgwood, 10 November 1915, Lord Barlaston Papers JCW/3, PP/MCR/104, IWM.
34 Lieutenant-Colonel E.M. Woulfe Flanagan to Edmonds, 19 December 1934, CAB45/133, PRO.

35 L. Green to Edmonds, 1 August 1936, CAB45/134, PRO.
36 Lieutenant-General Sir George Macdonogh to Edmonds, 22 November 1922, CAB45/141, PRO.
37 Cavan to Edmonds, 9 April 1936, CAB45/132, PRO.
38 G.C.S. Hodgson to Edmonds, 14 January 1928; General Sir Thomas Snow to General Sir Hugh Jeudwine, 5 February 1923, Jeudwine Papers 72/82/2, IWM; see also General Sir Ronald Charles to Edmonds, 14 January 1929, CAB45/139, PRO.
39 Haldane, War Diary, 30 June 1915, Haldane Papers, NLS.
40 General Sir Percy Radcliffe to Edmonds, 23 November 1923, CAB45/141, PRO.
41 Macdonogh to Edmonds, 14 November 1922, CAB45/141, PRO.
42 Macdonogh to Edmonds, 11 October 1922, and Notes and Suggestions by General [Sir George] Macdonogh, undated, CAB45/141, PRO.
43 General Sir Percy Radcliffe to Edmonds, 21 January 1924, CAB45/141, PRO.
44 Field-Marshal Sir Henry Wilson, Diary, 28 June 1915, Wilson Papers, IWM.
45 Howell to his wife, 19 July 1915, Howell Papers IV/C/2/196, LHCMA.
46 General Sir Hubert Gough to Edmonds, 12 July 1926, CAB45/120, PRO.
47 Haig, Diary, 7 June 1916, Haig Papers, WO256/10, PRO.
48 Wilson, Diary, 31 August 1916 and 5 June 1917, Wilson Papers, IWM.
49 Haig, Diary, 28 July 1916, Haig Papers, WO256/11, PRO.
50 Ibid., 27 September and 2 October 1916, Haig Papers, WO256/13, PRO.
51 Haig, Operations on the Western Front, 1916–1918, 30 December 1920, p. 24, Haig Papers, WO256/38, PRO.
52 Haig to Field-Marshal Sir William Robertson, 19 April 1917, Haig Papers, WO256/17, PRO.
53 Haig to Lord Milner, 11 June 1917, CAB21/22, PRO.
54 Haig, GHQ Letter OAD478, Present Situation and Future Plans, 12 June 1917, Haig Papers, WO256/19, PRO.
55 Haig to Army and Corps Commanders, OA 799, 5 June 1917, Haig Papers, WO256/19, PRO.
56 Haig to Robertson, 22 August 1917, Haig Papers, WO256/21, PRO.
57 Haig, Diary, 19 June 1917, Haig Papers, WO256/19, PRO.
58 Haig, GHQ Letter OAD 478, Present Situation and Future Plans, 12 June 1917, Haig Papers, WO256/19, PRO.
59 Haig to Robertson, 22 June 1917, Haig Papers, WO256/19, PRO.
60 Haig, Diary, 23 and 28 September 1917, Haig Papers, WO256/22, PRO.
61 Haig, Diary, 9 and 10 June 1917, Haig Papers, WO256/19, PRO.
62 Wilson, Diary, 11 June 1917, Wilson Papers, IWM; Haig, Diary, 15 October 1917, Haig Papers, WO256/23, PRO; Haig to Field-Marshal Sir William Robertson, 13 August 1917, Haig Papers, WO256/21, PRO.
63 Haig to Robertson, OAD 652, 16 October 1917, Haig Papers, WO256/23, PRO.
64 Robertson to Haig, Telegram R 142, 13 June 1917, Haig Papers, WO256/19, PRO; Robertson to Field-Marshal Lord Plumer, 10 December 1917, Robertson Papers 8/3/41, LHCMA; Robertson to Haig, 28 April 1917, Haig Papers, WO256/17, PRO.
65 Macdonogh to Brigadier-General J. Charteris, 8 August 1916, Macdonogh Papers, WO158/897, PRO; *Note by the Director of Military Intelligence*, Cabinet Committee on War Policy Memo No. WP49, The Man-Power and Internal Conditions of The Central Powers, 1 October 1917, Haig Papers, WO256/23, PRO.
66 Robertson to Haig, 13 June 1917, Haig Papers, WO256/19, PRO.
67 Macdonogh to Charteris, 24 October 1916, 23 and 25 July 1916, Macdonogh Papers, WO158/897, PRO.
68 Earl of Derby to Haig, 20 February 1917, Haig Papers, WO256/15, PRO.
69 Lieutenant-Colonel A.N. Lee, Memoirs, pp. 118–119, Lee Papers, IWM; Haldane, War Diary, 8 March 1917, Haldane Papers, NLS; General Sir James Marshall-Cornwall, *Wars and Rumours of Wars*, p. 27.

70 Haig, Diary, 21 June 1917, Haig Papers, WO256/19, PRO.
71 Robertson to Haig, Telegram No. 47259, 5 December 1917, Haig Papers, WO256/25, PRO.
72 Robertson to Haig, 6 December 1917, Haig Papers, WO256/25, PRO.
73 Charteris, Ia/35273, 'Note on the Strategical Situation with Special Reference to the Present Condition of German resources and Probable German Operations, 11 June 1917, Haig Papers, WO256/19, PRO.
74 General Sir Walter Kirke, Obituary of Lieutenant-General Sir George M. W. Macdonogh, GBE, KCB, KCMG, p. 9, Kirke Papers WMK10, IWM.
75 Wilson, Diary, 30 November, 3 December 1916, 19 April 1917, and 26, 30, 31 May 1917, Wilson Papers, IWM.
76 Robertson to Haig, 20 April and 15 and 27 September 1917, Haig Papers, WO256/17 and 22, PRO.
77 Haig to Robertson, 8 October 1917, and Haig, Diary, 18 October 1917, Haig Papers, WO256/23, PRO.
78 Kirke, 'Lecture on Secret Service', 27 November 1925, Kirke Papers, Intelligence Corps Museum; quoted in M. Occleshaw, *Armour Against Fate*, p. 366.
79 Wilson, Diary, 16 October and 3 September 917, Wilson Papers, IWM.
80 Kirke, Lieutenant-General Sir George M.W. Macdonogh, GBE, KCB, KCMG, pp. 8–9, Kirke Papers, IWM.
81 Macdonogh to Brigadier-General E.L. Spears, 1 February 1933, Spears Papers 2/3/70, LHCMA.
82 Marshall-Cornwall, *Wars and Rumours of Wars*, p. 26.
83 General Sir Sidney Clive, Diary, 1 and 4 October 1917, Clive Papers II/4/61, LHCMA.
84 General Sir Charles Bonham-Carter, Autobiography, Chapter VII, p. 14, and Chapter IX, p. 5, Bonham-Carter Papers 9/1 and 9/2, CCC; Captain Sir Basil Liddell Hart, Talk with Sir Charles Bonham-Carter, 12 December, 1935, Liddell Hart Papers 11/1935/114, LHCMA; Major-General J.F.C. Fuller, *Memoirs of an Unconventional Soldier*, p. 141; General Sir Henry Rawlinson, Diary, 29 August 1917, Rawlinson Papers 1/9, CCC.
85 Wilson, Diary, 3 September 1916, Wilson, IWM.
86 Bonham-Carter, Autobiography, Chapter VII, p. 14, Bonham-Carter Papers 9/1, CCC; see also Fuller, *Memoirs of an Unconventional Soldier*, p. 141.
87 Haig, Diary, 9 December 1917, Haig Papers, WO256/25, PRO.
88 Haig to his wife, 23 November 1917, Haig Papers No. 148, NLS.
89 Note by Colonel E.R. Clayton, n.d., CAB45/132, PRO.
90 J.L. Weston to Captain C. Falls, 21 July 1937, CAB45/116, PRO.
91 Kelly, *The Ruling Few*, p. 107.
92 Game to his wife, 27 September 1915, Game Papers PWG/8, IWM, and Major-General S.C.M. Archibald, Memoir, p. 118, Archibald Papers, IWM.
93 Haldane, War Diary, 19 March 1916, Haldane Papers, NLS.
94 Haig, Diary, 19 April 1916, Haig Papers, WO256/9, PRO.
95 Brigadier-General H.C. Rees to Edmonds, 14 November 1929, CAB45/137, PRO.
96 Robertson to Lieutenant-General Sir Launcelot Kiggell, 27 July 1917, Kiggell Papers IV/7, LHCMA.
97 Lieutenant-General Sir Charles Kavanagh to Lieutenant-General Sir Launcelot Kiggell, 11 May 1917, Kiggell Papers IV/105, LHCMA.
98 *SS544, Experiences of the Recent Fighting At Verdun*, Berlin, 25 December 1916, GHQ, 28 February 1917, Montgomery-Massingberd Papers 95, LHCMA.
99 *SS553, Experience of the German 1st Army in the Somme Battle, 24 June–26 November 1916*, General von Below, 30 January 1917, GHQ, 3 May 1917, Montgomery-Massingberd Papers 95, LHCMA.
100 F.A. Wilson to Edmonds, 17 June 1930, CAB45/138, PRO.
101 Lieutenant-General Sir Thomas Hutton, War Diary: Battle of the Somme, p. 6, Hutton Papers, LHCMA.

102 Major-General S.C.M. Archibald, Memoir, p. 118, Archibald Papers, IWM.
103 General Sir Herbert Lawrence, The Influence of Increased Strength on German Intentions during 1918, Ia/43614, 1 January 1918, Haig Papers, WO256/27, PRO.
104 General Lord Rawlinson to Lieutenant-Colonel O.A.G. FitzGerald, 24 May 1915, Kitchener Papers WB/21B, PRO 30/57.
105 Copy of letter from Colonel G. Crossman, CAB45/120, PRO.
106 Lieutenant-Colonel Rowland Feilding to his wife, 16 September 1915, *War Letters to a Wife*, p. 37.
107 Colonel C.G. Stewart to Major A.F. Becke, 3 August 1925, CAB45/121, PRO.
108 Copy of letter from Lieutenant-Colonel J.A.G. Rainsford, 14 March 1926, CAB45/121, PRO.
109 Comments by Brigadier-General R.M. Ovens, 3 February 1926, CAB45/121, PRO.
110 Lieutenant-Colonel C.R. Simonds to Edmonds, 3 February 1930, CAB45/137, PRO.
111 Lieutenant-Colonel John L. Hartley to Edmonds, 5 November 1929, CAB45/134, PRO.
112 Ian Grant to Edmonds, 29 October 1929, CAB45/134, PRO.
113 Charles Howard to Edmonds, 6 November 1929, CAB45/134, PRO.
114 Major J. Collis Browne to Edmonds, 12 November 1929, CAB45/132, PRO.
115 Colonel L.A.C. Southam to Edmonds, 3 July 1929, CAB45/137, PRO.
116 Major E.J. Snalding to Edmonds, 20 July [?1929], CAB45/137, PRO.
117 O.G. Wynne to Edmonds, 11 July 1930, CAB45/138, PRO.
118 Haig, Diary, 29 and 30 June 1916, Haig Papers, WO256/10, PRO.
119 Howell, Pocket Diary, 6 July 1916, Howell Papers IV/D/13, LHCMA.
120 Ibid., 14 September 1916.
121 Milward, 22 June 1916, War Diary, Volume III, Milward Papers, 6510-143-5, NAM.
122 Wilson, Diary, 29 August 1916, Wilson Papers, IWM.
123 Note by Colonel E.R. Clayton to [Edmonds], undated, CAB45/132, PRO.
124 Howell, Diary, 28 August 1916, Howell Papers IV/D/13, LHCMA.
125 Brian Bond and Simon Robbins, *Staff Officer: The Diaries of Lord Moyne, 1914–1918*, 23 July 1917, p. 162.
126 Haldane, Diary, 8 October 1917, Haldane Papers, NLS.
127 Haldane to Edmonds, 14 December 1944, CAB45/118, PRO.
128 Major-General Sir John Davidson to Edmonds, 31 January 1945, CAB45/118, PRO.
129 Wilson, Diary, 9 and 13 November 1916, Wilson Papers, IWM.
130 Davidson to Brigadier-General Sir James Edmonds, 3 July 1938, CAB45/133, PRO.
131 Wilson, Diary, 2 September 1916, Wilson Papers, IWM.
132 Wilson, Diary, 1 November 1916, Wilson Papers, IWM; see also General Sir Sidney Clive, Diary, 13 September 1916, Clive Papers II/3/58, LHCMA; Major-General T.H. Shoulbridge to General Sir Ivor Maxse, 30 July 1916, Maxse Papers 69/57/7, IWM.
133 R.H. Andrew to Field-Marshal Earl Wavell, 13 August 1937, Allenby Papers 6/VII/6, LHCMA.
134 Lord Gorell, *One Man... Many Parts*, p. 205.
135 Brigadier-General C.D'A. Baker-Carr, *From Chauffeur to Brigadier*, pp. 245–247; General Sir Charles Bonham-Carter, Autobiography, Chapter IX, pp. 5–6, Bonham-Carter Papers 9/2, CCC.
136 Major-General B.R. Mitford to Edmonds, 1 February 1934, CAB45/137, PRO.
137 Lieutenant-General Sir Hew Fanshawe to Haldane, War Diary, 31 December 1930, Haldane Papers, NLS.
138 Captain Sir Basil Liddell Hart, Talk with Edmonds, 7 October 1927, Liddell Hart Papers, 11/1927/17, LHCMA; Liddell Hart, *The Real War*, p. 367.
139 Haldane, War Diary, 22 March 1917, Haldane Papers, NLS.
140 General Sir John Burnett-Stuart, Memoir, p. 80, Burnett-Stuart Papers, LHCMA.
141 Brigadier-General E.N. Tandy to Edmonds, 4 December 1944, CAB45/118, PRO.
142 Bonham-Carter, Autobiography, Chapter IX, pp. 5–6, Bonham-Carter Papers 9/2, CCC.
143 Wilson, Diary, 24 December 1917 Wilson Papers, IWM.

144 Major-General Sir Frederick Maurice to his wife, 19 January 1915, Maurice Papers 3/1/4/70, LHCMA.
145 Wilson, Diary, 6 and 14 March 1915 Wilson Papers, IWM.
146 Wilson, Diary, 1 September 1916, Wilson Papers, IWM.
147 Bonham-Carter, Autobiography, Chapter IX, pp. 5–6, Bonham-Carter Papers 9/2, CCC.
148 Colonel A.C. Jeffcoat to Edmonds, 3 August 1937, CAB45/116, PRO.
149 Report by Major Gort to BGO re 17 Division, 3 November 1916, WO158/235, PRO; Brigadier-General P. Howell, Diary, 19, 23 and 25 September 1916, Howell Papers IV/D/12, LHCMA.
150 Liddell Hart, Talk with Sir Charles Bonham-Carter, 12 December 1935, Liddell Hart Papers 11/1935/114; Talk with Major-General C.C. Armitage, 15 May 1936, Liddell Hart Papers 11/1936/62; Talk with Sir Edward Grigg, 15 May 1936, Liddell Hart Papers 11/1936/63, LHCMA.
151 Colonel E.M. Birch to Captain Cyril Falls, 24 September 1938, CAB45/116, PRO.
152 Major-General E.G. Miles to 2nd Earl Haig, 28 November 1957, Haig Papers 347/1, Acc. 3155, NLS.
153 Liddell Hart, Talk with [Major-General] J.F.C. Fuller, 1 October 1929, Liddell Hart Papers 11/1929/16, LHCMA.
154 Miles to 2nd Earl Haig, 28 November 1957, Haig Papers 347/1, Acc. 3155, NLS.
155 Colonel B.C.T. Paget to Liddell Hart, 15 November 1936, Liddell Hart Papers 11/1936/105; Sir Edward Grigg to Liddell Hart, 15 May 1936, Liddell Hart Papers 11/1936/63; Major-General C.C. Armitage to Liddell Hart, 15 May 1936, Liddell Hart Papers 11/1936/62; Field-Marshal Lord Gort to Liddell Hart, 14 May 1936, Liddell Hart Papers 11/1936/61; Brigadier [D.F.] Anderson to Liddell Hart, 13 and 14 May 1936, Liddell Hart Papers 11/1936/60 and 15/2/6; Liddell Hart, Talk with General Sir Charles Bonham-Carter, 12 December 1935, Liddell Hart Papers 11/1935/114; Talk with J.F.C. Fuller on 1 October 1929, Liddell Hart Papers 11/1929/1b; General Sir Ivor Maxse to Liddell Hart, Diary Notes, 10 February 1928, Liddell Hart Papers 11/1928/1b, LHCMA.
156 Bonham-Carter, Memoir, Chapter VII, pp. 17–18, and Chapter IX, p. 13, Bonham-Carter Papers 9/1-2, CCC.
157 Haldane, War Diary, 11 March 1918, Haldane Papers, NLS.
158 Haig, Diary, 28 May 1918, Haig Papers, WO256/27, PRO.
159 Lieutenant-General A.N. Floyer-Acland, The Journal of Arthur Nugent Floyer, p. 95, Floyer-Acland Papers, IWM.
160 General Lord Jeffrrys to Edmonds, 23 October 1936, CAB45/135, PRO.
161 Lieutenant-Colonel E.M. Woulfe Flanagan to Edmonds, 19 December 1934, CAB45/133, PRO.
162 Major K.B. Godsell to Edmonds, 13 October 1936, CAB45/134, PRO.
163 Brigadier-General W. Robertson to Edmonds, 15 July [?1930], CAB45/137, PRO.
164 Haldane, Note on War Diary, 15 December 1914, Haldane Papers, NLS.
165 Haldane, War Diary, 15 August 1915, Haldane Papers, NLS.
166 Major-General A.I. MacDougall, Diary, 4–13 May 1915, MacDougall Papers DS/MISC/92, IWM.
167 Charles A.S. Page to Edmonds, 1 June 1929, CAB45/136, PRO.
168 Game to his wife, 1 August 1915, Game Papers PWG/12, IWM.
169 Haig, Diary, 19 July 1916, Haig Papers, WO256/11, PRO.
170 MacDougall, Diary, 16 September 1916, MacDougall Papers DS/MISC/92, IWM.
171 Lieutenant-Colonel E.M. Woulfe Flanagan to Edmonds, 19 December 1934, CAB45/133, PRO.
172 Brigadier-General S.V.P. Weston to Edmonds, 29 March 1937, CAB45/138, PRO.
173 Sir William Darling, *So It Looks to Me*, p. 170.
174 Robertson, GHQ Confidential Letter OB/888 to the First, Second, and Third Armies, Cavalry and Indian Cavalry Corps, 3 October 1915, WO95/2, PRO.

175 Haldane, War Diary, 5 October 1915, Haldane Papers, NLS; Major-General Sir Hugh Tudor, Diary of the War, 1917, p. 38, Tudor Papers, RAI.

176 Brigadier-General F.P. Crozier to Edmonds, 23 March 1930, CAB45/132, PRO.

177 Haig, Diary, 11 April 1917, Haig Papers, WO256/17, PRO.

178 Brigadier-General F.A. Maxwell to his wife, 16 April and 20 September 1917, Maxwell Papers 7402–31–24/31, NAM.

179 Major-General R.M. Luckock to Edmonds, 25 January 1931, CAB45/135, PRO.

180 Lieutenant-Colonel K. Henderson, Memoirs, pp. 168–169, Henderson Papers DS/MISC/2, IWM.

181 Brigadier-General S.G. Craufurd to Edmonds, 19 November 1933, CAB45/132, PRO.

182 Haldane, War Diary, 15 August 1915, Haldane Papers, NLS.

183 Haig, Diary, 4 November 1916, Haig Papers, WO256/14, PRO.

184 Field-Marshal Lord Birdwood to Colonel D. Rintoul, 13 April 1917, Birdwood Papers WRB/1, IWM.

185 Wilson, Diary, 12 June 1917, Wilson Papers, IWM.

186 Major-General Sir Neill Malcolm, Fifth Army SG 657/502, 1 October 1917; General Sir Herbert Plumer, Second Army G 924, 30 September 1917, WO158/250, PRO; and General Sir Charles Harington to Major-General Sir Frederick Maurice, 9 November 1934, Maurice Papers 3/2/7, LHCMA.

187 Howell, Pocket Diary, 17 July 1916, Howell Papers IV/D/13, LHCMA.

188 General Lord Rawlinson to Lieutenant-Colonel O.A.G. Fitzgerald, 24 April 1915, Kitchener Papers, PRO 30/57/51/WB/19B.

189 Haldane, Diary, 10 July 1916, Haldane Papers, NLS.

190 Ibid., 11 July 1916.

191 Howell, Pocket Diary, 16 July 1916, Howell Papers IV/D/13, LHCMA.

192 Haldane, War Diary, 5 June 1917, Haldane Papers, NLS.

193 General Sir Hubert Gough to Edmonds, 12 July 1926, CAB45/121, PRO.

194 Haldane, Autobiography, Volume II, p. 421, Haldane Papers, NLS.

195 Lieutenant-Colonel K. Henderson, Memoirs, p. 167, Henderson Papers DS/MISC/2, IWM.

196 Cavan to Edmonds, 9 April 1936, CAB45/132, PRO.

197 Tudor, Diary of the War, 1917, p. 38, Tudor Papers RAI.

198 Jeffreys to Edmonds, 31 July 1931, CAB45/123, PRO.

199 R.H. Andrew to Field-Marshal Lord Wavell, 13 August 1937, Allenby Papers 6/VII/6, LHCMA.

200 Haldane, War Diary, 7 June 1915; Haldane, Autobiography, Volume II, p. 327, Haldane Papers, NLS; Captain Rt Hon Sir Basil Brooke, Bart, to Edmonds, 15 May 1945, CAB45/118, PRO.

201 Liddell Hart, Diary Notes, 31 March 1927, Liddell Hart Papers 11/1927/1b, LHCMA; General Sir Charles Harington, *Plumer of Messines*, pp. 316–317.

202 Bonham-Carter, Autobiography, Chapter IX, p. 31, Bonham-Carter Papers, CCC.

203 Birdwood to Rintoul, 23 July 1916, Birdwood Papers WRB/1, IWM.

204 Colonel A.S. Bates to Edmonds, 10 June 1929, CAB45/132, PRO.

205 Milward, War Diary, 30 July and 8 August 1916, Milward Papers 6510-143-5, NAM.

206 A.T. Miller to Captain Cyril Falls, 24 January 1939, CAB45/116, PRO.

207 Colonel Hon I.L. Melville to 2nd Earl Haig, 14 May 1963, Haig Papers 347/11 Acc. 3155, NLS.

208 Major-General G.P. Dawnay to his wife, 5 April 1918, Dawnay Papers 69/21/3, IWM.

209 Major-General Sir Winston Dugan to Edmonds, 13 July 1937, CAB45/116, PRO.

210 Brigadier-General P.R. Wood to Captain Cyril Falls [June 1937], CAB45/116, PRO.

211 T.G. Taylor to Edmonds, 13 January 1930, CAB45/138, PRO.

212 Tudor to Edmonds, 2 December 1933, CAB45/138, PRO.

213 R.H. Andrew to Field-Marshal Wavell, 5 April 1937, Allenby Papers 6/I/6, LHCMA; General Sir George Barrow to Wavell, [3 June 1938], Allenby Papers 6/III/3, LHCMA.

214 Cavan to Edmonds, 9 April 1936, CAB45/132, PRO.

215 Liddell Hart, Diary Notes, 31 March 1927, Liddell Hart Papers 11/1927/1b, LHCMA; Harington, *Plumer of Messines*, pp. 316–317.
216 Haldane, War Diary, 9 September 1918, Haldane Papers, NLS.
217 General Sir Herbert Lawrence, The Influence of Increased Strength on German Intentions during 1918, Ia/43614, 1 January 1918, Haig Papers, WO256/27, PRO.
218 Lieutenant-General Lord Freyberg, *A Linesman in Picardy*, Chapter VII, pp. 2–3, CAB45/208, PRO.
219 General Sir Hugh Elles to Edmonds, Notes on Official History – Battle of Cambrai, 23 March 1944, CAB45/118, PRO.
220 Brigadier-General E.N. Tandy to Edmonds, *Personal Note on Cambrai Plan*, 4 December 1944, CAB45/118, PRO.
221 *SS218, Operations by the Australian Corps against Hamel, Bois de Hamel and Bois de Vaire, 4 July 1918*, Note by the General Staff, GHQ, July 1918, Major-General G.P. Dawnay Papers, IWM.
222 GHQ, T/9, Notes on Recent Fighting No. 19, Attack carried out by the Australian Corps near Hamel on the 4 July 1918, 5 August 1918, WO58/70, PRO.
223 Lieutenant-Colonel C.J. Aston, MC, to Edmonds, 3 October 1937, CAB45/184, PRO.
224 Lieutenant-Colonel C.R. Newman, Second Army Artillery Instructions No. 1, 20 September 1918, WO158/211, PRO.
225 Lieutenant-Colonel F.H. Lister, Notes on Operations of First French Army, 29 July and 2 August 1918, Lister Papers, LHCMA.
226 Haig, Diary, 7 August 1918, Haig Papers, WO256/34, PRO.
227 Major-General A.A. Montgomery to Major-General J.S.M. Shea, 28 October 1918, Montgomery-Massingberd Papers 91, LHCMA.
228 Haig, Diary, 8 August 1918, Haig Papers, WO256/34, PRO.
229 Freyberg, A Linesman in Picardy, Chapter IX, 'The Turning of the Tide', p. 12, CAB45/208, PRO.
230 Wilson, Diary, 25 August, 1918, Henry Wilson Papers, IWM.
231 Field-Marshal Viscount Alanbrooke to his mother, 1 September 1918, Alanbrooke Papers I/1/11/23, LHCMA.
232 Field-Marshal Viscount Montgomery to his mother, 3 September 1918, Montgomery Papers BLM1/65, IWM.
233 Lieutenant-Colonel O.S. Nelthorpe, Appreciation by the General Staff, 10 September, 1918, WO158/20, PRO.
234 Haig to his wife, 7 October 1918, Haig Papers 152, NLS.
235 Major-General A.A. Montgomery to Major-General J.S.M. Shea, 28 October 1918, Montgomery-Massingberd Papers 91, LHCMA.
236 Alanbrooke to his mother, 1 November 1918, Alanbrooke Papers I/1/11/35, LHCMA.
237 Haig to his wife, 27 August 1918, Haig Papers, Acc. 3155, No. 152, NLS.
238 Floyer-Acland, Journal, pp. 103–104, Floyer-Acland Papers, IWM.
239 Lieutenant G.H. Thomas to his parents, 5 September 1918, Thomas Papers, IWM.
240 Freyberg, *A Linesman in Picardy*, Chapter X, p. 1, CAB45/208, PRO.
241 Wilson, Diary, 11 August 1918, Henry Wilson Papers, IWM.
242 Haig, *Appreciation of the Present Situation*, OAD 90, 1 August 1916, WO158/21, PRO.
243 Wilson, Diary, 9 and 23 September 1918, Wilson Papers, IWM.
244 Haig, Diary, 31 October 1918, Haig Papers, WO256/37, PRO.
245 Brigadier-General R. FitzMaurice to Edmonds, 7 November 1936, CAB45/133, PRO.

6 Training for victory

1 GHQ, *SS109, Training of Divisions for Offensive Action*, 8 May 1916, p. 2.
2 General Sir John Burnett-Stuart, Memoirs, Chapter VIII, p. 86, Burnett-Stuart Papers, LHCMA.

3 Field-Marshal Sir Henry Wilson, Diary, 12 and 13 September 1916, Wilson Papers, IWM.

4 Brigadier-General F.P. Crozier, *Impressions and Recollections*, pp. 217, 221.

5 Field-Marshal Earl Haig to Lord Haldane, 4 August 1914, Haig Papers, WO256/1, PRO.

6 Major-General Sir Reginald Pinney, Diary, 29 January 1917, Pinney Papers, IWM.

7 Wilson, Diary, 5 August 1914, Wilson Papers, IWM.

8 Haig, Diary, 18 November 1914, Haig Papers, WO256/2, PRO.

9 General Sir Sidney Clive, Diary, 27 November 1914, Clive Papers II//1/65, LHCMA.

10 General Sir Aylmer Haldane, War Diary, 1 August 1916, Haldane Papers, NLS.

11 Haldane, War Diary, 1 August 1916, Haldane Papers, NLS.

12 Brigadier-General Philip Howell to [Wickham] Steed, 11 November, 1914, Howell Papers IV/C/2/67, LHCMA.

13 Howell to his wife, 3 November [1914], Howell Papers IV/C/3/82, LHCMA.

14 General Sir Ivor Maxse, Notes on the New Armies by a Divisional Commander, 3 February 1915, Maxse Papers, IWM 69/53/5.

15 Clive, Diary, 5 January 1915, Clive Papers II//1/83, LHCMA.

16 Wilson, Diary, 9 January 1915, Wilson Papers, IWM.

17 Haig, Diary, 4 January 1915, and *Expansion of the British Army in the Field*, 11 January 1915, Haig Papers, WO256/3, PRO.

18 Haig, Diary, 20 January 1915, Haig Papers, WO256/3, PRO.

19 Ibid., 26 January 1915.

20 General Sir Ivor Maxse, Notes on the New Armies by a Divisional Commander, November 1914, Maxse Papers, IWM 69/53/5.

21 Lieutenant-General Sir George Macdonogh to Brigadier-General Sir James Edmonds, undated, CAB45/120, PRO.

22 Howell to [Wickham] Steed, 11 November 1914, Howell Papers IV/C/2/67, LHCMA.

23 General Sir John Monash to his wife, 22 April 1916, quoted in P.A. Pedersen, *Monash As Military Commander*, p. 133.

24 Haldane, War Diary, 30 July 1915, Haldane Papers, NLS.

25 Howell to Steed, 10 November 1914, Howell Papers IV/C/2/64, LHCMA.

26 Howell to his wife, 20 February 1915, Howell Papers IV/C/3/113, LHCMA; see also Major-General Lord Loch to George V, 19 April 1915, Loch Papers 71/12/1, IWM.

27 Major-General A.A. Montgomery to [Major-General W.P. Braithwaite], 28 August 1916, Montgomery-Massingberd Papers 48/21, LHCMA.

28 General Lord Rawlinson to Field-Marshal Lord Kitchener, 23 and 24 February 1915, Kitchener Papers WB/13 and 15, PRO 30/57.

29 Brigadier Hon William Fraser, 1 November 1917, quoted in General Sir David Fraser (editor), *In Good Company: The First World War Letters and Diaries of The Hon. William Fraser, Gordon Highlanders*, p. 173.

30 General Sir Reginald Stephens, Points from the late Operation [October 1917], p. 8, Stephens Papers 69/70/1, IWM.

31 Maxse, Note by a member of the Court of Enquiry, p. 1, par. 1–2, 28 January 1918, WO158/53, PRO.

32 Lieutenant-General G.M. Harper, Notes on Tactics and Training, IV Corps, September 1918, Montgomery-Masssingberd Papers 92, LHCMA.

33 Major-General C.G. Fuller to Captain Cyril Falls, 8 July 1938, CAB45/116, PRO.

34 Colonel E.M. Birch to Falls, 24 September 1938, CAB45/116, PRO.

35 Haldane, War Diary, 6 April 1916, Haldane Papers, NLS.

36 Ibid., 22 June 1916.

37 Howell to Steed, 11 November 1914, Howell Papers IV/C/2/67, LHCMA.

38 Colonel R. Macleod, Memoir, p. 107, Macleod Papers, LHCMA.

39 General Sir Charles Grant to the Earl of Rosebery, 24 January 1916, Grant Papers, LHCMA.

40 Rawlinson to the Adjutant-General (AG) of the Forces, 24 June 1915, Kitchener Papers WB/23, PRO 30/57.
41 Haldane, War Diary, 25 February 1916, Haldane Papers, NLS.
42 GHQ, *SS109, Training of Divisions for Offensive Action*, 8 May 1916, p. 2.
43 Haig, Diary, 10 May 1916, Haig Papers, WO256/10, PRO.
44 Colonel C.J.L. Allanson, Diary, 3 December 1916, quoted in *Allanson of the 6th*, edited by H. Davies, p. 123.
45 Rawlinson, Diary, 9 March 1917, Rawlinson Papers 1/7, CCC.
46 Field-Marshal Sir Cyril Deverell to Falls, 24 November 1938, CAB45/116, PRO.
47 Rawlinson to Field-Marshal Lord Kitchener, 24 September 1914, Kitchener Papers WB/2, PRO 30/57.
48 Rawlinson to Colonel B. FitzGerald, 21 June 1915, Kitchener Papers WB/23, PRO 30/57.
49 Colonel T.E. Sandall to Edmonds, 27 June 1926, CAB45/120, PRO.
50 Haig, Diary, 23 October 1915, Haig Papers, WO256/6, PRO.
51 V.H.B. Majendie to Edmonds, 25 October 1929, CAB45/136, PRO.
52 Wilson, Diary, 13 August 1916, Wilson Papers, IWM.
53 Major-General C.G. Fuller to Falls, 12 December 1938, CAB45/116, PRO.
54 Major J. Buckley to Edmonds, 1 January 1927, CAB45/120, PRO.
55 C.T. Atkinson to Edmonds, 3 December 1927, CAB45/120, PRO.
56 Lieutenant-Colonel R.R. Gibson to Edmonds, 10 August 1926, CAB45/120, PRO.
57 Major-General Sir George Forestier-Walker to Edmonds, 24 January 1927, CAB45/120, PRO.
58 Forestier-Walker to Edmonds, 10 December 1927, CAB45/121, PRO.
59 Brigadier G.R.P. Roupell, VC, Memoirs, pp. 23, 65, Roupell Papers PP/MCR/56/GR1, IWM.
60 Forestier-Walker to Brigadier-General Sir James Edmonds, 10 December 1927, CAB45/121, PRO.
61 Haldane, War Diary, 21 February and 22 June 1916, Haldane Papers, NLS.
62 Haig, Diary, 11 May 1917, Haig Papers, WO256/18, PRO.
63 General C.A. Milward, War Diary, 13 September, 5–7 October, and 5 November 1916, Milward Papers 6510-143-5, NAM.
64 Second-Lieutenant A.M. Jameson to his mother, [August 1916], Jameson Papers, IWM.
65 Haig, to his wife, 14 October 1915, Haig Papers 141, NLS.
66 Lieutenant-General Sir Francis Nosworthy to Edmonds, 29 July 1935, CAB45/134, PRO.
67 General Sir Reginald Stephens, Lessons from the recent offensive Operations, [?September 1916], Stephens Papers 69/70/1, IWM.
68 GHQ, *SS478* (Translation of a German Document), *Experiences of the IV German Corps in the Battle of the Somme During July 1916*, GHQ Ia/20245, 30 September 1916, Montgomery-Massingberd Papers 49, LHCMA.
69 GHQ, *SS156, Notes on Recent Operations Compiled by G.S. Fourth Army*, GHQ OB 1782/A, April 1917, p. 5, Montgomery-Massingberd Papers 51, LHCMA.
70 Haig, Diary, 14 April 1917, Haig Papers, WO256/17, PRO.
71 Colonel C.E. Vickery to Falls, 11 February 1938, CAB45/116, PRO.
72 Brigadier-General C. Yatman to Falls, 2 November 1937, CAB45/116, PRO.
73 Earl Stanhope to Falls, 21 September 1938, CAB45/116, PRO.
74 Wilson, Diary, 17 April 1918, Wilson Papers, IWM.
75 Ibid., 2 May 1918.
76 Brigadier-General F.A. Maxwell to his wife, 20 September 1917, Maxwell Papers 7402-31-31, NAM.
77 Brigadier-General C.G. Stewart to Falls, 16 January 1938, CAB45/116, PRO.
78 Major-General W.L.O. Twiss to Edmonds, 18 September 1938, CAB45/116, PRO.
79 Brigadier W.E. Clark to Edmonds, 21 November 1934, CAB45/132, PRO.
80 Haig, Diary, 13 October 1916, Haig Papers, WO256/13, PRO.

81 Colonel H.D. Buchanan-Dunlop to Falls, 11 December 1938, CAB45/116, PRO.
82 74th Infantry Brigade, *Operations 10th, 11th August 1917* [August 1917], Montgomery-Massingberd Papers 94, LHCMA.
83 General Sir Charles Bonham-Carter, Memoir, Chapter IX, p. 6, Bonham-Carter Papers, CCC.
84 Lieutenant-Colonel E. Hewlett to Lieutenant-General Sir Ivor Maxse, 18 July 1918, Maxse Papers 69/53/11, IWM.
85 Haldane, War Diary, 26 December 1917, Haldane Papers, NLS.
86 Bonham-Carter, Memoir, Chapter IX, p. 6, Bonham-Carter Papers, CCC.
87 Lieutenant-Colonel C.W.H. Birt to Edmonds, 11 August 1931, CAB45/122, PRO.
88 Major General J.K. Dick-Cunyngham to Edmonds, 8 July 1931, CAB45/122, PRO.
89 Major-General D.N. Wimberley, Memoir, p. 223, Wimberley Papers, IWM.
90 Brigadier-General R.J. Kentish to 3rd Division, 76th Brigade No. B175, 3 August 1916, Montgomery-Massingberd Papers 47, LHCMA.
91 Brigadier W.F. Jefferies to Edmonds, 29 March 1930, Jefferies Papers, LHCMA.
92 Major-General C.N. Nicholson to Lieutenant-General Sir Ivor Maxse, 10 October 1918; Major-General John Ponsonby to Maxse, 11 October 1918; Lieutenant-General A.E.A. Holland to Maxse, 7 October 1918; Lieutenant-General R.B. Stephens to Maxse, 14 September 1918, Maxse Papers, 69/53/12, IWM.
93 Brigadier-General C. Bonham-Carter, Training in France, 8 July 1918, Maxse Papers 69/57/11, IWM.
94 Brigadier-General M.L. Hornby, 116th Brigade, to Maxse, XVIII Corps, 28 July 1917, Maxse Papers 69/53/8A, IWM.
95 Brigadier S.G. Francis, 111th Brigade, to Major-General H. Bruce Williams, 37th Division, 5 September 1918, Maxse Papers 69/53/12, IWM.
96 Major-General H.R. Davies to Maxse, 2 September 1918, Maxse Papers 69/53/12, IWM.
97 J.L. Weston to Falls, 21 July 1937, CAB45/116, PRO.
98 Haig, Diary, 23 October 1917, Haig Papers, WO256/22, PRO.
99 Major-General W. Douglas Smith, 20th Division, to XVIII Corps, 3 March 1918, Maxse Papers 69/53/11, IWM.
100 Brigadier-General R.J. Kentish to Maxse, 21/22 February 1917, Maxse Papers 69/57/7, IWM.
101 Major-General J.F.C. Fuller to his mother, 12 October 1915, Fuller Papers IV/3/163, LHCMA.
102 Haig, Diary, 23 December 1915 and 11 March 1916, Haig Papers, WO256/7 and 9, PRO.
103 Wilson, Diary, 8 April 1916, Wilson Papers, IWM.
104 Major-General J.F.C. Fuller, *Memoirs of An Unconventional Soldier*, pp. 56–57.
105 Wilson, Diary, 8 and 13 January 1916, Wilson Papers, IWM.
106 See Brigadier Sir Edward Beddington, Memoir, p. 91, Beddington Papers, LHCMA and Air Vice-Marshal Sir Philip Game to his wife, 9 November 1915, Game Papers PWG9, IWM.
107 Haig, Diary, 10 May 1916, Haig Papers, WO256/10, PRO.
108 Ibid., 19 and 20 December 1916, 12, 13, and 14 February 1917, Haig Papers, WO256/14, PRO.
109 Ibid., 23 September 1917, Haig Papers, WO256/22, PRO.
110 Brigadier-General C. Bonham-Carter, Training in France, 8 July 1918, Maxse Papers 69/57/11, IWM.
111 GHQ, *Summary of Schools of Training for the British Expeditionary Force during Winter 1916–1917*, n.d. [?December 1916], Haig Papers, WO256/15, PRO.
112 Ibid.
113 Fourth Army: Courses of Instruction During the Winter, 1 November 1916–1 April 1917, Fourth Army GS 318, 8 January 1918, Montgomery-Massingberd Papers 93, LHCMA.

114 GHQ, *SS152, Instructions for the Training of the British Armies in France*, quoted in Lieutenant-General G.M. Harper, Notes on Tactics and Training, IV Corps, September 1918, Montgomery-Masssingberd Papers 92, LHCMA.

115 Major-General Beauvoir de Lisle, *Report on Operations by 29th Division, January 27th, 1917*, 30 January 1917, Montgomery-Massingberd Papers 93, LHCMA.

116 Colonel R. Macleod, Memoirs, p. 99, Macleod Papers 1/1, LHCMA.

117 Maxse, Draft No. 4 on Reform of Schools in France, [August 1918], Maxse Papers, 69/53/12, IWM.

118 Major-General G.P. Dawnay to Major-General Sir Arthur Lynden-Bell, 27 July 1918, Dawnay Papers 69/21/3, IWM.

119 Edmonds, Memoir, Chapter XXVI, Edmonds Papers III/10/6, LHCMA.

120 Major L.H. Cockran to Edmonds, 23 January 1934, CAB45/132, PRO.

121 Lieutenant-Colonel T.S. Wollocombe, Diary, p. 170, Wollocombe Papers, IWM.

122 Major-General J.S.M. Shea to Major-General A.A. Montgomery, *The Preliminary Notes on the Tactical Lessons of the Recent Operations*, 10 August 1916, Montgomery-Massingberd Papers 47, LHCMA.

123 Brigadier-General W.D. Croft to Edmonds, 28 November 1929, CAB45/132, PRO.

124 Lieutenant-Colonel R. Oakley to Edmonds, 11 August 1935, CAB45/136, PRO.

125 Lieutenant-Colonel R.V. Turner to Edmonds, November 1934 and 22 September 1930, CAB45/138, PRO.

126 Bonham-Carter, Autobiography, Chapter IX, p. 8, Bonham-Carter Papers 9/1 and 9/2, CCC.

127 GHQ, *SS135, The Training and Employment of Divisions, 1918*, GHQ OB/1635, January 1918, Montgomery-Massingberd Papers 92, LHCMA.

128 Special Points with regard to the Training of Infantry, Third Army G 192, [July 1915], Montgomery-Massingberd Papers 37, LHCMA.

129 General Sir William Heneker, Diary, 3 and 5 August 1915, Heneker Papers, IWM.

130 Brigadier-General W.D. Croft to Edmonds, 28 November 1929, CAB/132, PRO.

131 IXth Corps Notes on Information collected from Various Sources including Troops who have been engaged in the Recent Fighting, 31 July 1916, Montgomery-Massingberd Papers 47, LHCMA.

132 Colonel R.V. Turner to Edmonds, November 1934, CAB45/138, PRO.

133 Lieutenant-Colonel J.G. Dill, *Training in the Bomy Area*, 37 Division No. G 1475, pp. 1–2, 7 June 1917, Dill Papers I/3/2, LHCMA.

134 Colonel W.D.B. Thompson, Biography of Brigadier-General R.B. Bradford, VC, MC, p. 12, Bradford Papers, IWM.

135 Maxse, Lecture by Corps Commander on Organization for Training, Senior Officers' Conference, XVIII Corps, 17 February 1918, Maxse Papers 69/53/10, IWM.

136 Major-General A. Solly-Flood, *42nd East Lancashire Division, 'Go One Better'*, published by Gale & Polden Ltd, Aldershot, 20 February 1918, Brigadier-General Hon A.M. Henley Papers, IWM.

137 Brigadier-General Hon A.M. Henley, Lecture: 'February 1918', February 1918, Henley Papers, IWM.

138 *SS135, The Training and Employment of Divisions, 1918*, GHQ OB/1635, January 1918, Montgomery-Massingberd Papers 92, LHCMA.

139 Colonel H.D. Buchanan-Dunlop to Falls, 11 December 1938, CAB45/116, PRO.

140 Lieutenant A. Thompson, Statement regarding the circumstances of his capture by the enemy, p. 3, Thompson Papers, IWM.

141 Haig, Diary, 19 September 1918, Haig Papers, WO256/36, PRO.

142 Henley, Diary, 4 September 1918, Henley Papers, IWM.

143 General Sir Julian Byng to Maxse [July 1918], Maxse Papers 69/57/11, IWM.

144 Colonel H.D. Buchanan-Dunlop to Falls, 11 December 1938, CAB45/116, PRO.

145 Brigadier G.R.P. Roupell, VC, Memoir, p. 1, Roupell Papers PP/MCR/56/GR5, IWM.

146 Major-General G.D. Jeffrey to Maxse, 9 September 1918, Maxse Papers 69/53/12, IWM.

147 Lieutenant-General G.M. Harper, Notes on Tactics and Training, IV Corps, September 1918, Montgomery-Masssingberd Papers 92, LHCMA.

148 Major-General J.F.C. Fuller, *Memoirs of An Unconventional Soldier*, p. 278.

149 General Sir Reginald Stephens, Bedfords at Falfamount [1916], p. 1, Stephens Papers 69/70/1, IWM.

150 Major-General H.L. Reed, VC, to Maxse, 1 September 1918, Maxse Papers 69/53/12, IWM.

151 Harper, Notes on Tactics and Training, IV Corps, September 1918, Montgomery-Masssingberd Papers 92, LHCMA.

152 Major-General A.A. Montgomery, MGGS Fourth Army, to III, XIV, I Anzac, and XV Corps, Fourth Army No. 414 (G), 10 November 1916, Montgomery-Massingberd Papers 48/4, LHCMA.

153 Montgomery, Notes on Tactical Schemes, Fourth Army No. GS 623, 15 April 1917, Montgomery-Massingberd Papers 92, LHCMA.

154 *SS159, Notes on Tactical Schemes Compiled by Fourth Army*, GHQ OB 1793/35, May 1917, Montgomery-Massingberd Papers 92, LHCMA.

155 Montgomery, MGGS Fourth Army, to III, XIV, I Anzac, and XV Corps, Fourth Army No. 414 (G), 10 November 1916, Montgomery-Massingberd Papers 48/4, LHCMA.

156 Major-General C.H. Harington, Comments On Operations, 20th Sept., 1917, Second Army, 28 September 1917, Montgomery-Massingberd Papers 94, LHCMA.

157 *SS135, The Division In Attack, November 1918*, Montgomery-Massingberd Papers 92, LHCMA.

158 Field-Marshal Lord. Byng to Maxse, 25 October 1918, Maxse Papers, 69/53/12, IWM.

159 Haig, Diary, 5 November 1918, Haig Papers, WO256/37, PRO.

160 Major-General W.H. Anderson to Maxse, 14 October 1918, Maxse Papers, 69/53/12, IWM.

161 5th Division Report on Operations, August 21st to September 4th, pp. 6–7, 15, General Sir John Ponsonby Papers 6306-69-1, NAM.

162 Wilson, Diary, 1 January and 15 March 1916, Wilson Papers, IWM.

163 Ibid., 11 and 28 August, 6 September, 21 October 1916; Haldane, War Diary, 24 October 1916, Haldane Papers, NLS.

164 Brigadier-General R.J. Kentish to General Sir Ivor Maxse, 21/22 February 1917, Maxse Papers 69/57/7, IWM.

165 Haldane, War Diary, 9 December 1916, Haldane Papers, NLS.

166 Precis of the Remarks made by the Army Commander at the Conference held on 27 December 1916, Fifth Army GA 68/0/29, 28 December 1916, Maxse Papers 69/53/8A, IWM.

167 Maxse to Major-General A.A. Montgomery, 31 July 1916, Maxse Papers, 69/53/7, IWM.

168 Field-Marshal Earl of Lord Cavan to Fourth Army, 30 January 1917, Montgomery-Massingberd Papers 93, LHCMA.

169 Major-General A.A. Montgomery to Lieutenant-General Sir Richard Butler, 27 January 1917, Montgomery-Massingberd Papers 93, LHCMA.

170 Edmonds, *Official History, 1916*, Volume II, pp. 571–572.

171 Major-General J.F.C. Fuller, *Memoirs of An Unconventional Soldier*, p. 242.

172 Kentish to Maxse, 21/22 February 1917, Maxse Papers 69/57/7, IWM.

173 Bonham-Carter, Autobiography, Chapter IX, p. 7, Bonham-Carter Papers 9/2, CCC.

174 *SS143, Instructions for the Training of Platoons for Offensive Action*, GHQ OB/1919T, February 1917, Maxse Papers 69/53/11.

175 Siegfried Sassoon, *Memoirs of an Infantry Officer*, pp. 186–187.

176 GHQ, *SS143, The Training and Employment of Platoons, 1918*, February 1918, Maxse Papers, IWM.

177 Lord Gorell, *One Man . . . Many Parts*, p. 204.

178 GHQ, *SS135, The Training and Employment of Divisions, 1918*, GHQ OB/1635, January 1918, Montgomery-Massingberd Papers 92, LHCMA.
179 *Recent Publications*, Appendix II of GHQ, *SS143* (The Training and Employment of Platoons, 1918), GHQ OB/1919T, February 1918, Maxse Papers 69/53/11, IWM.
180 Bonham-Carter, Autobiography, Chapter IX, p. 24, Bonham-Carter Papers 9/2, CCC.
181 Major-General H.C.C. Uniacke to Maxse, 30 June 1918, Maxse Papers, 69/53/10, IWM.
182 Major-General Sir A.A. Montgomery to [Major-General G.P. Dawnay], Fourth Army, 2 November 1918, Montgomery-Massingberd Papers 91, LHCMA.
183 Dawnay, MGGS (Staff Duties) GHQ, to the Director of Military Operations (DMO), War Office, GHQ OB/2266, 8 July 1918, Maxse Papers 69/53/11, IWM.
184 Haig to The Secretary, the War Office, GHQ OB/2255, 16 June 1918, Maxse Papers 69/53/11, IWM.
185 Dawnay to the Director of Staff Duties, War Office, GHQ OB/2266, 9 July 1918, Maxse Papers 69/53/11, IWM.
186 Dawnay, Appendix 'A', Duties of Inspector General of Training, GHQ OB/2255, 20 June 1918, Maxse Papers 69/53/11, IWM.
187 Maxse, Inspector General's Conferences, July–August 1918, Maxse Papers, 69/53/12, IWM.
188 General Sir Herbert Lawrence, *Record of a Conference of Army Commanders held at HESDIN on Friday, 5th July, 1918*, OAD 291/34/2, 5 July 1918, Haig Papers, WO256/33, PRO.
189 Major-General Lord Dugan, Visit to Xth Corps School, 28 August 1918; Maxse to Lawrence, 29 August 1918; General Sir Reginald Stephens to Lieutenant-Colonel J.C.H. Hamilton, 25 September 1918, Stephens Papers 69/70/1, IWM.
190 Dawnay to his wife, 14 June and 17 September 1918, Dawnay Papers 69/21/3, IWM.
191 Lieutenant-General Sir Aylmer Hunter-Weston to Maxse, 18 October 1918, Maxse Papers, 69/53/12, IWM.
192 Major-General W.H. Anderson to Maxse, 14 October 1918, Maxse Papers, 69/53/12, IWM.
193 Sir Basil Liddell Hart to Captain G.C. Wynne, 17 June 1958, Wynne Papers, LHCMA.
194 General Sir Peter Strickland, Diary, 16 August 1918, Strickland Papers, p. 362, IWM.
195 Major-General Arthur Solly-Flood to Edmonds, 26 November 1930, CAB 45/137, PRO.

7 Tactical innovation

1 Captain A.O. Pollard, VC, MC, DCM, *Fire-Eater: The Memoirs of a VC*, p. 249.
2 Major-General R.C. Money quoted by Major-General E.K.G. Sixsmith, *British Generalship in the Twentieth Century*, p. 157.
3 Field-Marshal Sir William Robertson to Lieutenant-General Sir Launcelot Kiggell, 20 June 1915, Kiggell Papers IV/1, LHCMA.
4 Brigadier-General J.A.L. Haldane, 10th Brigade, to 4th Division, 26 September 1914, and 4th Division G 100 to III Corps, Suggestions for Short Instructions for Benefit of Formations and Individuals arriving in the Theatre of War based on the Experience gained in the Campaign, 28 September 1914, Montgomery-Massingberd Papers 32, LHCMA.
5 General Lord Rawlinson to Field-Marshal Lord Kitchener, 23 March 1915, Kitchener Papers WB/17, PRO 30/57.
6 Rawlinson to Kitchener, 23 March 1915, Kitchener Papers WB/17, PRO 30/57.
7 Rawlinson to Kitchener, 5 June 1915, Kitchener Papers WB/22, PRO 30/57.
8 General Sir Walter Kirke to his wife, 30 April 1917, Kirke Papers, IWM.
9 Lieutenant-General Sir Aylmer Hunter-Weston to Lieutenant-General Sir Richard Butler, 29 October 1916, Butler Papers 69/10/1, IWM.

10 Notes on the Lessons of the Operations on the Somme as regards Infantry Attack formations and the Employment of Specialists, Fourth Army No. GS 360, 1 December 1916, Maxse Papers 69/53/8A, IWM.
11 Major-General A.A. Montgomery to XIII, XV and IX Corps, Fourth Army No. 264 (G), 20 July 1916, Montgomery-Massingberd Papers 48/16, LHCMA.
12 MGRA, First Army, *Control of Fire during the Operations 10–16 March, 1915*, undated, WO95/154, PRO.
13 Lieutenant-Colonel G.C.W. Gordon-Hall to Brigadier-General Sir James Edmonds, 19 October 1934, CAB45/134, PRO.
14 Major O.M.T. Frost to Edmonds, 5 July 1930, CAB45/133, PRO.
15 Major-General R. Wanless O'Gowan to Captain Cyril Falls, 8 October 1938, CAB45/116, PRO.
16 General Sir Reginald Stephens, 'Lessons from the recent offensive operations', c. September 1916, p. 6, Stephens Papers 69/70/1, IWM.
17 General Sir John Shea to Major-General Lord Loch, 8 December 1916, Loch Papers 71/12/5, IWM.
18 Field-Marshal Sir John French to Kitchener, 8 August 1915, Kitchener Papers WA/118, PRO 30/57.
19 *Organization of the Infantry Battalion*, GHQ OB1919, 7 February 1917, Montgomery-Massingberd Papers 93, LHCMA.
20 Kiggell, *The Normal Formation for the Attack*; outlining the principles to be adopted throughout all Armies in France, GHQ OB1919/T, 14 February 1917, Montgomery-Massingberd Papers 93, LHCMA.
21 Captain A.O. Pollard, VC, MC, DCM, *Fire-Eater: The Memoirs of a VC*, p. 249.
22 Stephens, Points from the late Operation [October 1917], p. 8, Stephens Papers 69/70/1, IWM.
23 *SS143, Instructions for the Training of Platoons for Offensive Action*, GHQ OB1919T, February 1917, Maxse Papers 69/53/11.
24 Major-General Beauvoir de Lisle, *Report on Operation by 29th Division, January 27th, 1917*, 29th Division, 30 January 1917, Montgomery-Massingberd Papers 93, LHCMA.
25 Brigadier-General Berkeley Vincent to Edmonds, 4 September 1944, CAB45/118, PRO.
26 Lieutenant-General Sir Ivor Maxse, IGT, to General Sir Herbert Lawrence, CGS, GHQ, 12 August 1918, Maxse Papers 69/53/11, IWM.
27 Inspector-General of Training, British Armies in France, Training Leaflet No. 4, *Training Leaflets, September 1918–February 1919*, Crecy-en-Ponthieu, February 1919, Maxse Papers 69/53/12, IWM.
28 *SS135, The Division In Attack*, p. 5, GHQ T/1635, November 1918, Montgomery-Massingberd Papers 92, LHCMA.
29 Brigadier E.C. Anstey, *The History of the Royal Artillery*, p. 183, Anstey Papers, RAI.
30 Lieutenant-Colonel W.F. Weber, 30th Division G 902, 15 July 1916, Montgomery-Massingberd Papers 47, LHCMA.
31 XIII Corps, *Lessons Deduced*, [August 1916], p. 5, Montgomery-Massingberd Papers 47, LHCMA.
32 XVIII Corps No. GS 70, 21 August 1917, Maxse Papers, IWM.
33 Major-General C.H. Harington, *Further Notes On Operations, 26th Sept. and 4th Oct., 1917*, Second Army, 12 October 1917, Montgomery-Massingberd Papers 94, LHCMA.
34 Major-General C.H. Harington, *Comments On Operations, 20th Sept., 1917*, Second Army, 28 September 1917, Montgomery-Massingberd Papers 94, LHCMA.
35 4th Seaforth Highlanders, *The Counter-Stroke: A Proposed Method of Assembly and Assault* [1917], Maxse Papers 69/53/10, IWM.
36 See Plate IA and Plate IB from *SS143, The Training and Employment of Platoons, 1918*, GHQ OB/1919T, February 1918, Maxse Papers 69/53/11, IWM.

37 Some Notes Made by a Battalion Commander after our Successful Attack on Wurst Farm Ridge on 20th September 1917, n.d., Montgomery-Massingberd Papers 94, LHCMA.
38 Brigadier-General W. Dugan, Some Points brought out during a visit to 31st Division on 29–8–18, 29 August 1918, Maxse Papers 69/53/12, IWM.
39 Lieutenant-General G.M. Harper, Notes on Tactics and Training, IV Corps, September 1918, Montgomery-Masssingberd Papers 92, LHCMA.
40 Stephens, *Lessons from the Recent Offensive Operations* [1916], p. 5, Stephens Papers 69/70/1, IWM.
41 Major-General W.T. Furse to Major-General A.A. Montgomery, 9th Division, 26 July 1916, Montgomery-Massingberd Papers 47, LHCMA.
42 XIII Corps, Lessons Deduced, [August 1916], p. 5, Montgomery-Massingberd Papers 47, LHCMA.
43 Stephens, [Bedfords at Falfamount 1916], p. 2, Stephens Papers 69/70/1, IWM.
44 Stephens, *Points from the late Operation* [October 1917], p. 8, Stephens Papers 69/70/1, IWM.
45 *SS143, Instructions for the Training of Platoons for Offensive Action*, GHQ OB1919T, February 1917, Maxse Papers 69/53/11.
46 Major-General H.R. Davies to Maxse (XVIII Corps), *Narrative of Operations, 8–30 August 1917*, 11 Division No. GS 640, 5 September 1917, p. 21, Maxse Papers, 69/53/8, IWM.
47 *Some Notes Made by a Battalion Commander after our Successful Attack on Wurst Farm Ridge on 20th September, 1917*, n.d., Montgomery-Massingberd Papers 94, LHCMA.
48 Major-General A.B.E. Cator to Maxse (XVIII Corps), *Narrative of Operations, 19–27 September 1917*, 58 (London) Division No. GS 1023/77/55, 18 October 1917, pp. 1–2, Maxse Papers, 69/53/8, IWM.
49 Major H.E. Franklyn to 51st and 58th Divisions, XVIII Corps No. GS 66/114, 28 August 1917, Maxse Papers 69/53/11, IWM.
50 Lieutenant-Colonel W.S. Whetherby, 61st Division GC 40/28, 2 September 1918, Maxse Papers 69/53/12, IWM.
51 Harper, *Guiding Principles in Tactics and Training for Platoon and Section Commanders*, IV Corps, 23 October 1918, Maxse Papers, 69/53/12, IWM.
52 Inspector-General of Training, British Armies in France, *Training Leaflet No 4, Training Leaflets, September 1918–February 1919*, Crecy-en-Ponthieu, February 1919, Maxse Papers 69/53/12, IWM.
53 *SS135, The Division In Attack*, pp. 8–9, 20–23, GHQ T/1635, November 1918, Montgomery-Massingberd Papers 92, LHCMA.
54 *SS135, The Division In Attack*, p. 8, GHQ T/1635, November 1918, Montgomery-Massingberd Papers 92, LHCMA.
55 Brigadier-General W. Dugan, *Notes on a Visit to II American Corps*, 10 November 1918, Maxse Papers, 69/53/12, IWM.
56 Inspector-General of Training, British Armies in France, *Training Leaflet No 13, Training Leaflets, September 1918–February 1919*, Crecy-en-Ponthieu, February 1919, Maxse Papers 69/53/12, IWM.
57 Major-General H.D. de Pree, *The 38th (Welsh) Division in the Last Five Weeks of the Great War*, Chapter III, p. 473, *Journal of the Royal Artillery*, Volume LVIII, No. 3, NAM.
58 Stephens, Lecture [September 1918], Stephens Papers 69/70/1, IWM.
59 Inspector-General of Training, British Armies in France, *Training Leaflet No 4, Training Leaflets, September 1918–February 1919, Crecy-en-Ponthieu, February 1919*, Maxse Papers 69/53/12, IWM.
60 General W.R. Birdwood to Maxse, 30 October 1918, Maxse Papers, 69/53/12, IWM.
61 Field-Marshal Earl Haig, Diary, 5 November 1918, Haig Papers, WO256/37, PRO.
62 General Sir Aylmer Haldane to Field-Marshal Lord Plumer, 16 April 1917, Spears Papers 2/2, LHCMA.

63 *Operations 10th, 11th August, 1917*, 74th Infantry Brigade [August 1917], Montgomery-Massingberd Papers 94, LHCMA.

64 Harper to Maxse (XVIII Corps), *Report on the Advance towards Poelcappelle by the 51st (Highland) Division, 20 September 1917*, undated, Maxse Papers, 69/53/8, IWM.

65 Field-Marshal Sir Henry Wilson, Diary, 28 September 1917, Wilson Papers, IWM.

66 Edmonds, Memoirs, Chapter XXVI, Edmonds Papers III/10/6, LHCMA.

67 *SS135, The Training and Employment of Divisions, 1918*, GHQ OB 1635, January 1918, Montgomery-Massingberd Papers 92, LHCMA.

68 Lieutenant-General Sir Richard Butler, Memo., III Corps, 24 May 1918, Butler Papers 69/10/1, IWM.

69 *5th Division Report on Operations, August 21st–September 4th*, pp. 1–7, General Sir John Ponsonby Papers 6306-69-1, NAM.

70 *SS135, The Division In Attack*, p. 5, GHQ T/1635, November 1918, Montgomery-Massingberd Papers 92, LHCMA.

71 Lieutenant-General Lord Freyberg, *A Linesman in Picardy*, Chapter X, p. 14, CAB45/208, PRO.

72 *IXth Corps Notes on Information Collected from Various Sources Including Troops who have been Engaged in the Recent Fighting*, 31 July 1916, Montgomery-Massingberd Papers 47, LHCMA.

73 *SS156, Notes on Recent Operations Compiled by G.S. Fourth Army*, GHQ OB 1782/A, April 1917, p. 6, Montgomery-Massingberd Papers 51, LHCMA.

74 Kiggell to the five Army Commanders, OB/2089, 7 August 1917, Haig Papers, WO256/21, PRO.

75 Maxse to Fifth Army, XVIII Corps No. GS 69, 12 August 1917, Maxse Papers, 69/53/8A, IWM.

76 *SS135, The Training and Employment of Divisions, 1918*, GHQ OB/1635, January 1918, Montgomery-Massingberd Papers 92, LHCMA.

77 Maxse to Fifth Army, XVIII Corps No. GS 69, 12 August 1917, Maxse Papers, 69/53/8A, IWM.

78 *Artillery Lessons drawn from the Battle of the Somme* [November 1916], p. 5, Montgomery-Massingberd Papers 48/12, LHCMA.

79 Harper, *Notes on Tactics and Training*, IV Corps, September 1918, Montgomery-Masssingberd Papers 92, LHCMA.

80 Major C.C. May, Diary, 22 January 1916, May Papers, IWM.

81 *The IV Corps Artillery at the Battle of Loos*, pp. 27–28, December 1915, Montgomery-Massingberd Papers 45, LHCMA.

82 *SS486, Extracts from German Documents Dealing with 'Lessons Drawn from the Battle of the Somme'*, General Staff (Intelligence) GHQ Ia/20958, 11 October 1916, Montgomery-Massingberd Papers 49, LHCMA.

83 *Artillery Lessons drawn from the Battle of the Somme* [November 1916], p. 6, Montgomery-Massingberd Papers 48/12, LHCMA.

84 Anstey, *The History of the Royal Artillery*, p. 112, Anstey Papers, RAI.

85 Field-Marshal Sir Archibald Montgomery-Massingberd, *The Autobiography of a Gunner*, p. 22, Montgomery-Massingberd Papers 159/1, LHCMA.

86 Anstey, *The History of the Royal Artillery*, p. 169, Anstey Papers, RAI.

87 Colonel C.E. Callwell to Colonel J.H. Boraston, 24 April 1926, Boraston Papers 71/13/1, IWM.

88 Haldane, War Diary, 7 July 1916, Haldane Papers, NLS.

89 General Sir Charles Bonham-Carter, Autobiography, Chapter VIII, p. 10, Bonham-Carter Papers 9/2, CCC.

90 *IXth Corps Notes on Information Collected from Various Sources Including Troops who have been Engaged in the Recent Fighting*, 31 July 1916, Montgomery-Massingberd Papers 47, LHCMA.

91 Lieutenant-Colonel R.M. Johnson, *Notes on the Recent Operations – 2nd Phase: 20th–30th July 1916*, 19th Division, September 1916, Montgomery-Massingberd Papers 47, LHCMA.
92 Rawlinson, Diary, 19 December 1916, Rawlinson Papers 1/7, CCC.
93 Major-General J.E. Capper to V Corps, 25 October 1915, CAB45/121, PRO.
94 General Sir Edward Bulfin to Edmonds, 11 December 1927, CAB 45/120, PRO.
95 Major-General G.T.M. Bridges, *Some Further Notes on the Recent Operations, by the Divisional Commander*, 9 September 1916, Montgomery-Massingberd Papers 47, LHCMA.
96 Major-General J.S.M. Shea to Major-General A.A. Montgomery, *The Preliminary Notes on the Tactical Lessons of the Recent Operations*, 10 August 1916, Montgomery-Massingberd Papers 47, LHCMA.
97 *Artillery Lessons drawn from the Battle of the Somme* [November 1916], pp. 2, 7–8, Montgomery-Massingberd Papers 48/12, LHCMA.
98 Lieutenant-Colonel G.P. MacClellan to Edmonds, 15 March 1936, CAB45/132, PRO.
99 Edmonds, Memoir, Chapter XXVI, Edmonds Papers III/10/6, LHCMA.
100 Brigadier General T.H. Shoubridge to Maxse, 30 July 1916, Maxse Papers, 69/53/7, IWM.
101 Haldane, War Diary, 8 November 1918, Haldane Papers, NLS.
102 Anstey, *The History of the Royal Artillery*, p. 85, Anstey Papers, RAI.
103 Field-Marshal Lord Alanbrooke, Notes For My Memoirs, Alanbrooke Papers 3/1/85, LHCMA.
104 Colonel S.W.H. Rawlins, *A History of the Development of the British Artillery in France, 1914–18*, p. 124, Rawlins Papers 1162, RAI.
105 R.H. Andrew to Field-Marshal Earl Wavell, 13 August 1937, Allenby Papers 6/VII/6; General Sir Charles Grant to Wavell, 21 November 1936, Allenby Papers 6/VII/26, LHCMA; see also Field-Marshal Lord Allenby to his wife, 10 and 12 April [1917], Allenby Papers 1/8/2 and 1/8/4, LHCMA.
106 Extract from Field-Marshal Lord Alanbrooke to General Sir Clement Armitage [1934], Spears Papers 2/3/2, LHCMA.
107 Allenby to Major-General Sir Edward Spears, 31 October 1934, Spears Papers 2/3/2, LHCMA; R.H. Andrew to Wavell, 13 August, 1937, Allenby Papers 6/VII/6; General Spencer E. 'Tom' Hollond to Wavell, 4 December [1936–1938], Allenby Papers 6/VII/30 and 6/VII/31; General Sir Charles Grant to Wavell, 21 November 1936, Allenby Papers 6/VII/26, LHCMA; Extract from Field-Marshal Lord Alanbrooke to General Sir Clement Armitage [1934], Spears Papers 2/3/2, LHCMA.
108 Falls to Wavell, 10 December, 1936, Allenby Papers 6/VII/23; General Sir Charles Grant to Wavell, 21 November 1936, Allenby Papers 6/VII/26, LHCMA.
109 Rawlinson, Diary, 21 January 1917, Rawlinson Papers 1/7, CCC.
110 Falls to Wavell, 10 December 1936, Allenby Papers 6/VII/23; General Sir Beauvoir de Lisle to Wavell, 3 September 1936, Allenby Papers 6/V/28, LHCMA.
111 Haldane to Major-General Sir Edward Spears, 31 October 1934, Spears Papers 2/3/52-56, LHCMA.
112 General Sir Percy Radcliffe to General Sir Noel Birch, 8 July 1918, Colonel S.W.H. Rawlins Papers 1162, RAI.
113 Anstey, The History of the Royal Artillery, p. 229, Anstey Papers, RAI.
114 Haig, Diary, 9 March 1918, Haig Papers, WO256/28, PRO.
115 *Artillery Lessons drawn from the Battle of the Somme* [November 1916], p. 10, Montgomery-Massingberd Papers 48/12, LHCMA.
116 Maxse to Fifth Army, XVIII Corps No. G.S 70, 21 August 1917, Maxse Papers, 69/53/8A, IWM; Lieutenant-Colonel W.D. Croft, *Three Years With the 9th (Scottish) Division*, p. 87.
117 *Artillery Lessons drawn from the Battle of the Somme* [November 1916], p. 9, Montgomery-Massingberd Papers 48/12, LHCMA.

118 Anstey, *The History of the Royal Artillery*, p. 158, Anstey Papers, RAI.
119 Bonham-Carter, Autobiography, Chapter VIII, pp. 10–11, Bonham-Carter Papers 9/2, CCC.
120 Anstey, *The History of the Royal Artillery*, p. 227, Anstey Papers, RAI.
121 MGRA's remarks on proof copy of *SS214, Tanks and Their Employment in Co-operation with Other Arms* [July 1918], WO158/832, PRO.
122 *SS135, The Division In Attack*, p. 20, GHQ T/1635, November 1918, Montgomery-Massingberd Papers 92, LHCMA.
123 Haig, Diary, 18 September 1914, Haig Papers, WO256/1, PRO.
124 Ibid., 25 February 1915, Haig Papers, WO256/3, PRO.
125 Brigadier-General John Charteris, *At GHQ*, 24 February 1915, p. 77.
126 H.A. Jones, *War in the Air*, Volume II, pp. 87–91; General Sir James Marshall-Cornwall, *Wars and Rumours of Wars*, p. 19.
127 Brigadier-General A.A. Montgomery, Lecture given on action of IV Corps at Loos, 25th September 1915, 14 December 1915, Montgomery-Massingberd Papers 45, LHCMA.
128 Haig, Diary, 28 November 1917, Haig Papers, WO256/14, PRO.
129 XIII Corps, *Lessons Deduced* [August 1916], p. 2, Montgomery-Massingberd Papers 47, LHCMA.
130 Haig, Diary, 28 November 1917, Haig Papers, WO256/14, PRO.
131 *SS131, Co-operation of Aircraft with Artillery* (December 1917) and *SS135, Co-operation between Aircraft and Infantry* (April 1918).
132 *SS478* (Translation of a German Document), *Experiences of the IV German Corps in the Battle of the Somme During July 1916*, GHQ Ia/20245, 30 September 1916, Montgomery-Massingberd Papers 49, LHCMA.
133 Adv[anced] HQ RFC, 'A Review of the Principles Adopted by the Royal Flying Corps Since the Battle of the Somme', 23 August 1917, WO256/22, PRO.
134 Maxse to Fifth Army, XVIII Corps No. GS 70, 21 August 1917, Maxse Papers, 69/53/8A, IWM.
135 See J.C. Slessor, *Air Power and Armies*, p. 105; Edmonds, *Military Operations: France and Belgium, 1918*, Volume IV, pp. 323–327 and 380 et seq.
136 Major-General A.A. Montgomery to Shea, 28 October 1918, Montgomery-Massingberd Papers 91, LHCMA.
137 *SS135, The Division In Attack*, p. 29, GHQ T/1635, November 1918, Montgomery-Massingberd Papers 92, LHCMA.
138 Brigadier-General H.C. Rees, 11th Brigade, to 4th Division, 3 November 1916, p. 2, Montgomery-Massingberd Papers 48/3, LHCMA.
139 Croft, *Three Years With The 9th (Scottish) Division*, pp. 146–147.
140 *SS135, The Training and Employment of Divisions, 1918*, GHQ OB/1635, January 1918, Montgomery-Massingberd Papers 92, LHCMA.
141 *SS135, The Division In Attack*, p. 6, GHQ T/1635, November 1918, Montgomery-Massingberd Papers 92, LHCMA.
142 *SS214, Tanks and Their Employment in Co-operation with Other Arms*, p. 3, August 1918, WO158/832, PRO.
143 Harper, *Notes on Tactics and Training*, IV Corps, September 1918, Montgomery-Masssingberd Papers 92, LHCMA.
144 *SS135, The Division In Attack*, p. 7, GHQ T/1635, November 1918, Montgomery-Massingberd Papers 92, LHCMA.
145 *SS135, Instructions for the Training of Divisions for Offensive Action*, issued by the General Staff, December 1916, p. 41, Major-General Sir Hugh Bruce-Williams Papers 77/189/6, IWM.
146 Major Hon D.G. Fortescue to Falls, 6 February 1938, CAB45/116, PRO.
147 Preliminary Report on Tank Corps Operations with the Third Army 20th Nov.–1st Dec. 1917, Tank Corps SG 500/233, 14 December 1917, Maxse Papers 69/53/12, IWM.

148 Bonham-Carter, Autobiography, Chapter IX, p. 41, Bonham-Carter Papers, CCC.
149 Maxse to Fifth Army, XVIII Corps No. GS 70, 21 August 1917, Maxse Papers, 69/53/8A, IWM.
150 Brigadier-General J. Hardress Lloyd, Report on 3rd Brigade Tank Corps Operations with Third Army Nov[ember] 20th to Nov[ember] 27th 1917, 3rd Brigade Tank Corps GS No. 1140, 22 December 1917, and Preliminary Report on Tank Corps Operations with the Third Army 20th Nov[ember]–1st Dec[embe]r. 1917, Tank Corps SG 500/233, 14 December 1917, Maxse Papers 69/53/12, IWM.
151 Notes on the Offensive against Cambrai, unsigned, n.d., Maxse Papers 69/53/8A, IWM.
152 Kiggell to General Sir Hubert Gough, 7 August 1918, Kiggell Papers V/114, LHCMA.
153 Rawlinson, Diary, 3 February 1918, Rawlinson Papers 1/9, CCC.
154 Haldane, War Diary, 9 July 1918, Haldane Papers, NLS.
155 Rawlinson, Diary, 30 June 1918, Rawlinson Papers 1/11, CCC.
156 Major-General A.A. Montgomery to Shea, 8 July 1918, Montgomery-Massingberd Papers 91, LHCMA.
157 Edmonds, *Military Operations: France and Belgium, 1918*, Volume V, pp. 521–534.
158 Haig to Lawrence, 12 August 1918, Lawrence Papers, NLS Acc. 3678.
159 Lieutenant-Colonel J.H. Boraston, *Sir Douglas Haig's Despatches (December 1915–April 1919)*, 21 December 1918, p. 302.
160 Major-General A.A. Montgomery to Shea, 28 October 1918, Montgomery-Massingberd Papers 91, LHCMA.
161 B.I. Gudmundson, *Stormtroop Tactics*, p. 175; see also Martin Samuels, *Doctrine and Dogma*, pp. 152 ff.

8 A strategy for victory

1 General Sir Beauvoir de Lisle, *Reminiscences of Sport and War*, p. 253.
2 J.G.G. MacKenzie and Brian Holden Reid (editors), *The British Army and the Operational Level of War*, p. i.
3 John English, *The Canadian Army and the Normandy Campaign*, p. xiii.
4 Brian Bond, *British Military Policy Between the Two World Wars*, pp. 5–6.
5 Brigadier-General C.D. Baker-Carr, *From Chauffeur to Brigadier*, p. 89.
6 Field-Marshal Sir William Robertson, *From Private to Field-Marshal*, pp. 195–196; General Sir Walter Kirke, Lieutenant-General Sir George Macdonogh, GBE, KCB, KCMG, p. 6, Kirke Papers, IWM.
7 General Sir Archibald Murray to Glyde, 22 December 1930, Spears Papers 2/3/77-85, LHCMA.
8 Robertson, *From Private to Field-Marshal*, p. 198.
9 Major-General Lord Loch, Diary, 24 August 1914, Loch Papers 71/12/1, IWM.
10 General Lord Rawlinson, Diary, 4 December 1914, Rawlinson Papers 1/1, CCC.
11 Brigadier-General Philip Howell to his wife, 27 February 1915, Howell Papers IV/C/3/115, LHCMA.
12 Field-Marshal Sir Henry Wilson, Diary, 14 September 1914, Wilson Papers, IWM.
13 Loch, Diary, 24 August 1914, Loch Papers 71/12/1, IWM.
14 Wilson, Diary, 7 September 1914, Wilson Papers, IWM.
15 General Sir Sidney Clive, Diary, 18 September 1914, Clive Papers II/1/24, LHCMA.
16 Howell to his wife, 27 August 1915, Howell Papers IV/C/3/216, LHCMA.
17 Margot Asquith to Field-Marshal Sir John French, 2 July 1915, French Papers, IWM.
18 Howell to his wife, 28 September 1914, Howell Papers IV/C/3/70, LHCMA.
19 Lord Esher to French, 26 June 1915, French Papers, IWM; M.V. Brett (editor), *The Journals and Letters of Reginald Viscount Esher*, Volume III, pp. 247–248.
20 Rawlinson, Diary, 30 October 1914, Rawlinson Papers 1/1, CCC.
21 Wilson, Diary, 28 September 1914, Wilson Papers, IWM.

22 Ibid., 6 September 1914.
23 Rawlinson, Diary, 28 November 1914, Rawlinson Papers 1/1, CCC.
24 Ibid., 6 December 1914.
25 Clive, Diary, 29 December 1914, Clive Papers II/1/82, LHCMA.
26 Rawlinson, Diary, 6 December 1914, Rawlinson Papers 1/1, CCC.
27 Brigadier-General Sir James Edmonds, Memoirs, August 1914, Edmonds Papers III/9/5-6 and 11, LHCMA; Wilson, Diary, 27 August 1914, Wilson Papers DS/MISC/80/V, IWM; Lieutenant-Colonel R.M. Luckock, Lecture IV, Mons and the Retreat, p. 15a, Lectures on the Western Front in The Great War to the Staff College, Camberley, February 1920, Dill Papers (Old List) 3/2, LHCMA.
28 Loch, Diary, 28 August 1914, Loch Papers 71/12/1, IWM; see also Luckock, Lecture IV, Mons and the Retreat, pp. 15–15a, Lectures on the Western Front in The Great War to the Staff College, Camberley, February 1920, Dill Papers (Old List) 3/2, LHCMA; Edmonds, Memoirs, War: August 1914, Edmonds Papers III/9/11, LHCMA.; General Sir Horace Smith-Dorrien, *Memories of Forty-Eight Years Service*, pp. 416–417.
29 General Sir Aylmer Haldane, War Diary, 28 August 1914, Haldane Papers, NLS.
30 General Sir George Macdonogh to Edmonds, 16 March 1927; see also Edmonds, GHQ Pessimism during the Mons Retreat, undated, CAB45/129, PRO.
31 Brigadier-General E.L. Spears, *Liaison, 1914*, p. 240.
32 Rawlinson, Diary, 25 January 1915, Rawlinson Papers 1/1, CCC.
33 Haldane, War Diary, 30 June 1915, Haldane Papers, NLS; Field-Marshal Earl Haig, Diary, 22 January 1915, Haig Papers, WO256/3, PRO.
34 Clive, Diary, 29 December 1914 and 21 January 1915, Clive Papers II/1/82 and 88-89, LHCMA.
35 Robertson, *From Private to Field-Marshal*, p. 218.
36 General Sir James Marshall-Cornwall, *Haig As Military Commander*, p. 138.
37 Robertson, *From Private to Field-Marshal*, p. 222.
38 Clive, Diary, 13 October 1915, Clive Papers II/2/68, LHCMA.
39 Major-General Sir C.E. Callwell, *Field-Marshal Sir Henry Wilson*, Volume I, p. 205.
40 Haldane, War Diary, 30 June 1915, Haldane Papers, NLS.
41 General Sir Walter Kirke, Lieutenant-General Sir George M.W. Macdonogh, GBE, KCB, KCMG, p. 3, Kirke Papers, IWM.
42 Rawlinson, Diary, 29 January and 8 February 1915, Rawlinson Papers 1/1, CCC.
43 Ibid., 12 June 1915, Rawlinson Papers 1/3, CCC.
44 Wilson, Diary, 8, 18, 26 February, 6 and 21 March, and 2 and 6 May 1915, Wilson Papers, IWM.
45 Clive, Diary, 28 January 1915, Clive Papers II/1/90-91, LHCMA.
46 Howell to his wife, 8 February 1915, Howell Papers IV/C/3/108, LHCMA.
47 Kirke, Lieutenant-General Sir George M.W. Macdonogh GBE, KCB, KCMG, p. 6, Kirke Papers, WMK10, IWM.
48 Robertson, *From Private to Field-Marshal*, p. 221.
49 Clive, Diary, 22 March 1916, Clive Papers II/2/141, LHCMA.
50 Major-General Sir Frederick Maurice to Edmonds, 10 January 1926, CAB 45/120, PRO.
51 See, for example, 'G.S. Notes on Operations 1915', WO 158/17, PRO.
52 Howell to his wife, 16 January 1915, Howell Papers IV/C/3/103, LHCMA.
53 French to Field-Marshal Earl Kitchener, 15 December 1914, Kitchener Papers WA/46, PRO 30/57.
54 Haig, Diary, 17 March 1915, WO256/3, PRO.
55 Edmonds, Memoirs, Chapter III, Edmonds Papers III/8 and III/10, LHCMA.
56 Brian Bond, *The Victorian Army and the Staff College*, pp. 301, 313.
57 Wilson, Diary, 29 July 1915, Wilson Papers, IWM.
58 Ibid., 27 May 1915.
59 Kirke to his wife, 16 March and May 1915, Kirke Papers, IWM.
60 Haig, Diary, 24 September and 9 October 1915, Haig Papers, WO256/5-6, PRO.

61 Edmonds, 'Memoirs', Chapter XXVI, p. 1, Edmonds Papers, LHCMA.
62 Captain Sir Basil Liddell Hart, Talk with Edmonds, 1938, Liddell Hart Papers 11/1938/59, LHCMA.
63 General Sir Hubert Gough to Edmonds, 27 May 1945, CAB45/140, PRO.
64 Edmonds to Haldane, 17 March 1931, Haldane Papers, NLS; Captain Sir Basil Liddell Hart, Talk with Edmonds, 23 September 1929, Liddell Hart Papers, 11/1929/15, LHCMA; Wilson, Diary, 12 July and 22 June 1916, Wilson Papers, IWM.
65 General Sir George Barrow to Field-Marshal Earl Wavell, [3 June 1938], Allenby Papers 6/III/3, LHCMA.
66 Liddell Hart, Tea with General [Sir John] Dill, 24 August 1931, Liddell Hart Papers, 11/1931/1c, LHCMA.
67 Lord Esher, Diary, 1 June 1916, 2/16.
68 Clive, Diary, 4 January 1918, Clive Papers II/4/88, LHCMA.
69 Liddell Hart, Talk with [General] Sir Hubert Gough, 9 April 1935, Liddell Hart Papers 11/1935/72, LHCMA; Brigadier-General John Charteris, *At GHQ*, p. 74; Clive, Diary, 6 December 1917, Clive Papers II/4/80, LHCMA.
70 Major-General G.P. Dawnay to his wife, 27 February 1918, Dawnay Papers 69/21/3, IWM; Kirke to his wife, 6 February 1917, Kirke Papers, IWM; General Sir Charles Bonham-Carter, Autobiography, Chapter VII, p. 13, and Chapter IX, p. 6, Bonham-Carter Papers 9/1-2, CCC; Major-General J.F.C. Fuller, *Memoirs of An Unconventional Soldier*, pp. 140–141; Liddell Hart, Talk with J.F.C. Fuller on 1 October 1929, Liddell Hart Papers 11/1929/1b, & Talk with General Sir Charles Bonham-Carter, 12 December 1935, Liddell Hart Papers 11/1935/114, LHCMA.
71 Clive, Diary, 5 June 1918, Clive Papers II/4/133, LHCMA.
72 Major-General S.S. Butler, Memoirs, p. 34, Butler Papers, IWM; Major-General Sir John Davidson, Notes on 'Haig & Lawrence', 3 March 1954, Lawrence Papers, NLS; Bonham-Carter, Autobiography, Chapter IX, p. 13, Bonham-Carter Papers 9/2, CCC; Charteris, *At GHQ*, p. 286; Lieutenant-Colonel A.N. Lee, Memoirs, p. 165, Lee Papers, IWM.
73 Charteris, *At GHQ*, p. 286; [Colonel Hon I.L. Melville], Note on 'Gen[eral] The Hon Sir H.A. Lawrence', May 1960, Lawrence Papers, NLS.
74 Clive, Diary, 5 January 1918, Clive Papers II/4/89, LHCMA.
75 Haig, Diary, 30 January; 7, 13, 15 and 27 February; 4 March; 28 and 29 April; 16, 17, and 31 May 1918, Haig Papers, WO256/27, 28, 29 and 30, PRO.
76 [Colonel Hon I.L. Melville], Note on 'Gen The Hon Sir H.A. Lawrence', May 1960, Lawrence Papers, NLS.
77 Davidson, Notes on 'Haig & Lawrence', 3 March 1954, Lawrence Papers, NLS.
78 Lieutenant-Colonel J.H. Boraston (editor), *Sir Douglas Haig's Despatches*, p. 240.
79 Davidson, Notes on 'Haig & Lawrence', 3 March 1954, Lawrence Papers, NLS.
80 Clive, Diary, 5 June 1918, Clive Papers II/4/133, LHCMA.
81 Reverend G.S. Duncan, *Douglas Haig as I Knew Him*, p. 70.
82 General Sir Beauvoir de Lisle, *Reminiscences of Sport and War*, p. 253.
83 Davidson, Notes on 'Haig & Lawrence', 3 March 1954, Lawrence Papers, NLS.
84 Marshall-Cornwall, *Haig as Military Commander*, p. 257.
85 Davidson, Notes on 'Haig & Lawrence', 3 March 1954, Lawrence Papers, NLS.
86 Davidson to Fulford, 4 March 1954, Lawrence Papers, NLS.
87 Davidson, Notes on 'Haig & Lawrence', 3 March 1954, Lawrence Papers, NLS.
88 Butler, Memoirs, p. 39, Butler Papers, IWM.
89 Boraston, *Sir Douglas Haig's Despatches*, p. 350.
90 Bonham-Carter, Autobiography, Chapter IX, p. 13, Bonham-Carter Papers 9/2, CCC.
91 Bonham-Carter, Memoir, Chapter IX, p. 6, Bonham-Carter Papers, IWM; Butler, Memoirs, p. 34, Butler Papers, IWM.
92 Kirke, Lieut.-General Sir George M.W. Macdonogh, GBE, KCB, KCMG, p. 9, Kirke Papers, IWM; Dawnay to his wife, 30 August 1918, Dawnay Papers 69/21/3, IWM;

Brigadier E.C. Anstey, The History of the Royal Artillery, p. 313, Anstey Papers 1159/10, RAI.

93 Clive, Diary, 2 and 6 March 1918, Clive Papers II/4/100-102, LHCMA.

94 *Field Service Regulations*, Part I, *Operations, 1909* (Reprinted, with Amendments, 1912), General Staff, War Office, pp. 127–128, 157, 162–163.

95 Clive, Diary, 19 December 1914, Clive Papers 11/1/77, LHCMA.

96 General Sir Reginald Stephens, Outline of a Scheme for a General Offensive, BR 73, 24 December 1914, Stephens Papers 69/70/1, IWM.

97 General Sir John Burnett-Stuart, Memoirs, Chapter VIII, p. 86, Burnett-Stuart Papers, LHCMA.

98 *Notes on Conference held at Bethune on 5 March 1915*, First Army HQ, WO 95/154, PRO.

99 Memorandum by GOC First Army, 28 February, 1915, WO158/181, PRO.

100 Haig, Diary, 2 March 1915, Haig Diaries, PRO.

101 First Army, Notes at Conference held at Bethune on 3rd March, 1915, undated, WO95/154, PRO.

102 Memorandum by GOC First Army, 28 February, 1915, WO158/181, PRO.

103 Haig to Lieutenant-General Sir Launcelot Kiggell, 2 April 1915, Kiggell Papers II/I, LHCMA.

104 Rawlinson, Diary, 14 March 1915, Rawlinson Papers 1/1, CCC.

105 Rawlinson to Kitchener, 1 April and 15 March 1915, Kitchener Papers WB/16 and /18, PRO 30/57.

106 Rawlinson, Diary, 25 March 1915, Rawlinson Papers 1/1, CCC.

107 Rawlinson to Kitchener, 1 April 1915, Kitchener Papers WB/18, PRO 30/57.

108 Brigadier-General J.P. du Cane, Memo. on Neuve Chapelle, pp. 1–4, 15 March 1915, WO158/17, PRO.

109 GHQ, 'General Staff Notes on the Offensive' [April 1915], WO 158/17, PRO.

110 Rawlinson to Kitchener, 21 April 1915, Kitchener Papers WB/19A, PRO 30/57.

111 Major-General H. de F. Montgomery, Siege Operations, pp. 1–3 [May–June 1915], WO158/17, PRO.

112 Montgomery, Co-operation with the French in the Offensive, pp. 1–2, 19 June 1915, WO158/17, PRO.

113 Rawlinson, Proposals for the Attack of Loos Village and Hill 70, Fourth Corps No HRS 503, 22 August 1915, WO95/157, PRO.

114 First Army GS 164 (a), General Principles for the Attack, 6 September 1915, WO95/158, PRO.

115 Haig, Diary, 14 September 1915, Haig Papers, WO256/5, PRO.

116 General Sir Hubert Gough to First Army, I Corps No 494 (G)51, p. 2, 17 September 1915, WO95/592, PRO.

117 [Brigadier-General A.A. Montgomery] to [Brigadier-General F.B. Maurice], HQ IV Corps, 13 October 1915, Montgomery-Massingberd Papers 40, LHCMA.

118 [Montgomery], *Lecture Given at Head-Quarters, 3rd Army, on 14th December, 1915 on action of IV Corps at Loos, 25th September, 1915*, WO95/711, PRO.

119 Brigadier-General A.A. Montgomery, Lecture given on action of IV Corps at Loos, 25th September 1915, 14 December 1915, Montgomery-Massingberd Papers 45, LHCMA.

120 Stephens, Memo. to 8th Division, BR75, 25 December 1915, Stephens Papers 69/70/1, IWM.

121 Anstey, The History of the Royal Artillery, p. 112, Anstey Papers, RAI.

122 General Staff, *General Factors to be Weighed in Considering the Allied Plan of Campaign during the Next Few Months*, pp. 2–3, 16 January 1916, WO158/19, PRO.

123 Haldane, War Diary, 25 March 1916, Haldane Papers, NLS.

124 Rawlinson, Diary, 29 and 30 March 1916, Rawlinson Papers 1/5, CCC.

125 Clive, Diary, 26 July 1915, Clive Papers II/2/26, LHCMA.

126 Robertson to Kiggell, 5 July 1916, Kiggell Papers IV/3, LHCMA.
127 Rawlinson, Diary, 31 March 1916, Rawlinson Papers 1/5, CCC.
128 Rawlinson, Plan for Offensive By Fourth Army, GX 3/1, 3 April 1916, WO158/233, PRO.
129 Ibid., Diary, 23 May 1916, Rawlinson Papers 1/5, CCC.
130 Ibid., Plan for Offensive By Fourth Army, GX 3/1, 3 April 1916, WO158/233, PRO.
131 Ibid., Plan for Offensive Operations by Fourth Army, Fourth Army GX 3/1, 19 April, 1916, WO158/233, PRO.
132 Haig, Diary, 12 May 1916, Haig Papers, WO256/10, PRO.
133 Ibid., Diary, 7 and 8 April 1916, Haig Papers, WO256/9, PRO.
134 Ibid., 5 April 1916.
135 Rawlinson, Diary, 1 and 4 April 1916, Rawlinson Papers 1/5, CCC.
136 Haldane, War Diary, 7 July 1916, Haldane Papers, NLS.
137 Major-General Hon W. Lambton to [Robertson], 18 July 1916, Maurice Papers 3/5/28, LHCMA.
138 Haldane, War Diary, 10 and 22 October 1916, Haldane Papers, NLS.
139 Field-Marshal Lord Byng to Field-Marshal Lord Chetwode, 30 May 1917, Chetwode Papers P183, IWM.
140 Robertson to Haig, 20 April 1917, Haig Papers, WO256/17, PRO.
141 Wilson, Note by Lieutenant-General Sir H.H. Wilson KCB, DSO, 30 April 1917, WO106/1512, PRO.
142 Lieutenant-Colonel C.N. Macmullen, *Summary of the Proposed Northern Operations in Chronological Order*, 20 February 1917, WO158/ 214, PRO.
143 Field-Marshal Lord Plumer to GHQ, 30 January 1917, WO158/38, PRO and Rawlinson to GHQ, 9 February 1917, WO158/214, PRO.
144 Rawlinson, Diary, 7 December 1916, Rawlinson Papers 1/7, CCC.
145 Major-General Sir John Davidson to the CGS, 'Operations by Second and Fifth Armies for the capture of the Passchendaele-Staden Ridge', 26 June 1917, WO158/ 249, PRO.
146 Rawlinson, Diary, 3 July 1917, Rawlinson Papers 1/7, CCC.
147 *Memo by General Sir Hubert Gough on the GS Note of 26 June, addressed by General Davidson to CGS, dated 26 June 1917*, WO 158/249, PRO.
148 Major-General N. Malcolm, Fifth Army, 'Notes for Conference – 24/5/1917', 23 May 1917, Maxse Papers, 69/53/8A, IWM.
149 Malcolm, Note by MGGS on principles upon which Fifth Army Commander proposes to carry out the forthcoming operations, Fifth Army SG671/1, 7 June 1917, WO158/249, PRO.
150 Rawlinson, Diary, 21 July 1917, Rawlinson Papers 1/7, CCC; *Memo by General Sir H. Gough on the GS Note of 26 June, addressed by General Davidson to CGS*, 26 June 1917, WO158/249, PRO.
151 Haig, Diary, 14 June 1917, Haig Papers, WO256/19, PRO.
152 Anstey, *The History of the Royal Artillery*, pp. 192, 169, Anstey Papers, RAI.
153 Haldane, War Diary, 4 September 1917, Haldane Papers, NLS.
154 Kiggell to Gough, 7 August 1918, Kiggell Papers V/114, LHCMA.
155 Kiggell to the five Army Commanders, OB/2089, 7 August 1917, Haig Papers, WO256/21, PRO.
156 Rawlinson to GHQ, Fourth Army No. 806 (G), 9 August 1917, Montgomery-Massingberd Papers 94, LHCMA.
157 Lieutenant-Colonel C.H. Mitchell, *The Enemy's Tactical Methods East of Ypres*, Second Army Intelligence, 16 September 1917, Montgomery-Massingberd Papers 95, LHCMA.
158 Major-General C.H. Harington, *Notes on Training and Preparations for Offensive Operations, Second Army, 31 August 1917*, Montgomery-Massingberd Papers 94, LHCMA.

159 Anstey, The History of the Royal Artillery, pp. 180, 169, Anstey Papers, RAI.
160 General Sir Charles Harington to Major-General Sir Frederick Maurice, 9 November 1934, Maurice Papers 3/2/7, LHCMA.
161 Edmonds, *Military Operations, France and Belgium, 1917*, Volume II, pp. xi, 303.
162 Translation of 5th [German] Guards Brigade Order I Br 1125, General von Radowitz, 29 September 1917, GHQ Ia/40569, 7 October 1917, Montgomery-Massingberd Papers 95, LHCMA.
163 Field-Marshal Lord Alanbrooke, Notes For My Memoirs, Alanbrooke Papers 3/1/85, LHCMA.
164 Haldane, Autobiography, Volume II, p. 421, Haldane Papers, NLS.
165 Ibid., War Diary, 14 November 1917, Haldane Papers, NLS.
166 Stephens to Field-Marshal Sir John Dill, 6 March 1918, Dill Papers I/8, LHCMA.
167 Field-Marshal Sir Archibald Montgomery-Massingberd, *The Autobiography of a Gunner*, p. 34, Montgomery-Massingberd Papers 159/1, LHCMA.
168 Haig to Lieutenant-General the Hon Sir Herbert Lawrence, 12 August 1918, Lawrence Papers, NLS.
169 Haig, Diary, 10 and 14 August 1918, Haig Papers, WO256/34, PRO.
170 C.R.M.F. Cruttwell, *A History of the Great War*, pp. 169, 554.
171 Rawlinson, Diary, 16 July, 14 August, and 15 August 1918, Rawlinson Papers, CCC.
172 Haig, Diary, 29 July 1918, Haig Papers, WO256/33, PRO.
173 Ibid., 30 August 1918, Haig Papers, WO256/35, PRO.
174 Ibid., 31 August and 1 September 1918, Haig Papers, WO256/36, PRO.
175 *SS135, The Training and Employment of Divisions, 1918*, GHQ OB 1635, January 1918, Montgomery-Massingberd Papers 92, LHCMA.
176 *SS135, The Division In Attack*, p. 8, GHQ T/1635, November 1918, Montgomery-Massingberd Papers 92, LHCMA.
177 Haig, Diary, 26 and 18 August 1918, Haig Papers, WO256/35, PRO.
178 GHQ, T/9, Notes on Recent Fighting No. 20, 6 September 1918, WO58/70, PRO.
179 General Sir Noel Birch to General Sir Percy Radcliffe, 5 July 1918, Colonel S.W.H. Rawlins Papers 1162, RAI.
180 Major-General A.A. Montgomery to Major-General J.S.M. Shea, 28 October 1918, Montgomery-Massingberd Papers 91, LHCMA.
181 War Office, *Statistics of the Military Effort of the British Empire during the Great War, 1914–1920*, HMSO, p. 727.
182 Montgomery to Shea, 28 October 1918, Montgomery-Massingberd Papers 91, LHCMA.
183 Montgomery, *The Autobiography of a Gunner*, p. 36, Montgomery-Massingberd Papers 159/1, LHCMA.
184 Major-General H.D. de Pree, *The 38th (Welsh) Division in the Last Five Weeks of the Great War*, Chapter 1V, p. 336, *Journal of the Royal Artillery*, Volume LVIII, No. 3, NAM.

Appendices

Appendix 1: List of the sample of war managers

This book is based on research on a sample of officers (700 in total) who were the War Managers, forming the military elite of the Imperial Forces holding the principal senior command, administrative, medical and staff posts within the BEF and managing the operations of the British Army on the Western Front, 1914–1918. The names of these men, including the holders of the senior posts at GHQ; the commanders of Armies, Corps, Divisions, Tank and RFC Brigades; and the Staff Officers holding the posts of MGGS, BGGS and GSO1 within the BEF, are listed below:

Adair, Lieutenant-Colonel H.S.
Alanbrooke, Field-Marshal Viscount
Alderson, Lieutenant-General Sir Edwin A.H.
Alexander, Major-General E.W.
Alexander, Major-General H.L.
Alexander, Major-General R.O.
Allanson, Colonel C.J.L.
Allardyce, Brigadier J.G.B.
Allen, Lieutenant-Colonel R.S.
Allenby, Field-Marshal Viscount
Anderson, Lieutenant-General Charles A.
Anderson, Lieutenant-General Sir Desmond F.
Anderson, Lieutenant-General Sir (Warren) Hastings
Anley, Brigadier-General B.D.L.G.
Anstey, Brigadier E.C.
Armes, Colonel R.J.
Armitage, General Sir (Charles) Clement
Ashmore, Major-General E.B.
Aspinall-Oglander, Brigadier-General C.F.
Asser, General Sir (Joseph) John
Atkinson, Lieutenant-General E.H. de V.

Babington, Lieutenant-General Sir James M.
Baillie, Colonel H.F.
Bainbridge, Major-General Sir (Edmund) Guy (Tulloch)
Baker-Carr, Brigadier-General C. D'A.B.S.
Baldock, Major-General T.S.
Bannatine-Allason, Major-General Sir Richard
Barnardiston, Major-General N.W.
Barne, Brigadier W.B.G.
Barnes, Major-General Sir Reginald W.R.
Barratt, Air Chief Marshal Sir Arthur S.
Barrow, General Sir George de S.
Barter, Lieutenant-General Sir Charles St L.
Bartholomew, General Sir William H.
Barton, Group Captain R.J.F.
Battye, Colonel B.C.
Bayley, Colonel A.G.
Beck, Major-General E.A.
Becke, Brigadier-General J.H.W.
Beckwith, Major W.M.
Beddington, Brigadier Sir Edward H.L.
Belgrave, Lieutenant-Colonel J.D.
Bernard, Lieutenant-General Sir Denis J.C.K.
Bertram, Lieutenant-Colonel W.R.
Bethell, Major-General Sir (Hugh) Keppel
Biddulph, Brigadier-General H.
Bingham, Major-General Hon Sir Cecil E.
Birch, Colonel E.M.
Birch, General Sir (James Frederick) Noel
Birdwood, Field-Marshal Lord
Black, Lieutenant-Colonel C.H.G.
Blackader, Major-General C.G.
Blacklock, Major-General C.A.
Blair, Brigadier-General A.
Blair, Colonel J.M.
Blamey, Field-Marshal Sir Thomas A.
Blewitt, Lieutenant-Colonel G.
Blore, Lieutenant-Colonel H.R.
Boileau, Colonel F.R.F.
Bols, Lieutenant-General Sir Louis J.
Bonham-Carter, General Sir Charles
Boscawen, Major Hon G.E.
Bourne, General Sir Alan G.B.
Bowdler, Lieutenant-Colonel B.W.B.
Bowly, Colonel W.A.T.
Boyce, Major-General Sir William G.B.

Boyd, Major-General Sir Gerald F.
Boyd-Rochfort, Lieutenant-Colonel H.
Bradford, Lieutenant-Colonel E.A.
Braine, Brigadier H.E.R.R.
Braithwaite, General Sir Walter P.
Bray, Major-General Sir Claude A.
Bridges, Colonel A.H.
Bridges, Lieutenant-General Sir (George) Tom (Molesworth)
Bridgford, Brigadier-General R.J.
Briggs, Lieutenant-General Sir Charles J.
Brind, General Sir John E.S.
Broad, Lieutenant-General Sir Charles N.F.
Broadwood, Lieutenant-General R.G.
Brooke-Popham, Air Chief Marshal Sir (Henry) Robert (Moore)
Bruce, Colonel G.D.
Bruce-Williams, Major-General Sir Hugh B.
Bryant, Lieutenant-Colonel A.
Buckland, Major-General Sir Reginald U.H.
Buckle, Brigadier-General A.S.
Buckle, Major-General C.R.
Budworth, Major-General C.E.D.
Bulfin, General Sir Edward S.
Burkhardt, Colonel V.R.
Burnett-Hitchcock, Lieutenant-General Sir Basil F.
Burnett-Stuart, General Sir John T.
Burrowes, Brigadier-General A.R.
Burstall, Lieutenant-General Sir Henry E.
Burtchaell, Lieutenant-General Sir Charles H.
Butler, Lieutenant-General Sir Richard H.K.
Butler, Major-General S.S.
Buzzard, Brigadier-General F.A.
Byng, Field-Marshal Viscount

Caldecott, Lieutenant-Colonel E.L.
Cameron, General Sir Archibald R.
Cameron, Major-General N.J.G.
Campbell, General Sir David G.M.
Campbell, Major-General J.
Campbell, Colonel R.B.
Campbell, Lieutenant-General Sir Walter
Capper, Major-General Sir John E.
Capper, Major-General T.
Carey, Major-General G.G.S.
Carr, Lieutenant-General L.
Carter, Major-General Sir Evan E.
Carter-Campbell, Colonel G.T.C.

Carthew, Lieutenant-Colonel T.W.C.
Cator, Major-General A.B.E.
Cavan, Field-Marshal Earl of
Cavendish, Brigadier-General F.W.L.S.H.
Cayley, Major-General D.E.
Cecil, Lieutenant-Colonel R.E.
Charles, Lieutenant-General Sir (James) Ronald (Edmonston)
Charles, Lieutenant-Colonel W.G.
Charlton, Air Commodore L.E.O.
Charrington, Lieutenant-Colonel S.H.
Charteris, Brigadier-General J.
Charteris, Colonel N.K.
Chetwode, Field-Marshal Lord
Chichester, Major-General Sir Arlington A.
Church, Colonel G.R.M.
Clarke, Colonel A.L.C.
Clarke, Lieutenant-Colonel M.O.
Clarke, Colonel R.G.
Clarke, Lieutenant-General Sir Travers E.
Clayton, Colonel E.R.
Clayton, Lieutenant-General Sir Frederick T.
Clive, General Sir (George) Sidney
Cobbe, General Sir Alexander S.
Cochrane, Brigadier-General J.K.
Coffin, Major-General C. (VC)
Coleridge, General Sir John F.S.D.
Collins, Major-General R.J.
Congreve, General Sir Walter N.
Constable-Maxwell-Scott, Major-General Sir Walter J.
Cookson, Major-General G.A.
Cory, Lieutenant-General Sir George N.
Cosens, Lieutenant-Colonel G.P.L.
Couper, Major-General Sir Victor A.
Courage, Brigadier-General A.
Cox, Brigadier-General E.W.
Cox, General Sir (Herbert) Vaughan
Crookenden, Colonel A.
Crookshank, Major-General Sir Sidney D'A.
Crossman, Colonel G.L.
Crozier, Major-General B.B.
Cubitt, General Sir Thomas A.
Cuffe, Colonel J.A.F.
Cumming, Brigadier-General H.R.
Cuninghame, Colonel Sir Thomas A.A.M.
Curling, Brigadier-General B.J.
Currie, General Sir Arthur W.

Currie, Brigadier-General R.A.M.
Cuthbert, Major-General G.J.

Dalby, Major-General T.G.
Dallas, Major-General A.G.
Daly, Major-General A.C.
Daniell, Lieutenant-Colonel F.E.L.
Davidson, Lieutenant-Colonel E.H.
Davidson, Major-General Sir John H.
Davidson, Lieutenant-Colonel N.R.
Davies, Lieutenant-Colonel C.M.
Davies, General Sir Francis J.
Davies, Major-General H.R.
Davies, Colonel R.H.
Davies, Brigadier-General W.P.L.
Dawkins, Major-General Sir Charles T.
Dawnay, Major-General G.P.
Dawson, Brigadier-General R.
De Brett, Brigadier-General H.S.
de Burgh, General Sir Eric
Deedes, General Sir Charles P.
de Lisle, General Sir (Henry de) Beauvoir
de Pree, Major-General H.D.
De Rougemont, Brigadier-General C.H.
Deverell, Field-Marshal Sir Cyril J.
Dick-Cunyngham, Major-General J.K.
Diggle, Lieutenant-Colonel W.H.
Dill, Field-Marshal Sir John G.
Dillon, Brigadier Viscount
Dobbie, Lieutenant-General Sir William G.S.
Dooner, Lieutenant-Colonel J.G.
Doran, Major-General B.J.C.
Dorling, Colonel F.H.
Douglas, Major-General Sir William
Drake, Lieutenant-Colonel R.J.
Drew, Major-General Sir James S.
Dreyer, Major-General J.T.
Du Cane, General Sir John P.
Dudgeon, Major-General F.A.
Dugan, Major-General Lord
Duncan, Major-General F.J.
Durand, Lieutenant-Colonel H.M.

Edmonds, Brigadier-General Sir James E.
Elles, General Sir Hugh J.

Ellington, Marshal of the RAF Sir Edward L.
Evans, Brigadier-General C.

Fanshawe, Lieutenant-General Sir Edward A.
Fanshawe, Lieutenant-General Sir Hew D.
Fanshawe, Major-General Sir Robert
Fasken, Major-General C.G.M.
Faunthorpe, Lieutenant-Colonel J.C.
Feetham, Major-General E.
Feilding, Major-General Sir Geoffrey P.T.
Ferguson, General Sir Charles; Bt
Festing, Lieutenant-Colonel M.C.
Fisher, Lieutenant-General Sir Bertie D.
Fitzgerald, Brigadier-General P.D.
Follett, Lieutenant-Colonel R.S.
Ford, Major-General Sir Reginald
Forestier-Walker, Major-General Sir George T.
Forster, Brigadier D.
Foss, Brigadier C.C. (VC)
Foulkes, Major-General C.H.
Fowke, Lieutenant-General Sir George H.
Fowler, Lieutenant-General Sir John S.
Franklyn, General Sir Harold E.
Franks, Major-General Sir George McK
Freeman, Air Chief Marshal Sir Wilfred R.
French, Field-Marshal Sir John (later Earl of Ypres)
Friend, Major-General Rt Hon Sir Lovick B.
Fry, Major-General Sir William
Fuller, Major-General C.G.
Fuller, Major-General J.F.C.
Furse, Lieutenant-General Sir William T.

Gage, Brigadier-General M.F.
Game, Air Vice-Marshal Sir Philip W.
Gathorne-Hardy, General Hon Sir (John) Francis
Geddes, Major-General Rt Hon Sir Eric C.
Geiger, Lieutenant-Colonel G.J.P.
Gellibrand, Major-General Sir John
Gepp, Major-General Sir (Ernest) Cyril
Gerrard, Major-General J.J.
Giles, Major-General E.D.
Girdwood, Major-General Sir Eric S.
Glasfurd, Colonel A.I.R.
Glasfurd, Lieutenant-Colonel D.J.
Glasgow, Major-General Sir (Thomas) William

Gleichen, Major-General Lord
Glubb, Major-General Sir Frederic M.
Glyn, Lieutenant-Colonel A. St L.
Godley, General Sir Alexander J.
Godwin, Lieutenant-General Sir Charles A.C.
Gogarty, Colonel H.E.
Goldsmith, Colonel H.D.
Gordon, Lieutenant-General Sir Alexander Hamilton
Gordon, Lieutenant-Colonel E.B.
Gordon, Major-General Hon Sir Frederick
Gordon-Hall, Lieutenant-Colonel G.C.W.
Goringe, Lieutenant-General Sir George F.
Gorton, Brigadier R. St G.
Gosset, Colonel F.W.
Gough, General Sir Hubert de la P.
Gough, Major-General J.E.
Graham, Brigadier Lord (Douglas) Malise
Graham, Major-General Sir Edward R.C.
Graham, Brigadier M.
Grant, Lieutenant-Colonel A.K.
Grant, General Sir Charles J.C.
Grant, Major-General Sir Philip G.
Greenly, Major-General W.H.
Grierson, Lieutenant-General Sir James M.
Grigg, Colonel Sir Edward W.M. (later Lord Altrincham)
Grove, Colonel T.T.
Guggisberg, Brigadier-General Sir (Frederick) Gordon
Guise-Moores, Major-General Sir (Samuel) Guise (nee Moores)
Guy, Lieutenant-Colonel R.F.
Gwynn, Major-General Sir Charles W.

Haig, Field-Marshal Earl Haig
Haking, General Sir Richard C.B.
Haldane, General Sir (James) Aylmer (Lowthrop)
Halliday, General Sir Lewis S.T. (VC)
Hambro, Major-General Sir Percy O.
Hamilton, Major-General H.I.W.
Hanbury-Williams, Major-General Sir John
Hankey, Brigadier-General E.B.
Hare, Brigadier-General R.H.
Hare, Brigadier-General R.W.
Harington, General Sir Charles H.
Harman, Lieutenant-General Sir (Antony Ernest) Wentworth
Harper, Lieutenant-General Sir George M.
Harrison, Lieutenant-Colonel E.F.

Harrison, Major-General J.M.R.
Harvey, Lieutenant-Colonel F.H.
Harvey, Major-General R.N.
Haskard, Brigadier-General J. McD
Hay, Major-General C.J.B.
Hayter, Brigadier R.J.F.
Headlam, Lieutenant-Colonel Rt Hon Sir Cuthbert M.
Headlam, Major-General Sir John E.W.
Heard, Lieutenant-Colonel E.S.
Heath, Major-General Sir Gerald M.
Heath, Major-General H.N.C.
Henderson, Lieutenant-General Sir David
Heneker, General Sir William C.G.
Henley, Brigadier-General Hon A.M.
Hewitt, Brigadier C.C.
Hewlett, Brigadier-General E.
Heywood, Major-General C.P.
Hickie, Major-General Sir William B.
Higgins, Air Marshal Sir John F.A.
Higgins, Air Commodore T.C.R.
Higginson, Major-General H.W.
Hill, Lieutenant-Colonel H.
Hill, Major-General J.
Hill-Whitson, Lieutenant-Colonel T.E.L.
Hoare-Nairne, Brigadier-General E.S.
Hobbs, Lieutenant-General Sir (Joseph John) Talbot
Hobbs, Major-General P.E.F.
Hodgson, Brigadier W.T.
Hogg, Brigadier-General R.E.T.
Holdich, Lieutenant-Colonel G.W.V.
Holland, Lieutenant-General Sir Arthur E.A. (born Butcher)
Holland, Lieutenant-Colonel H.W.
Hollond, Major-General S.E.
Holman, Lieutenant-General H.C.
Holmes, Major-General W.
Holt, Air Vice-Marshal F.V.
Home, Brigadier-General Sir Archibald F.
Hopwood, Brigadier-General H.R.
Hordern, Brigadier-General G.V.
Hore-Ruthven, Brigadier Hon A.G.A. (later Earl of Gowrie)
Hore-Ruthven, Colonel Hon C.M.
Hore-Ruthven, Major-General Hon W.P. (later Lord Ruthven)
Horne, General Lord
Hoskins, Major-General Sir (Arthur) Reginald
Howard, Lieutenant-General Sir Geoffrey W.

Howard, Colonel H.C.L.
Howard-Vyse, Major-General Sir Richard G.H.
Howell, Brigadier-General P.
Hudson, General Sir Haverlock
Hudson, Brigadier-General T.R.C.
Hull, Major-General Sir (Charles Patrick) Amyatt
Hume-Spry, Lieutenant-Colonel L.
Humphreys, Lieutenant-General Sir (Edward) Thomas
Hunter-Weston, Lieutenant-General Sir Aylmer G.
Huskisson, Major-General W.
Hutchison, Major-General Sir Robert (later Lord Hutchison)

Ingouville-Williams, Major-General E.C.
Ironside, Field-Marshal Lord
Irwin, Major-General Sir James M.
Isacke, Major-General H.

Jack, Brigadier E.M.
Jackson, Colonel C.H.I.
Jackson, Major-General G.H.N.
Jackson, General Sir Henry C.
Jackson, Colonel L.C.
Jacob, Field-Marshal Sir Claud W.
James, Wing Commander Sir Archibald W.H.
James, Colonel B.R.
James, Lieutenant-Colonel R.E.H.
James, Major-General Sir (William) Bernard
Jeffreys, General Lord
Jerram, Lieutenant-Colonel C.F.
Jess, Lieutenant-General Sir Carl H.
Jeudwine, Lieutenant-General Sir Hugh S.
Johnson, Major-General F.E.
Johnson, Lieutenant-Colonel R.H.
Johnson, Brigadier-General R.M.
Jones, Major-General L.C.
Jury, Colonel E.C.

Karslake, Lieutenant-General Sir Henry
Kavanagh, Lieutenant-General Sir Charles (Toler McMurragh)
Kay, Lieutenant-Colonel Sir William A.I.
Kay, Major-General W.H.
Kearsley, Brigadier-General R.H.
Keary, Lieutenant-General Sir Henry D'U.
Keir, Lieutenant-General Sir John L.
Kelly, Brigadier E.H.
Kennedy, Major-General A.A.

Kenyon, Major-General E.R.
Ker, Major-General C.A.
Kerr, Colonel F.W.
Kiggell, Lieutenant-General Sir Launcelot E.
Kirke, General Sir Walter M. St G.
Kirwan, Lieutenant-General Sir Bertram R.
Knox, General Sir Harry H.S.

Lambe, Air Vice-Marshal Sir Charles L.
Lambert, Colonel T.S.
Lambton, Major-General Hon Sir William
Landon, Major-General H.J.S.
Laskey, Lieutenant-Colonel F.S.
Lavarack, Lieutenant-General Sir John D.
Lawford, Lieutenant-General Sir Sidney T.B.
Lawrence, General Hon Sir Herbert A.
Lawrie, Major-General C.E.
Lawson, Lieutenant-General Sir Henry M.
Leader, Major-General H.P.
Lecky, Major-General R. St C.
Lee, Colonel Sir Arthur H. (later Viscount Lee of Fareham)
Lee, Lieutenant-Colonel A.N.
Lee, Major-General Sir Richard P.
Lee, Colonel R.T.
Legard, Brigadier-General D'A.
Legge, Lieutenant-General J.G.
Levey, Lieutenant-Colonel J.H.
Lewin, Major-General E.O.
Liddell, Major-General Sir William A.
Lindsay, Major-General G.M.
Lindsay, Major-General Sir Walter F.L.
Lipsett, Major-General L.J.
Lister, Lieutenant-Colonel F.H.
Livesay, Brigadier-General R.O'H.
Lloyd, Brigadier-General J. Hardress
Loch, Major-General Lord
Lomax, Lieutenant-General S.H.
Longcroft, Air Vice-Marshal Sir Charles A.H.
Longmore, Lieutenant-Colonel C.M.
Longridge, Lieutenant-Colonel J.A.
Loomis, Major-General Sir Frederick O.W.
Lowther, Major-General Sir (Henry) C.
Lucas, Major-General C.H.T.
Luckock, Major-General R.M.
Ludlow-Hewitt, Air Chief Marshall Sir Edgar R.

Lukin, Major-General Sir Henry T.
Lyall Grant, Lieutenant-Colonel H.F.
Lynden-Bell, Major-General Sir Arthur L.
Lyon, Brigadier-General F.

Macandrew, Major-General H.J.M.
McCay, Lieutenant-General Sir James W.
McClintock, Lieutenant-Colonel R.S.
McColl, Lieutenant-Colonel J.T.
McCracken, Lieutenant-General Sir Frederick W.N.
Macdonnell, Lieutenant-General Sir Archibald C.
Macdonogh, Lieutenant-General Sir George M.W.
McDouall, Brigadier-General R.
MacInnes, Lieutenant-Colonel D.S.
MacIntyre, Lieutenant-Colonel D.E.
Mackenzie, Major-General Sir Colin J.
MacKenzie, Colonel J.H.
MacKenzie-Kennedy, Major-General Sir Edward C.W.
Macmullen, General Sir (Cyril) Norman
McNamara, Lieutenant-General Sir Arthur E.
MacPherson, Major-General Sir William G.
Macready, General Rt Hon Sir (Cecil Frederick) Nevil
Madocks, Brigadier-General W.R.N.
Maitland-Makgill-Crichton, Brigadier H.C.
Makin, Lieutenant-Colonel E.L.
Malcolm, Major-General Sir Neill
Mangles, Brigadier-General R.H.
Marden, Major-General Sir Thomas O.
Marindin, Major-General A.H.
Marshall, Major-General F.J.
Matheson, General Sir Torquhil G.
Mathew, Major-General Sir Charles M.
Maude, Lieutenant-General Sir Frederick S.
Maunsell, Brigadier-General F.G.
Maurice, Major-General Sir Frederick B.
Maxse, General Sir (Frederick) Ivor
Maxwell, General Rt Hon Sir John G.
Maxwell, Lieutenant-General Sir Ronald C.
Meinertzhagen, Colonel R.
Mercer, Major-General Sir (Harvey) Frederick
Mercer, Major-General M.S.
Micklem, Brigadier-General J.
Miles, Lieutenant-General C.G.N.
Milne, Field-Marshal Lord
Mitchell, Brigadier-General C.H.

Mitford, Major-General B.R.
Moir, Brigadier-General A.J.G.
Monash, General Sir John
Monro, General Sir Charles C.
Montagu-Stuart-Wortley, Lieutenant-General Hon Sir (Alan) Richard
Montagu-Stuart-Wortley, Major-General Hon E.J.
Montgomery, Field-Marshal Viscount
Montgomery, Lieutenant-Colonel H.F.
Montgomery, Major-General H.M. de F.
Montgomery, Major-General Sir Robert A.K.
Montgomery-Massingberd, Field-Marshal Sir Archibald
Moore, Lieutenant-Colonel F.H.
Morland, General Sir Thomas L.N.
Mudie, Brigadier T.C.
Muirhead, Lieutenant-Colonel J.A.
Mullens, Major-General R.L.
Munby, Major-General J.E.
Murray, General Sir Archibald J.
Murray, Colonel K.D.B.
Muspratt, General Sir Sidney F.

Napier, Brigadier V.M.C.
Nash, Major-General Sir Philip A.M.
Neame, Lieutenant-General Sir Philip
Neilson, Colonel W.G.
Newall, Marshal of the RAF Lord
Newcome, Major-general H.W.
Newland, Major-General Sir Foster R.
Newman, Major-General C.R.
Nichol, Colonel C.E.
Nicholson, Major-General Sir Cecil L.
Nicholson, Major-General O.H.L.
Norie, Major-General C.E. de M.
Nosworthy, Lieutenant-General Sir Francis P.
Nugent, Major-General Sir Oliver S.W.
Nunn, Lieutenant-Colonel T.H.C.

O'Connor, Lieutenant-Colonel P.B.
O'Donnell, Major-General Sir Thomas J.
O'Keefe, Major-General Sir Manus W.
O'Leary, Brigadier-General T.E.
Ollivant, Brigadier-General A.H.
Onslow, Colonel Earl of
Osborne, Lieutenant-General E.A.
Oxley, Brigadier-General R.S.

Paget, Lieutenant-Colonel A.E.S.L.
Pakenham, Colonel G. de la P.B.
Paley, Colonel A.T.
Panet, Brigadier-General E. de B.
Paris, Major-General Sir Archibald
Parker, Brigadier-General A.
Parker, Brigadier-General R.G.
Parsons, Major-General Sir Harold D.E.
Parsons, Brigadier J.L.R.
Peck, Major-General A.W.
Peck, Lieutenant-Colonel J.H.
Peck, Major-General S.C.
Perceval, Major-General Sir Edward M.
Percival, Lieutenant-Colonel A.J.-B.
Percy, Major-General Sir (John Samuel) Jocelyn
Pereira, Major-General Sir Cecil E.
Peyton, General Sir William E.
Philipps, Major-General Sir Ivor
Piggott, Major-General F.S.G.
Pigot, Brigadier-General Sir Robert
Pike, Major-General Sir William W.
Pilcher, Major-General T.D.
Pinney, Major-General Sir Reginald J.
Pinwill, Lieutenant-Colonel W.R.
Pitcher, Air Commodore D. le G.
Pitman, Major-General T.T.
Pitt-Taylor, General Sir Walter W.
Place, Colonel C.O.
Platt, General Sir William
Plumer, Field-Marshal Viscount
Pollok-Morris, Lieutenant-Colonel T.A.
Ponsonby, Major-General Sir John
Porter, Major-General Sir Robert
Price, Brigadier-General T.R.C.
Pritchard, Brigadier-General C.G.
Pryce, Lieutenant-General Sir Henry (Edward) ap Rhys
Pulteney, Lieutenant-General Sir William

Radcliffe, General Sir Percy P. de B.
Ramsay, Major-General F.W.
Ramsay, Major-General Sir John G.
Ramsay-Fairfax, Commander W.G.A.
Rawlins, Colonel S.W.H.
Rawlinson, General Lord
Reed, Major-General H.L.

Renny, Colonel L.F.
Rice, Major-General Sir (Spring) Robert
Rimington, Major-General Sir Michael F.
Ritchie, Major-General Sir Archibald B.
Robb, Major-General Sir Frederick S.
Robertson, Major-General Sir Philip R.
Robertson, Brigadier-General W.
Robertson, Field-Marshal Sir William R.
Romer, General Sir Cecil F.
Rosenthal, Major-General Sir Charles
Ross, Lieutenant-Colonel A.M.
Ross, Major-General C.
Rowan, Lieutenant-Colonel P.S.
Ruggles-Brise, Major-General Sir Harold G.
Russell, Brigadier-General Hon A.V.F.
Russell, Major-General Sir Andrew H.
Ryan, Lieutenant-Colonel R.S.
Rycroft, Major-General Sir William H.

Sackville, Lieutenant-Colonel Lord
Sackville-West, Major-General C.J. (later Lord Sackville)
St John, Colonel E.F.
Salmond, Marshal of the RAF Sir John M.
Sandbach, Major-General A.E.
Sanders, Brigadier-General A.R.C.
Sandilands, Brigadier H.R.
Sargent, Major-General H.N.
Sceales, Lieutenant-Colonel G.A. McL
Scobell, Major-General Sir (Sanford) John (Palairet)
Scott, Major-General Sir Arthur B.
Scott, Major-General C.W.
Scrase-Dickens, Major-General S.W.
Seagrave, Brigadier-General W.H.-E.
Shea, General Sir John S.M.
Shephard, Brigadier-General G.S.
Sherbrooke, Colonel N.H.C.
Shoubridge, Major-General T.H.
Shute, General Sir Cameron D.
Sillem, Major-General Sir Arnold F.
Simpson-Baikie, Brigadier-General Sir Hugh A.D.
Sinclair-Maclagen, Major-General E.G.
Skeffington-Smyth, Lieutenant-Colonel G.H.J. (later FitzPatrick)
Skinner, Major-General B.M.
Skinner, Major-General Sir (Percy) Cyriac (Burrell)
Sloggett, Lieutenant-General Sir Arthur T.

Sloman, Brigadier-General H.S.
Smith, Major-General Sir William D.
Smith-Dorrien, General Sir Horace L.
Smyth, Major-General Sir Nevill W. (VC)
Smyth-Osbourne, Air Commodore H.P.
Snow, General Sir Thomas D'O.
Solly-Flood, Major-General A.
Soutry, Lieutenant-Colonel T.L.B.
Spender, Lieutenant-Colonel Sir Wilfred B.
Stephens, General Sir Reginald B.
Stericker, Lieutenant-Colonel A.W.
Stewart, Brigadier-General C.G.
Stewart, Brigadier-General I.
Stewart, Major-General Sir (John Henry) Keith
Stewart, Colonel P.A.V.
Stirling, Major P.D.
Stranack, Lieutenant-Colonel C.E.
Strick, Major-General J.A.
Strickland, General Sir Edward P.
Stuart, Lieutenant-Colonel A.G.
Stuart, Major-General Sir Andrew M.
Studd, Brigadier-General H.W.
Sutton, Major-General H.C.
Sutton Nelthorpe, Colonel O.
Swinton, Major-General Sir Ernest D.
Sykes, Major-General Rt Hon Sir Frederick H.
Symons, Brigadier-General A.

Tagart, Major-General Sir Harold A.L.
Tandy, Brigadier-General E.N.
Tanner, Lieutenant-Colonel F.C.
Taylor, Brigadier-General R.O'B.
Teck, Duke of (later Lieutenant-Colonel Marquess of Cambridge)
Teck, Prince Alexander of (later Brigadier-General Earl of Athlone)
Temperley, Major-General A.C.
Thesiger, Major-General G.H.
Thompson, Major-General Sir Harry N.
Thomson, Lieutenant-Colonel A.G.
Thomson, Major-General J.
Thorp, Colonel H.W.B.
Thorpe, Major-General G.
Thuillier, Major-General Sir Henry F.
Thwaites, General Sir William
Trail, Lieutenant-Colonel W.H.
Treherne, Major-General Sir Francis H.

Trenchard, Marshal of the RAF Viscount
Tudor, Major-General Sir (Henry) Hugh
Tulluch, Brigadier-General J.B.G.
Turner, Brigadier-General A.J.
Turner, Colonel J.E.
Turner, Lieutenant-General Sir Richard E.W.
Twining, Major-General Sir Philip G.
Twiss, Major-General Sir William L.O.

Uniacke, Lieutenant-General Sir Herbert C.C.

Van Straubenzee, Major-General Sir Casimir Cartwright
Vaughan, Major-General J.
Vaughan, Lieutenant-General Sir Louis R.
Vincent, Brigadier-General Sir Berkeley
Vivian, Lieutenant-Colonel V.

Wace, Brigadier-General E.G.
Wagstaff, Major-General C.M.
Wake, Major-General Sir Hereward
Walcot, Lieutenant-Colonel B.
Walker Brigadier-General H.A.
Walker, Lieutenant-General Sir Harold B.
Walker, Major-General W.G.
Wallace of that Ilk, Colonel R.F.H.
Wanless O'Gowan, Major-General R.
Wardrop, General Sir Alexander E.
Watkis, General Sir Henry B.B.
Watson, Brigadier-General C.F.
Watson, Major-General Sir David
Watt, Brigadier-General D.M.
Watts, Lieutenant-General Sir Herbert E.
Weatherby, Lieutenant-Colonel J.T.
Webb-Bowen, Air Vice-Marshal Sir Tom I.
Webber, Brigadier-General N.W.
Weber, Colonel W.H.F.
Western, Major-General Sir William G.B.
Wethered, Colonel J.R.
Whetherly, Lieutenant-Colonel W.S.
Whigham, General Sir Robert D.
White, General Sir (Cyril) Brudenell (Bingham)
Whitton, Lieutenant-Colonel F.E.
Wieck, Lieutenant-Colonel G.F.G.
Wigram, Brigadier-General K.
Wilkins, Lieutenant-Colonel H. St C.
Wilkinson, Major-General Sir Percival S.

Willcocks, General Sir James
Williams, Colonel A.F.C.
Williams, Brigadier E.M.
Williams, Major-General W. de L.
Wilson, Brigadier-General C.S.
Wilson, Lieutenant-General Sir Henry F.M.
Wilson, Field-Marshal Sir Henry H.
Wilson, Field-Marshal Lord Wilson
Wilson, Brigadier-General Sir Samuel H.
Wing, Major-General F.D.V.
Wintour, Major-General FitzG
Wood, Brigadier-General P.R.
Woodhouse, Major-General Sir (Tom) Percy
Woods, Brigadier-General H.K.
Woollcombe, Lieutenant-General Sir Charles L.
Wright, Brigadier-General W.D.
Wynter, Brigadier H.W.

Yarde-Buller, Brigadier-General Hon Sir Henry

Appendix 2: Breakdown of sample by occupation

Service	Number of officers	% of sample (700)
Serving British Army Officer	575	82.14
Serving Indian Army Officer	46	6.57
Retired British Army Officer	25	3.57
Serving Commonwealth Officer	17	2.43
Serving Commonwealth Militia Officer	15	2.14
Serving British Territorial Officer	6	0.86
Serving Royal Marine Officer	6	0.86
British Civilian	4	0.57
Serving Royal Naval Officer	3	0.43
Retired Indian Army Officer	3	0.43
Total	700	100.00

Appendix 3: Service of British officers

Branch	Number of officers	% of officers (655)	% of sample (700)
British Infantry	280	42.75	40.00
Royal Artillery	112	17.10	16.00
Cavalry	65	9.92	9.29
Royal Engineers	64	9.77	9.14
Guards	33	5.04	4.71
Indian Infantry	29	4.43	4.14

Indian Cavalry	20	3.05	2.86
R.A.M.C.	17	2.595	2.43
Royal Flying Corps	17	2.595	2.43
Army Service Corps	5	0.76	0.71
Household Cavalry	4	0.61	0.57
Royal Marines Light Infy.	4	0.61	0.57
Royal Marines Artillery	2	0.31	0.29
Army Ordnance Department	2	0.31	0.29
Army Pay Department	1	0.15	0.14
Total	655	100.00	

Most popular corps/regiment of British regular officers

Corps/regiment	Number of officers	% of officers (600)	% of sample (700)
Royal Artillery	112	18.66	16.00
Royal Engineers	64	10.67	9.14
Rifle Brigade	22	3.67	3.14
R.A.M.C.	17	2.83	2.43
Royal Flying Corps	17	2.83	2.43
K.R.R.C.	15	2.50	2.14
Grenadier Guards	14	2.34	2.00
Coldstream Guards	14	2.34	2.00
Gordon Highlanders	13	2.17	1.86
Queen's Royal West Surrey	13	2.17	1.86
Total	301	50.17	43.00

Appendix 4: Leading forty schools

School	Number of officers	% of sample (700)
Eton College	93	13.3
Wellington College	44	6.3
Harrow School	38	5.4
Marlborough College	35	5.0
Charterhouse	33	4.7
Winchester	33	4.7
Clifton College	30	4.3
Cheltenham College	26	3.7
Haileybury	19	2.7
Rugby	19	2.7
Bedford School	14	2.0
United Services College	12	1.7
St Paul's School	9	1.3
Fettes	8	1.1

(Continued)

School	Number of officers	% of sample (700)
Radley	8	1.1
Wimbledon School	8	1.1
H.M.S. Britannia	7	1.0
Malvern	7	1.0
Uppingham	7	1.0
Felsted	6	0.9
King's, Canterbury	6	0.9
Shrewsbury	6	0.9
Brighton College	5	0.7
Sherborne	5	0.7
Stubbington House	5	0.7
Beaumont	4	0.6
Bishop's College, Canada	4	0.6
Dulwich	4	0.6
Eastbourne College	4	0.6
Merchiston Castle School	4	0.6
Repton	4	0.6
St Columba's College	4	0.6
Sedburgh	4	0.6
Victoria College, Jersey	4	0.6
Edinburgh Academy	3	0.4
Newtown College	3	0.4
Rossall	3	0.4
Royal School, Armagh	3	0.4
Tonbridge	3	0.4
Westminster	3	0.4

Appendix 5: Numbers of officers at public schools

School	Number of officers	% of sample (700)
Leading school (Eton)	93	13
5 leading schools	244	35
10 leading schools	371	53
15 leading schools	421	60
20 leading schools	456	65
25 leading schools	483	69
30 leading schools	503	71
35 leading schools	522	74
40 leading schools	537	77

Appendix 6: Universities attended by officers

University	Number of officers	% of sample (700)	% of total (73)
Oxford University	25	3.5	35
Cambridge University	19	2.5	25
Trinity College, Dublin	7	1.0	10
Canadian Universities	4	0.5	6
Australian Universities	3	0.5	4
Dublin University	3	0.5	4
European Universities	3	0.5	4
London University	3	0.5	4
Aberdeen University	3	0.5	4
Glasgow University	2	0.3	3
Edinburgh University	1	0.2	1
Total	73	10.5	100.00

University	Number of officers	% of sample (700)	% of total (73)
Oxbridge Universities	44	6.0	60
Irish Universities	10	1.0	14
Dominion Universities	7	1.0	10
Scottish Universities	6	1.0	8
English Universities	3	0.5	4
European Universities	3	0.5	4
Total	73	10.0	100.0

Appendix 7: Father's occupation

Occupation	Number of officers	% of sample (700)
Army Officer	228	32.5
Landed Gentry	183	26.0
Unknown	159	23.0
Clergy	73	10.5
Aristocracy	59	8.5
Civil Service	31	4.5
The Law	20	3.0
Royal Navy	15	2.0
Doctor	9	1.0
M.P.	9	1.0
Merchant	8	1.0
Academic	6	1.0

(Continued)

Occupation	Number of officers	% of sample (700)
Other professions	5	0.5
Banker	3	0.5
Working Class	3	0.5
Railway Engineer	2	0.5
Royal Marine	2	0.5
Shipping	2	0.5

Occupation	Number of officers	% of sample (700)
Armed Services	245	35.0
Landed Gentry	183	26.0
Unknown	159	23.0
Clergy	73	10.5
Aristocracy	59	8.5
Civil Service	31	4.5
M.P.	9	1.0
Professional/Business Class	57	8.0
Working Class	3	0.5
Total	700	100.0

Appendix 8: Graduates from staff college

	Number of officers	% of sample (700)
Non-psc	316	45
psc	384	55

Age groups of graduates from staff college

Birth	Number of officers	% of sample (700)	Non psc	% of age group	psc	% of age group
1850s	61	8.5	42	69	19	31
1860s	216	31.0	113	52	103	48
1870s	311	44.5	95	31	216	69
1880s	109	15.5	63	59	46	42
1890s	3	0.5	3	100	0	0
Total	700	100.0	316		384	

Appendix 9: Staff experience within the BEF, 1914

Post	Number of officers	% of sample (700)
With Commonwealth Forces	52	7.5
Egyptian Army	27	4.0
King's African Rifles	17	2.5
West African Frontier Force	21	7.0
War Office	141	20.0
HQ, India	20	3.0
HQ, South Africa	5	0.7
Staff College	43	6.0
R.M.C, R.M.A., etc.	60	8.5
No Staff Experience	230	33.0
Administrative Post	101	14.5
Junior General Staff Post	268	38.0
Senior General Staff Post	89	13.0
Corp level Commanders	9	2.0
Divisional Commanders	28	4.0
Brigade Commanders	63	9.0
Regimental Commanders	91	13.0

Battle experience within the BEF, 1914

Campaign	Number of officers	% of sample (700)
No battle experience	123	18.0
South Africa	485	69.0
North-West Frontier, 1897–98	73	10.5
Nile Expedition, 1897–99	64	9.0
Tirah Campaign, 1897–98	42	6.0
Burma	35	5.0
Chitral Relief Force, 1895	29	4.0
Egypt, 1882–85	24	3.5
China, 1900–1901	22	3.0
Nigeria, 1897–1904	21	3.0
Somaliland, 1903–04	20	3.0
Afghan War, 1879–80	16	2.0
Ashanti Wars, 1895–1900	16	2.0
Dongola, 1896	15	2.0
Waziristan, 1894–95	14	2.0

Appendix 10: Analysis of senior officers

Corps/regt.	Number of officers	% of total	psc	% of group	Non psc	% of group
		Commanders-in-chief of the BEF				
Cavalry	2	100	1	50	1	50
		Army commanders of the BEF				
Infantry	3	30	3	100	0	0
Guards	1	10	1	100	0	0
Cavalry	4	40	4	100	0	0
Artillery	1	10	0	0	1	100
Indian Army	1	10	1	100	0	0
Total	10	100	9	90	1	10
		Corps commanders of the BEF				
Infantry	19	40	14	74	5	26
Guards	6	12	3	50	3	50
Cavalry	10	21	6	60	4	40
Artillery	7	15	2	29	5	71
Engineers	2	4	2	100	0	0
Indian Army	2	4	0	0	2	100
Dominion	2	4	0	0	2	100
Total	48	100	27	56	21	44

Corps/regt.	Number of officers	% of total	psc	% of group	Non psc	% of group
		Divisional commanders of the BEF				
Infantry	91	47.0	57	63	34	37
Guards	15	8.0	7	47	8	53
Cavalry	27	14.0	15	56	12	44
Artillery	22	11.0	10	45	12	55
Engineers	9	4.5	5	56	4	44
Indian Army	14	7.0	3	21	11	79
Marines	1	0.5	1	100	0	0
Dominion	16	8.0	1	6	15	94
Total	195	100.0	99	51	96	49

Appendix 11: Analysis of staff officers

Corps/regt.	Number of officers	% of total	psc	% of group	Non psc	% of group
		MGGS, Army				
Infantry	8	53	8	100	0	0
Artillery	3	20	3	100	0	0

Engineers	1	7	1	100	0	0
Indian Army	2	13	2	100	0	0
Dominion	1	7	1	100	0	0
Total	15	100	15	100	0	0
		BGGS, Corps				
Infantry	28	42	28	100	0	0
Guards	3	4	3	100	0	0
Cavalry	5	8	5	100	0	0
Artillery	17	25	15	88	2	12
Engineers	5	8	5	100	0	0
Indian Army	7	10	4	57	3	43
Dominion	2	3	2	100	0	0
Total	67	100	62	93	5	7

Corps/regt.	Number of officers	% of total	psc	% of group	Non psc	% of group
		GSO1, Division				
Infantry	133	48.0	109	82	24	18
Guards	8	3.0	6	75	2	25
Cavalry	22	8.0	17	77	5	23
Artillery	50	18.0	44	88	6	12
Engineers	18	6.5	13	72	5	28
Indian Army	26	9.5	24	92	2	8
Marines	4	1.5	3	75	1	25
Civilian	1	0.5	0	0	1	100
Dominion	13	5.0	2	6	11	94
Total	275	100.0	218	79	57	21

Appendix 12: Analysis of staff at GHQ

Corps/regt.	Number of officers	% of total	psc	% of group	Non psc	% of group
		CGS, GHQ				
Cavalry	2	100	2	100	0	0
Infantry	2	100	2	100	0	0
Total	4	100	4	100	0	0
		MGGS, GHQ				
Infantry	3	75	3	100	0	0
Guards	1	25	1	100	0	0
Total	4	100	4	100	0	0
		BGGS, GHQ				
Infantry	8	40	8	100	0	0
Guards	1	5	1	100	0	0

(Continued)

Corps/regt.	Number of officers	% of total	psc	% of group	Non psc	% of group
Cavalry	2	10	2	100	0	0
Artillery	2	10	2	100	0	0
Engineers	6	30	5	83	1	17
Indian Army	1	5	1	100	0	0
Total	20	100	19	95	1	5

Corps/regt.	Number of officers	% of total	psc	% of group	Non psc	% of group
		GSO1, GHQ				
Infantry	15	31.3	11	73	4	27
Guards	2	4.2	2	100	0	0
Cavalry	1	2.0	1	100	0	23
Artillery	16	33.3	14	88	2	12
Engineers	8	16.7	6	75	2	25
Indian Army	2	4.2	2	100	0	0
Civilian	4	8.3	0	0	4	100
Total	48	100.0	36	75	12	25

Appendix 13: Average ages of army commanders

Corps/regt.	Number of officers	% of total	psc	Non psc	Average age
		5 August 1914			
Cavalry	1	100	0	1	62
		10 March 1915			
Infantry	1	50	1	0	57
Cavalry	1	50	1	0	54
Total	2	100	2	0	55
		25 September 1915			
Infantry	2	67	2	0	57
Cavalry	1	33	1	0	54
Total	3	100	3	0	56
		1 July 1916			
Infantry	2	50	2	0	58
Guards	1	25	1	0	52
Cavalry	1	46	1	0	55
Total	4	100	4	0	54

Corps/regt.	Number of officers	% of total	psc	Non psc	Average age
		31 July 1917			
Infantry	1	20	1	0	60
Guards	1	20	1	0	53
Cavalry	2	40	2	0	51
Artillery	1	20	0	1	56
Total	5	100	4	1	54
		11 November 1918			
Infantry	1	20	1	0	61
Guards	1	20	1	0	54
Cavalry	1	20	1	0	56
Artillery	1	20	0	1	57
Indian Army	1	20	0	1	51
Total	5	100	3	2	56

Appendix 14: Average ages of corps commanders

Corps/regt.	Number of officers	% of total	psc	Non psc	Average age
		5 August 1914			
Infantry	1	50	1	0	56
Cavalry	1	50	1	0	53
Total	2	100	2	0	54.5
		10 March 1915			
Infantry	2	25.0	2	0	57
Guards	3	37.5	1	2	52
Cavalry	2	25.0	1	1	56
Indian Army	1	12.5	0	1	58
Total	8	100.0	4	4	55
		25 September 1915			
Infantry	5	35.71	4	1	55
Guards	3	21.43	1	2	52
Cavalry	4	28.57	2	2	53
Artillery	2	14.29	1	1	59
Total	14	100.00	8	6	54

Corps/regt.	Number of officers	% of total	psc	Non psc	Average age
		1 July 1916			
Infantry	5	26.32	4	1	54
Guards	4	21.05	1	3	52
Cavalry	4	21.05	2	2	52
Artillery	3	15.79	2	1	58

(Continued)

Corps/regt.	Number of officers	% of total	psc	Non psc	Average age
Engineers	1	5.26	1	0	52
Indian Army	2	10.53	0	2	52
Total	19	100.00	10	9	54
		31 July 1917			
Infantry	7	33.33	5	2	57
Guards	5	23.81	2	3	53
Cavalry	1	4.76	0	1	53
Artillery	4	19.05	2	2	56
Engineers	1	4.76	1	0	53
Indian Army	2	9.52	0	2	53
Dominion	1	4.76	0	1	42
Total	21	100.00	10	11	55

Corps/regt.	Number of officers	% of total	psc	Non psc	Average age
		11 November 1918			
Infantry	8	44.44	7	1	54
Guards	2	11.11	1	1	53
Cavalry	2	11.11	1	1	54
Artillery	1	5.56	0	1	56
Engineers	2	11.11	2	0	54
Indian Army	1	5.56	0	1	55
Dominion	2	11.11	0	2	48
Total	18	100.00	11	7	53

Appendix 15: Average ages of divisional commanders

Corps/regt.	Number of officers	% of total	psc	Non psc	Average age
		5 August 1914			
Infantry	4	57.14	4	0	55
Guards	1	14.29	0	1	49
Cavalry	1	14.29	1	0	53
Artillery	1	14.29	1	0	58
Total	7	100.00	6	1	55
		10 March 1915			
Infantry	9	50.00	7	2	53
Guards	1	5.56	1	0	50
Cavalry	4	22.22	3	1	50
Artillery	2	11.11	0	2	55
Indian Army	2	11.11	0	2	54
Total	18	100.00	12	7	53

		25 September 1915			
Infantry	15	36.59	10	5	54
Guards	2	4.88	1	1	52
Cavalry	5	12.20	0	5	52
Artillery	7	17.07	3	4	53
Engineers	1	2.44	1	0	50
Indian Army	8	19.51	1	7	55
Dominion	3	7.32	0	1	46
Total	41	100.00	16	25	53

Corps/regt.	Number of officers	% of total	psc	Non psc	Average age
		1 July 1916			
Infantry	28	46.66	16	12	54
Guards	4	6.67	4	0	53
Cavalry	9	15.00	5	4	47
Artillery	5	8.33	2	3	54
Engineers	2	3.33	1	1	53
Indian Army	6	10.00	3	3	52
Domimion	5	8.33	0	5	48
Royal Marine	1	1.67	1	0	55
Total	60	100.00	31	29	52
		31 July 1917			
Infantry	30	44.78	18	12	51
Guards	6	8.96	2	4	52
Cavalry	12	17.91	6	6	50
Artillery	6	8.96	3	3	54
Engineers	5	7.46	2	3	51
Indian Army	1	1.49	0	1	51
Dominion	7	10.45	1	6	51
Total	67	100.00	32	35	50

Corps/regt.	Number of officers	% of total	psc	Non psc	Average age
		11 November 1918			
Infantry	34	51.51	19	15	48
Guards	4	6.06	0	4	47
Cavalry	9	13.64	3	6	48
Artillery	5	7.58	2	3	50
Engineers	6	9.09	3	3	50
Dominion	8	12.12	1	7	49
Total	66	100.00	28	38	49

Appendix 16: Schooling of senior commanders

Corps/regt.	Total of officers	% of total	Public school	% of group	Non-public school	% of group
		Commanders-in-Chief of the BEF				
Cavalry	2	100	1	50	1	50
		Army commanders of the BEF				
Infantry	3	30	1	33.3	2	66.7
Guards	1	10	1	100.0	0	0
Cavalry	4	40	4	100.0	0	0
Artillery	1	10	1	0	0	0
Indian Army	1	10	1	100.0	0	0
Total	10	100	9	80	2	20
		Corps commanders of the BEF				
Infantry	19	40	14	74	5	26
Guards	6	12	6	100	0	0
Cavalry	10	21	9	90	1	10
Artillery	7	15	5	71	2	29
Engineers	2	4	1	50	1	50
Indian Army	2	4	2	100	0	50
Dominion	2	4	0	0	2	100
Total	48	100	37	77	23	44

Corps/regt.	Total of officers	% of total	Public school	% of group	Non-public school	% of group
		Divisional commanders of the BEF				
Infantry	90	46.0	65	72	25	28
Guards	15	8.0	14	93	1	7
Cavalry	27	14.0	19	70	8	30
Artillery	22	11.0	14	64	8	36
Engineers	9	4.5	7	78	2	22
Indian Army	15	8.0	9	60	6	40
Marines	1	0.5	1	100	0	0
Dominion	16	8.0	2	13	14	88
Total	195	100.0	131	67	64	33

Appendix 17: Schooling of senior staff officers

Corps/regt.	Total of officers	% of total	Public school	% of group	Non-public school	% of group
		MGGS, Army				
Infantry	8	53	8	100	0	0
Artillery	3	20	3	100	0	0

Engineers	1	7	1	100	0	0
Indian Army	2	13	2	100	0	0
Dominion	1	7	1	100	0	0
Total	15	100	15	100	0	0

BGGS, Corps

Infantry	28	42	28	100	0	0
Guards	3	4	3	100	0	0
Cavalry	5	8	5	100	0	0
Artillery	17	25	15	88	2	12
Engineers	5	8	5	100	0	0
Indian Army	7	10	4	57	3	43
Dominion	2	3	2	100	0	0
Total	67	100	62	93	5	7

Corps/regt.	Number of officers	% of total	psc	% of group	Non psc	% of group
			GSO1, Division			
Infantry	133	48.0	109	82	24	18
Guards	8	3.0	6	75	2	25
Cavalry	22	8.0	17	77	5	23
Artillery	50	18.0	44	88	6	12
Engineers	18	6.5	13	72	5	28
Indian Army	26	9.5	24	92	2	8
Marines	4	1.5	3	75	1	25
Civilian	1	0.5	0	0	1	100
Dominion	13	5.0	2	6	11	94
Total	275	100.0	218	79	57	21

Appendix 18: Changes in senior commands during the war

Year	Division comdrs	% of total	Corps comdrs	% of total	Army comdrs	% of total
1914	12	14	2	5.0	0	0
1915	64	22	9	22.0	3	33.4
1916	62	21	13	31.5	2	22.2
1917	70	24	4	10.0	2	22.2
1918	83	29	13	31.5	2	22.2
Total	291	100	41	100.0	9	100.0

Bibliography

Unpublished official records

Public Record Office of England and Wales, Kew, London

Papers of the Cabinet and its Committees

CABINET FILES

CAB1/25	Cabinet Minutes, 1917
CAB1/27	Cabinet Minutes, 1917
CAB21/22	Cambrai Enquiry, 1917

OFFICIAL WAR HISTORIES CORRESPONDENCE AND PAPERS

CAB45/116	Arras, 1917
CAB45/118	Cambrai, 1917
CAB45/119	La Becque, 1918
CAB45/120	Loos, 1915
CAB45/122–125	Lys, 1918
CAB45/127	Messines, 1914
CAB45/129	Mons and Le Cateau, 1914
CAB45/130	St. Eloi, 1916
CAB45/132–138	Somme, 1916
CAB45/139	Vimy Ridge, 1916
CAB45/140–145	Ypres, 1917
CAB45/184	Third Army
CAB45/192–193	March 1918
CAB45/208	Memoir of General Lord Freyberg

Papers of the War Office

WAR OFFICE REGISTERED FILES

WO32/3116	Report of Committee to study Lessons of the Great War
WO32/4730	Staff Duties in the Field
WO32/4731	War Office: Staff Manual 1912
WO32/5095B	Cambrai Enquiry

WO32/5097	Operations of Fifth Army, April 1918
WO32/5146–7	Transport on the Western Front
WO32/5153	Staff Reorganisation
WO32/5154	Conferences to consider tactical use of tanks, 1917
WO32/5163–4	Transport – Investigation by Sir E. Geddes
WO32/5754	Formation of Tank Supply Committee
WO32/5933	Proposals for Formation of Tank Armies
WO32/6941	Staff College
WO32/8937	Visit of H.H. Wilson to Paris
WO32/8938	Staff College
WO32/8940	Staff College
WO32/9288	Foundation of Duties of Mechanised Warfare (Overseas & Allies) Department of Ministry of Munitions, 1917–18
WO32/10776	History of DMI
WO32/11239	Formation of Machine Gun Corps, 1915
WO32/11393	Progress Reports by GOC Machine Gun Corps (Heavy)
WO32/11394	Future Organisation of Machine Gun Corps in France, 1917–18

O AND A PAPERS

WO33/723	Registration of Targets and Calibration, 1915
WO33/831	Sound Ranging, 1917
WO33/11376	Report on Special Brigade RE, 1919

WAR DIARIES

WO95/1–24	GHQ, 1914–18
WO95/91–5	Tank Corps, 1917–20
WO95/120	Special Brigade RE, 1915–19
WO95/127	Camouflage Park RE, 1915–18
WO95/154–65	First Army, 1914–16
WO95/172	First Army, 1917
WO95/187	RE Committee, 1919–20
WO95/275	Second Army, 1917
WO95/366–70	Third Army, 1917–18
WO95/433–8	Fourth Army, 1917–18
WO95/520	Fifth Army, 1917
WO95/590–2	I Corps, 1915
WO95/707–12	IV Corps, 1915
WO95/880	XI Corps, 1915
WO95/895	XIII Corps, 1916

DIRECTORATE OF MILITARY OPERATIONS AND INTELLIGENCE

WO106/45	History of Ib, GHQ
WO106/49A/9	Mobilization Appointments
WO106/360	Organization of GHQ
WO106/401–28	DMO's files
WO106/1510–7	DMI's files

MILITARY HEADQUARTERS PAPERS

WO158/17–20	GHQ: General Staff Notes on Operations, 1915–18
WO158/21–25	GHQ: Secretary of State for War and CIGS File, 1915–18
WO158/70	GHQ: Notes on Recent Fighting, 1918
WO158/181–92	First Army
WO158/199	First Army: Vimy and Thelus, 1917
WO158/201–15	Second Army
WO158/221–8	Third Army, 1916–18
WO158/233–43	Fourth Army, 1916–18
WO158/245–54	Fifth Army, 1916–18
WO158/258	First Army: Neuve Chapelle, 1915
WO158/261–68	First Army: Loos, 1915
WO158/298	Lessons of Messines, 1917
WO158/304–8	Messines, 1917
WO158/314–20	Cambrai, 1917
WO158/321–31	Fourth Army, 1916
WO158/344	Fifth Army, 1916
WO158/374	IV Corps: Neuve Chapelle, 1915
WO158/831–65	GHQ: Questions relating to Tanks, 1915–18
WO158/897–8	Charteris-Macdonogh Correspondence
WO158/961	Reorganization of Intelligence Branch, GHQ, 1917

Unpublished private records

PRO30/57	Field-Marshal Lord Kitchener
WO79/62	General Sir Archibald Murray
WO79/66	Field-Marshal Earl of Cavan
WO256	Diaries of Field-Marshal Earl Haig

Unpublished private records

Churchill Archive Centre, Churchill College, Cambridge

Bonham-Carter, General Sir Charles
Cavan, Field-Marshal Earl
Rawlinson, General Lord

Imperial war museum, Lambeth, London

Department of Documents

Allanson, Colonel C.J.L.
Anderson, Lieutenant-General Sir Hastings
Archibald, Major-General S.C.M.
Ashmore, Major-General E.B.
Athlone, Brigadier-General Earl of
Barnardiston, Major-General N.W.
Barrow, Squadron Leader P.
Battine, Captain C.W.

Birdwood, Field-Marshal Lord
Blumenfeld, R.D.
Boraston, Lieutenant-Colonel J.H.
Bowly, Colonel W.A.T.
Bradford, Brigadier-General R.B.
Bruce-Williams, Major-General Sir Hugh
Bush, Captain E.W. (R.N.)
Butler, Lieutenant-General Sir Richard
Butler, Major-General S.S.
Carleton, Brigadier-General F.M.
Chetwode, Field-Marshal Lord
Clark, Captain C.
Craig-Brown, Brigadier-General E.
Crookenden, Colonel A.
Cunliffe-Owen, Lieutenant-Colonel F.
Cude, R.
Dartford, Captain R.C.G.
Dawnay, Major-General G.P.
Deverell, Field-Marshal Sir Cyril
Dillon, Brigadier Viscount
Dudgeon, Major-General F.A.
Dunnington-Jefferson, Lieutenant-Colonel Sir John
Egerton, Major-General G.G.A.
Fanshawe, Lieutenant-General Sir Hew
Fife, Lieutenant-Colonel R.D'A.
Fitzgerald, Lieutenant-Colonel B.
FitzGerald, Lieutenant-Colonel P.P.
Floyer-Acland, Lieutenant-General A.N.
Foot, Brigadier R.C.
Forward, R.G.
Fourth Army, Records of
French, Field-Marshal Sir John
Game, Air Vice Marshal Sir Philip
Gattie, Major-General K.D.B.
Hawksley, Brigadier-General R.P.T.
Henderson, Lieutenant-Colonel K.
Heneker, General Sir William
Henley, Brigadier-General Hon A.M.
Hodgkin, Brigadier A.E.
Home, Brigadier-General Sir Archibald
Hore-Ruthven, Colonel C.M.
Horne, General Lord
Hotblack, Major-General F.E.
Ironside, Field-Marshal Lord
James, Wing Commander Sir Archibald
Jeudwine, Lieutenant-General Sir Hugh
Johnson, A.
Keary, Lieutenant-General Sir Henry
Kirke, General Sir Walter
Kirkpatrick, Sir Ivone

Lambert, Colonel T.S.
Lanyon, Major O.M.
Lee, Lieutenant-Colonel A.N.
Lloyd-Williams, Lieutenant-Colonel H.
Loch, Major-General Lord
Lush, Brigadier M.S.
Lynden-Bell, Maajor-General Sir Arthur
MacDougall, Major-General A.I.
Maxse, General Sir Ivor
May, Captain C.C.
Micklem, Brigadier R.
Miller, Captain C.C.
Montgomery, Field-Marshal Viscount
Morland, General Sir Thomas
Murray, General Sir Archibald
Murray, Lieutenant-Colonel W.A.
Muspratt, General Sir Sydney
Nicholson, Major-General Sir Cecil
Paris, Major-General Sir Archibald
Patterson, Second Lieutenant W.
Peel, Lieutenant-Colonel W.R.
Pigot, Brigadier-General Sir Robert
Pinney, Major-General Sir Reginald
Reynolds, Lieutenant-Colonel L.L.C.
Robins, P.
Robins, W.
Roupell, Brigadier G.R.P.
Rylands, H.J.
Schweder, Major R.P.
Sceales, Lieutenant-Colonel G.A.McL.
Seymour, Lieutenant-Colonel G.A.
Slingsby, Lieutenant-Colonel T.
Smith, H.W.
Smith-Dorrien, General Sir Horace
Snow, Lieutenant-General Sir Thomas
Spurrell, Lieutenant-Colonel H.W.
Stephens, General Sir Reginald
Sterndale-Bennett, Captain J.B.
Stevens, Brigadier-General G.A.
Strickland, General Sir Peter
Surtees, Major-General G.
Thomas, Lieutenant G.H.
Thompson, Lieutenant A.
Trevor, Lieutenant-Colonel H.E.
Wedgwood, Colonel J.C. (later Lord Barlaston)
Whitefoord, Major-General P.G.
Wilson, Field-Marshal Sir Henry
Wimberley, Major-General D.N.
Wollocombe, Lieutenant-Colonel T.S.

Woodroffe, Brigadier-General C.R.
Woods, Brigadier-General H.K.
Woodward, Captain O.H.

Department of Printed Books

CDS 1–388   Large Collection of Stationery Service publications issued by GHQ and
             the War Office, 1914–19
SS 29–1035

Liddell Hart Centre for Military Archives, King's College, London

Alanbrooke, Field-Marshal Viscount Alanbrooke
Allenby, Field-Marshal Viscount
Barnardiston, Major-General N.W.
Beddington, Brigadier Sir Edward
Bonham-Carter, Victor
Burnett-Stuart, General Sir John
Cadoux-Hudson, Brigadier P.H.
Carr, Lieutenant-General Sir Laurence
Clive, General Sir (George) Sidney
Davidson, Major-General F.H.N.
Dill Field-Marshal Sir John
Edmonds, Brigadier-General Sir James
Fuller, Major-General J.F.C.
Godley, General Sir Alexander
Grant, General Sir Charles
Howell, Brigadier-General P.
Hutton, Lieutenant-General Sir Thomas
Jeffries, Brigadier W.F.
Kiggell, Lieutenant-General Sir Launcelot
Liddell Hart, Captain Sir Basil
Lister, Lieutenant-Colonel F.H.
McCrae, Colonel Sir George
Macleod, Colonel R.
Maurice, Major-General Sir Frederick
Maze, Paul
Montgomery-Massingberd, Field-Marshal Sir Archibald
Robertson, Field-Marshal Sir William
Simpson-Baikie, Brigadier-General H.A.D.
Swinton, Major-General Sir Ernest
Wynne, Captain G.C.

National Army Museum, Chelsea, London

Barley, Lieutenant H.
Barrow, General Sir George
Broadwood, Lieutenant-General R.G.

Central Training Camp, Etaples
Cunningham, General Sir Alan
de Burgh, General Sir Eric
de Pree, Major-General H.D.
Fergusson, Lieutenant-Colonel R.H.
Grove, Colonel T.T.
Hunter-Weston, Lieutenant-General Sir Aylmer
Loch, Major-General Lord
Marker, Colonel R.J.
Maxwell, Brigadier-General F.A.
Maxwell, Brigadier-General L.L.
Milward, General C.A.
Monro, General Sir Charles
Oliver, Captain O.M.
Ponsonby, General Sir John
Rawlinson, General Lord
Ruggles-Brise, Major-General Sir Harold
Spence Edge, W.M.

National Library of Scotland, Edinburgh

Davidson, Major-General Sir John
Field-Marshal Earl Haig
Haldane, General Sir Aylmer
Lawrence, General Hon Sir Herbert

Royal Artillery Institution, Woolwich, London

Anstey, Brigadier E.C.
Rawlins, Colonel S.W.H.
Tudor, Major-General Sir Hugh
Uniacke, Lieutenant-General Sir Herbert

Scottish Record Office, Edinburgh

Hope of Craighall Muniments
Matthew of Gourdiehall Muniments
Papers of Major J.A.B. Urquhart
Papers of Lord Waring of Lennel

Printed primary sources (published in London except where stated)

Manuals and pamphlets

Addresses on Leadership, Esprit De Corps and Moral, Brigadier-General R.J. Kentish (Gale & Polden, 1917)

Artillery Survey in the First World War, Sir Lawrence Bragg (Field Survey Association, 1971)

Cavalry Studies, Major-General D. Haig (1907)

Company Training, Brigadier-General R.C.B. Haking (Hugh Rees, 1914)

The Operation of War, Sir Edward Hamley (1907)

Field Service Pocket Book, 1914, General Staff, War Office (HMSO, 1914)

Field Service Regulations, Part 1, Operations, 1909, General Staff, War Office (HMSO, 1912)

Field Service Regulations, Part 1, Operations, 1909, General Staff, War Office (HMSO, 1914)

A General's Letters to His Son on Obtaining His Commission, [Major-General T.D. Pilcher] (Cassell, 1917)

German Notes On Minor Tactics, US Army War College (Government Printing Office, Washington, 1918)

Impressions and Reflections of a French Company Commander Regarding the Attack (HMSO, 1916)

Infantry Training, 1914, General Staff, War Office (HMSO, 1914)

Lecture delivered by Brig.-General R.A.K. Montgomery, CB, DSO, at the Camp of the 8th Division, near Winchester, on the 30th October, 1914 (HMSO, 1914)

Manual of Field Engineering, 1911, General Staff, War Office (HMSO, 1916)

Manual of Map Reading and Field Sketching, 1912, General Staff, War Office (HMSO, 1912)

The Maxims of the late Field-Marshal Viscount Wolseley, Brigadier-General R.J. Kentish (Gale & Polden, 1917)

Minor Tactics, Brigadier-General C. Francis Clery (Kegan Paul, 1893)

Our Military Problem For Civilian Readers, Captain F.I. Maxse (J.M. Dent, 1896)

Notes on Platoon and Company Drill, General Staff, War Office (Harrison & Sons, 1916)

The Principles of War, Major-General E.A. Altham (2 volumes, Macmillan, 1914)

The Rifle Brigade Chronicle, Anon. (1914)

The Solution of Tactical Problems: A Logical and Easy Way of Working Out the Tactical Schemes Set at Examinations, Lieutenant-Colonel J. Layland Needham (Hugh Rees, 1911)

Staff Rides and Regimental Tours, Brigadier-General R.C.B. Haking (Hugh Rees, 1912)

School Registers and War Memorial Lists for

Aberdeen Grammar School
Aldenham School
Bedford School
Birkonians
Bishops Stortford College
Bradfield College
Brighton College
Carlisle Grammar School
Charterhouse
Cheltenham College
Clifton College
Dover College

Downside
Dragon School
Dulwich College
Old Dunelmians
Dumferline High School
Eastbourne College
Epsom College
Eton College
Fettes College
George Heriot's School
Glasgow Academicals
Haileybury
Harrow
Hillhead High School
Kelly's College, Tavistock
King Edward's School, Birmingham
Lancing College
Leys School
Loretto
Malvern College
Marlborough College
Merchant Taylors
Merchiston Castle School
Mill Hill
Old Ride School
Oundle
Radley College
Repton
Rossall
Royal Grammar School, Newcastle
Royal High School
Rugby
St Edward's School, Oxford
St Paul's School
Sedburgh
Sherborne
Shrewsbury
Stonyhurst
Stowe
Tonbridge
United Services College, Westward Ho!
University College School, London
Uppingham
Victoria College, Jersey
Watford Grammar School
Watsonians
Wellington College
Whitgift
Winchester College

Works of reference

Army Lists [British Army], 1900–45
Australian Encyclopedia
British Regiments, 1914–1918, Brigadier E.A. James (Samson Books, 1978)
Canadian Who's Who
Concise Dictionary of National Biography
Debrett's Illustrated Peerage, Baronetage and Knightage
Debrett's Peerage, Baronetage, Knightage, and Companionage
Dictionary of National Biography
Dictionary of New Zealand Biography
Handbook of British Regiments, Christopher Chant (Routledge, 1988)
Indian Army Lists, 1914–47
Kelly's Handbook to the Titled, Landed and Official Classes, 1914–77
Obituaries from The Times, 1950–1975
Officers Died in the Great War, 1914–1919 (HMSO, 1919)
Orders of Battle of Divisions, History of the Great War, Major A.F. Becke (compiler Parts 1–4, HMSO, 1934–45) and F.W. Perry (compiler Part 5, Ray Westlake, 1992–93)
Oxford Companion to Australian Military History (Oxford University Press Australia, 1995)
Register of the Victoria Cross
Statistics of the Military Effort of the British Empire during the Great War, War Office (HMSO, 1922)
The VC and DSO, Sir O'Moore Creagh and E.M. Humphris (3 volumes, Standard Art Book Co, no date)
Who Was Who, 1897–1980
Who's Who, 1900–1994
Who's Who in Australia
Who's Who in New Zealand
The Wisden Book of Obituaries: Obituaries from Wisden Cricketers' Almanack, 1892–1985

Secondary sources (published in London except where stated)

Articles, pamphlets, and unpublished theses

Badsey, Dr Stephen, *The Trench Raid at Cherisy, 15 September 1917* (Imperial War Museum Review No. 4, 1989)
Bailey, Jonathan, *The First World War and the Birth of the Modern style of Warfare* (Strategic & Combat Studies Institute, The Occasional, No. 22, 1996)
Bittner, Dr Donald F., *A Ghost of a General: Royal Marine Officers and the Promotion Crisis of the Pre-World War I Era* (Royal Marines Historical Society, Eastney, 1984)
Broad, Lieutenant-Colonel C.N.F., *The Development of Artillery Tactics, 1914–1918* (*Journal of the Royal Artillery*, May and June 1922)
Cave, Colonel Terry, *The Dismissal of Major General Barter* (STAND TO!, The Journal of the Western Front Association, No. 34, 1992)
Cook, Donald, *Divisional Commander in France: General Sir David Campbell* (The Quarterly and Defence Journal, Volume 118, No. 2, April 1988)

De Groot, Gerard J., *The Pre-War Life and Military Career of Douglas Haig* (PhD Thesis, Edinburgh University, 1983)

de Pree, Major-General H.D., *The 38th (Welsh) Division in the Last Five Weeks of the Great War*, Chapters I–III, p. 486, *Journal of the Royal Artillery*, Volume LVIII, No. 3.

Edmonds, Brigadier-General Sir James E. *et al.*, *Four Generations of Staff College Students – 1896 to 1952* (The Army Quarterly, Volume LXV, October 1952)

Falls, Captain Cyril, *Contacts With Troops: Commanders and Staffs in the First World War* (The Army Quarterly, Volume LXXXVIII, No. 2, July 1964)

Hammond, Bryn, *General Harper and the Failure of 51st (Highland) Division at Cambrai, 20 November 1917* (Imperial War Museum Review No. 10, 1995)

Holden Reid, Brian, *War Studies at the Staff College, 1890–1930* (Strategic and Combat Studies Institute, 1991)

Holloway, S.M., *From Trench and Turret: Royal Marines Letters and Diaries 1914–1918* (Royal Marines Museum, no date)

Hughes, Albert Colin, The Capture of Mametz Wood: A Study of Lloyd George's 'Welsh Army' at the Battle of the Somme 1916 (MPhil Thesis, London University, 1975)

Hussey, John, *A Hard Day at First Ypres: The Allied Generals and their Problems: 31st October 1914* (The British Army Review, No. 107, 1994)

Jones, Robert F., *The Kipkororor Chronicles* [Meinertzhagen in East Africa] (MHO: The Quarterly Journal of Military History, Volume 3, No. 3, 1991)

Kirke, Brian St. George, *General Sir Walter Kirke, Part I: Subaltern to Major – 1896 to 1914* (The Army Quarterly and Defence Journal, Volume 115, No. 4, October 1985)

Kirke, Brian St. George, *General Sir Walter Kirke, Part II – 1914 to 1933: Half Pay and 'Odd Jobs'* (The Army Quarterly and Defence Journal, Volume 116, No. 1, January 1986)

Kirke, Brian St. George, *General Sir Walter Kirke, Part III: Champion of the TA, 1933–40* (The Army Quarterly and Defence Journal, Volume 116, No. 2, April 1986)

Little, Matthew, *Royal Marine Victoria Crosses* (Royal Marines Museum, n.d.)

MacLeod Ross, Brevet Major G., *The Death of a Division: The 39th Division in March 1918* (The Fighting Forces, Volume VII, No. 1, April 1930)

Mallinson, Allan, *Charging Ahead: Transforming Britain's Cavalry, 1902–14* (History Today, Volume 42, 1992)

Montgomery-Massingberd, Field-Marshal Sir Archibald, *The Autobiography of a Gunner* (Journal of the Royal Artillery, Volume LXXIII, No. 4, and Volume LXXIV, Nos 1–2, 1946–47).

Otley, Christopher Blackwood, *The Origins and Recruitment of the British Army Elite, 1870–1959* (PhD Thesis, University of Hull, 1965)

Otley, C.B., *The Educational Background of British Army Officers* (Sociology, Volume 7, Clarendon Press, 1973)

Perry, Nicholas, *General Nugent and the Ulster Division in the March 1918 Retreat* (Imperial War Museum Review No. 12, 1999)

Philpott, William, *The Great Landing: Haig's Plan to Invade Belgium from the Sea in 1917* (Imperial War Museum Review No. 10, 1995)

Pitman, Major-General T.T., *Cavalry in the Trenches* (Cavalry Journal No. 80)

Preston, Major T., *The Cavalry at Arras, 1917* (Cavalry Journal, No. 82)

Preston, Major T., *The Cavalry in France, 1918* (Cavalry Journal, [1942])

Rawlinson, Brigadier-General Sir H.S., *Night Operations* (Journal of the RUSI, Volume 52, No. 364, June 1908)

Razzell, P.E., *Social Origins of the Indian and British Home Army: 1758–1962* (The British Journal of Sociology, Volume 14, Routledge & Kegan Paul, 1963)

Robbins, Simon, *The Ethos of the British Army during the First World War* (Imperial War Museum Review No. 5, 1991)

Robinson, Andrew, *Eton and the First World War* (Imperial War Museum Review No. 8, 1993)

Scales, Robert H., Jr, *Artillery in Small Wars: The Evolution of British Artillery Doctrine, 1860–1914* (PhD Thesis, Duke University, 1976)

Simkins, Peter, *Somme Footnote: The Battle of the Ancre and the Struggle for Frankfurt Trench, November 1916* (Imperial War Museum Review No. 9, 1994)

Thorne, I.D.P., *Kiggell* (Army Quarterly & Defence Journal, Volume 119, No. 4, October 1989)

Towle, Philip, *The Russo-Japanese War and British Military Thought* (RUSI Journal, Volume 116, No. 664, 1971)

Travers, T.H.E., *The Offensive and the Problem of Innovation in British Military Thought, 1870–1915* (The Journal of Contemporary History, Volume 13, 1978)

Travers, T.H.E., *The Hidden Army: Structural Problems in the British Officer Corps, 1900–1918* (The Journal of Contemporary History, Volume 17, 1982)

Travers, T.H.E., *Learning and Decision-making on the Western Front, 1915–16* (Canadian Journal of History, April 1983)

Autobiographies, biographies and novels

Adair, Major-General Sir Allan, *A Guards' General* (Hamish Hamilton, London, 1986)

Adams, Bernard, *Nothing of Importance: A Record of Eight Months at the Front with a Welsh Battalion* (Reissued, The Strong Oak Press/Tom Donovan Publishing, Stevenage, Herts, 1988)

Adye, Major-General Sir John, *Soldiers and Others I Have Known* (Herbert Jenkins, London, 1925)

Aitken, Alexander, *Gallipoli to the Somme: Recollections of a New Zealand Infantryman* (Oxford University Press, Oxford, 1963)

Alderson, Brevet-Lieutenant-Colonel E.A.H., *With the Mounted Infantry and the Mashonaland Field Force, 1896* (Methuen, London, 1898)

Aldington, Richard, *Death of A Hero* (Consul Books, London, 1965)

Alexander, Michael, *True Blue: The life and Adventures of Colonel fred Burnaby, 1842–85* (Rupert hart-Davis, London, 1957)

Allanson, Colonel C.J.L. (edited by Harry Davies), *Allanson of the 6th: An Account of the Life of Colonel Cecil John Lyons Allanson CMG CIE DSO, 6th Gurkha Rifles* (A Square One Publication, Worcester, 1990)

Applin, Colonel R.V.K., *Across the Seven Seas* (Chapman & Hall, London, 1937)

Arthur, Sir George, *Lord Haig* (William Heinemann, London, 1928)

Arthur, Sir George, *General Sir John Maxwell* (John Murray, London, 1932)

Ash, Bernard, *The Lost Dictator: A Biography of Field-Marshal Sir Henry Wilson* (Cassell, London, 1968)

Ash, Eric, *Sir Frederick Sykes and the Air Revolution, 1912–1918* (Frank Cass, London, 1999)

Ashurst, George (edited by Richard), *My Bit: A Lancashire Fusilier at War, 1914–1918* (The Crowood Press, Marlborough, Wiltshire, 1987)

Ashmead-Bartlett, Major S., *From the Somme to the Rhine* (Bodley Head, London, 1921)

Asquith, Herbert H. (edited by Michael and Eleanor Brock), *H.H. Asquith: Letters to Venetia Stanley* (Oxford University Press, Oxford, 1982)

Asquith, Herbert H., *Moments of Memory: Recollections and Impressions* (Hutchinson, London, n.d.)

Aston, Sir George, *Secret Service* (Faber & Faber, London, 1930)

Bacon, Captain A.F.L., *The Wanderings of a Temporary Warrior* (Witherby, London, 1922)

Baker-Carr, Brigadier-General C.D., *From Chauffeur to Brigadier* (Ernest Benn, London, 1930)

Ballard, Brigadier-General C.R., *Kitchener* (Faber & Faber, London, 1930)

Ballard, Brigadier-General C.R., *Smith-Dorrien* (Constable, London, 1931)

Barnett, Corelli, *The Swordbearers: Studies in Supreme Command in the First World War* (Eyre & Spottiswoode, London, 1966)

Barrow, General Sir George, *Life of Sir Charles Carmichael Monro* (Hutchinson, 1931)

Barrow, General Sir George de S., *The Fire of Life* (Hutchinson, London, n.d.)

Barton, E.C., *Let the Boy Win His Spurs* (Resarch Publishing, London, 1976)

Baynes, John, *The Forgotten Victor: General Sir Richard O'Connor* (Brassey's, London, 1989)

Baynes, John, *Far From A Donkey: The Life of General Sir Ivor Maxse* (Brassey's, London, 1995)

Bean, C.E.W., *Two Men I Knew: William Bridges and Brudenell White, Founders of the A.I.F.* (Angus & Robertson, London, Sydney, 1957)

Beauman, Brigadier-General A.B., *Then a Soldier* (P.R. Macmillan, London, 1959)

Beaverbrook, Lord, *Men and Power, 1917–1918* (Hutchinson, London, 1956)

Beaverbrook, Lord, *Politicians and the War* (Oldbourne, London, 1960)

Beckett, Ian F.W. (editor), *The Army and the Curragh Incident, 1914* (Army Records Society, London, 1986)

Beckett, Ian F.W., *Johnnie Gough, V.C.* (Tom Donovan, London, 1989)

Beckett, Ian F.W., *The Judgement of History: Sir Horace Smith-Dorrien, Lord French and 1914* (Tom Donovan, London, 1993)

Behrend, Arthur, *As from Kemmel Hill: An Adjutant in France and Flanders* (Eyre & Spottiswoode, London, 1963)

Bell, Captain D.H., *A Soldier's Diary of the Great War* (Faber & Faber, London, 1929)

Bion, Wilfred R. (edited by Francesca Bion), *The Long Week-end, 1897–1919: Part of a Life* (Free Association Books, London, 1986)

Birdwood, Field-Marshal Lord, *Khaki and Gown* (Ward, Lock & Co., London, 1941)

Birdwood, Field-Marshal Lord, *In My Time* (Skeffington, London, 1945)

Blacker, General Sir Cecil, *Monkey Business: The Memoirs of General Sir Cecil Blacker* (Quiller Press, London, 1993)

Blunden, Edmund, *Undertones of War* (Penguin Modern Classics, London, 1982)

Bond, Brian and Cave, Nigel (editors), *Haig: A Reappraisal 70 Years On* (Leo Cooper, London, 1999)

Bonham-Carter, Victor, *Soldier True: The Life and Times of Field-Marshal Sir Robertson* (Frederick Muller, London, 1963)

Boyle, Andrew, *Trenchard: Man of Vision* (Collins, London, 1962)

Bridges, Lieutenant-General Sir Tom, *Alarms and Excursions* (Longmans Green, London, 1938)

Brooke, Major-General Geoffrey, *The Brotherhood of Arms* (William Clowes, London, 1941)

Brownrigg, Lieutenant-General Sir Douglas, *Unexpected* (Hutchinson, London, no date)

Bruckshaw, Horace (edited by Martin Middlebrook), *The Diaries of Private Horace Bruckshaw, 1915–1916* (Scolar Press, London, 1979)

Buchan, John, *Memory Hold-the-Door* (Hodder & Stoughton, London, 1940)

Burgoyne, Gerald Achilles (edited by Claudia Davison), *The Burgoyne Diaries* (Thomas Harmsworth Publishing, 1985)

Byrne, Charlie (edited by Joy Cave), *I Survived Didn't I: The Great War Reminiscences of 'Ginger' Byrne* (Leo Cooper, London, 1992)

Callwell, Major-General Sir C.E., *The Life of Sir Stanley Maude* (Constable, London, 1920)

Callwell, Major-General Sir C.E., *Experiences of a Dug-out, 1914–1918* (Constable, London, 1920)

Callwell, Major-General Sir C.E., *Stray Recollections* (2 volumes, Edward Arnold, 1923)

Callwell, Major-General Sir C.E., *Field-Marshal Sir Henry Wilson* (2 volumes, Cassell, London, 1927)

Campbell, P.J., *The Ebb and the Flow* (Hamish Hamilton, London, 1977)

Campbell, P.J., *In the Cannon's Mouth* (Hamish Hamilton, London, 1979)

Carlisle, Christopher (editor), *My Own Darling: Letters from Monty to Kitty Carlisle* (Carlisle Books, 1989)

Carrington, C.E., *Soldier From the Wars Returning* (Hutchinson, London, 1965)

Carstairs, Carroll, *A Generation Missing* (Reissued, The Strong Oak Press with Tom Donovam Publishing, Stevenage, Herts, 1989)

Carton de Wiart, Lieutenant-General Sir Adrian, *Happy Odyssey* (Jonathon Cape, London, 1950)

Carnarvon, Earl of, *No Regrets: Memoirs of the Earl of Carnarvon* (Weidenfeld & Nicolson, London, 1976)

Carnarvon, Earl of, *Ermine Tales: More Memoirs of the Earl of Carnarvon* (Weidenfeld & Nicolson, London, 1980)

Carr, William (edited by Elizabeth Marshall), *A Time to Leave the Ploughshares: A Gunner Remembers, 1917–18* (Robert Hale, London, 1985)

Cassar, George H., *The Tragedy of Sir John French* (University of Delaware Press, Newark, 1985)

Cave Brown, Anthony, *The Secret Servant: The Life of Sir Stewart Menzies, Churchill's Spymaster* (Michael Joseph, London, 1988)

Chandos, Oliver Lyttelton, Lord, *The Memoirs of Lord Chandos* (The Bodley Head, London, 1962)

Chandos, Oliver Lyttelton, Lord, *From Peace to War: A Study in Contrast, 1857–1918* (Bodley Head, London, 1968)

Chapman, Guy (editor), *Vain Glory* (Cassell, London, 1937)

Chapman, Guy, *A Passionate Prodigality* (Reprint, Buchan & Enright, London, 1985)

Chapman, Guy, *A Kind of Survivor* (Victor Gollancz, London, 1975)

Chapman-Houston, D. and Rutter, O., *General Sir John Cowans* (2 volumes, Hutchinson, London, 1924)

Chalfont, Lord, *Montgomery of Alamein* (Weidenfeld & Nicolson, London, 1977)

[Charlton, Air Commodore L.E.O.], *Charlton* (Faber & Faber, London, 1931)

Charteris, Brigadier-General John, *Field-Marshal Earl Haig* (Cassell, London, 1929)

Charteris, Brigadier-General John, *At GHQ* (Cassell, London, 1931)

Charteris, Brigadier-General John, *Haig* (Duckworth, London, 1933)

Childs, Major-General Sir Wyndham, *Episodes and Reflections* (Cassell, London, 1930)

Chisholm, Cecil, *Sir John French* (Herbert Jenkins, London, 1915)

Churchill, Randolph, *Lord Derby, 'King of Lancashire'* (Heineman, London, 1959)

Churchill, Winston S., *The Story of the Malakand Field Force* (Mandarin Paperbacks, London, 1990)

Churchill, Winston S., *The World Crisis, 1911–18* (2 volumes, Odhams Press, 1938)

Clarke, David A. (Compiler), *Great War Memories: Soldiers' Experiences, 1914–1918* (T.H.C.L. Books, Blackburn, 1987)

Clayton, Anthony, *Three Marshals of France* (Brassey's, London, 1992)

Clayton, C.P., *The Hungry One* (Gomer Press, Llandysul Dyfed, 1978)

Cliff, Norman D., *To Hell and Back with the Guards* (Merlin Books, Braunton, Devon, 1988)

Cloete, Stuart, *How Young They Died* (Collins, London, 1969)

Cloete, Stuart, *A Victorian Son* (Collins, London, 1972)

Cocker, Mark, *Richard Meinertzhagen: Soldier, Scientist & Spy* (Secker & Warburg, London, 1989)

Collier, Basil, *Brasshat: A Biography of Field-Marshal Sir Henry Wilson* (Secker & Warburg, London, 1961)

Collins, Major-General R.J., *Lord Wavell* (Hodder & Stoughton, London, 1947)

Colville, Sir John, *Those Lambtons!: A Most Unusual Family* (Hodder & Stoughton, London, 1988)

Congreve, Commander Sir Geoffrey, *The Congreve Family* (printed privately, 1980)

Congreve, Major W. la T. (edited by Terry Norman), *Armageddon Road: A VC's Diary, 1914–1916, Billy Congreve* (William Kimber, London, 1982)

Connell, John, *Wavell: Scholar and Soldier* (Collins, London, 1961)

Cook, Charles St.G. (edited by Don Cook), *1914 Letters from a Volunteer* (Cranbourn Press, London, 1984)

Cooper, Artemis, *A Durable Fire: The Letters of Duff and Diana Cooper, 1913–1950* (Collins, London, 1983)

Coppard, George, *With a Machine-gun to Cambrai* (Imperial War Museum, 1969)

Craster, J.M. (editor), 'Fifteen Rounds a Minute', *The Grenadiers at War 1914: Edited from the Diaries of Major 'Ma' Jeffreys and Others* (Macmillan, London, 1976)

Critchley, Brigadier-General A.C., *Critch!: The Memoirs of Brigadier-General A.C. Critchley* (Hutchinson, London, 1961)

Croft, Lieutenant-Colonel W.D., *Three Years With the 9th (Scottish) Division* (John Murray, London, 1919)

Crozier, Brigadier-General F.P., *Impressions and Recollections* (T. Werner Laurie, London, 1930)

Crozier, Brigadier-General F.P., *A Brass Gat In No Man's Land* (Jonathon Cape, London, 1930)

Crozier, Brigadier-General F.P., *Five Years Hard* (1932)

Crozier, Brigadier-General F.P., *The Men I Killed* (Michael Joseph, London, 1937)

Crutchley, C.E., *Machine Gunner, 1914–1918: Personal Experiences of the Machine Gun Corps* (Revised Edition, Purnell Book Services, 1975)

Cumming, Brigadier-General Hanway R., *A Brigadier in France, 1917–1918* (Jonathon Cape, London, 1922)

Danchev, Alex, *Alchemist of War: The Life of Basil Liddell Hart* (Weidenfeld and Nicolson, London, 1998)

Dancocks, Daniel G., *Sir Arthur Currie: A Biography* (Methuen, Ontario, London, 1985)

Darling, Sir William Y., *So It Looks To Me* (Odhams Press, n.d.)

Davidson, Major-General Sir John, *Haig: Master of the Field* (Peter Nevill, London, 1953)

Dawson, Brigadier-General Sir Douglas, *A Soldier-Diplomat* (John Murray, London, 1927)

De Groot, Gerard J., *Douglas Haig, 1861–1928* (Unwin Hyman, London, 1988)

De Groot, Gerard J. (editor), *The Reverend George S. Duncan at GHQ, 1916–1918* (Military Miscellany I, Army Records Society, Volume 12, 1997)

De la Grange, Baroness, *Open House in Flanders 1914–1918* (John Murray, London, 1929)

de Lisle, General Sir Beauvoir, *Reminiscences of Sport and War* (Eyre & Spottiswoode, London, 1939)

De Montmorency, Hervey, *Sword and Stirr Up: Memories of an Adventurous Life* (G. Bell, London, 1936)

De Pierrefeu, Jean, *French Headquarters, 1915–1918* (Geoffrey Bles, no date)

Desagneaux, Henri, *A French Soldier's War Diary, 1914–1918* (Translation by The Elmfield Press, Morley, Yorkshire, 1975)

Dillon, Brigadier The Viscount, *Memories of Three Wars* (Allan Wingate, 1951)

Dobbie, Sybil, *Faith & Fortitude: The Life and Work of General Sir William Dobbie* (Major P.E. Johnston, Gillingham, Kent, 1979)

Dodden, A. Stuart, *Cannon Fodder: An Infantryman's Life on the Western Front, 1914–18* (Blandford Press, Poole, Dorset, 1980)

Douie, Charles, *The Weary Road: Recollections of a Subaltern of Infantry* (Reissued, The Strong Oak Press with Tom Donovan Publishing, 1988)

Duff Cooper, Lord, *Haig* (2 volumes, Faber & Faber, London, 1935–36)

Duff Cooper, Lord, *Old Men Forget* (Rupert Hart-Davis, London, 1955)

Duncan, G.S., *Douglas Haig As I Knew Him* (George Allen & Unwin, London, 1966)

Dunn, Captain, J.C., *The War the Infantry Knew, 1914–1919* (Reprinted, Jane's, London, 1987)

Dunsterville, *Stalky's Adventures* (Reprinted, Jonathan Cape, 1933)

Eberle, Lieutenant-Colonel V.F., *My Sapper Venture* (Pitman Publishing, 1973)

Eden, Anthony, *Another World, 1897–1917* (Allen Lane, London, 1976)

Edmonds, Charles, *A Subaltern's War* (reprinted Anthony Mott, 1984)

Egremont, Max, *Under Two Flags: The Life of Major General Sir Edward Spears* (Weidenfeld and Nicolson, London, 1997)

Elton, Oliver, *C.E. Montague* (Chatto & Windus, London, 1929)

Evans, Brigadier-General U.W., *Thoughts and Memories of a Long Life* (privately printed, 1945)

Ewart, Wilfred, *Scots Guard* (Rich & Cowan, London, 1934)

Ewart, Wilfred, *Way of Revelation* (Reprinted, Alan Sutton, 1986)

Falkenhayn, E. von, *General Headquarters 1914–1916 and its Critical Decisions* (Hutchinson, London, 1919)

Farrar-Hockley, Anthony, *Goughie: The Life of General Sir Hubert Gough* (Hart-Davis, MacGibbon, London, 1975)

Fay, Sir Sam, *The War Office at War* (Hutchinson, London, 1937)

Feilding, Colonel Rowland, *War Letters to a Wife, France and Flanders, 1915–1919* (Medici Society, 1929)

Foch, Marshal Ferdinand, *The Memoirs of Marshal Foch* (William Heinemann, London, 1931)

Foot, Stephen, *Three Lives and Now: An Autobiography* (William Heinemann, London, 1934)

Forester, C.S., *The General* (Michael Joseph, London, 1936)

Frankland, Noble, *Witness of a Century: The Life and Times of Prince Arthur Duke of Connaught, 1850–1942* (Shepheard-Walwyn, London, 1993)

Fraser, General Sir David, *Alanbrooke* (Collins, London, 1982)

Fraser, Brigadier Hon William (edited by General Sir David Fraser), *In Good Company: The First World War Letters and Diaries of the Hon. William Fraser, Gordon Highlanders* (Michael Russell, Salisbury, 1990)

Fraser, P., *Lord Esher: A Political Biography* (Hart-Davis, London, 1973)

Fraser-Tytler, *Lieutenant-Colonel Neil, Field Guns in France* (Hutchinson, London, 1922)

French, Anthony, *Gone for a Soldier* (The Roundwood Press, Kineton, Warwick, 1972)

French, Major The Hon Gerald, *The Life of Field-Marshal Sir John French* (Cassell, London, 1931)

French, Major The Hon Gerald, *French Replies To Haig* (Hutchinson, London, 1936)

Freyberg, Paul, *Bernard Freyberg, V.C.* (Hodder & Stoughton, London, 1991)

Fuller, Major-Gen J.F.C., *The Army in My Time* (Rich & Cowan, London, 1935)

Fuller, Major-Gen J.F.C., *Memoirs of an Unconventional Soldier* (Ivor Nicholson and Watson, 1936)

Fuller, Major-Gen J.F.C., *The Last of the Gentlemen's Wars: A Subaltern's Journal of the War in South Africa, 1899–1902* (Faber & Faber, London, 1937)

Furbank, P.N., *E.M. Forster: A Life* (Volume 2, Secker and Warburg, London, 1978)

Gardner, Brian, *Allenby* (Cassell, London, 1965)

Geddes, Lord, *The Forging of a Family* (Faber & Faber, London, 1952)

Gibbs, Philip, *The Realities of War* (Heinemann, London, 1920)

Gibbs, Sir Philip, *The Pageant of the Years* (Heinemann, London, 1946)

Gibbs, Sir Philip, *The War Dispatches* (Anthony Gibbs and Phillips with Times Press, London, 1964)

Gibbs, Captain Stormont Gibbs (edited by Richard Devonald-Lewis), *From the Somme to the Armistice: The Memoirs of Captain Stormont Gibbs, MC* (William Kimber, London, 1986)

Gilbert, Martin, *Winston S. Churchill: Volume III, 1914–1916* (Heinemann, London, 1971)

Gilbert, Martin, *Winston S. Churchill: Companion Volume III, 1914–1916* (2 volumes, Heinemann, London, 1972)

Gilbert, Martin, *Winston S. Churchill: Volume IV, 1917–1922* (Heinemann, London, 1975)

Gladden, Norman, *Ypres, 1917* (Book Club Edition, 1967)

Gladden, Norman, *The Somme, 1916* (William Kimber, London, 1974)

Gleichen, General Lord Edward, *A Guardsman's Memoirs* (William Blackwood, Edinburgh, London, 1932)

Glubb, Lieutenant-General Sir John, *Into Battle: A Soldier's Diary of the Great War* (Cassell, London, 1978)

Glubb, Lieutenant-General Sir John, *The Changing Scenes of Life: An Autobiography* (Quartet Books, London, 1983)

Godley, General Sir Alexander, *Life of an Irish Soldier* (John Murray, London, 1939)

Godley, The Hon Eveline, *Letters of Arthur, Lord Kilbracken, GCB, and General Sir Alexander Godley, GCB, KCMG, 1898–1932* (published privately, n.d.)

Goodall, H.B., *Beloved Imperialist: Sir Gordon Guggisberg* (The Pentland Press, Bishop Auckland, Durham, 1998)

Gordon, Huntley, *The Unreturning Army: A Field-gunner in Flanders, 1917–18* (J.M. Dent, London, 1967)

Gorell, Lord, *One Man, Many Parts* (Odhams, London, 1956)

Gough, General Sir Hubert, *Soldiering On* (Arthur Barker, London, 1954)

Graham, Stephen, *A Private in the Guards* (Macmillan, London, 1919)

Graves, Richard Perceval, *Robert Graves: The Assault Heroic 1895–1926* (Papermac, London, 1987)

Graves, Robert, *Goodbye to All That* (Cassell, London, 1957)

Gray, John G., *Prophet in Primsoles: An Account of the Life of Colonel Ronald B. Campbell* (Edina Press, Edinburgh, no date)

Greacen, Lavinia, *Chink: A Biography [of Major-General Eric Dorman-Smith]* (Macmillan, London, 1989)

Green, Brigadier-General A.F.U., *Evening Tattoo* (Stanley Paul, London, 1941)

Greenwell, Graham H., *An Infant in Arms: War Letters of a Company Officer, 1914–1918* (reprinted, Allen Lane, 1972)

Griffith, Wyn, *Up to Mametz* (Faber & Faber, London, 1931)

Griffiths, Richard, *Marshal Petain* (Constable, London, 1970)

Grimshaw, Captain Roly, *Indian Cavalry Officer, 1914–15* (Costello, London, 1986)

Groom, W.H.A., *Poor Bloody Infantry* (William Kimber, London, 1976)

'GSO' [Sir Frank Fox], *GHQ (Montreuil-sur-Mer)* (Philip Allan, London, 1920)

Guinness, Walter (edited by Brian Bond and Simon Robbins), *Staff Officer: The Diaries of Walter Guinness (Lord Moyne), 1914–1918* (Leo Cooper, London, 1987)

Gurney, Ivor (edited by R.K.R. Thornton), *War Letters* (The Hogarth Press, London, 1984)

Haig, The Countess, *The Man I Knew* (The Moray Press, Edinburgh, 1936)

Haig, Field-Marshal Earl (edited by Robert Blake), *The Private Papers of Douglas Haig* (Eyre & Spottiswoode, London, 1952)

Haig, Field-Marshal Earl (edited by Lieutenant-Colonel J.H. Boraston), *Sir Douglas Haig's Despatches* (J.M. Dent, London, 1919)

Haigh, R.H. and Turner, P.W., *Not Glory: A Personal History of the 1914–18 War* (Robert Maxwell, London, 1969)

Haldane, General Sir Aylmer, *A Soldier's Saga* (William Blackwood, Edinburgh, 1948)

Hamilton, General Sir Ian, *Listening for the Drums* (Faber & Faber, London, 1944)

Hamilton, General Sir Ian, *When I was a Boy* (Faber & Faber, London, 1939)

Hamilton, Nigel, *Monty: The Making of a General, 1887–1942* (Hamish Hamilton, London, 1981)

Hamilton, Lieutenant-Colonel The Hon Ralph G.A., Master of Belhaven, *The War Diary of The Master of Belhaven, 1914–1918* (Reprint, Wharncliffe, London, 1990)

Hanbury-Sparrow, Lieutenant-Colonel A.A., *The Land-Locked Lake* (Arthur Barker, London, 1932)

Hankey, Lord, *The Supreme Command* (2 volumes, Allen & Unwin, London, 1961)

Hankey, Donald, *A Student in Arms* (Melrose, London, 1916)

Harding, Lieutenant-Colonel Colin, *Far Bugles* (Simpkin Marshall, London, 1933)

Harington, General Sir Charles, *Plumer of Messines* (John Murray, London, 1935)

Harington, General Sir Charles, *Tim Harington Looks Back* (John Murray, London, 1940)

Harris, John, *Covenant with Death* (Hutchinson, London, 1961)

Harris, Brigadier L.H., *Signal Venture* (Gale & Polden, Aldershot, London, 1951)

Harrison, Eric, *Gunners, Game & Gardens: An Autobiography* (Leo Cooper, London, 1978)

Hawkings, Frank, *From Ypres to Cambrai: The Diary of an Infantryman, 1914–1919* (Elmfield Press, London, 1974)

Haworth, Christopher, *March to Armistice, 1918* (William Kimber, London, 1968)

Head, Lieutenant-Colonel C.O., *No Great Shakes* (Robert Hale, London, 1943)

Henderson-Bland, R., *Actor – Soldier – Poet* (Heath Cranton, London, 1939)

Hesketh-Prichard, Major H., *Sniping In France: With Notes on the Scientific Training of Scouts, Observers, and Snipers* (Hutchinson, n.d.)

Hetherington, John, *Blamey: The Biography of Field-Marshal Sir Thomas Blamey* (F.W. Cheshire, Melbourne, 1954)

Hetherington, John, *Conroversial Soldier: A Biography of Field-Marshal Sir Thomas Blamey* (Australian War Memorial and the Australian Government Publishing Service, Canberra, 1973)

Hindenburg, Marshal Paul von, *Out of My Life* (Cassell, London, 1920)

Hiscock, Eric, *The Bells of Hell Go Ting-Aling-Aling: An Autobiographical Fragment Without Maps* (Arlington Books, London, 1976)

Hitchcock, Captain F.C., *'Stand To': A Diary of the Trenches, 1915–1918* (Reprinted, Gliddon Books, Norwich, 1988)

Hobhouse, Charles (edited by Edward David), *Inside Asquith's Cabinet: From the Diaries of Charles Hobhouse* (John Murray, London, 1977)

Holden Reid, Brian, *J.F.C. Fuller: Military Thinker* (Macmillan Press, London, 1987)

Holmes, Richard, *The Little Field-Marshal: Sir John French* (Jonathon Cape, London, 1981)

Home, Brigadier-General Sir Archibald (edited by Diana Briscoe), *The Diary of a World War I Cavalry Officer* (Costello, Tunbridge Wells, 1985)

Horn, Lieutenant T.L., *Lancer Dig In: 1914 Diary* (Ellison's Edition, Orwell, Cambridgeshire, 1983)

Horner, D.M. (editor), *The Commanders: Australian Military Leadership in the Twentieth Century* (George Allen & Unwin, Sydney, 1984)

Housman, Laurence (editor), *War Letters of Fallen Englishmen* (Victor Gollancz, 1930)

Howell, Mrs Philip, *Philip Howell, A Memoir by his Wife* (Allen & Unwin, London, 1942)

Huguet, General M., *Britain and the War: A French Indictment* (Cassell, London, 1928)

Hurd, Michael, *The Ordeal of Ivor Gurney* (Oxford University Press Paperback, 1984)

Hutchison, Lieutenant-Colonel G.S., *Footslogger* (Hutchinson, London, 1933)

Hutchison, Lieutenant-Colonel G.S., *Pilgrimage* (Rich & Cowan, London, 1935)

Hyatt, A.M.J., *General Sir Arthur Currie* (University of Toronto Press, London, 1987)

Ironside, Lord (editor), *High Road to Command: The Diaries of Major-General Sir Edmund Ironside, 1920–22* (Leo Cooper, London, 1972)

Jack, Brigadier-General J.L., *General Jack's Diary, 1914–1918* (Eyre & Spottiswoode, London, 1964)

Jackson, Stanley, *The Sassoons* (Heinemann, London, 1968)

James, David, *Lord Roberts* (Hollis & Carter, London, 1954)

James, Lawrence, *Imperial Warrior: The Life and Times of Field-Marshal Viscount Allenby, 1861–1936* (Weidenfeld & Nicolson, London, 1993)

Jeffery, Keith (editor), *The Military Correspondence of Field-Marshal Sir Henry Wilson, 1918–1922* (Army Records Society, 1985)

Jerrold, Douglas, *Georgian Adventure* (Collins, London, 1937)

Jerrold, Walter, *Field-Marshal Sir John French* (W.A. Hammond, London, n.d.)

Joffre, Marshal Joseph, *The Memoirs of Marshal Joffre* (2 volumes, Geoffrey Bles, 1932)

Jolliffe, John, *Raymond Asquith: Life and Letters* (Collins, London, 1980)

Jones, Ira, *An Air Fighters Scrapbook* (Reprinted, Vintage Aviation Library, 1990)

Joynt, Lieutenant-Colonel W.D., *Saving the Channel Ports – 1918* (Wren Publishing, North Blackburn, Australia, 1975)

Judd, Alan, *Ford Madox Ford* (Collins, London, 1990)

Keegan, John (editor), *Churchill's Generals* (Grove Weidenfeld, New York, 1991)

Kelly, Sir David, *The Ruling Few: The Memoirs of Sir David Kelly* (Hollis & Carter, London, 1952)

Kentish, Basil, *This Foul Thing Called War: The Life of Brigadier General R.J. Kentish, CMG, DSO (1876–1956)* (The Book Guild Ltd, Lewes, Sussex, 1998)

Kirkpatrick, Sir Ivone, *The Inner Circle* (Macmillan, London, 1959)

Knox, Ronald, *Patrick Shaw-Stewart* (William Collins, London, 1920)

Laffin, John, *Swifter Than Eagles: The Biography of Marshal of the Royal Air Force Sir John Maitland Salmond* (William Blackwood, Edinburgh, 1964)

Lane, Major-General Ronald B. (editor), *Memoirs of Field-Marshal Lord Grenfell* (Hodder & Stoughton, London, [1925])

Law, Colonel Francis, *A Man at Arms: Memoirs of Two World Wars* (Collins, London, 1983)

Lawrence, Lieutenant B.L. (edited by Ian Fletcher), *Letters from the Front: The Great War Correspondence of Lieutenant Brian Lawrence, 1916–17* (Parapress Ltd, Tunbridge Wells, Kent, 1993)

Leask, G.A., *Sir William Robertson: The Life Story of the Chief of the Imperial General Staff* (Cassell, London, 1917)

Lees-Milne, James, *The Enigmatic Edwardian: The Life of Reginald 2nd Viscount Esher* (Sidgwick & Jackson, London, 1986)

Lewin, Ronald, *Montgomery as Military Commander* (Batsford, London, 1971)

Lewis, Wing Commander G.H., *Wings Over the Somme, 1916–18* (Bridge Books, Wrexham, Clwyd, 1994)

Liddell Hart, Captain B.H., *Reputations* (John Murray, London, 1928)

Liddell Hart, Captain B.H., *Foch: Man of Orleans* (Eyre & Spottiswoode, London, 1931)

Liddell Hart, Captain B.H., *Through the Fog of War* (Faber & Faber, London, 1938)

Liddell Hart, Captain Sir Basil, *Memoirs* (2 volumes, Cassell, London, 1965)

Limerick, Countess of, *Mark, A Memoir of Edmund Colquhoun Pery, 5th Earl of Limerick* (Privately published, 1972)

Lindley, Rt Hon Sir Francis, *Lord Lovat, 1871–1933: A Biography* (Hutchinson, London, n.d.)

Lindsay, Donald, *Forgotten General: A Life of Andrew Thorne* (Michael Russell, Salisbury, 1987)

Liveing, Edward G.D., *Attack: An Infantry Subaltern's Impressions of July 1st 1916* (Heinemann, London, 1918)

Lloyd, R.A., *A Trooper in the 'Tins'* (Hurst & Blackett, London, 1938)

Lloyd, T., *The Blazing Trail of Flanders* (Heath Cranton, London, 1933)

Lloyd George, D., *War Memoirs of Lloyd George* (2 volumes, Odhams, London, 1938)

Lonsdale, Jeremy, *The Army's Grace: The Life of Brigadier General R.M. Poore* (Spellmount Limited, Tunbridge Wells, Kent, 1992)

Lord, John, *Duty, Honour, Empire: The Life and Times of Colonel Richard Meinertzhagen* (Hutchinson, London, 1971)

Lowther, Lieutenant-Colonel H.C., *From Pillar to Post* (Edward Arnold, London, 1912)

Ludendorff, E., *My War Memories* (2 volumes, Hutchinson, London, n.d.)

Lunt, Major-General James, *Glubb Pasha: A Biography* (Harvill Press, London, 1984)

Lyttleton, General Sir Neville, *Eighty Years: Soldiering, Politics, Games* (Hodder & Stoughton, London, 1926)

McCalmont, Major-General Sir Hugh (edited by Major-General Sir C.E. Callwell), *The Memoirs of Major-General Sir Hugh McCalmont* (Hutchinson, London, 1924)

MacGregor, Tom, *Tom's Letters* (privately printed, no date)

Macksey, Kenneth J., *Armoured Crusader: A Biography of Major-General Sir Percy Hobart* (Hutchinson, London, 1967)

Macmillan, Harold, *Winds of Change, 1914–1939* (Macmillan, London, 1966)

Macmillan, Wing Commander Norman, *Sir Sefton Brancker* (William Heineman, London, 1935)

Macmillan, Wing Commander Norman, *Into the Blue* (revised, Jarrolds, 1969)

Macready, Lieutenant-General Sir Gordon, *In the Wake of the Great* (William Clowes, London, 1965)

Macready, General The Rt. Hon Sir Nevil, *Annals of An Active Life* (2 volumes, Hutchinson, London, n.d.)

Manning, Frederic, *The Middle Parts of Fortune: Somme and Ancre 1916* (Buchan & Enright, London, 1986)

MARK VII [Mark Plowman], *A Subaltern on the Somme in 1916* (J.M. Dent, London, 1927)

Marling, Colonel Sir Percival, *Rifleman and Hussar* (John Murray, London, 1931)

Marriott, Major-General Sir John, *Military Memories* (Privately printed, 1960)

Marshall, Lieutenant-General Sir William, *Memories of Four Fronts* (Ernest Benn, London, 1929)

Marshall-Cornwall, General Sir James, *Foch as Military Commander* (Batsford, London, 1972)

Marshall-Cornwall, General Sir James, *Haig as Military Commander* (Batsford, London, 1973)

Marshall-Cornwall, General Sir James, *Wars and Rumours of Wars: A Memoir* (Leo Cooper, London, 1984)

Martel, Lieutenant-General Sir Giffard, *In the Wake of the Tank* (Sifton Praed, London, 1931)

Martel, Lieutenant-General Sir Giffard, *An Outspoken Soldier: His Views and Memoirs* (Sifton Praed, London, 1949)

Martin, Bernard, *Poor Bloody Infantry: A Subaltern on the Western Front 1916–17* (John Murray, London, 1987)

Maurice, Major-General Sir Frederick, *The Life of General Lord Rawlinson of Trent* (Cassell, London, 1928)

Maurice, Major-General Sir Frederick, *Haldane: The Life of Viscount Haldane of Cloan* (2 volumes, Faber & Faber, London, 1937–39)

Maurois, Andre, *The Silence of General Bramble* (Bodley Head, London, 1930)

Maurois, Andre, *General Bramble* (Bodley Head, London, 1931)

Maxse, Colonel F.I., *Seymour Vandeleur* (The National Review Office, 1905)

Maxwell, Mrs F.A. (editor), *Brigadier-General Frank Maxwell, V.C.: A Memoir and Some Letters* (John Murray, London, 1921)

May, Major-General Sir Edward S., *Changes and Chances of a Soldier's Life* (Philip Allan, London, 1925)

Maze, Paul, *A Frenchman in Khaki* (William Heinemann, London, 1934)

McCourt, Edward, *Remember Butler: The Story of Sir William Butler* (Routledge & Kegan Paul, London, 1967)

McLachlan, Donald, *In the Chair: Barrington-Ward of The Times, 1927–1948* (Weidenfeld & Nicolson, London, 1971)

Mearsheimer, John J., *Liddell Hart and the Weight of History* (Brassey's, London, 1988)

Meinertzhagen, Richard, *Army Diary, 1899–1926* (Oliver & Boyd, London, 1960)

Mellersh, H.E.L., *Schoolboy into War* (William Kimber, London, 1978)

Melvill, Colonel T.P., *Ponies and Women* (Jarrolds, London, 1932)

Menzies, Mrs Stuart, *Sir Stanley Maude and Other Memories* (Herbert Jenkins, London, 1920)

Mizener, Arthur, *The Saddest Story: A Biography of Ford Madox Ford* (The Bodley Head)

Monash, Lieutenant-General Sir John, *The Australian Victories in France in 1918* (Hutchinson, London, 1920)

Monash, Lieutenant-General Sir John (edited by F.M. Cutlack), *War Letters of General Monash* (Angus & Robertson, Sydney, London, 1935)

Montague, C.E., *Disenchantment* (MacGibbon & Kee, London, 1968)

Montgomery, Field-Marshal Viscount, *The Memoirs of Field-Marshal The Viscount Montgomery of Alamein, KG* (The Companion Book Club, 1960)

Montgomery, Lieutenant-Colonel Brian, *A Field-Marshal in the Family* (Constable, London, 1973)

Montgomery-Cuninghame, Colonel Sir Thomas, *Dusty Measure: A Record of Troubled Times* (John Murray, London, 1939)

Montgomery Hyde, H., *Strong For Service: The Life of Lord Nathan of Churt* (W.H. Allen, London, 1968)

Morehead, Alan, *Montgomery* (Hamish Hamilton, London, 1967)

Morgan, General Sir Frederick, *Peace and War: A Soldier's Life* (Hodder & Stoughton, London, 1961)

Morris, A.J.A., *The Letters of Lieutenant-Colonel Charles a Court Repington CMG: Military Correspondent of The Times, 1903–1918* (Army Records Society, 1999)

Mottistone, Lord [Major-General the Rt Hon J.E.B. Seely], *My Horse: Warrior* (Hodder & Stoughton, London, 1934)

Mottram, R.H., *The Spanish Farm Trilogy, 1914–1918* (Chatto & Windus, London, 1927)

Mottram, R.H., *John Easton and Eric Partridge, Three Personal Accounts of the War* (The Scholartis Press, London, 1929)

Murray, Joseph, *Call to Arms: From Gallipoli to the Western Front* (William Kimber, London, 1980)

Nagle, Fritz (edited by Richard A. Baumgartner), *Fritz: The World War I Memoirs of a German Lieutenant* (Der Angriff Publications, Huntington, West Virginia, USA, 1981)

Nash, T.A.H. (edited by T.A.M. Nash), *The Diary of an Unprofessional Soldier* (Picton, Chippenham, 1991)

Neame, Lieutenant-General Sir Philip, *Playing With Strife: The Autobiography of a Soldier* (George G. Harrap, London, 1947)

Nettleton, John, *The Anger of the Guns: An Infantry Officer on the Western Front* (William Kimber, London, 1979)

Nichol, Graham, *Uncle George: Field-Marshal Lord Milne of Salonika and Rubislaw* (Reedminster Publications, London, 1976)

Nicholson, Colonel W.N., *Behind the Lines* (Jonathon Cape, London, 1939)

Nicolson, Nigel, *The Life of Field-Marshal Earl Alexander of Tunis* (Weidenfeld & Nicolson, London, 1973)

North, Lieutenant-Colonel Piers William, *Reminiscences of a Younger Son* (printed privately, 1957)

Ogle, Captain Henry (edited by Michael Glover), *The Fateful Battle Line: The Great War Journals and Sketches of Captain Henry Ogle, MC* (Leo Cooper, London, 1993)

Ole Luk-Oie [E.D. Swinton], *The Green Curve and Other Stories* (William Blackwood, Edinburgh, 1909)

Oliver, F.S., *Ordeal By Battle* (Macmillan, London, 1915)

Oliver, F.S., *The Anvil of War* (Macmillan, London, 1936)

Onslow, The Earl of, *Sixty-Three Years* (Hutchinson, London, n.d.)

Orange, Vincent, *Coningham: A Biography of Air Marshal Sir Arthur Coningham* (Methuen, London, 1990)

Parker, Ernest, *Into Battle, 1914–1918* (Longmans, London, 1964)

Peacock, Basil, *Tinker's Mufti: An Autobiography* (Seeley Service, 1974)

Pedersen, P.A., *Monash As Military Commander* (Melbourne University Press, Melbourne, 1985)

Pershing, General J.J., *My Experiences in the World War* (Hodder & Stoughton, London, 1931)

Piggott, Major-General F.S.G., *Broken Thread: An Autobiography* (Gale & Polden, London, 1950)

Plowman, Max (edited by D.L.P.), *Bridges into the Future: The Letters of Max Plowman* (Andrew Dakers, London, 1944)

Pollard, Captain A.O., *Fire-eater: The Memoirs of a VC* (Hutchinson's, London, n.d.)

Portway, Colonel Donald, *Militant Don* (Robert Hale, London, 1964)

Pound, Reginald and Harmsworth, Geoffrey, *Northcliffe* (Cassell, London, 1959)

Pound, Reginald, *A.P. Herbert: A Biography* (Michael Joseph, London, 1976)

Powell, Geoffrey, *Plumer: The Soldier's General* (Leo Cooper, London, 1990)

Prescott, John F., *In Flanders Fields: The Story of John McCrae* (The Boston Mills Press, Ontario, Canada, 1985)

Prior, Robin and Wilson, Trevor, *Command on the Western Front: The Military Career of Sir Henry Rawlinson, 1914–18* (Blackwell Publishers, Oxford, 1992)

Protheroe, Ernest, *Earl Haig* (Hutchinson, London, n.d.)

Raw, David, *'It's Only Me': A Life of The Reverend Theodore Bayley Hardy VC, DSO, MC, 1863–1918* (Frank Peters Publishing, Gatebeck, near Kendal, Cumbria, 1988)

Ravenscroft, P.D. (edited by Antony Bird), *Unversed In Arms: A Subaltern on the Western Front* (The Crowood Press, Swindon, 1990)

Read, Anthony and Fisher, David, *Colonel Z: The Secret Life of a Master of Spies [Lieutenant-Colonel Sir Claude Dansey]* (Hodder & Stoughton, 1984)

Read, I.L., *Of Those We Loved* (The Pentland Press, Durham, 1994)

Reid, Gordon (Editor), *Poor Bloody Murder: Personal Memoirs of the First World War* (Mosaic Press Publishers, Ontario, Canada, 1980)

Reitz, Denys, *Trekking On* (Faber & Faber, London, 1933)

Repington, Colonel C. a Court, *The First World War, 1914–1918* (2 volumes, Constable, London, 1919)

Richards, Frank, *Old Soldiers Never Die* (Faber & Faber, London, 1933)

Richardson, General Sir Charles, *From Churchill's Secret Circle to the BBC: The Biography of Lieutenant General Sir Ian Jacob* (Brassey's, London, 1991)

Rizzi, Joseph N. (edited by Richard A. Baumgartner), *Joe's War: Memoirs of a Doughboy* (Der Angriff Publications, Huntington, West Virginia, USA, 1983)

Roberts, Field-Marshal Lord, *Forty-One Years in India* (Macmillan, London, 1901)

Roberts, G.D., *Witness These Letters: Letters from the Western Front, 1915–18* (Gee & Son, Denbigh, Clwyd, Wales, 1983)

Robertson, Field-Marshal Sir William, *From Private To Field-Marshall* (Constable, London, 1921)

Robertson, Field-Marshal Sir William, *Soldiers and Statesmen, 1914–1918* (2 volumes, Cassell, London, 1926)

Robertson, Field-Marshal Sir William (edited by David R. Woodward), *The Military Correspondence of Field-Marshal Sir William Robertson, 1915–1918* (Army Records Society, 1989)

Robson, Brian, *Roberts In India: The Military Papers of Field-Marshal Lord Roberts, 1876–1893* (Army Records Society, 1993)

Rogers, Major Vivian Barry, *An Autobiography* (privately printed, 1965)

Rogerson, Sidney, *Twelve Days* (Arthur Barker, London, n.d.)

Rogerson, Sidney, *The Last of the Ebb* (Arthur Barker, London, 1937)

Roskill, Captain S.W., *Hankey, Man of Secrets* (3 volumes, Collins, London, 1970–74)

Ross, Captain Robert B., *The Fifty-First in France* (Hodder & Stoughton, London, n.d.)

Rowell, Lieutenant-General Sir Sydney, *Full Circle* (Melbourne University Press, Melbourne, 1974)

Rowland, Peter, *David Lloyd George: A Biography* (Macmillan, New York, 1976)

Royle, Trevor, *Glubb Pasha: The Life and Times of Sir John Bagot Glubb, Commander of the Arab Legion* (Abacus, London, 1993)

Russell, Arthur, *The Machine Gunner* (The Roundwood Press, Kineton, Warwick, London, 1977)

Sanderson of Ayot, Basil, Lord, *Ships and Sealing Wax: Memoirs* (Heinemann, London, 1967)

Sassoon, Siegfried, *Memoirs of a Fox-hunting Man* (Faber & Faber, London, 1928)

Sassoon, Siegfried, *Memoirs of an Infantry Officer* (Faber & Faber, London, 1930)

Sassoon, Siegfried, *Sherston's Progress* (Faber & Faber, London, 1936)

Sassoon, Siegfried, *Diaries, 1915–1918* (Faber & Faber, London, 1983)

Savage, Raymond, *Allenby of Armageddon* (Hodder & Stoughton, London, [1925])

Scott, Ralph, *A Soldier's Diary* (W. Collins & Sons, Second Edition, London, 1930)

Secrett, Sergeant T., *Twenty-Five Years With Earl Haig* (Jarrods, London, 1929)

Seely, Major-General the Rt Hon J.E.B., *Adventure* (William Heinemann, London, 1930)

Seely, Major-General the Rt Hon J.E.B., *Fear, And Be Slain* (Hodder & Stoughton, London, 1931)

Serle, A.G., *John Monash: A Biography* (Melbourne University Press, Melbourne, 1982)

Sheffield, G.D. and Inglis, G.I.S., *From Vimy Ridge to the Rhine: The Great War Letters of Christopher Stone DSO MC* (The Crowood Press, Marlborough, Wiltshire, 1989)

Shephard, Ernest (edited by Bruce Rosser and Dr Richard Holmes), *A Sergeant-Major's War: From Hill 60 to the Somme* (The Crowood Press, Marlborough, Wiltshire, 1987)

Sherriff, R.C. and Bartlett, Vernon, *Journey's End* (Victor Gollancz, London, 1930)

Sherriff, R.C., *No Leading Lady: An Autobiogrpahy* (Gollancz, London, 1968)

Sholto Douglas, Marshal of the RAF Lord, *Years of Combat* (Collins, London, 1963)

Siepmann, Harry, *Echo of the Guns: Recollections of an Artillery Officer, 1914–18* (Robert Hale, London, 1987)

Singleton-Gates, Peter, *General Lord Freyburg VC* (Michael Joseph, London, 1963)

Sitwell, Osbert, *Great Morning: An Autobiography* (Reissued, Reprint Society, 1949)

Sixsmith, Major-General E.K.G., *Douglas Haig* (Weidenfeld & Nicolson, London, 1976)

Slater, Guy (editor), *My Warrior Sons: The Borton Family Diary 1914–1918* (Military Book Society, London, n.d.)

Slessor, Marshal of the RAF Sir John, *The Central Blue: Recollections and Reflections* (Cassell, London, 1956)

[Smith, Aubrey M.], *Four Years on the Western Front, by a Rifleman: Being the Experiences of a Ranker in the London Rifle Brigade* (Odhams, London, 1922)

Smith-Dorrien, General Sir Horace, *Memories of Forty-Eight Years' Service* (John Murray, London, 1925)

Smithers, A.J., *The Man Who Disobeyed: Sir Horace Smith-Dorrien and his Enemies* (Leo Cooper, London, 1970)

Smithers, A.J., *Sir John Monash* (Leo Cooper, London, 1973)

Smyth, Brigadier Sir John, *The Only Enemy: An Autobiography* (Hutchinson, London, 1959)

Smyth, Brigadier Sir John, *Milestones* (Sidgwick & Jackson, London, 1979)

Smythe, Donald, *Pershing: General of the Armies* (Indiana University Press, Bloomington, 1986)

Spears, Brigadier-General E.L., *Liaison 1914: A Narrative of the Great Retreat* (William Heinemann, London, 1930)

Spears, Brigadier-General E.L., *Prelude To Victory* (Jonathon Cape, London, 1939)

Spears, Major-General Sir Edward, *The Picnic Basket* (Secker & Warburg, London, 1967)

Spicer, Lancelot Dykes, *Letters From France, 1915–1918* (Robert Yorke, London, 1979)

Spiers, Edward, *Haldane: An Army Reformer* (Edinburgh University Press, London, 1980)

Spring, Howard, *In the Meantime* (Constable, London, 1942)

Stallworthy, Jon, *Wilfred Owen* (Oxford University Press Paperback, Oxford, 1977)

Stotherd, Lieutenant-Colonel E.A.W., *Sabre and Saddle* (Seeley Service, n.d.)

Strange, Lieutenant-Colonel L.A., *Recollections of an Airman* (John Hamilton, The Airman's Bookshelf Edition, 1935)

Stuart Dolden, A., *Cannon Fodder: An Infantryman's Life on the Western Front, 1914–1918* (Blandford Press, London, 1980)

Swinton, Major-General Sir Ernest D., *Eyewitness* (Hodder & Stoughton, London, 1932)

Swinton, Major-General Sir Ernest D., *Over My Shoulder* (George Ronald, Oxford, 1951)

Sykes, Major-General The Rt. Hon Sir Frederick, *From Many Angles* (George G. Harrap, London, 1942)

Talbot Kelly, R.B. (edited by R.G. Loosmore), *A Subaltern's Odyssey: A Memoir of the Great War, 1915–17* (William Kimber, London, 1980)

Terraine, John, *Douglas Haig: The Educated Soldier* (Hutchinson, London, 1963)

Thomas, Alan, *A Life Apart* (Victor Golancz, London, 1968)

Thomas, R. George, *Edward Thomas: A Portrait* (Oxford University Press, Oxford, 1987)

Thomason, John W., *Fix Bayonets!: With the US Marine Corps in France, 1917–1918* (reissued, Greenhill Books, 1989)

Thornton, Lieutenant-Colonel L.H. and Fraser, Pamela, *The Congreves: Father and Son* (John Murray, London, 1930)

Trythall, Anthony John, *'Boney' Fuller: The Intellectual General, 1878–1966* (Rutgers Cassell, London, 1977)

Tucker, John F., *Johnny Get Your Gun: A Personnal Narrative of the Somme, Ypres and Arras* (William Kimber, London, 1978)

Turner, Major-General Sir Alfred E., *Sixty Years of a Soldier's Life* (Methuen, London, 1912)

Urquhart, Hugh M., *Arthur Currie* (J.M. Dent, Toronto, 1950)

Vaughan, Edwin Campion, *Some Desperate Glory: The Diary of a Young Officer, 1917* (Frederick Warne, London, 1981)

Verney, David (editor), *The Joyous Patriot: The Correspondence of Ralph Verney, 1900–1916* (Leo Cooper, London, 1989)

Villiers-Stuart, Brigadier-General W.D. (edited by Lieutenant-Colonel R.M. Maxwell), *Villiers-Stuart: On the Frontier, 1894–1914* (Pentland Press, Edinburgh, 1989)

Villiers-Stuart, Brigadier-General W.D. (edited by Lieutenant-Colonel R.M. Maxwell), *Villiers-Stuart: Goes to War* (Pentland Press, Edinburgh, 1989)

Wade, Major A.G., '*Counterspy!*' (Stanley Paul, London, 1938)

Wade, Aubrey, *The War of the Guns: Western Front, 1917 & 1918* (B.T. Batsford, London, 1936)

Wallace, Major Claude, *From Jungle to Jutland* (Nisbet, London, 1932)

Warner, Philip, *Field Marshal Earl Haig* (Bodley Head, London, 1991)

Warren, Second Lieutenant Frank (edited by Antony Bird), *Honour Satisfied: A Dorset Rifleman at War 1916–1918* (Crowood Press, London, 1990)

Webb, Barry, *Edmund Blunden: A Biography* (Yale University Press, New Haven and London, 1990)

Wheatley, Dennis, *The Time Has Come . . . , The Memoirs of Dennis Wheatley: Officer and Temporary Gentleman, 1914–1918* (Hutchinson, London, 1978)

White, Lieutenant A.P. (edited by Michael Hammerson), *No Easy Hopes Or Lies: The World War I Letters of Lt. Arthur Preston White, 1st Battalion, Northamptonshire Regiment, 1914–1918* (The London Stamp Exchange, 1991)

Wilkes, Lyall, *Festing – Field Marshal: A Study of 'Front Line Frankie'* (The Book Guild Limited, Lewes, Sussex, 1991)

William, Crown Prince of Germany, *My War Experiences* (Hurst & Blackett, London, 1926)

Williams, Jeffrey, *Byng of Vimy* (Leo Cooper, 1983)

Williamson, Henry, *The Patriot's Progress* (Geoffrey Bles, 1930)

Willcocks, Brigadier-General Sir James, *From Kabul to Kumassi* (John Murray, London, 1904)

Willcocks, General Sir James, *The Romance of Soldiering and Sport* (Cassell, London, 1925)

Wilson, A. Gordon, *Walter Wilson: Portrait of an Inventor* (Duckworth, London, 1986)

Wilson, Keith, *The Rasp of War: The Letters of H.A. Gwynne to the Countess Bathurst, 1914–1918* (Sidgwick & Jackson, London, 1988)

Winter, Denis, *Haig's Command: A Reassessment* (Viking, London, 1991)

Winter, Brigadier-General Sir Ormonde de L'Epee, *Winter's Tale* (Richards Press, London, 1955)

Wright, Captain Peter E., *At the Supreme War Council* (Eveleigh Nash, London, 1921)

Young, [Brigadier] Desmond, *Try Anything Twice* (Hamish Hamilton, London, 1963)

Young, Keith, Harry, *Lord Roseberry* (Hodder & Stoughton, London, 1974)

Younghusband, Major-General Sir George, *Forty Years A Soldier* (Herbert Jenkins, London, 1923)

Campaign and official histories

Adams, R.J.Q., *Arms and the Wizard: Lloyd George and the Ministry of Munitions, 1915–1916* (Cassell, 1978)

Adams, R.J.Q. and Poirier, Philip P., *The Conscription Controversy in Great Britain, 1900–18* (Ohio State University Press with Macmillan, 1987)

Allinson, Sidney, *The Bantams: The Untold History of World War I* (Howard Baker, 1981)

Andrew, Christopher, *Secret Service: The Making of the British Intelligence Community* (Heinemann, 1985)

Applin, Captain R.V.K., *Machine Gun Tactics* (Hugh Rees, 1910)

Ascoli, David, *The Mons Star: The British Expeditionary Force, 1914* (George Harrap, 1981)

Ashworth, Tony, *Trench Warfare, 1914–1918: The Live and Let Live System* (Macmillan, 1980)

Asprey, Robert B., *The First Battle of the Marne* (Weidenfeld & Nicolson, 1962)

Atkinson, C.T., *The Seventh Division, 1914–1918* (John Murray, 1927)

Babington, Anthony, *For the Sake of Example* (Leo Cooper, 1983)

Barclay, Brigadier C.N., *Armistice, 1918* (J.M. Dent & Sons, 1968)

Barnett, Corelli, *Britain and her Army* (Allen Lane, 1970)

Barrie, Alexander, *War Underground* (Frederick Muller, 1962)

Baynes, John, *Morale: A Study of Men and Courage* (Leo Cooper, 1967)

Bean, C.E.W., *The Official History of Australia in the War of 1914–1918: The AIF in France* (Volumes III–VI, Angus & Robertson, Sydney, 1929–42)

Beckett, Ian F.W., *The Army and the Curragh Incident, 1914* (Army Records Society, 1986)

Beckett, Ian F.W. and Simpson, Keith (editors), *A Nation In Arms* (Manchester University Press, 1985)

Berton, Pierre, *Vimy* (Penguin, 1987)

Best, Geoffrey and Wheatcroft, Andrew, *War, Economy and the Military Mind* (Croom Helm, 1976)

Bidwell, Brigadier [R.G.] Shelford *Gunners at War: A Tactical Study of the Royal Artillery in the Twentieth Century* (Arms & Armour Press, 1970)

Bidwell, Brigadier [R.G.] Shelford and Graham, Dominick, *Fire-power: British Army Weapons and Theories of War 1904–1945* (George Allen & Unwin, 1982)

Bidwell, Brigadier [R.G.] Shelford and Graham, Dominick, *Coalitions, Politicians and Generals: Some Aspects of Command in Two World Wars* (Brasseys, 1993)

Blaxland, Gregory, *Amiens: 1918* (Frederick Muller, 1968)

Bond, Brian, *The Victorian Army and the Staff College, 1854–1914* (Eyre Methuen, 1972)

Bond, Brian, *Liddell Hart: A Study of his Military Thought* (Cassell, 1977)

Bond, Brian, *British Military Policy between the Two World Wars* (Clarendon Press, Oxford, 1980)

Bond, Brian (editor), *The First World War and British Military History* (Clarendon Press, Oxford, 1991)

Bourne, J.M., *Britain and the Great War, 1914–1918* (Edward Arnold, 1989)

Braim, Paul F., *The Test of Battle: The American Expeditionary Force in the Meuse-Argonne Campaign* (University of Delaware Press, Newark, 1987)

Bristow, Adrian, *A Serious Disappointment: The Battle of Aubers Ridge, 1915, and the Subsequent Munitions Scandal* (Leo Cooper, 1995)

Brook-Shepherd, Gordon, *November, 1918: The Last Act of the Great War* (Collins, 1981)

Brown, Ian Malcolm, *British Logistics on the Western Front, 1914–1919* (Praeger, Westport, Connecticut, 1998)

Brown, Malcolm, *The Imperial War Museum Book of the First World War* (Sidgwick & Jackson, 1991)

Brown, Malcolm, *The Imperial War Museum Book of The Somme* (Sidgwick & Jackson, 1996)

Cave, Nigel, *Beaumont Hamel, Somme* (Leo Cooper, 1994)

Charlton, Peter, *Australians on the Somme: Pozieres, 1916* (Leo Cooper, 1986)

Cheyne, G.Y., *The Last Great Battle of the Somme: Beaumont Hamel 1916* (John Donald, Edinburgh, 1988)

Clarke, Alan, *The Donkeys* (Hutchinson, 1963)

Coffman, Edward M., *The War to End Wars: The American Military Experience in World War I* (Reprint, University of Wisconsin Press, Madison, 1986)

Coop, The Rev J.O., *The Story of the 55th (West Lancashire) Division* (Liverpool 'Daily Post' Printers, Liverpool, 1919)

Cooper, Bryan, *The Ironclads of Cambrai* (Souvenir Press, 1967)

Cooper, Bryan, *Tank Battles of World War 1* (Ian Allen, 1974)

Corum, James S., *The Roots of Blitzkrieg: Hans von Seeckt and German Military Reform* (University of Kansas, Lawrence, Kansas, 1992)

Cruttwell, C.R.M.F., *A History of the Great War 1914–18* (Clarendon Press, 1934, reprinted Granada, 1982)

Cruttwell, C.R.M.F., *The Role of British Strategy in the Great War* (Cambridge University Press, Cambridge, 1936)

Currie, Lieutenant-General Sir Arthur, *Canadian Corps Operations during the Year 1918: Interim Report* (Department of Militia and Edefence, Ottawa, 1919)

Dallas, Gloden and Gill, Douglas, *The Unknown Army: Mutinies in the British Army in World War I* (Verso, 1985)

Davies, Frank and Maddocks, Graham, *Bloody Red Tabs: General Officer Casualties of the Great War, 1914–1918* (Leo Cooper, 1995)

Denman, Terence, *Ireland's Unknown Soldiers: The 16th (Irish) Division in the Great War, 1914–1918* (Irish Academic Press, Blackrock, Ireland, 1992)

Dewar, G.A.B., assisted by Lieutenant-Colonel J.H. Boraston, *Sir Douglas Haig's Command, 1915–1918* (2 volumes, Constable, 1922)

Dixon, Norman F., *On the Psychology of Military Incompetence* (Jonathon Cape, 1976)

Dupuy, Colonel T.N., *A Genius for War: The German Army and General Staff, 1807–1945* (Macdonald & Janes, 1977)

Edmonds, Brigadier-General Sir J.E. (editor), *History of the Great War: Military Operations, France and Belgium, 1914–1918* (14 volumes, HMSO and Macmillan, 1922–49)

Elliott, Major-General J.G., *Field Sports in India, 1800–1947* (Gentry Books, 1973)

Ellis, John, *Eye-deep in Hell; The Western Front, 1914–1918* (Croom Helm, 1976)

English, Colonel J.A., *The Canadian Army and the Normandy Campaign* (Praeger, New York, 1991)

Essame, Major-General H., *The Battle for Europe 1918* (B.T. Batsford, 1972)

Falls, Captain Cyril, *The First World War* (Capricorn Books, New York, 1961)

Farndale, General Sir M., *History of the Royal Regiment of Artillery: Western Front, 1914–1918* (The Royal Artillery Institution, Woolwich, 1986)

Farrar-Hockley, A.H., *The Somme* (B.T. Batsford, 1954)

Farrar-Hockley, A.H., *Death of an Army [Ypres, 1914]* (Arthur Barker, 1970)

Farrar-Hockley, General Sir Anthony, *The Army in the Air: The History of the Army Air Corps* (Alan Sutton Stroud, 1994)

Ferguson, Niall, *The Pity of War* (Allen Lane, The Penguin Press, 1998)

Fergusson, Sir James, *The Curragh Incident* (Faber & Faber, 1964)

Ferris, John (editor), *The British Army and Signals Intelligence during the First World War* (Army Records Society, 1992)

Ferro, Marc, *The Great War, 1914–1918* (Routledge & Kegan Paul, 1973)

Foley, John, *The Boilerplate War* (Frederick Muller, 1963)

Foulkes, Charles Howard, *Gas! The Story of the Special Brigade* (Blackwood, Edinburgh and London, 1934)

French, Field-Marshal Viscount, *1914* (Constable, 1919)

French, David, *British Economic and Strategic Planning, 1905–1915* (Allen & Unwin, 1982)

French, David, *British Strategy and War Aims, 1914–1916* (Allen & Unwin, 1986)

Fuller, Colonel J.F.C., *Tanks in the Great War, 1914–1918* (John Murray, 1920)

Fuller, Major-General J.F.C., *The Decisive Battles of the Western World and their Influence upon History, Volume Three: From the American Civil War to the End of the Second World War* (Eyre & Spottiwoode, 1956)

Gardner, Brian, *The Big Push [Somme, 1916]* (Cassell, 1961)

Germains, V.W., *The Kitchener Armies* (Peter Davies, 1930)

Godwin-Austen, Major A.R., *The Staff and the Staff College* (Constable, 1927)

Gollin, Alfred, *No Longer An Island* (Heinemann, 1984)

Gooch, John, *The Plans of War: The General Staff and British Military Planning c. 1900–1916* (Routledge & Kegan Paul, 1974)

Goodspeed, D.J., *The Road Past Vimy: The Canadian Corps, 1914–1918* (Macmillan of Canada, Toronto, 1969)

Gough, General Sir Hubert, *The Fifth Army* (Hodder & Stoughton, 1931)

Gough, General Sir Hubert, *The March Retreat [March, 1918]* (Cassell, 1934)

Grieves, Keith, *The Politics of Manpower, 1914–18* (Manchester University Press, 1988)

Griffith, Paddy, *Forward into Battle: Fighting Tactics from Waterloo to Vietnam* (Antony Bird, 1981)

Griffith, Paddy, *Battle Tactics of the Western Front: The British Army's Art of Attack, 1916–18* (Yale University Press, New Haven, 1994)

Griffith, Paddy, *British Fighting Methods in the Great War* (Cass, London, 1996)

Gudmundsson, Bruce I., *Stormtroop Tactics: Innovation in the German Army, 1914–1918* (Praeger, New York, 1989)

Haber, Ludwig F., *The Poisonous Cloud: Chemical Warfare in the First World War* (Oxford, 1986)

Hallion, Richard P., *Strike from the Sky: The History of Battlefield Air Attack, 1911–1945* (Smithsonian History of Aviation Series published in the UK by Airlife Publishing Ltd, Shrewsbury, 1989)

Hamer, W.S., *The British Army: Civil-Military Relations, 1885–1905* (Oxford University Press, Oxford, 1970)

Hamilton, Lord Ernest, *The First Seven Divisions: Being a Detailed Account of the Fighting from Mons to Ypres* (Hurst & Blackett, 1916)

Harbord, Major-General James G., *The American Army In France, 1917–1919* (Little, Brown, and Company, Boston, 1936)

Harris, J.P. and Toase, F.N. (editors), *Armoured Warfare* (Batsford, 1990)

Harris, J.P., *Men, Ideas and Tanks: British Military Thought and Armoured Forces, 1903–1939* (Manchester University Press, Manchester, 1995)

Harris, J.P. and Barr, Niall, *Amiens to the Armistice: The BEF in the Hundred Days' Campaign, 8 August–11 November 1918* (Brassey's, London, 1998)

Haswell, Jock, *British Military Intelligence* (Weidenfeld & Nicolson, 1973)

Hay, Ian, *The First Hundred Thousand* (Blackwood, Edinburgh, 1916)

Hay, Ian, *Carrying on – after the First Hundred Thousand* (Blackwood, Edinburgh, 1917)

Haywood, Colonel A. and Clarke, Brigadier F.A.S., *The History of the West African Frontier Force* (Gale & Polden, Aldershot, 1964)

Heniker, Colonel A.M., *Transportation on the Western Front, 1914–1918* (HMSO, 1937)

Hittle, Brigadier-General J.D., *The Military Staff: Its History and Development* (Third Edition, The Stackpole Company, Harrisburg, Pennsylvania, 1961)

Hughes, Colin, *Mametz: Lloyd George's 'Welsh Army' at the Battle of the Somme* (Orion Press, 1982)

James, Lawrence, *The Savage Wars: British Campaigns in Africa 1870–1920* (Robert Hale, 1985)

James, Lawrence, *Mutiny: In the British and Commonwealth Forces, 1797–1956* (Buchan & Enright, 1987)

Janovitz, Morris, *The Professional Soldier* (The Free Press, New York, 1964)

Johnson, Hubert C., *Break-through: Tactics, Technology, and the Search for Victory on the Western Front in World War I* (Presidio Press, Novato, Clifornia, 1994)

Kearsey, Lieutenant-Colonel A., *1915 Campaign in France: The Battles of Aubers Ridge, Festubert & Loos* (Gale & Polden, Aldershot, n.d.)

Kearsey, Lieutenant-Colonel A., *The Battles of Amiens, 1918, and Operations 8th August – 3rd September 1918: The Turn of the Tide on the Western Front* (Gale & Polden, Aldershot, 1950)

Kennedy, P.M. (editor), *The War Plans of the Great Powers* (Allen & Unwin, 1979)

Kluck, Alexander von, *The March on Paris and the Battle of the Marne, 1914* (Edward Arnold, 1920)

Larson, Robert H., *The British Army and the Theory of Armored Warfare, 1918–1940* (University of Delaware Press, Newark, 1984)

L'Etang, Hugh, *The Pathology of Leadership* (Heinemann, 1969)

Liddell Hart, B.H., *The Real War, 1914–1918* (Faber & Faber, 1930)

Liddell Hart, B.H., *The Tanks: History of the Royal Tank Regiment* (Volume 1, Cassell, 1959)

Liddell Hart, B.H., *Strategy: The Indirect Approach* (Fourth Edition, Faber & Faber, 1967)

Liddell Hart, B.H., *History of the First World War* (Pan Books, 1972)

Livesay, J.F.B., *Canada's Hundred Days: With the Canadian Corps from Amiens to Mons, August 8–November 11, 1918* (Thomas Allen, Toronto, 1919)

Lupfer, Timothy T., *The Dynamics of Doctrine: The Changes in German Tactical Doctrine during the First World War* (U.S. Army Command and General Staff College, Fort Leavenworth, Kansas, 1981)

Luvaas, Jay, *The Education of an Army: British Military Thought, 1815–1940* (Cassell, 1964)

MacKenzie, J.G.G. and Reid, Brian Holden (editors), *The British Army and the Operational Level of War* (Tri-Servicer Press, 1989)

Mackesy, Major Kenneth, *The Shadow of Vimy Ridge* (William Kimber, 1965)

Macpherson, Major-General Sir W.G., *History of the Great War: Medical Services* (12 volumes, HMSO, 1928–31)

Marwick, Arthur, *The Deluge: British Society and the First World War* (The Norton Library, W.W. Norton, New York, 1970)

Maurice, Major-General Sir F., *Forty Days In 1914* (Constable, 1919)

Maurice, Major-General Sir F., *The Last Four Months: The End of the War in the West* (Cassell, 1919)

Maurice, Major-General Sir F., *British Strategy: A Study of the Application of the Principles of War* (Constable, 1929)

Maurice, Nancy, *The Maurice Case: From the Papers of Major-General Sir Frederick Maurice* (Leo Cooper, 1972)

McKee, Alexander, *Vimy Ridge* (Souvenir Press, 1966)

McWilliams, James L. and Steel, R. James, *Gas! The Battle for Ypres, 1915* (Vanwell Publishing, St. Catharines, Ontario, n.d.)

Mead, [Brigadier] Peter, *The Eye in the Air: History of Air Observation and Reconnaissance for the Army, 1785–1945* (HMSO, 1983)

Middlebrook, Martin, *The First Day on the Somme, 1 July 1916* (Allen Lane, 1971)

Middlebrook, Martin, *The Kaiser's Battle, 21 March 1918: The First Day of the German Spring Offensive* (Allen Lane, 1978)

Millet, Allan R. and Murray, Williamson, *Military Effectiveness: The First World War* (Unwin Hyman, 1988)

Mitchell, [Lieutenant] Frank, *Tank Warfare: The Story of the Tanks in the Great War* (Reissued, Spa Books with Tom Donovan Publishing, Stevenage, Herts, 1987)

Montgomery, Major-General Sir A., *The Story of the Fourth Army* (Hodder & Stoughton, 1919)

Moore, William, *See How They Ran [March 1918]* (Leo Cooper, 1970)

Moore, William, *The Thin Yellow Line* (Leo Cooper, 1974)

Moore, William, *A Wood Called Bourlon: The Cover-up After Cambrai, 1917* (Leo Cooper, 1988)

Moran, Lord, *The Anatomy of Courage* (Constable, 1945)

Morton, Desmond and Granatstein, J.L., *Marching to Armageddon: Canadians and the Great War, 1914–1919* (Lester & Open Dennys)

Moynihan, Michael, *God On Our Side: The British Padre in World War I* (Leo Cooper with Secker & Warburg, 1983)

Muffett, D.J.M., *Concerning Brave Captains: Being a History of the British Occupation of Kano and Sokoto and the Last Stand of the Fulanie Forces* (Andre Deutsch, 1964)

Nalder, Major-General R.F.H., *The Royal Corps of Signals: A Short History of its Antecedents and Development, 1800–1955* (Royal Signals Institution, 1958)

Neame, Brevet Lieutenant-Colonel Philip, *German Strategy in the Great War* (Edward Arnold, 1923)

Neillands, Robin, *The Great War Generals on the Western Front, 1914–18* (Robinson Publishing Ltd, London, 1999)

Neilson, K., *Strategy and Supply: The Anglo-Russian Alliance 1914–1917* (Allen & Unwin, 1984)

Nichols, Jonathon, *Cheerful Sacrifice: The Battle of Arras 1917* (Leo Cooper, 1990)

Nicholson, Colonel G.W.L., *Official History of the Canadian Army in the First World War, Canadian Expeditionary Force, 1914–1919* (Queen's Printer, Ottawa, 1964)

Norman, Terry, *The Hell They Called High Wood* (William Kimber, 1984)

Occleshaw, Michael, *Armour Against Fate: British Military Intelligence in the First World War* (Columbus Books, 1989)

Palazzo, Albert, *Seeking Victory on the Western Front: The British Army and Chemical Warfare in World War I* (University of Nebraska, Lincoln, Nebraska and London, 2000)

Parker, Peter, *The Old Lie: The Great War and the Public-School Ethos* (Constable, 1987)

Pascall, Rod, *The Defeat of Imperial Germany* (Algonquin Books, Chapel Hill, 1989)

Passingham, Ian, *Pillars of Fire: The Battle of Messines Ridge, June 1917* (Sutton, Stroud, Gloucestershire, 1998)

Pitt, Barrie, *1918: The Last Act* (Cassell, 1962)

Pollard, A.F., *A Short History of the Great War* (Methuen, 1920)

Ponsonby, Lord Arthur, *Falsehood in War-Time: Containing an Assortment of Lies Circulated Throughout the Nations during the Great War* (Eighth Edition, George Allen & Unwin, 1940)

Pound, Reginald, *The Lost Generation* (Constable, 1964)

Priestley, Major R.E., *Breaking the Hindenburg Line: The Story of the 46th (North Midland) Division* (T. Fisher Unwin, 1919)

Priestley, R.E., *The Signal Service in the European War of 1914 to 1918* (Royal Engineers, Chatham, 1921)

Prior, Robin and Wilson, Trevor, *Passchendaele: The untold story* (Yale University Press, New Haven and London, 1996)

Raleigh, Sir Walter and Jones H.A., *The War in the Air* (6 volumes, Clarendon Press, Oxford, 1922–37)

Rawling, Bill, *Surviving Trench Warfare: Technology and the Canadian Corps, 1914–1918* (University of Toronto Press, Toronto, 1992)

Reid, Brian Holden (editor), *Military Power: Land Warfare in Theory and Practice* (Frank Cass, 1997)

Richter, Donald, *Chemical Soldiers: British Gas Warfare in World War One* (Leo Cooper, 1994)

Robertson, Bruce, *The Army and Aviation: A Pictorial History* (Robert Hale, 1981)

Samuels, Martin, *Doctrine and Dogma: German and British Infantry Tactics in the First World War* (Greenwood Press, New York, 1992)

Samuels, Martin, *Command or Control? Command, Training and Tactics in the British and German Armies, 1888–1918* (Frank Cass, 1995)

Schreiber, Shane B., *Shock Army of the British Empire: The Canadian Corps in the Last 100 Days of the Great War* (Praeger, Westport, Connecticut, 1997)

Schwink, Captain Otto (translation by G.C.W[ynne]), *Ypres, 1914: An Official Account Published by Order of the German General Staff* (Constable, 1919)

Scott, J.D., *Vickers: A History* (Weidenfeld and Nicolson, 1962)

Shaw Sparrow, A., *The Fifth Army in March 1918* (Bodley Head, 1921)

Sheffield, G.D., *Leadership and Command: The Anglo-American Military Experience Since 1861* (Brassey's, 1997)

Sheffield, Gary, *Forgotten Victory: The First World War Myths and Realities* (Headline, 2001)

Sheffield, Gary, *The Somme* (Cassell, 2003)

Simkins, Peter, *Kitchener's Army: The Raising of the New Armies, 1914–16* (Manchester University Press, 1988)

Simpson, Andy, *The Evolution of Victory: British Battles on the Western Front, 1914–1918* (Tom Donovan, 1995)

Sixsmith, Major-General E.K.G., *British Generalship in the Twentieth Century* (Arms & Armour Press, 1970)

Slessor, J.C., *Air Power and Armies* (Oxford University Press, 1936)

Smithers, A.J., *A New Excalibur; The Development of the Tank, 1909–1939* (Leo Cooper, 1986)

Smithers, A.J., *Cambrai: The First Great Tank Battle, 1917* (Leo Cooper, 1992)

Spiers, E.M., *The Army and Society* (Longman, 1980)

Spiers, Edward M., *Haldane: An Army Reformer* (Edinburgh University Press, 1980)

Strong, Major-General Sir Kenneth, *Men of Intelligence: A Study of the Roles and Decisions of Chiefs of Intelligence from World War I to the Present Day* (Giniger, 1970)

Swettenham, John, *To Seize the Victory: The Canadian Corps in World War I* (Ryerson Press, Toronto, 1965)

Swinson, Arthur, *North-West Frontier* (Hutchinson, 1967)

Terraine, John, *Mons [August 1914]* (B.T. Batsford, 1960)

Terraine, John, *Impacts of War 1914 and 1918* (Hutchinson, 1970)

Terraine, John, *The Road to Passchendaele: The Flanders Offensive of 1917* (Leo Cooper, 1977)

Terraine, John, *To Win a War, 1918: The Year of Victory* (Sidgwick & Jackson, 1978)

Terraine, John, *The Smoke and the Fire: Myths and Anti-Myths of War, 1861–1945* (Sidgwick & Jackson, 1980)

Terraine, John, *White Heat: The New Warfare, 1914–18* (Book Club Associates, 1982)

Thompson, Julian, *The Imperial War Museum Book of Victory in Europe* (Sidgwick & Jackson in Association with the Imperial War Museum, 1994)

Toland, J., *No Man's Land* (Eyre Methuen, 1980)

Travers, Tim, *The Killing Ground: The British Army, the Western Front and the Emergence of Modern Warfare, 1900–1918* (Allen & Unwin, 1987)

Travers, Tim, *How the War Was Won: Command and Technology in the British Army on the Western Front, 1917–1918* (Routledge, 1992)

Turner, E.S., *Gallant Gentlemen: A Portrait of the British Officer, 1600–1956* (Michael Joseph, 1956)

Turner, John (Editor), *Britain and the First World War* (Unwin Hyman, 1988)

Tyng, Sewell, *The Campaign of the Marne, 1914* (Humphrey Milford, 1935)

Walker, Jonathon, *The Blood Tub: General Gough and the Battle of Bullecourt, 1917* (Spellmount, Staplehurst, Kent, 1998)

Warner, Philip, *The Battle of Loos* (William Kimber, 1976)

Warner, Philip, *Passchendaele* (Sidgwick & Jackson, 1987)

Watt, Richard M., *Dare Call it Treason* (Chatto & Windus, 1964)

Wilkinson, Rupert, *The Prefects: British Leadership and the Public School Tradition* (Oxford University Press, Oxford, 1964)

Williams, John, *Mutiny, 1917* (William Heinemann, 1962)

Winter, Denis, *Death's Men: Soldiers of the Great War* (Allen Lane, 1978)

Winton, Harold, *To Change an Army: General Sir John Burnett-Stuart and British Armoured Doctrine, 1927–1938* (Brassey's, 1988)

Wolf, Leon, *In Flanders Fields* (Longmans Green, 1959)

Wood, [Colonel] Herbert Fairlie, *Vimy!* (Macdonald, 1967)

Woodall, David, *The Mobbs' Own: The 7th Battalion The Northamptonshire Regiment, 1914–1918* (Published Privately, 1994)

Woodward, David R., *Lloyd George and the Generals* (University of Delaware Press, Newark, 1983)

Woollcombe, *The First Tank Battle, Cambrai 1917* (Arthur Barker, 1967)

Wynne, Captain G.C., *If Germany Attacks: The Battle in Depth in the West* (Faber & Faber, 1940)

Zabecki, David T., *Steel Wind: Colonel Georg Bruchmüller and the Birth of Modern Artillery* (Praeger, Westport, Connecticut, 1994)

Index

2854862R00145

Printed in Great Britain
by Amazon.co.uk, Ltd.,
Marston Gate.